QUAID-I-AZAM MOHAMMAD ALI JINNAH
His Personality and His Politics

Frontispiece: Quaid-i-Azam Muhammad Ali Jinnah

QUAID-I-AZAM MOHAMMAD ALI JINNAH
His Personality and His Politics

S. M. Burke
and
Salim AL-Din Quraishi

Karachi
Oxford University Press
Oxford New York Delhi
1997

Oxford University Press, Walton Street, Oxford OX2 6DP
Oxford   New York
Athens   Auckland   Bangkok   Bombay
Calcutta   Cape Town   Dar es Salaam   Delhi
Florence   Hong Kong   Istanbul   Karachi
Kuala Lumpur   Madras   Madrid   Melbourne
Mexico City   Nairobi   Paris   Singapore
Taipei   Tokyo   Toronto
and associated companies in
Berlin   Ibadan

Oxford is a trade mark of Oxford University Press

© Oxford University Press, 1997

All rights reserved. No part of this publication may be reproduced, stored in a retrieval system, or transmitted, in any form or by any means, without the prior permission in writing of Oxford University Press.

This book is sold subject to the condition that it shall not, by way of trade or otherwise, be lent, re-sold, hired out or otherwise circulated without the publisher's prior consent in any form of binding or cover other than that in which it is published and without a similar condition including this condition being imposed on the subsequent purchaser.

ISBN 0 19 577783 2

Printed in Pakistan at
Challenger Paper Products, Karachi.
Published by
Ameena Saiyid, Oxford University Press
5-Bangalore Town, Sharae Faisal
P.O. Box 13033, Karachi-75350, Pakistan.

CONTENTS

	page
Acknowledgements	xi
Preface	xiii

1. **The Background**
   The Birth of Indian Nationalism
   and the Hindu-Muslim Problem — 1
   Hinduism and Islam — 2
   Mohammad Ali Jinnah and
   Mohandas Karamchand Gandhi — 7

2. **The First Thirty Years**
   Ancestry, Birth and Education — 32
   The Sad Homecoming and the Hard Road to Success — 42
   His Genius in Advocacy — 44
   Entrance into Politics — 48

3. **The Quaid-i-Azam's Character and Political Style**
   Integrity — 52
   Independence of India, His Lifelong Passion — 54
   His Sang-froid — 54
   His Constitutionalism — 55
   His Secular Politics — 58
   Reserved but Correct — 59

4. **The Birth of Indian Nationalism and Muslim Nationalism**
   India in 1906 — 63
   The Birth of Indian Nationalism — 63
   Sir Syed Ahmed Khan, the Father of Muslim Nationalism — 68

The Aga Khan Delegation	74
The Foundation of the Muslim League	77

5. On the Ladder to Leadership, 1906-1913

Idealists versus Realists	81
The Quaid's First Congress, 1906	83
1907-1913	88

6. Ambassador of Hindu-Muslim Unity, 1914-1918

World War I	100
The Lucknow Pact	101
The War Conferences	108
The Jinnah People's Memorial Hall	110

7. India in a Ferment, 1919-1923

Constitutional Developments	114
The Quaid's Views on the Montagu-Chelmsford Report, the Rowlatt Bill and Khilafat	116
Mahatma Gandhi's 'Himalayan Miscalculation'	118
The Quaid-i-Azam's Response to the Rowlatt Act	120
The Royal Proclamation and its Calming Effect	121
The End of the Truce	123
Jinnah and Gandhi's Respective Responses	126
The Special Sessions of the Muslim League and the Congress at Calcutta	127
Jinnah Resigns from the Home Rule League as well as from the Congress	129
Non-Cooperation in Action	132
Muslim Politics in the Doldrums	139
Jinnah and Ruttie	140

8. Jinnah Resumes His Efforts to Bring About Hindu-Muslim Unity, 1924-1929

The Nature of Jinnah's Differences with Congress	143
The All-India Muslim League's Fifteenth Session, Lahore, 24-25 May 1924	144
Jinnah's Triumphant Return to the Central Legislative Assembly	146
The Delhi Muslim Proposals, 20 March 1927	149
Appointment of the Simon Commission	150

The Muslim League Splits into Two		152
Origin of the Nehru Committee		154
The Nehru Report		157
Jinnah and the Nehru Report		158
The Burial of the Nehru Report		160
The Legacy of the Nehru Report		164
Jinnah's Fourteen Points		166
Death of Ruttie, 20 February 1929		168

9. The Round Table Conference and Jinnah's Self-Imposed Exile in England, 1930-1933

Lord Irwin's Goodwill for India	173
Lord Irwin's Declaration of 31 October 1929	174
The Lahore Congress, 29-31 December 1929	176
The Civil Disobedience Movement	177
The Simon Report	178
The First Session of the Round Table Conference, 21 November 1930 to 19 January 1931	179
Presidential Address of Dr Muhammad Iqbal at the Allahabad Session of the All-India Muslim League, 29 December 1930	183
The Second Session of the Round Table Conference, 7 September 1931 to 1 December 1931	185
The Third Session of the Round Table Conference, 17 November to 24 December 1932	190
The 'Communal Award'	190
Why the Quaid was not Invited to the Third Session of the Round Table Conference	191
Resumption and end of Civil Disobedience Movement by Congress and Gandhi's Resignation from the Congress Party	192
Choudhary Rahmat Ali, 1897-1951	194
The Quaid's Self-Imposed Exile in England	197

10. The Quaid-i-Azam at the Helm, 1934-1939

The Quaid Resumes His Mission of Forging Hindu-Muslim Unity	202
The Himalayan Odds Facing the Quaid	203
The Act of 1935	208
The Attitude of the Congress Toward the Reforms	212

Jinnah's Attitude Toward the Reforms and His Unceasing Efforts to Achieve Hindu-Muslim Unity	212
The Quaid Defuses the Shahidganj Crisis	214
The Twenty-Fourth Session of the All-India Muslim League, Bombay, 11-12 April 1936	215
The Muslim League Manifesto, 11 June 1937	216
Election Results	217
Congress Spurns Jinnah's Olive Branch	219
The Muslims Get a Taste of Hindu Rule	222
Communal Rioting	228
The Muslim Reaction to Congress Rule	229
A Step Toward Pakistan	233
World War II	235
Indian Reaction to World War II	235

11. The Struggle for Pakistan, 1940-1946

The Pakistan Resolution	246
The Quaid Defuses the Khaksar Crisis	251
The Quaid-i-Azam's Further Advocacy of the Demand for Pakistan	251
The Hindu Exponents of the Two Nation Doctrine	253
The German Blitzkrieg and its Repercussions in India	254
Twenty-Eighth Session of the Muslim League, Madras, 12-15 April 1941	258
The Cripps Mission, 23 March to 12 April 1942	259
Gandhi's Quit India Rebellion	264
The Muslim League Attitude Toward the Quit India Rebellion	266
A Murderous Attack on the Quaid-i-Azam	267
The Bengal Famine	268
Wavell's Appointment as Viceroy	269
The Jinnah-Khizar Rift	270
Gandhi Offers to Trade Non-Violence for a Declaration of Immediate Indian Independence	271
Jinnah-Gandhi Negotiations, 9-26 September 1944	272
The Simla Conference	276
The Labour Party Takes Office in the United Kingdom	282
Wavell's Breakdown Plan	285
The Parliamentary Delegation	286

CONTENTS ix

Election Results 287
The Cabinet Mission 288
Statement by the Cabinet Delegates and the Viceroy
    Issued in New Delhi on 16 May 1946 295
The Interim Government 304
Intensification of the Civil War 308
The London Conference, 3-6 December 1946 ... 309

12. Pakistan Zindabad
Attlee's Statement on New Indian Policy and
    Mountbatten's Appointment as Viceroy 317
Congress Requests the British Government to
    Partition India 322
The Opening Phase of Mountbatten's Viceroyalty 325
Plan Balkan 330
Developments in the North-West Frontier Province 332
Proposal for a United Independent Bengal 334
Plan Dominion Status 335
The Plan of 3 June 1947 339
The Consitutional and Legal Formalities of Partition
    and Independence 343
The Quaid-i-Azam's Wisdom in Preventing
    Mountbatten from Becoming Governor-General
    of Pakistan 345
The Radcliffe Boundary Awards 351
The Last Year 354
The Quaid-i-Azam's Conception of the State
    of Pakistan 366
The Quaid-i-Azam's Place in History 372

Bibliography 385

Index 401

Acknowledgements

The two authors most of all wish to thank Professor Burke's daughter, Mrs P. P. Cass. She not only diligently typed the script but also joined the authors in doing research. Her contribution to the production of this book is on a par with that of the authors. They next offer their thanks to Syed Sharifuddin Pirzada. He generously provided the authors with research material and stimulated them with lively exchange of views. They also express their gratitude to Professor Burke's former colleague in the Indian Civil Service, Mr Ronald H. Belcher, CMG, for taking the trouble to read the typescript and offering valuable advice. Finally, they wish to express their warm appreciation for the encouragement and helpful suggestions which Salim AL-Din Quraishi's wife, Margarita, has continuously offered them.

The division of labour between the two authors has been that Burke has written the text and Quraishi has done the research.

Preface

Quaid-i-Azam Mohammad Ali Jinnah was a luminary in three walks of life. He was one of India's leading legal practitioners; he was one of India's leading legislators; and he was one of India's leading politicians. But it is as a politician that he attained world stature and won a permanent place in history. He did not only win independence from colonial rule for an existing country, but performed the extraordinary feat of bringing an altogether new independent country into existence against seemingly impossible odds. And it is with this aspect of his life that our book principally deals.

We propose to leave his professional activities as a barrister to other pens, and to refer to his performance within the precincts of the central legislature only to the extent that it supplements and illustrates the main theme.

The proponents of united India—the departing British and the followers of the mainly Hindu Indian National Congress—have written more massively and eloquently in support of their standpoint than have the Muslim Leaguers to explain the rationale for the creation of Pakistan. This has built up the widely held misconception that Jinnah gratuitously divided the Indian nation by introducing religion into politics.

We hope to demonstrate that in fact the peoples and the regions of the subcontinent of India began to weld into a single nation only under the unifying influence of the British administration and the phenomenal growth of the contagious conceptions of democracy and freedom in the contemporary world. But they never convincingly achieved it. Also, that it was Gandhi, not Jinnah who first introduced religion into politics.

At this stage, all we can reasonably ask of the reader is to suspend final judgement till he or she has examined the entire argument presented in these pages and to ponder over the following submissions.

From the very beginning of their rule, British statesmen were aware that India probably could never manage to become a single nation. In the last years of British rule, three possibilities competed with each other. The Indian National Congress wanted the whole of the British Indian Empire to be treated as a single nation; the Muslim League wished it to be partitioned into two independent states; and the British, while preferring to leave behind a united India, recognized the reality of provincial nationalism and left open the possibility that some provinces might opt for independence. Thus, the ultimate division of the empire into only two independent states was a compromise between the alternatives of one independent state or several independent states.

When Queen Victoria assumed sovereignty over India, John Bright in his speech on the India Bill in 1858 said, 'Does any man with the smallest glimmering of common sense believe that so great a country with its twenty different nations and twenty languages, can ever be bound up and consolidated into one compact and enduring empire? I believe such a thing to be utterly impossible.'[1]

Not surprisingly, it was at the provincial level that the Act of 1919 first partly transferred power to Indian ministers. The Act of 1935 carried the process further and made the provinces administratively autonomous.

The Indian National Congress themselves pleaded the cause of provincial nationalism in their resolution protesting against the proposal to partition Bengal. Resolution XIV of the Twentieth Session at Bombay on 26-28 December 1904 condemned Partition on the ground that it would result in 'the division of the Bengali nation into separate units'.

When it became clear that Indian independence had become inevitable, the British began to favour transfer of power to a united India. This was due to two main reasons. First, this boon would serve as visible proof that British Imperialism had been good for India. Secondly, it was believed that a divided India would be less able to shield itself against the traditional threat from the north-west, which previously stemmed from the expansionary imperial Russia and now from the rampant Communist USSR. At the same time, they could not disregard the existence of provincial nationalism.

Consequently, British proposals for the actual transfer of power—the Cripps Declaration, the Cabinet Mission Proposals and Prime Minister Attlee's statement of 20 February 1947 that the British would definitely leave India by the end of June 1948—though biased in favour of a united India, all recognized the right of the provinces to opt for independence if that proved to be their ultimate choice.

As to whether it was Gandhi or Jinnah who was more responsible for introducing religion into politics, we wish to point out that long before Jinnah started his campaign for a separate homeland for the Muslims, Gandhi himself had frankly proclaimed, 'I can say without the slightest hesitation, and yet in all humility, that those who say that religion has nothing to do with politics do not know what religion means'.[2]

'Gandhiji,' noted a troubled Jawaharlal Nehru, 'indeed, was continuously laying stress on the religious and spiritual side of the movement. His religion was not dogmatic, but it did mean a definitely religious outlook on life, and the whole movement was strongly influenced by this and took a revivalist character so far as the masses were concerned.'[3]

In spelling, place names such as Sind and Baluchistan, we have followed *The Imperial Gazetteer of India,* New and Revised edition published under the authority of the Government of India at Oxford, The Clarendon Press, 1931.

S. M. Burke
and
Salim AL-Din Quraishi

Record of an Interview between Rear-Admiral Viscount Mountbatten of Burma and Quaid-i-Azam Mohammad Ali Jinnah on 9 April 1947

I [Mountbatten] told him [Jinnah] that I regarded it as a very great tragedy that he should be trying to force me to give up the idea of a united India. I painted a picture of the greatness that India could achieve—four hundred million people of different races and creeds, all bound together by a central Union Government, with all the economic strength that would accrue to them from increased industrialization, playing a great part in world affairs as the most progressive single entity in the Far East...

He said that nothing would have given him greater pleasure than to have seen such unity, and he entirely agreed that it was indeed tragic that the behaviour of the Hindus had made it impossible for the Muslims to share in this.[4]

Notes

1. Quoted by Jinnah in his Presidential address at the Thirty-first Session of the All-India Muslim League at Karachi in December 1943.
2. M. K. Gandhi, *An Autobiography or the Story of My Experiments With Truth*, Penguin Books, p. 453. The autobiography containing this declaration by Gandhi was first published in India in two parts, Volume I in 1927 and Volume II in 1929.
3. Jawaharlal Nehru, *An Autobiography*, Oxford University Press, Delhi, 1985, p. 72.
4. *The Transfer of Power*, X, p. 164.

CHAPTER 1

The Background

The Birth of Indian Nationalism and the Hindu-Muslim Problem

In order to comprehend and assess Quaid-i-Azam Mohammad Ali Jinnah's political career fairly, it will be helpful first to elucidate certain forces which conditioned the development of his thinking and conduct.

Hindu and Muslim nationalists are agreed on two important matters:

First, that it was the administrative unity and Western education provided by the British rule in India that originated the feeling that the diverse peoples and regions of the subcontinent of India constituted a single nation.

Secondly, that the ideal outcome of the Indian struggle for freedom would be the emergence of the British empire in India as a united, peaceful and strong independent country, and that the biggest obstacle to the achievement of that shining goal was discord between the two major communities—the Hindus and the Muslims.

That an all-India national feeling owed its birth to the British connection was acknowledged by the very first speaker on the first resolution at the inaugural session of the Indian National Congress at Bombay in 1885. Subramania Ayar, a Hindu delegate from Madras, declared that 'by a merciful dispensation of Providence' Britain had rescued India from centuries of external aggression and internal strife, and summed up the benefits of British rule 'in one remarkable fact, that for the first time in the history of the Indian populations there is to be held the phenomenon of national unity among them, of a sense of national existence'.[1]

And in his presidential address at the Ninth Session of the All-India Muslim League at Lucknow in December 1916, Quaid-i-

Azam Mohammad Ali Jinnah similarly referred to the following 'two cardinal facts'. The first was that the

> British rule in India with its Western character and standards of administration...has maintained, for many decades, unbroken peace and order in the land, administered evenhanded justice, brought the Indian mind through a widespread system of Western education, into contact with the thought and ideals of the West, and thus led to the birth of a great and living movement for the intellectual and moral regeneration of the people.

Secondly, there was

> ...the fact of the existence of a powerful unifying process—the most vital and interesting result of Western education in the country—which is creating out of the diverse mass of race and creed a new India, fast growing into unity of thought, purpose and outlook, responsive to new appeals of territorial patriotism and nationality, stirring with new energy and aspiration and becoming daily more purposeful and eager to recover its birthright to direct its own affairs and govern itself.[2]

In our view two factors were principally responsible for the frustration of the dream that the British empire in India would join the comity of independent nations as a single, powerful and respected member. The first was the inherent incompatibility of Hinduism and Islam, and the second, an accident of history, the incompatibility of temperament and style of leadership of Jinnah and Gandhi, the two controlling players in the final stages of the drama of India's struggle for freedom.

Hinduism and Islam

It was natural that, in their irritation with British imperialism, Indian nationalists should have found it more soothing to ascribe all their misfortunes to their alien rulers rather than to the lack of unity in their own society.

In truth, there are no two great religions more incompatible than Hinduism and Islam. Islam is the youngest of the great religions of the world. It is also the simplest and the most explicit.

The sole requirement is belief in one all-powerful God, in Muhammad (PBUH) as His messenger, and in the Koran as the message. Muhammad (PBUH), of course, was not the first messenger of God. The first prophet was Adam, sent as soon as the world itself was created. Others followed from time to time, such as Abraham, Moses, and Christ. But Muhammad's (PBUH) message, being the last in time, is the final one, taking precedence over all the others. According to the poet-philosopher Muhammad Iqbal: 'The simple faith of Muhammad (PBUH) is based on two propositions—that God is One, and that Muhammad (PBUH) is the last of the line of those holy men who have appeared from time to time in all countries and in all ages to guide mankind to the right ways of living'.[3]

There is no caste system in Islam. All Muslims are supposed to be equal and form a single brotherhood under God, transcending the barriers of race and geography. The word Islam means 'submission' (to the will of God) and Muslim means 'one who submits'. Muslims do not like to be described as Muhammadans because this might suggest they worship the Prophet Muhammad (PBUH), who was not a saviour but just one through whom God revealed his message to the world. Belief in one living God is so strong that the making of images not only is forbidden, but is a cardinal sin. The Koran contains a record of Muhammad's (PBUH) utterances, as revealed to him by God, and collected into an authorized version after his demise.

Hinduism on the other hand, is rooted in the ancient past and is not a religion at all in the usual sense of a faith having a prescribed dogma and scripture. Perhaps the best way of exploring its essence is to find out what it has meant to the leading Hindus of our time: 'Hinduism, as a faith, is vague, amorphous, many-sided, all things to all men. It is hardly possible to define it, or indeed to say definitely whether it is a religion or not, in the usual sense of the word' (Nehru).[4] 'If I were asked to define the Hindu creed, I should simply say: Search after truth through non-violent means. A man may not believe in God and still call himself a Hindu. Hinduism is a relentless pursuit after truth.' Hinduism is 'the religion of truth. Truth is God. Denial of God we have known. Denial of truth we have not known...I believe in the Bible as I believe in the Gita. I regard all the great faiths of the world as equally true with my own' (Gandhi).[5] However, 'many eminent and undoubted Hindus say that non-violence as Gandhi understands it, is no essential part of the Hindu creed. We thus have truth left by itself as the distinguishing mark of Hinduism. That, of course, is no definition at all' (Nehru).[6] Jawaharlal Nehru is not the only Hindu who rejects the Gandhian proposition linking Hinduism with non-violence. Swami Vivekananda asserts: 'Our Shastras say, you are a householder; if anybody slaps you once on your face, you must return it tenfold, otherwise you will be committing a sin'.[7] K. M. Panikkar thinks Indian vision has been obscured by an 'un-Indian wave of pacifism' and states that India rejected the creed of ahimsa when she refused to follow Gautama Buddha.[8] Sarvepalli Radhakrishnan points out that Hindu society made room for Kshatriyas, a group dedicated to the use of force, and surmises that as a long as human nature is what it is, the use of force will be required.[9]

Directly raising the question of what is the spirit of Hinduism, Radhakrishnan explains

> The spirit of science is not dogmatic certainty but the disinterested pursuit of truth, and Hinduism is infused by the same spirit… Fixed intellectual beliefs mark off one religion from another, but Hinduism sets itself no such limits. It is comprehensive and synthetic, seeking unity not in a common creed but in a common quest for truth. Hinduism is more a way of life than a form of thought. It insists not on religious conformity but on a spiritual and ethical outlook in life. It is a fellowship of all who accept the law of right and earnestly seek for the truth.[10]

Gandhi had said that in Hinduism there is 'room enough' for prophets such as Jesus, Muhammad (PBUH), Zoroaster, and Moses.[11] Consequently, Mrs Vijaya Lakshmi Pandit points out, 'Hinduism, Buddhism, Jainism, Islam, Sikhism, and Christianity, have all helped enrich the fabric of India's spiritual life. Hinduism cannot be described as a particular system of thought. Rather it is a commonwealth of systems: not a particular faith but a fellowship of faiths'.[12] Radhakrishnan explains further

> In the long and diversified history of man's quest for reality represented by Hinduism, the object which haunts the human soul as a presence at once all-embracing and infinite is envisaged in many different ways. The Hindus are said to adopt polytheism, monotheism, and pantheism as well as belief in demons, heroes, and ancestors. It is easy to find

texts in support of each of these views. The cults of Siva and Sakti may have come down from the Indus people. Worship of trees, animals, rivers, and other cults associated with fertility ritual may have had the same origin, while the dark powers of the underworld, who are dreaded and propitiated, may be due to aboriginal sources. The Vedic Aryans contributed the higher gods comparable to the Olympians of the Greeks, like the Sky and the Earth, the Sun and the Fire. The Hindu religion deals with these different lines of thought and fuses them into a whole by means of its philosophical synthesis.[13]

As a result of this tolerant attitude, Hinduism itself has become a mosaic of almost all the types and stages of religious aspiration and endeavour. It has adapted itself with infinite grace to every human need and it has not shrunk from the acceptance of every aspect of God conceived by man, and yet preserved its unity by interpreting the different historical forms as modes, emanations, or aspects of the Supreme.[14]

Altogether the Hindu pantheon comprises some 350 million gods. Radhakrishnan says that all the gods stand for some aspect of the Supreme.[15]

Because of its almost unlimited receptiveness, Hinduism has survived the onslaughts of other religions through the ages. Though in time it became laden with social abuses, its theory has a noble and attractive aspect. It does not enclose the mind with mandatory restrictions. But its unbounded toleration also deprives it of positiveness. Its followers lack any central theme to unite them into a single-minded homogeneous unit. They are like an army with no visible flag to protect.

Hindu society stands internally divided not only by doctrinal disunity, which has been discussed, but also by an equally pervasive social disunity. Nehru called Hindu society 'anarchistic'.[16] It subscribes to four principal castes and some three thousand sub-castes. Members of one caste, however meritorious, cannot aspire to promotion to a higher rung, and the fresh convert to the Hindu faith simply remains outside the pale of the caste system, an outcaste and an untouchable. 'What is to be the caste of the convert?' asked B.R. Ambedkar, and answered: 'According to the Hindus, for a person to belong to a caste he must be born in it. A convert is not born in a caste, therefore he belongs to no caste.'[17]

It is far easier to join the brotherhood of Islam. To be converted it is sufficient to proclaim the creed, 'There is no God but Allah;

Muhammad (PBUH) is the messenger of Allah.' Islam thus does not uncompromisingly slam the door in the face of non-believers, who can enter the fold, if they so choose, and make all of humanity one big brotherhood. The sense of equality among the members of the brotherhood is visibly emphasized on congregational occasions. At the various daily prayers and the weekly Friday prayers, worshippers occupy places of their own choice without regard to anyone's worldly status, and at the annual pilgrimage to Mecca, Muslims from all over the world, rich and poor, belonging to different countries and races, wear identical flowing white robes.

Though far less restrictive than Hinduism, Islam, of course, is not without a formidable barrier of its own. It classifies mankind into two mutually exclusive categories, Muslims and non-Muslims. The spiritual bond which holds all the Muslims together serves also to segregate them from all the other peoples on the face of the earth. 'The Believers are but one Brotherhood', declares the Koran. Accordingly, argued the poet-philosopher Muhammad Iqbal, 'there is only one *millat* [community] confronting the Muslim community, that of the non-Muslims taken collectively',[18] and Quaid-i-Azam Mohammad Ali Jinnah averred that Islam imposes a duty on its followers not to merge their identity and individuality in any alien society. Maulana Muhammad Ali, who was Gandhi's right hand man during the civil disobedience movement of the early 1920s, had no compunction in stating publicily that 'however pure Mr Gandhi's character may be, he must appear to me from the point of view of religion inferior to any Mussulman, even though he be without character'.[19]

Thus, forbidden by their respective faiths to merge into a single homogeneous society, Hindus and Muslims continued to exist side by side for several centuries as two distinct entities.

The task before the modern Indian nationalists was to devise a political formula that would make the newly-planted Western conception of majority representative government acceptable to the Muslims who formed a substantial permanent minority.

Mohammad Ali Jinnah and Mohandas Karamchand Gandhi

Jinnah and Gandhi were both intensely patriotic. Gandhi, till the very end of his natural existence, and Jinnah, for most of his political life, yearned for a united India. A narration of their respective roles in the struggle for freedom belongs to the body of this book. At this stage we wish to investigate their personalities and styles of leadership in the hope that this will enable the reader to appreciate the ever-present fundamentals that kept these highly intelligent and responsible leaders apart, and made it impossible for them to present a united front to their alien rulers.

Edward Thompson said that Gandhi was 'the greatest Indian since the days of Buddha'.[20] And the poet Tagore had prophesied in Gandhi's lifetime, 'Perhaps he will not succeed. Perhaps he will fail as the Buddha failed and as Christ failed to wean men from their iniquities, but he will always be remembered as one who made his life a lesson for all ages to come.'[21] When Gandhi was assassinated in January 1948, the United Nations lowered its flag to half-mast.

What was the secret of success of the insignificant looking half-naked Gandhi?

Subhas Chandra Bose explains

> The asceticism of Gandhiji, his simple life, his vegetarian diet, his adherence to truth and his consequent fearlessness—all combined to give him a halo of saintliness. His loin-cloth was reminiscent of Christ, while his sitting posture at the time of lecturing was reminiscent of Buddha. Now all this was a tremendous asset to the Mahatma in compelling the attention and obedience of his countrymen... A large and influential section of the intelligentsia was against him, but this opposition was gradually worn down through the enthusiastic support given by the masses... In some parts of the country the Mahatma began to be worshipped as an Avatar...[22] In 1922 when the writer was in prison, Indian warders in the service of the Prison's Department would refuse to believe that the Mahatma had been cast in prison by the British Government. They would say in all seriousness that since Gandhiji was a Mahatma, he could assume the shape of a bird and escape from prison any moment he liked.[23]

Furthermore

> There is something in Mahatma Gandhi, which appeals to the mass of the Indian people. Born in another country he might have been a complete misfit. What, for instance, would he have done in a country like Russia or Germany or Italy? His doctrine of non-violence would have led him to the cross or to the mental hospital. In India it is different. His simple life, his vegetarian diet, his goat's milk, his day of silence every week, his habit of squatting on the floor instead of sitting on a chair, his loin-cloth—in fact everything connected with him—has marked him out as one of the eccentric Mahatmas of old and has brought him nearer to his people. Wherever he may go, even the poorest of the poor feels that he is a product of the Indian soil—bone of his bone, flesh of his flesh. When the Mahatma speaks, he does so in a language that they comprehend not in the language of Herbert Spencer and Edmund Burke, as for instance Sir Surendra Nath Banerji would have done, but in that of the *Bhagavad-Gita* and the *Ramayana*. When he talks to them about Swaraj, he does not dilate on the virtues of provincial autonomy or federation, he reminds them of the glories of Ramajya [the kingdom of King Rama of old][24] and they understand. And when he talks of conquering through love and ahimsa [non-violence], they are reminded of Buddha and Mahavira and they accept him.[25]

Mountbatten who presided over the transfer of power in India also found that Gandhi 'was not compared with some great statesman like Roosevelt or Churchill. They classified him simply in their minds with Muhammad and with Christ'.[26]

Gandhi deliberately introduced religion into politics. In his own words

> To see the universal and all-pervading Spirit of Truth face to face one must be able to love the meanest of creation as oneself. And a man who aspires after that cannot afford to keep out of any field of life. That is why my devotion to Truth has drawn me into the field of politics; and I can say without the slightest hesitation, and yet in all humility, that those who say that religion has nothing to do with politics do not know what religion means.[27]

Again

> If I seem to take part in politics, it is only because politics today encircles us like the coils of a snake from which one cannot get out

no matter how one tries. I wish to wrestle with the snake... I am trying to introduce religion into politics.²⁸

In South Africa where he fought apartheid for over twenty years, he called his political technique satyagraha, in India he described it as non-co-operation.

The term 'satyagraha' is composed of two words: *'sat'* which means truth and *'agraha'* which means firmness. Gandhi explained that this meant holding on to truth by truth-force or soul-force. 'In satyagraha physical force is forbidden even in the most favourable circumstances...there is not the remotest idea of injuring the opponent. Satyagraha postulates the conquest of the adversary by suffering in one's own person.'²⁹

Annie Besant was of the opinion that 'Gandhi believes in suffering and he is not happy if he achieves his object through evolutionary methods. He wants to build character through suffering. That is not my way. He is the martyr type and believes more in suffering than in achievement.'³⁰

Gandhi himself extolled suffering in these words

> Suffering is the mark of the human tribe. It is an eternal law. The mother suffers so that her child may live. Life comes out of death. The condition of wheat growing is that the seed grain should perish. No country has ever risen without being purified through the fire of suffering... It is impossible to do away with the law of suffering which is the one indispensable condition of our being. Progress is to be measured by the amount of suffering undergone...the purer the suffering, the greater is the progress.³¹

In an article 'The Doctrine of the Sword' he wrote

> I have ventured to place before India the ancient law of self-sacrifice. For satyagraha and its offshoots, non-cooperation and civil resistance, are nothing but new names for the law of suffering. The *rishis* who discovered the law of non-violence in the midst of violence were greater geniuses than Newton. They were themselves greater warriors than Wellington... Non-violence in its dynamic condition means conscious suffering. It does not mean meek submission to the will of the evil-doer, but it means the putting of one's whole soul against the will of the tyrant. Working under this law of our being, it is possible for a single individual to defy the whole might of an unjust empire to save his honour, his religion, his soul, and lay the foundation

for that empire's fall or regeneration. And so I am not pleading for India to practice non-violence because it is weak. I want her to practice non-violence being conscious of her strength and power.³²

The technique of non-cooperation with the agencies of the state was designed to bring about the collapse of the government. His vision of independent India was a return to a system of self-sufficient village communities

> In our own civilization there naturally will be progress, retrogression, reforms, and reactions; but one effort is required, and that is to drive out Western civilization. All else will follow...³³
> Machinery has begun to desolate Europe. Ruination is now knocking at the English gates. Machinery is the chief symbol of modern civilization. I am convinced that it represents a great sin.³⁴

And he glorified India's ancient past

> It was not that we did not know how to invent machinery, but our forefathers knew that, if we set our hearts after such things, we would become slaves and lose our moral fibre. They, therefore, after due deliberation, decided that we should only do what we could with our hands and feet. They saw that our real happiness and health consisted in a proper use of our hands and feet. They further reasoned that large cities were a snare and a useless encumbrance and that people would not be happy in them, that there would be gangs of thieves and robbers, prostitution and vice flourishing in them and that poor men would be robbed by rich men. They were, therefore, satisfied with small villages.³⁵

At another place he said, 'I hold that economic progress...is antagonistic to real progress'.³⁶

When a patient asked for Gandh's advice, he wrote back, 'But you can expect nothing but licensed murders from that most empirical of professions. Whenever I hear of your illness, I feel like shooting some doctor or other but my ahimsa comes in the way.'³⁷ And hospitals he believed were 'institutions for propagating sin'.³⁸

It was in South Africa that the idea 'flashed' upon Gandhi that if he wanted to devote himself to the service of the community, he must relinquish the desire for children and wealth and live the life of a *vanaprastha*—of one retired from household cares.³⁹ And in 1906 he took the oath of *brahamcharya* which he defined as not only abstinence from sex but 'control of the senses in thought, word and deed'.⁴⁰ He gave up drinking cow's milk because he had not the least doubt that milk diets make the *brahamcharya* vow 'difficult to observe'.⁴¹ He had learnt that 'milk stimulated animal passion'.⁴²

Gandhi believed that he could not follow God unless he gave up all he had; words like non-possession 'gripped' him.⁴³ During his voyage from South Africa to London in 1914, he argued with his friend and travelling companion, Mr Kallenback, that the latter's possession of binoculars was not in keeping with the ideal of simple living, and with Kallenback's consent threw them into the sea.⁴⁴

Gandhi said that he followed his 'inner voice'.⁴⁵ Nehru explained that

> Gandhiji has often acted almost by instinct; by long and close association with the masses he appears to have developed, as great popular leaders often do, a new sense which tells him how the mass feels, what it does and what it can do. He reacts to this instinctive feeling and fashions his actions accordingly, and later, for the benefit of his surprised and resentful colleagues, tries to clothe his decisions with reasons. This covering is often very inadequate.⁴⁶

At another place Nehru stated that Gandhi's

> ...way of springing surprises upon us frightened me; there was something unknown about him which, in spite of the closest association for fourteen years, I could not understand at all and which filled me with apprehension. He admitted the presence of this unknown element in him, and said that he himself could not answer for it or foretell what it might lead to.⁴⁷

This lack of a carefully worked out plan of action disconcerted his colleagues at some critical junctures. At its annual session at Nagpur in December 1920, the Indian National Congress at Gandhi's behest passed a resolution holding out the amazing promise of *swarajya* within one year by following a programme of non-cooperation with the British Government. Subhas Chandra Bose has written an account of his disappointing interview with Gandhi designed to understand the Mahatma's 'mind and purpose'.

Bose had been successful in the competitive examination for the Indian Civil Service in England but had resigned his position and hurried back to India to participate in the national struggle. He landed at Bombay on 16 July 1921 and managed to secure an interview with Gandhi on the same day. He summed up the result as follows

> What was to him a question of faith...namely, that swaraj would be won within one year...was by no means clear to me, and personally speaking, I was prepared to work for a much longer period. However, I had no other course but to feel thankful for what I had been able to learn after an hour's conversation. But though I tried to persuade myself at the time that there must have been a lack of understanding on my part, my reason told me clearly, again and again, that there was a deplorable lack of clarity in the plan which the Mahatma had formulated and that he himself did not have a clear idea of the successive stages of the campaign which would bring India to her cherished goal of freedom.[48]

Bose plainly says that 'the promise of Swaraj within one year was not only unwise but childish. It made the Congress appear so foolish before all reasonable men.'[49]

Abul Kalam Azad who was president of the Indian National Congress when it passed the Quit India resolution in the summer of 1942, also tells us that while the resolution was in the making he 'pressed' Gandhi 'to tell us what exactly would be the programme of resistance' but 'he had no clear idea'.[50]

Even some of the senior-most colleagues of the Mahatma did not accept his basic conceptions. For Gandhi non-violence was a creed. Nehru unequivocally stated, 'For us and for the National Congress as a whole the non-violent method was not, and could not be, a religion or an unchallengeable creed or dogma. It could only be a policy and a method promising certain results'.[51] Rajendra Prasad explained, 'We were disarmed; we were unable to fight with arms, and not a few of us saw in Gandhiji's method a way out of our difficult position'.[52] Azad too affirmed, 'For me non-violence was a matter of policy, not of creed... Our decision to fight non-violently was...compelled by circumstances... If freedom could be obtained by fighting, we would certainly participate in the war.'[53]

Nehru also confessed, that he could not understand Gandhi's 'glorification of poverty...for poverty seemed to me a hateful thing, to be fought and rooted out and not to be encouraged in any way'.[54] Also, 'Few of us, I think, accepted Gandhiji's old ideas about machinery and modern civilization... Certainly most of us were not prepared to reject the achievements of modern civilization... Personally, I have always felt attracted toward big machinery and fast travelling.'[55]

Gandhi's observation with regard to the terrible earthquake in Bihar in January 1934, deeply shocked even his most ardent admirers. 'It is an ennobling thing,' the Mahatma wrote, 'for me to guess that the Bihar disturbance is due to the sin of untouchability.' But he made no reply to the poet Tagore's question why God had chastised so many innocent children in Bihar, not a few harijans (Untouchables) among them?[56] And Nehru confessed that he had read Gandhi's 'staggering remark' with a 'great shock' and thought that 'anything more opposed to the scientific outlook it would be difficult to imagine'.[57]

'How came we to associate ourselves with Gandhiji politically, and to become, in many instances, his devoted followers?' Nehru mused on one occasion, 'Personality is an undefinable thing, a strange force that has power over the soul of men'.[58]

There was 'a waning and waxing of Gandhi's popularity among the intelligentsia' but 'there has been no going back in popularity so far as the masses are concerned. There has been a progressive increase in his popularity.'[59]

Gandhi's

> stress was never on the intellectual approach to a problem but on character and piety. He did succeed amazingly in giving backbone and character to the Indian people. It was this extraordinary stiffening up of the masses that filled us with confidence. A demoralized, backward, and broken up people suddenly straightened their backs and lifted their heads.[60]

Gandhi's fads endeared him to the masses because they were Indian fads conforming to the country's ancient culture. To his Westernized colleagues they were a source of some amusement, and Nehru recorded in his autobiography that they would half-humorously say that after independence had been achieved these fads must not be encouraged.[61]

But, whether they agreed with him or not, they could not dispense with him while the struggle for freedom was continuing for 'without him where was the struggle, where was Civil Disobedience and Satyagraha? He was part of the living movement; indeed he was the movement itself.'[62]

Even to many of the Mahatma's admirers some of his own actions seemed to conflict with his ideal of non-violence. During the Boer War and the Zulu Rebellion he sided with the British and organized an ambulance corps during the former and a stretcher-bearer company during the latter with the title of Sergeant Major. During World War I he volunteered to work as a recruiting officer and tells us the people used to ask him, 'You are a votary of ahimsa, how can you ask us to take arms?'[63] He also issued leaflets in which he argued that enlistment in the armed forces offered the recruits 'a golden opportunity' to learn the use of arms.[64]

He was also criticized for those of his fasts which were not for self-purification or to atone for the sins of others, but were undertaken to get his own way in political causes. It was pointed out that they were a form of coercion inconsistent with his commitment to non-violence. His explanation was that

> Those who have to bring about radical changes in human conditions and surroundings cannot do so except by raising ferment in society. There are only two methods of doing this—violence and non-violence. Non-violent pressure exerted though self-suffering by fasting...touches and strengthens the moral fibre of those against whom it is directed.[65]

Gandhi certainly was a unique leader. To kindle self-respect and a longing for freedom in the slumbering masses was an extraordinary achievement. The Hindus had been ruled for some 800 years by the Muslims, and for about 100 years by the British. Only a Gandhi could rouse them. The liberal leader Gokhale said Gandhi could 'mould heroes out of common clay'. The Mahatma instilled pride, courage and hope into the minds of India's poor and made them independence conscious. Poverty no longer was a mark of inferiority; going to prison in the national cause became a signal honour. He eroded the fear of the foreign government in the masses thus weakening one important element of its control over India's millions. By shaking the foundation of imperialism in India, he certainly hastened the freedom of the country for the benefit of Hindus and Muslims alike.

The Mahatma was also the national movement's greatest propaganda asset. His lifestyle, mode of dress, philosophy and political technique were so utterly different from those of all other leaders of world stature that he became a magnet for writers, journalists, photographers and visitors from all over the globe. By becoming world-famous he gave the Indian problem a world dimension.

His utter commitment to non-violence fascinated the Western world which had suffered two devastating wars; perhaps the ancient East did have a message for the materialistic West.

Nevertheless, it is amply clear that the Mahatma's leadership was Hindu in character and unsuited to cure Hindu-Muslim discord which was India's greatest problem and ultimately resulted in the subcontinent's division into the two countries of India and Pakistan. Adherence to non-violence under all circumstances was not consistent with the Islamic doctrine that the faithful must fight in a just cause and would be rewarded in the hereafter should they perish in the line of duty. Gandhi himself was not unaware that non-violence was a purely Hindu doctrine; 'if ahimsa [non-violence] disappears, Hindu religion disappears', he warned.[66] Islam also does not glorify poverty. It permits the accumulation of wealth though it provides for its equitable distribution by laws of inheritance and charity.

The situation in India called for a practical political solution. It demanded recognition that the Westminster type of parliamentary democracy pure and simple would mean permanent Hindu majority rule, and that Muslim fears could be allayed only if the Constitution contained sufficient safeguards for them to feel that they would be free to pursue their own culture and religion and would have an effective share in the government and administration of the country.

This was by no means an impossible achievement. The Hindu community did not lack leaders of the highest calibre who were capable of reaching an agreement with Muslims on mutually acceptable terms. With the co-operation of one of them—Bal Gangadhar Tilak—Jinnah actually brought about the Congress-Muslim League Lucknow Pact in 1916. This was of course before Gandhi took control of the Congress in 1920. Under the Lucknow Pact the Congress had recognized that Hindus and Muslims were two separate political entities and Muslim rights needed constitutional protection if the two communities were to inhabit a common independent country. With another universally respected Hindu leader—Gopal Krishna Gokhale—Jinnah enjoyed a close relationship based on a common political outlook and mutual respect. With a third—Chitta Ranjan Das—Jinnah could have come to terms because Das was a practical politician willing to allay Muslim fears by allowing them constitutional concessions.

But providence had decided that there must be a Muslim homeland called Pakistan. It therefore decreed that Jinnah's opponent in the decisive political duel in the Indian independence movement should be the otherworldly Mahatma Gandhi and not a realistic Hindu politician. So the important question for us to examine is why Gandhi and Jinnah failed to reach an understanding with each other.

The short answer is that there was hardly any meeting ground between them. Their personalities and tactics were poles apart. Gandhi was a visionary throwback to ancient India; Jinnah was an utterly Westernized practical politician. Jinnah wore English suits of the finest cut and quality. Even after he had adopted national dress, his clothes were fashionable and elegant. He lived in a princely residence. He had a large income from his legal practice and he was a careful investor and accumulated a goodly nest-egg. When some members of the Muslim League advised him to travel third-class on the railway just as Gandhi did, he angrily said, 'Do not dictate to me what I should do or should not do. It is not your money I am spending, and I shall live and act as I choose.'[67] He had no compunction in admitting publicly that English was 'the only language in which I can make no mistake'.[68]

Romain Rolland, whom Gandhi visited in Villeneuve, Switzerland in December 1931, recalled

> The little man, bespectacled and toothless, was wrapped in his white burnoose, but his legs, thin as a heron's stilts, were bare. His shaven head with its few coarse hairs was uncovered and wet with rain. He came to me with a dry laugh, his mouth open, like a good dog panting, and flinging an arm around me leaned his cheek against my shoulder. I felt his grizzled head against my cheek. It was, I amuse myself thinking, the kiss of St Dominic and St Francis.[69]

Beverley Nichols, who called on Jinnah in December 1943,

said of him that he was

> ...tall, thin, and elegant, with a monocle on a grey silk cord, and a stiff white collar which he wears in the hottest weather. He suggests a gentleman of Spain, a diplomat of the old school; one used to see his like sitting in the window of the St James's Club, sipping Contrexeville while he read *Le Temps*, which was propped against a Queen Anne toast-rack stacked with toast Melba.[70]

As to the quality of Jinnah's politics, Nichols concluded that 'the difference between Jinnah and the typical Hindu politician was the difference between a surgeon and a witch doctor'.[71]

Jinnah believed that Islam is a modern religion and that its principles 'are as applicable in actual life as they were 1,300 years ago. Islam and its idealism have taught us democracy. It has taught equality of man, justice and fairplay to everybody.'[72] Also

> If Pakistan is to play its proper role in the world to which its size, manpower and resources entitle it, it must develop industrial potential side by side with its agriculture and give its economy an industrial bias. By industrializing our State, we shall decrease our dependence on the outside world for necessities of life, we will give more employment to our people and will also increase the resources of the State.[73]

With regard to democracy, Jinnah said that it

> ...is alien to the Hindu society. I do not want to show any disrespect to any other society but the Hindu society is caste-ridden and caste-bound. The Untouchables have no place socially, economically or any way at all. Democracy is in the blood of the Muslims who look upon complete equality of manhood... Mussulmans believe in fraternity, equality and liberty.[74]

Gandhi's conception of democracy, on the other hand, like everything else about him, was utterly unconventional. Nehru described it in these words

> Gandhiji's conception of democracy has nothing to do with numbers or majority or representation in the ordinary sense. It is based on service and sacrifice, and it uses moral pressure... True democracy is not inconsistent with a few persons representing the spirit, the hope, and the aspirations of those whom they claim to represent.[75]

He called the British Parliament a prostitute 'under the control of ministers who change from time to time... Today it is under Mr Asquith, tomorrow under Mr Balfour and the day after it will be somebody else.'[76]

Jinnah parted company with Gandhi on the issue of non-cooperation at the annual Congress Session at Nagpur in December 1920. Congress first adopted the non-cooperation resolution at a special session at Calcutta in September 1920 demanding the preservation of the territorial and spiritual status of the Sultan of Turkey and retribution for the martial law excesses in the Punjab.[77]

Jinnah was not opposed to non-cooperation in principle. At Calcutta he supported a motion by Bipin Chandra Pal to postpone the launching of the movement. 'Make preparation,' Jinnah advised, 'have your national schools and a court of arbitration. Find out in what other directions you are able to practice non-cooperation. When you have understood the whole situation you could begin to practice led by the best brains amongst you.' Speaking at the sixth anniversary of the death of Gokhale, Jinnah said on 19 February 1921 that

> ...he was convinced in his mind that the programme of Mahatma Gandhi for whom he had great respect and admiration was taking them to a wrong channel...what they wanted was a real political movement based on real political principles...he could not understand why they should not go to the Council and fight face to face with the bureaucrats. He said they were not proceeding according to the constitutional methods... If they were going to regulate everything in their country by the doctrine of non-violence he was afraid they were forgetting human nature. They were forgetting that they were human beings and not saints... Mr Gandhi's programme was based on soul force and it was an essentially spiritual movement... He said that it was not a political programme though it had for its object the political goal of the country.[78]

Indeed, given Indian mob mentality, it was unrealistic to expect that the non-cooperation movement would remain non-violent. Gandhi launched the first non-cooperation movement on 1 August 1920 and stopped it after an incident at Chauri Chaura in the United Provinces on 5 February 1922. Twenty-one policemen and a police inspector had taken shelter in a building, but the mob set fire to it and hacked to death all the members of the police force when they tried to escape.

On 16 February 1922 the Mahatma wrote in his organ *Young India*, 'God spoke clearly through Chauri Chaura... Non-violent non-cooperation can only succeed when they have succeeded in attaining control over the hooligan of India'.[79] Needless to say this impossible condition was never achieved. But this did not stop Gandhi from launching the non-cooperation movement whenever he thought it fit to do so. His most successful campaign was the famous salt march in the spring of 1930. On that occasion he had personally led a band of dedicated followers from his ashram and defied the government monopoly of salt by making salt from sea water at Dandi on 6 April. After masterminding the Quit India resolution in August 1942, he was asked in an interview what would happen if the Muslims did not accept Hindu rule. He said

> I have not asked the British to hand over India to the Congress or to the Hindus. Let them entrust India to God or, in modern parlance, to anarchy. Then all the parties will fight one another like dogs, or will, when real responsibility faces them, come to a reasonable agreement. I shall expect non-violence to arise out of that chaos.[80]

Not surprisingly, Jinnah blamed Gandhi for turning Congress into a Hindu body

> I have no hesitation in saying that it is Mr Gandhi who is destroying the ideal with which Congress was started. He is the one man responsible for turning the Congress into an instrument for the revival of Hinduism. His ideal is to revive the Hindu religion and establish Hindu Raj in this country, and he is utilizing the Congress to further this object.[81]

Nehru said much the same thing

> Gandhiji, indeed, was continually laying stress on the religious and spiritual side of the movement. His religion was not dogmatic, but it did mean a definitely religious outlook on life and the whole movement was strongly influenced by this and took on a revivalist character so far as the masses were concerned.[82]

'I am a very peculiarly constituted person', confessed Jinnah, 'I am guided by cold-blooded reason, logic and judicial training.'[83] At another place he said, 'I am essentially a practical man, I have been in practical politics for over quarter of a century'.[84] And he protested in a letter to Gandhi, 'All your thoughts and actions are guided by "inner voice". You have very little concern with realities, or what might be termed, by an ordinary mortal, "practical politics".'[85]

Everyone knew that Gandhi was the supremo of the Congress party. But when negotiating he often nonplussed the opposite party by declining to admit that he was a spokesman for the Congress. He took advantage of the fact that since 1934 he had held no office in the Congress organization and from October of that year had ceased to be even an ordinary member of the party.

That his formal resignation was a mere subterfuge was lost on no one. As R. Coupland has pointed out, Gandhi exercised 'virtual sovereignty' over 'the operation of the Congress constitution' and despite his resignation often attended the meetings of the Working Committee and took a leading part in the discussions of the AICC and the will of the Congress was 'almost always his in the last resort'. Thus, Gandhi was, 'to put it plainly, a dictator' who supervised and, with rare exceptions imposed his will on the operation of the Congress and at a crisis, took 'sole command of it'. Nehru described Gandhi's status as a kind of permanent 'super-President'.[86]

Of the 'rare occasions' on which the Mahatma's colleagues dared to differ from him we cite the following three well-known ones: first, when C. R. Das and Motilal Nehru decided to enter the legislature and founded the Swaraj party for that purpose; second, when during World War II the Working Committee of the Congress in the summer of 1940 felt 'unable to go the full length with Gandhiji' on the ideal of non-violence and offered to 'throw its full weight' behind the war effort provided the British Government promised complete independence to India and as an immediate step toward it constituted a provisional National Government at the centre; third, when Congress agreed to the partition of the British Empire in India into the two independent states of India and Pakistan. We will have more to say on these episodes in the pages that follow.

Jinnah who went by the book, found it impossible to come to terms with the unrealistic credentials which the Mahatma claimed for himself. This was amply brought out in the course of their well-known parleys from 9 to 27 September 1944.

At their very first meeting Gandhi gave notice that he was negotiating in his 'individual capacity'. In his letter of 10 September Jinnah protested

> With reference to our talk yesterday [9 September] I understood from you that you had come to discuss a Hindu-Muslim settlement with me in your individual capacity, and not in any representative character or capacity, on behalf of Hindus or the Congress; nor had you any authority to do so. I naturally pointed out to you that there must be someone on the other side with authority holding a representative status with whom I can negotiate and, if possible, come to a settlement of the Hindu Muslim question, and that for the position you had adopted there was no precedent, and that this raises great difficulties in my way.
>
> As you know, I can only speak on behalf of Muslim India and the All-India Muslim League, as the President of the organization which I represent, and as such I am subject to and governed by its constitution, rules and regulations. I think you realize and will admit that a settlement of the Hindu Muslim question is the foremost and major hurdle, and unless representatives of these two nations put their heads together, how is one to make any headway with it?[87]

Gandhi in his reply on the following day contented himself by simply saying, 'I have stated publicly that I am approaching you as an individual'.

When Gandhi said that he aspired to represent all the inhabitants of India, Jinnah wrote that he could not accept that claim and went on

> It is quite clear that you represent nobody else but Hindus, and as long as you do not realize your true position and realities, it is very difficult for me to argue with you, and it becomes still more difficult to persuade you, and hope to convert you to the realities and the actual conditions prevailing in India today.

But Gandhi persisted: 'Why can you not accept my statement that I aspire to represent all sections that compose the peoples of India? Do you not aspire? Should not every Indian? That the aspiration may never be realized is beside the point.'

In his last letter Jinnah summed up his frustration in the following terms

> When you arrived here and told me that you were approaching me in your individual capacity, I at once made it clear and informed you, both in our talks and in my letters, that the position you had taken up had no precedent for it, and further that it was not possible to negotiate and reach an agreement, unless both parties were fully represented. For it is a one-sided business, as it will not be binding upon any organization in any sense whatever, but you would as an individual only recommend it, if any agreement is reached, to the Congress and the country, whereas it will be binding upon me as the President of the Muslim League. I cannot accept this position. I hope you do see the unfairness and the great disadvantage to me, and it is so simple and elementary for any one to understand.[88]

At a later date Jinnah again complained about the difficulty of doing business with Gandhi

> When it suits him [Gandhi], he represents nobody, he can talk in an individual capacity; he is not even a four-anna member of the Congress; he undertakes fasts to decide the political issue; he reduces himself to zero and consults his inner voice; yet when it suits him, he is the supreme dictator of the Congress! He thinks he represents the whole of India.
> Mr Gandhi is an enigma... How can we come to a settlement with him?[89]

Gandhi also baffled the international community by pressing it to accept the non-violent way as the panacea for its conflicts.

He advised the Czechs to offer Hitler unarmed resistance.[90] His message to the Jews 'the Untouchables of Christianity' was the same

> I am convinced that if someone with courage and vision can arise among them to lead them in non-violent action, the winter of their despair can, in the twinkling of an eye, be turned into the summer of hope. And what has today become a degrading man-hunt can be turned into a calm and determined stand offered by unarmed men and women, possessing the strength of suffering given to them by Jehovah. It will then be a truly religious resistance offered against the godless fury of dehumanized man.[91]

The Mahatma wrote to Hitler on 23 July 1939 appealing to him to prevent a war which threatened to reduce humanity to the condition of savages.[92] And he wrote again on 24 December 1940 asking Hitler to stop the war and refer the issues at stake to an international tribunal.[93]

In an article in the *Harijan* of 6 July 1940, Gandhi appealed to 'every Briton' to lay down their arms and let Hitler and Mussolini take possession of their beautiful island. If 'these gentlemen' choose to occupy British homes 'you will vacate them. If they do not give you free passage out, you will allow yourself, man, woman and child, to be slaughtered but you will refuse to owe allegiance to them.'[94]

After issuing another appeal to the British to oppose Hitler with spiritual force, Gandhi met the viceroy, Lord Linlithgow, and pressed him to accept his point of view and communicate it to the British Government. Linlithgow was so taken aback that he forgot the usual courtesies to say goodbye to the caller and to ring the bell for an ADC to escort him to his motor car.[95]

Earlier in 1919 when war had broken out between British India and Afghanistan, Gandhi had advised the British Government not to fight the tribesmen but to win them over by non-violence. However, at his prayer meeting on 29 October 1947, he supported Nehru's action in sending troops to fight the tribesmen in Kashmir.[96]

With regard to resisting the tribesmen of North-West India, Gandhi had already explained more explicitly in 1916 that

> All you want to do is to train any army of strictly non-violent men who would offer themselves as willing sacrifices to the fury of the tribesmen and over whose corpses these tribesmen must tread before entering the gates of India. But I am sure that these chivalrous men would hate to strike and kill such non-resisting Satyagrahis and their stout hearts would, therefore easily succumb to the mighty powers of truth and love.[97]

A few hours before his death, Gandhi was asked by a journalist 'How would you meet the atom bomb...with non-violence?' He replied, 'I will come out in the open and let the pilot see I have not a trace of evil against him. The pilot will not see our faces from his great height, I know. But the longing in our hearts—that he will not come to harm—would reach up to him and his eyes would be opened.'[98]

Our purpose in discussing the extraordinary aspects of Mahatma Gandhi's philosophy and political tactics is not to question his saintliness nor to deny his status as the most venerated Hindu of modern times. But this book is not on the lofty subjects of religion and ethics. It is on the down-to-earth subject of politics and we needed to explain our view that Gandhi was not a practical politician and that he and not Jinnah was really responsible for wrecking the chances of Hindu-Muslim unity.

This will become increasingly clear as our story proceeds. At this stage we wish to illustrate our view by briefly referring to two episodes during which Jinnah and Gandhi each was able to unite Hindus and Muslims in a common cause. Jinnah was the driving force behind the making of the Lucknow Pact between the Congress and the Muslim League and Gandhi for bringing together the two communities under his flag four years later to fight the cause of Khilafat.[99]

The Lucknow Pact entered into by the Congress and Muslim League parties at Lucknow in December 1916 was a joint demand addressed to the British Government for the immediate grant of substantial steps toward the ultimate goal of full self-government.[100] It was the fruit mainly of the joint efforts of Jinnah and Tilak as we have already mentioned.

Jinnah explained that though Tilak 'was known in his earlier days to be a communalist...developed and showed broader and greater national outlook as he gained experience...[he] played a very important part in bringing about Hindu-Muslim unity which ultimately resulted in the Lucknow Pact in 1916...[Tilak] was a practical politician'.[101]

Tilak had said, 'I have great respect and admiration for Gandhiji, but I do not like his politics. If he would retire to the Himalayas and give up politics, I would send him fresh flowers from Bombay every day because of my respect for him.[102]

Romain Rolland who has written a sympathetic book on Gandhi's philosophy thinks that if Tilak had lived, Gandhi would have remained only the religious leader of the movement.[103] Tilak's death, therefore, was to be regretted 'not only' for Tilak's sake but for India's and even Gandhi's.[104]

The pressure exerted by the Lucknow Pact was one of the main factors which caused Secretary of State Montagu to announce in the House of Commons on 20 August 1917 that the policy of His Majesty's Government was 'that of the increasing association of Indians in every branch of the administration and the gradual development of self-governing institutions with a view to the progressive realization of responsible government in India'. This promise was followed by the reforms Act of 1919 which while falling far short of Indian expectations, for the first time transferred portfolios of some welfare departments to Indian ministers at the provincial level.

Had the spirit of the Lucknow Pact endured, there is every reason to believe that further advances toward independence would have been extracted and the fusion of Hindus and Muslims into one nation would have become a real possibility.

But Gandhi discarded constitutional methods and resorted to non-cooperation as the weapon both for the Khilafat cause of preserving the spiritual and territorial status of the Sultan of Turkey and for achieving redress for the Punjab martial law atrocities of 1919. This made the Indian political movement more emotional than rational, and cool-headed constitutional-minded leaders like Jinnah were eclipsed.

The Mahatma's philosophy of mixing religion with politics dismayed some prominent nationalists who stood for a united India. One such person was Muhammad Ali Cureem Chagla, a successful barrister of Bombay who after Independence became Chief Justice of the Bombay High Court, India's ambassador to the USA, and a member of the central Cabinet. He was originally a colleague of Jinnah in the Muslim League and explains that he parted company with Jinnah as soon as he became communal-minded and started his two-nation theory.[105] But Chagla makes it plain that it was Gandhi who was really responsible for transforming the secular character of the Muslim League

> ...the alliance between Mahatma Gandhi and the Khilafatists considerably accentuated the communal and religious aspects of Indian public life. Gandhiji was essentially a religious man, and it is very natural that he should feel that he could bring about unity on the basis of religion. As I have already stated, as soon as the Khilafat cause disappeared from the picture, the Khilafatists went back to their original fanatical and religious outlook on life. It also resulted in a great set-back both for Jinnah and men like him and for the Muslim League, which was working on secular lines.[106]

It remains for us to explain our observations with regard to Gokhale and Das.

Gokhale,[107] like Jinnah, regarded Hindu-Muslim unity of paramount importance. He said of Jinnah, 'He has true stuff in him, and that freedom from all sectarian prejudice which will make him the best ambassador of Hindu-Muslim unity'.[108] And Jinnah owned that it was his one ambition to become the Muslim Gokhale.[109] At a condolence meeting in Bombay in May 1915 Jinnah recalled that Gokhale 'was respected by the Muhammedans and the Hindus alike and trusted by both'.[110]

At a later date, Jinnah recalled that Gokhale had 'championed the cause of the Mussulmans' by supporting their demand for separate electorates in 1907 in these words

> Confronted by an overwhelming Hindu majority, Muslims are naturally afraid that release from the British yoke might in their case mean enslavement to the Hindus. (This is not a fear to be ridiculed.) Were the Hindus similarly situated as are the Muslims in regard to numbers and other things, would they not have entertained similar misgivings? We would undoubted have felt the same fears and adopted the identical policy which the Muslims are adopting today.[111]

Das, another 'practical politician',[112] also believed in the necessity of Hindu-Muslim unity based on a sensible political pact. To that end he forged the Bengal Pact and defended it in words which echoed Jinnah's repeated statement to the same effect

> So long as Hindus and Mohamedans do not unite, Swaraj will be an impossibility, and will always remain a theme of impractical fancy... To think that the two communities will merge their respective individuality and make up a new community is inconceivable. And, as I have already said on several occasions, they can only unite by a federation of the two communities based on sacrifice, mutual 'give and take' and understanding of each other's interests.[113]

Azad has appreciatively commented on the Bengal Pact

> In Bengal Muslims were the majority community but for various reasons they were educationally and politically backward. They had hardly any place in public life or Government service... Das was a great realist... He, therefore, made a declaration which took not only Bengal but India by surprise. He announced that when Congress

secured the reins of office in Bengal, it would reserve 60 per cent of all new appointments for Muslims till such time as they achieved proper representation according to population. He went even further to reserve 80 per cent of the new appointments on similar terms... Many of the Congress leaders violently opposed it... I am convinced that if he had not died a premature death, he would have created a new atmosphere in the country. It is a matter of regret that after he died, some of his followers assailed his position and the declaration was repudiated. The result was that the Muslims of Bengal moved away from the Congress and the first seeds of partition were sown.[114]

And who was the foremost critic of Das's Pact? It was none other than Mahatma Gandhi. He contributed an article to the 9 July 1925 issue of *Young India*, less than a month after Das's death.[115] The caption was 'The Science of Surrender'. 'Justice might have been satisfied,' Gandhi complained, 'if Deshabandhu[116] had not filled certain posts with Mussulmans, but he went out of his way to anticipate Mussulman wishes and placate Mussulman sentiment.' And he pronounced that it was Das's 'sensitiveness to placate them that hastened his death'.

Das also held the same view as Jinnah on two other important matters. First, he acknowledged that the Westminster type of Parliamentary system pure and simple was not suited to Indian conditions. In his address on the self-government resolution at the 1917 Congress session he declared, 'I want the power to build my own constitution in a way which is suited to this country'.[117] Secondly, like Jinnah, Das favoured council entry and in 1923 founded the Swaraj Party in cooperation with Motilal Nehru to carry on the fight for freedom from inside the legislature. Gandhi who had opposed the move, went into virtual political exile till the Calcutta Congress of December 1928 when, in the aftermath of the appointment of the Simon Commission, India once more had an important all-India issue to pursue and the Congress party needed the weight of the masses to back up its demands.

Notes

1. R. Coupland, *The Indian Problem, 1833-1935*, p. 23.
2. Syed Sharifuddin Pirzada, *The Collected Works of Quaid-e-Azam Mohammad Ali Jinnah*, Volume I, p. 191. Henceforth referred to as *Collected Works*.

3. 'Shamloo', ed., *Speeches and Statements of Iqbal*, p. 117.
4. Jawaharlal Nehru, *Discovery of India*, p. 63.
5. Quoted by S. Radhakrishnan, *Eastern Religions and Western Thought*, pp. 312-3. Radhakrishnan, President of India from 1962-1967, had earlier been Spalding Professor of Eastern Religions and Ethics at the University of Oxford.
6. Nehru, *Discovery of India*, op. cit., pp. 13-14. See also, Frank Moraes's article, 'Gandhi Ten Years After' in *Foreign Affairs* of January 1958. Moraes observes that Gandhi's effort to equate non-violence with Hinduism was 'vigorously contested by many Hindus who cited Krishna's address to Arjuna in the *Bhagvad-Gita* urging the latter to play his part in the destruction of the enemy in war'.
7. Quoted by Sinha, *Indian Independence in Perspective*, p. 109.
8. K. M. Panikkar, *India and the Indian Ocean*, p. 16.
9. S. Radhakrishnan, *The Hindu View of Life*, p. 78.
10. S. Radhakrishnan, 'Hinduism and the West', in *Modern India and the West*, ed., L.S.S. O'Malley, p. 339.
11. M. K. Gandhi, *Truth is God*, p. 61.
12. Vijaya Lakshmi Pandit, *The Evolution of India*, p. 6. Mrs Pandit, sister of Jawaharlal Nehru, was India's ambassador to the USSR and the USA.
13. S. Radhakrishnan, 'Hinduism', in the *Legacy of India*, ed., G. T. Garratt, p. 268.
14. S. Radhakrishnan, *Eastern Religions and Western Thought*, op.cit., p. 313.
15. S. Radhakrishnan, 'Hinduism', op. cit., p. 276.
16. Quoted by Tibor Mende, *Nehru: Conversations on India and World Affairs*, p. 34.
17. B. R. Ambedkar, *Pakistan or the Partition of India*, p. 119.
18. 'Shamloo', ed., *Speeches and Statements of Iqbal*, op.cit., p. 234.
19. B. R. Ambedkar, *Pakistan or the Partition of India*, op.cit., p. 196.
20. H.S.L., Polak, H. N. Brailsford and Lord Pethic-Lawrence, *Mahatma Gandhi*, p. 118.
21. Louis Fischer, *The Life of Mahatma Gandhi*, p. 408.
22. An Avatar is the embodiment of the supreme God Vishnu in human flesh, such as Rama and Krishna.
23. Subhas Chandra Bose, *The Indian Struggle*, New York, 1964, pp. 114-5.
24. Which, of course, was a Hindu kingdom.
25. Subhas Chandra Bose, *The Indian Struggle*, op. cit., p. 293.
26. Louis Fischer, *The Life of Mahatma Gandhi*, op.cit., p. 507.
27. M. K. Gandhi, *An Autobiography*, Penguin Books, p. 453.
28. Romain Rolland, *Mahatma Gandhi*, p. 149.
29. Polak, Brailsford, Pethick-Lawrence, *Mahatma Gandhi*, op.cit., p. 59.
30. Kanji Dwarkadas, *Gandhi Though My Diary Leaves*, p. 22.
31. Romain Rolland, *Mahatma Gandhi*, op.cit., p. 67.
32. Jawaharlal Nehru, *Mahatma Gandhi*, first published 1949, reprinted 1966, pp. 48-49.
33. Erik H. Erikson, *Gandhi's Truth*, p. 224.
34. Ibid., p. 225.
35. Ibid., p. 219.

36. Ibid., p. 281.
37. Ibid., p. 373.
38. Judith M. Brown, *Gandhi*, p. 88.
39. Gandhi, *Autobiography*, op.cit., p. 196.
40. Ibid., p. 199.
41. Ibid., p. 198.
42. Ibid., p. 300.
43. Ibid., pp. 244-5.
44. Ibid., pp. 314-5.
45. Ibid., pp. 134, 324.
46. Jawaharlal Nehru, *An Autobiography*, p. 85.
47. Ibid., p. 260.
48. Subhas Chandra Bose, *The Indian Struggle*, op. cit., pp. 54-55.
49. Ibid., p. 70.
50. Maulana Abul Kalam Azad, *India Wins Freedom*, p. 75.
51. Nehru, *Mahatma Gandhi*, op.cit., p. 49.
52. Speeches of President Rajendra Prasad, p. 216.
53. Maulana Abul Kalam Azad, *India Wins Freedom*, op.cit., p. 32.
54. Nehru, *Mahatma Gandhi*, op. cit., p. 59.
55. Ibid., pp. 44-45.
56. Polak, Brailsford, Pethic-Lawrence, *Mahatma Gandhi*, op. cit., p. 207.
57. Nehru, *Autobiography*, op.cit., p. 490.
58. Nehru, *Mahatma Gandhi*, op.cit., p. 71.
59. Ibid., p. 52.
60. Ibid., p. 44.
61. Nehru, *Autobiography*, op.cit., p. 73.
62. Ibid., p. 288.
63. Gandhi, *Autobiography*, op.cit., p. 402.
64. Ibid.
65. Polak, Brailsford, Pethic-Lawrence, *Mahatma Gandhi*, op.cit., p. 199.
66. Pyarelal, *Mahatma Gandhi, The Last Phase*, Vol. I, p. 386.
67. Hector Bolitho, *Jinnah*, p. 153.
68. M. H. Saiyid, *Mohammad Ali Jinnah*, 1962, p. 391. Saiyid had published the first edition of this book in 1945.
69. Romain Rolland, *Mahatma Gandhi*, op.cit., p. 27.
70. Beverley Nichols, *Verdict on India*, p. 188.
71. Ibid., p. 191.
72. Sharif AL Mujahid, *Quaid-i-Azam Jinnah*, p. 233.
73. Riaz Ahmad, *Quaid-i-Azam's Perception of Islam and Pakistan*, p. 63.
74. Jamil-UD-Din Ahmad, *Speeches and Writings of Mr Jinnah*, Vol. II, p. 391.
75. Nehru, *Mahatma Gandhi*, op.cit., 68-69.
76. Erik H. Erikson, *Gandhi's Truth*, pp. 219-20.
77. The Khilafat question and the Punjab atrocities will be discussed more fully later in their proper context. The Sultan of Turkey was the spiritual successor of the Prophet as Khalifa and the keeper of the holy places.
78. Pirzada, *Collected Works*, Vol. I, op.cit., pp. 408-10.
79. Romain Rolland, *Mahatma Gandhi*, op.cit., p. 202.

80. *Quit India Movement,* British Secret Report, edited by P.N. Chopra, p. 47.
81. Syed Sharifuddin Pirzada, *Foundations of Pakistan,* Vol. II, pp. 305-6.
82. Nehru, *Autobiography,* op.cit., p. 72.
83. Syed Sharifuddin Pirzada, *Quaid-i-Azam Mohamad Ali Jinnah and Pakistan,* p. 192.
84. Ibid., p. 193.
85. M. H. Saiyid, *Mohammad Ali Jinnah,* op.cit., p. 310.
86. R. Coupland, *Indian Politics, 1936-1942,* pp. 90-93.
87. G. Allana, *Pakistan Movement: Historic Documents,* p. 341. The quotations relating to the negotiations that follow are also taken from this book.
88. For the political questions discussed during these negotiations *see,* Chapter II.
89. Jamil-UD-Din Ahmad, *Speeches and Writings of Mr Jinnah,* Vol. II, op.cit., p. 192.
90. Judith M. Brown, *Gandhi,* op.cit., p. 320.
91. Polak, Brailsford, Pethic-Lawrence, *Mahatma Gandhi,* op.cit., p. 224.
92. Judith M. Brown, *Gandhi,* op.cit., p. 321.
93. Ibid., p. 322.
94. Kanji Dwarkadas, *Gandhiji Through My Diary Leaves,* pp. 80-81.
95. Maulana Abul Kalam Azad, *India Wins Freedom,* op.cit., 35.
96. This change of heart puzzled Kanji Dwarkadas and he gives a full account of it in his *Gandhiji Through My Diary Leaves,* op.cit., at pp. 80-85.
97. Indulal K. Yajnik, *Gandhi As I Know Him,* p. 16.
98. Erik H. Erikson, *Gandhi's Truth,* op.cit., p. 430.
99. These two episodes will be discussed more fully at an appropriate stage in this narrative.
100. For a fuller account of the Lucknow Pact *see* pp. 101-7.
101. Pirzada, *Collected Works,* Vol. I, op.cit., p. 386.
102. Kanji Dwarkadas, *India's Fight for Freedom,* p. 151.
103. Tilak died on 1 August 1920, which was the very day on which Gandhi launched the non-co-operation movement.
104. Romain Rolland, *Mahatma Gandhi,* op.cit., p. 30.
105. M. C. Chagla, *Roses in December,* p. 78.
106. Ibid., p. 81.
107. Gokhale died in February 1915.
108. Pirzada, *Collected Works,* Vol. I, op.cit., p. 128.
109. Ibid.
110. Ibid.
111. Pirzada, *Foundations of Pakistan,* Vol. II, op.cit., p. 407.
112. So described by Bose, *The Indian Struggle,* op.cit., p. 111.
113. From the English version of Das's speech on the 'necessity of Hindu-Muslim Pact' delivered at the Bengal Provincial Conference in June 1924, printed at p. 270 of *Deshbandhu Chitta Ranjan [Das], Brief Survey of Life and Work, Provincial Conferences Speeches, Congess Speeches,* published by Rajen Sen and B. K. Sen.
114. Abul Kalam Azad, *India Wins Freedom,* op.cit, pp. 23-24.
115. Das died on 16 June 1925 at the early age of 55.

116. Das had been given the title of 'Deshabandhu' by the people. It literally means 'friend of the country'.
117. *Dictionary of National Biography*, Vol. I, edited by S. P. Sen. p. 341. At a meeting of the Council of the All-India Muslim League at Bankipur on 31 December 1912, Jinnah had already pointed out that a system of self-government on 'colonial lines' was not feasible for India. Pirzada, *Collected Works,* Vol. I, op.cit., p. 48.

CHAPTER 2

The First Thirty Years

Ancestry, Birth and Education

On 25 December 1876 Jinnahbhai Poonja and his wife Mithibai[1] were blessed with a son who was destined to achieve an independent homeland for Indian Muslims against impossible odds. The baby was small, weak and underweight. However, when his anxious parents had him examined by a doctor he assured them that there was nothing physically or otherwise wrong with the newborn. The child was given the name Mahomedalli Jinnahbhai but on growing up he modified it to read Mohammad Ali Jinnah or M. A. Jinnah.

Jinnah was the eldest child of his parents. He was followed by six others, the last but one of whom was a girl named Fatima. She alone figured in his later life. He educated her to be a dentist. After he became a widower, she kept house for him and looked after him till he died.

The original home of Jinnah's family was Paneli, a village in the Princely State of Gondal in Kathiawar. It was not far from Porbandar where Mohandas Karamchand, the future Mahatma Gandhi, had been born on 2 October 1869. The mother tongue of both was thus Gujrati. Both moreover, belonged to mercantile communities. Jinnah's family were Khojas of the Ismaili sect of Shiahs and Gandhi's were Modh Banias, a subcaste of the Vaisya caste.

Poonja and Mithibai had moved from the small village of Paneli to the fast-growing port of Karachi in 1874 in search of greater prosperity. Poonja rented 'a modest two-room apartment on Newnham Road in Kharadar which was the business centre of the city. The apartment was on the first floor and had a spacious balcony of wood and iron above the pavement exposed to the cool sea breeze which came from the west throughout most of the year'.[2]

Poonja had not studied English at school but he was good at languages and soon learnt to converse in English. He conducted his business directly with the Managing Director of the British firm, Grahams Trading Company. As his business spread abroad he also learnt how to read and write English because it was the language of the commercial houses he traded with in Hong Kong and England. With Grahams his business was mainly in isinglass[3] and gum arabic.[4]

The entire trade of Sind, Baluchistan and the Punjab flowed through Karachi, but conventional banking facilities in Karachi at that time were inadequate. Monetary transactions were therefore usually channelled through trustworthy merchant houses. 'Jinnah Poonja and Company' conducted this business too on a large scale.

Though Poonja built up a flourishing business, he remained careful with his money and his family lived a simple life. 'He thought of fortune—in the idiom of Paneli—as a capricious deity' and it was on this principle that he ran his family budget. His example made a lasting impression on the minds of his growing children.[5]

Jinnah was the favourite child of Mithibai and she believed he would grow up to be a great man. She persuaded her busy and frugal husband to take their eldest son all the way to the shrine *(dargah)* of Hassan Pir in Ganod, ten miles from Paneli, for the *aqiqa* ceremony because as a child she had heard stories about the supernatural powers of the Pir. After the *aqiqa* ceremony, she insisted upon celebrating the occasion at Paneli by inviting the entire village community to a feast. 'On that day in Paneli not a single family lit a fire in their home; their pots and pans rested on the kitchen shelves and all because tiny Mohamed Ali was visiting his ancestral village'.[6]

When Jinnah was about six years old, his parents engaged a tutor to teach him Gujrati at home. He proved to be an indifferent student and 'positively loathed arithmetic'.[7] This loathing for arithmetic probably was one of the underlying reasons why he chose law and politics as a career instead of joining the family business which involved keeping accounts.

However, he liked games and became the leader of his playmates, in that field. His favourite pastimes were marbles, tops, *gilidanda* and cricket. His father owned a number of carriages and had some fine horses in his stables. Jinnah enjoyed riding them in the company of a school friend named Karim Kassim.

In December 1887, Jinnah was admitted to the first English standard of the Sind Madressah-tul-Islam which was about half a mile from his home.[8] It was run by the Anjuman-i-Islam Karachi and aimed at combining modern Western education with the teaching of the traditional subjects of religion and Arabic and Persian. However, young Jinnah's indifference to formal teaching and preference for games and sports remained unaffected.

Hoping that a change of environment might have a salutory effect on his difficult son, Poonja decided to send him to a school in Bombay. So, when Jinnah's paternal aunt Manbai, who lived in Bombay with her husband, visited Karachi, she took the youngster back with her. Mithibai felt unhappy at the prospect of parting with her beloved firstborn but Manbai who was 'a vivacious person, full of wit, humour and wisdom'[9] was able to obtain her consent.

At Bombay Jinnah joined the Anjuman-i-Islam School and the transfer had the desired effect. 'He passed his fourth Gujrati, qualifying him for first grade English'.[10]

But Mithibai's patience soon ran out and upon her insistence Poonja recalled Jinnah to Karachi and once more sent him to the Sind Madressah tul Islam.

Jinnah left the school in January 1891 to join his father in business. However, he soon got bored because 'everything depended on reading and writing; money received and paid had to be entered into account books'. He told his father that he would rather go back to school than continue in his office.[11]

Accordingly he returned to the Sind Madressah-tul-Islam on 9 February 1891 but had to leave it finally on 30 January 1892. The reason for this was that Frederick Leigh Croft, Managing Director of the Karachi office of Graham's Trading Company, had offered to attach young Jinnah to the firm's head office in London for three years as a paid apprentice to learn practical business administration, and Poonja had accepted the invitation hoping the training would equip his son to expand the family business on his return home.

But before leaving for England it was considered essential quickly to improve his proficiency in English. It was proposed to achieve this by moving him from the Madressah-tul-Islam to the Church Mission School.

Also, the misery of Mithibai had to be assuaged. She was shattered by the prospect of being separated from her dearest child for three long years and in particular feared that some English girl might entice her handsome son into marriage if he remained a bachelor. To avoid the possibility of such a family disaster, she made her consent to his going abroad conditional upon his acquiring a spouse before leaving the shores of his motherland. Furthermore, she personally selected the bride. Her choice fell on fourteen year old Emi Bai who came of an Ismaili Khoja family of Paneli, distantly related to herself.

So in February 1892, before Jinnah started at the Church Mission School, the family journeyed to Paneli where the marriage was performed with due pomp and ceremony.

Poonja's business at Karachi was suffering because of his absence. He was therefore anxious to return there along with the newly married couple as soon as possible. But the bride's father flatly refused to let his daughter leave home before the expiry of the customary period of at least one month after marriage. The impasse was unexpectedly resolved by the bold intervention of young Jinnah.

Fatima has described the incident in the following words

> The two families, newly joined in marriage, began to argue, but the differences remained unresolved. During the ensuing discussions Mohamed Ali remained silent, but once he knew that they were no nearer conclusion, he decided to intervene. Without informing my father or mother, he went to see his in-laws. They welcomed him with much cordiality and ceremony. The formalities over, Mohamed Ali said quietly that because of business reasons his father could no longer stay in Paneli; his mother must return with his father and he with them. His bride, he said, he would like to take with him, because he would leave Karachi for Europe soon and would be gone for three years. Perhaps they would like to send their daughter to Karachi in his absence and have her wait three years until his return from England?
>
> The following day his in-laws came to see my father and mother and surprised them by asking when they would like to take Emi Bai with them to Karachi, so that they could make the necessary arrangements.[12]

When Emi Bai first joined the Poonja family she followed the custom of concealing her face with her *orni* in the presence of her father-in-law. But in deference to her progressive husband's wishes she soon discarded the practice.

Immediately after returning to Karachi, Jinnah was enrolled in the Church Mission School and studied there till the end of October.

He sailed for England in the first week of November 1892, landing at Southampton three weeks later when he was about a month short of his sixteenth birthday.[13]

One of his cousins, Mrs Fatima Gangji Valji, recalled many years later, that when Jinnah bid her farewell her eyes were heavy with tears. He told her, 'Don't be a fool, bai. I will return a great man from England and not only you and the family but the whole country will be proud of me. Would you not be happy then?'[14]

During the voyage he was the youngest passenger on his own. An English gentleman was kind to him and engaged in friendly conversation with him every day giving useful tips regarding life in London. When the gentleman disembarked at Marseilles, he left his London address with Jinnah. During Jinnah's three and a half year stay in London, the said Englishman would invariably invite his young shipboard friend to a meal with himself and his family whenever he came 'home' on a visit.[15]

After landing at Southampton, Jinnah took a train to London. There the driver of a hackney cab guided him to an hotel which was inexpensive but comfortable. He rented a modest room in it.

November—at the time of Jinnah's years in London as a student—used to be the gloomiest part of the year. Coal was still the principal fuel for domestic and industrial use and produced depressingly damp and dark fogs.[16] Jinnah was not used to such conditions. Not surprisingly, he found life in London rather depressing. He was not used to such severe cold. He could seldom afford the luxury of a cab and had to walk considerable distances on foot every day in the damp winter. Years later he said to Fatima

> It was quite trying and tiring. I was lonely, far from home, far from my parents, I was in a new country where life was so different from all I had known in Karachi. Except for some colleagues at Grahams,

> I did not know a soul, and the immensity of London, which had first impressed me, now weighed heavily on me. The severe cold and the dreary drizzle chilled me to the bone. I felt miserable but I steeled myself and with much effort settled down to take on London on its terms. I began to like it before long.[17]

Finding a prolonged stay in the hotel beyond his means, he shifted before long to a one-room apartment at 40 Glazbury Road in West Kensington. In March 1894 he took up residence as a paying guest of one Mrs F. E. Page-Drake at 35 Russell Road, Kensington, and remained there for the rest of his stay in London.[18]

> In later years when he reminisced about London he would say that Mrs Page-Drake was a very kind old lady, with a large family, and that she treated him as if he were her son. She had an attractive daughter who was about the same age as Mohamed Ali. Miss Page-Drake liked my brother but he was not the flirtatious type and she could not break through his reserve. She would sometimes arrange mixed parties in her mother's house, and among the various games she would organize for her guests was one in which the penalty for a fault was a kiss. Mohamed Ali always counted himself out of this kissing game. 'One Christmas Eve,' he recalled, 'Miss Page-Drake threw her arms around me as I was standing under some mistletoe, the significance of which I did not then know, and said that I must kiss her. I told her gently that we too had our social rules and the mistletoe kiss was not one of them. She let me go and did not bother me again in this manner.[19]

Jinnah began his apprenticeship at Grahams Trading Company on the day after he had arrived in London. The company's office was located at Threadneedle Street in the heart of the commercial district of the metropolis. 'He was given a small table and a chair in one of the rooms where he sat with a number of office-hands learning how business was conducted'.[20]

London's rich political and cultural activities beckoned him but his sedentary and boring apprenticeship at Graham's afforded him little leisure to enjoy them. Even before leaving Karachi for London, he had displayed his attraction for the legal profession. He made his first visit to the law courts in Karachi in the company of his father. As soon as he saw an advocate there in gown and bands, he said 'I want to be a barrister'. 'Thus Jinnah's love for law was love at first sight'.[21]

He therefore decided to give up the apprenticeship and to qualify as a barrister instead. Of the four Inns of Court he chose Lincoln's Inn because on the inner side of New Hall's main entrance he saw a fresco depicting the image of the Prophet Muhammad (PBUH) among the group of lawgivers of the world.[22]

It is not surprising that Jinnah should have been influenced in favour of Lincoln's Inn because it had honoured the Prophet. He came from a devout Muslim family and his mother, whom he deeply loved and respected, was a deeply religious lady. Mian Abdul Aziz who was a law student in London during the same years as Jinnah, recalled that Jinnah at that time was 'an active member of the Muslim Society in England'.[23] He remained a good Muslim all his life but was too sophisticated ever to be a narrow-minded one.

He joined Lincoln's Inn in June 1893 and passed the Bar finals in April 1895. After completing the formality of attending the requisite number of dinners he was called to the Bar a year later. However, he did not leave for India till July 1896.

When Poonja learnt from his son that the latter had joined Lincoln's Inn and it would take him three years to qualify as a barrister, he ordered him to return home immediately. Jinnah, however, pleaded to be allowed to complete the course, promising not to ask for any more money and to live as frugally as possible. His father had no option but to reconcile himself to the situation and pray for the best.[24]

Living in London had a lasting effect on Jinnah's lifestyle and political philosophy. A few months before sailing home Jinnah petitioned Lincoln's Inn to have his name altered from Mahomed Ali Jinnahbhai to Mahomed Ali Jinnah. The Council of the Inn granted the request on 25 April 1896. However, he had already signed his name simply as M. A. Jinnah on the register of the British Museum in February 1895.[25] In later years he usually signed his full name as Mohammad Ali Jinnah.

The future ambassador of Hindu-Muslim unity reminisced in his presidential address at the Thirtieth Session of the All-India Muslim League at Delhi in April 1943 that he had learnt politics 'at the feet of that great man, Dadabhoy Naoroji' and that it was 'men of the character of that Great Dadabhoy that inspired us with some hope of a fair and equitable adjustment' between Hindus and Muslims.

Naoroji was born at Bombay on 4 September 1825 in a priestly Parsee family. He was the first Indian to be appointed a professor at the Elphinstone College Bombay in 1850. In 1855 he became a business partner of Cama and Co. and took charge of their London branch but left them in 1862 to start his own business under the name Dadabhai Naoroji & Co. However, he visited India regularly and took a leading part in the politics of the country.

One of the founding fathers of the Indian National Congress in 1885, he was elected its president thrice, in 1866, 1893 and 1906. In 1865 he founded the London India Society jointly with W.C. Bonnerjee and continued as its president till 1907 when he finally returned to India. He was respected by all sections of Indian society and affectionately called 'The Grand Old Man of India'.

Mahatma Gandhi recalled that when he arrived in London as a student in 1888

> I soon found that Indian students had free access to the GOM at all hours of the day. Indeed, he was in the place of father to every one of them, no matter to which province or religion they belonged. He was there to advise and guide them in their difficulties. I have always been a hero-worshipper. And so Dadabhai became real Dada to me.[26]

Naoroji stood for election to the British Parliament as a Liberal candidate for Central Finsbury and in July 1892 became the first Indian to enter the House of Commons.

In his maiden speech in the House of Commons on 9 August 1892 he acknowledged 'the spirit of British rule, the instinct of British justice and generosity' which had led to an Indian standing 'in this house, becoming a member of the great Imperial Parliament of the British Empire and being able to express his views openly and fearlessly before you'.

Replying to the felicitations offered to him at a meeting in London on 23 January 1893 celebrating his election victory, Naoroji expressed sentiments which Jinnah often expressed in years to come

> We hope to enjoy the same freedom, the same strong institutions which you in this country enjoy. We claim them as our birth-right

as British subjects. We are either British subjects or British slaves. If we are really British subjects, you are honestly bound to give us every one of your institutions as soon as we are prepared to receive them. I have now no doubt from my long knowledge of this country that as soon as the British people begin to understand what we are prepared for, they will be ready to give it.[27]

Indian students had enthusiastically campaigned for Naoroji during the election but Jinnah could not share this honour because in July he was still in Karachi.[28] However, he must have participated in the celebratory gathering in January.

The general election which took Naoroji to the House of Commons also installed Gladstone at 10 Downing Street to commence his fourth term as prime minister with John Morley as his Irish Secretary. The Liberals thus were very much in evidence in the United Kingdom during Jinnah's years as a student in London.

Jinnah told Dr Ashraf that, during the last two years in London his time was 'utilized for further independent studies, for the political career' he already 'had in mind'. Jinnah also said, 'Fortune smiled on me, and I happened to meet several important English Liberals with whose help I came to understand the doctrine of Liberalism. The Liberalism of Lord Morley was then in full sway. I grasped that Liberalism, which became part of my life and thrilled me very much.'[29]

Jinnah regularly attended the House of Commons as a visitor and subscribed to Hansard. On Sundays he occasionally went to listen to the soap-box orators at Hyde Park Corner and was 'as much amused by their lack of coherence or responsibility as he was impressed by the tolerance of their large or small audiences'.[30]

He also read in the library of the British Museum to broaden his mind and attended the law courts to familiarize himself with the working of the British system of justice.

In the cultural field he was mainly interested in the theatre, especially in Shakespearean plays. So much so that he nearly became a professional actor in London after completing his studies. On 19 March 1947 he gave the following account to Malik Wahedana[31]

I used to read out Shakespeare before my friends. Soon the news got around: 'Jinnah reads well.' After I was called to the Bar, I was taken by some friends to the manager of a theatrical company, who asked me to go up to the stage and read out pieces of Shakespeare. I did so.

His wife and he were immensely pleased, and immediately offered me a job. I was exultant, and I wrote to my parents craving for their blessings. I wrote to them that law was a lingering profession where success was so uncertain; a stage career was much better, and it gave me a good start, and that I would now be independent and not bother them with grants of money at all. My father wrote a long letter to me, strongly disapproving of my project; but there was one sentence in his letter which touched me most and which influenced a change in my decision: 'Do not be a traitor to the family.'

I went to my employers and conveyed to them that I no longer looked forward to a stage career. They were surprised, and they tried to persuade me, but my mind was made up. According to the terms of the contract I had signed with them, I was to have given them three months notice before quitting. But you know, they were Englishmen, and so they said: 'Well when you have no interest in the stage, why should we keep you, against your wishes, for three months with us? We relieve you now and you can go home.' My stage career, therefore was very short.[32]

Miss Fatima Jinnah recalled that,

An ambition of his those days was to play the role of Romeo at the Old Vic. Even in the days of most active political life, when he returned home tired and late, he would read Shakespeare in bed. Sometimes after dinner he would read aloud his favourite passages, and I still remember that whenever he was reading Shakespeare his voice would be resonant and well modulated as if he had had experience of the stage.[33]

Thus, the student who had left the shores of India in November 1892 as 'a tall thin boy in a funny long yellow coat'[34] bearing the cumbersome name of Mahomed Ali Jinnahbhai returned home as a westernized young man wearing the latest London clothes, enunciating the English language well enough to go on the London stage, imbued with Gladstonian liberalism and signing himself fashionably as M. A. Jinnah.

The Sad Homecoming and the Hard Road to Success

Circumstances outside his control had conspired to make the homecoming a sad one. On the eve of his departure from London he drew three cheques on 15 July 1896. The largest one was in favour of the National Bank of India Limited, Bombay, showing that he was not returning to Karachi but going to Bombay. Let us explain.

Soon after his departure for London in 1892, his wife had died. He had not known her for long. So it did not shock him as much as his mother's passing away later while giving birth to her youngest child, Bundeh Ali. 'He broke down and wept for hours for his tender mother, whom he loved more than anything else in the world'.[35]

Also, following litigation, his father had been declared insolvent in January 1893, and in July of that year had moved with his family to Durga Maula near Bombay.[36]

Soon after reaching Bombay Jinnah enrolled himself as an Advocate of the Bombay High Court (24 August 1896). He never made a secret of the fact that the opening years of his legal practice had been hard. Everyone involved in a lawsuit wishes to win his case and naturally prefers to engage a counsel who has already made a name for himself. Even under the best of circumstances a newcomer takes time to build up a reputation. That Jinnah was a Muslim was an additional handicap for him because the Bombay Bar was dominated by British, Parsee and Hindu practitioners.

Reminiscing about his early days at a party at the Karachi Club on 9 August 1947, Jinnah, now the governor-general designate of Pakistan, recalled that at Bombay 'he waited and waited for a long time for a brief. At last he got a brief'.[37] His sister also wrote

> Even after three years he was not earning much and was agonizing over his inability to help his distressed family... But he kept up the appearance of being a busy barrister, daily making the rounds of the courts, making social contacts and frequenting some of the best clubs of Bombay. In his early twenties, my brother was a very attractive

young man,[38] slim and tall, with a commanding personality a sensitive face, and always impeccably dressed.[39]

His social contacts paid off. A friend of Jinnah, impressed by his personality and talent, introduced him to John Molesworth MacPherson, acting Advocate General of Bombay, who invited the young barrister to read in his chambers. This concession had never before been granted to an Indian and caused quite a stir in legal circles.

Impressed by Jinnah's character and ability, MacPherson passed on some cases to him.

When the vacancy of a Presidency Magistrate fell vacant in 1900, Jinnah decided to apply for it thinking it would give him financial stability. He was too proud to seek the intercession of MacPherson. While gazing through the window and wondering how to proceed, he noticed a victoria cab passing by. He impulsively jumped into it and made for the office of Sir Charles Ollivant, Member in charge of the Judicial Department. Sir Charles told him that he had heard about him but would like to have a letter of recommendation from MacPherson who knew him personally.

Next morning when Jinnah hesitantly broached the subject with MacPherson he told him that Sir Charles had already spoken to him. At the same time he demanded to know why Jinnah had not told him earlier that he wanted to apply for the job. Jinnah explained that he had already felt so obliged for his kindness in letting him read in his chambers that he did not have the heart to ask for another favour.

Jinnah was appointed as a Third Presidency Magistrate for three months to fill a temporary vacancy. At the end of that period he was given a further three-month stint in another temporary vacancy.[40]

That he had acquitted himself well as a magistrate was obvious from the fact that when his term expired Sir Charles asked him to remain available for a permanent position on a salary rising to fifteen hundred rupees a month. But Jinnah's period as a magistrate had already earned him a high reputation in legal circles and had inspired sufficient confidence in himself for him to decline the offer stating that his ambition now was to earn fifteen hundred rupees a day.

Jinnah told his biographer, M. H. Saiyid

> After two years Sir Charles returned to India having spent some time in England in quiet retirement. He was invited to the Orient Club in Bombay of which I was a member and I attended the function. On seeing me there, he came over and enquired as to how I was doing in law; and when I told him I was earning more than rupees two thousand a month, he congratulated me on my courage, saying that I had done well to refuse his offer.[41]

His Genius in Advocacy

Before long Jinnah climbed to the uppermost echelons of the Bombay Bar. In October 1937 he publicly said

> I am not a poet. I am not an orator. I can only reason. One gentleman here has characterized me as the Mustafa Kamal Pasha of India. I wish I were Mustafa Kamal. In that case I could easily solve the problem of India. But I am not. I have not the army behind me. Therefore, I have got to reason. My strongest and longest gun is this reasoning.[42]

Sarojini Naidu diagnosed the secret of his success

> As a speaker Mohomed Ali Jinnah has the triple assets of a magnetic presence, an impressive delivery, and a voice which while lacking volume has an arresting timbre. But though occasionally he has attained a moment of wholly unconscious and stirring eloquence, he has the cogent force of a brilliant advocate rather than the glowing fervour of a brilliant orator. And it is not on a public platform, but at a round table conference that he finds full scope for his unusual powers of persuasion, luminous exposition, searching argument and impeccable judgement.[43]

It was in the field of advocacy that Jinnah's genius really lay. His polished delivery, incisive reasoning, carefully adjusted monocle and well drilled gestures were all more suited to the theatre and the courtroom than to an open air mass meeting.

It is true that after he had been recognized by his followers as their Quaid-i-Azam (The Supreme Leader) he mesmerized huge public gatherings but that was due mainly to the hero worship aroused by his personal magnetism and universally known promises of political salvation.

He never became nor wanted to become a demagogue because he spoke neither Urdu nor Hindi with facility—and mass audiences in India did not understand English. Nevertheless, during the Pakistan Movement, people came in thousands to his public meetings to see him, many of them, who knew no English, simply because his message had already reached them through his lieutenants and the Congress newspapers which criticized him. He could be devastating in parliamentary debates which were conducted in English.[44]

In India there always has been a well-established tradition that the mere sight *(darshan)* of an exalted person confers merit. Gandhi was a poor public speaker but the Hindu masses flocked to have his *darshan* because they revered him as a mahatma. After he had completed his studies in London, Gandhi was given a farewell dinner by fellow vegetarians. In trying to thank them for the honour he could utter only one sentence of thanks. He tried to practice as a barrister in Bombay but at the very first appearance in court was so overcome by shyness that when he rose to cross-examine a witness he sat down and made over the case to a colleague.

He never again appeared in an Indian court. 'It was only in South Africa that I got over this shyness,' he tells us in his autobiography, 'though I never completely overcame it. It was impossible for me to speak impromptu. I hesitated whenever I had to face a strange audience and avoided making a speech whenever I could.'[45]

The historic Lahore session of the Muslim League in March 1940, which demanded independence for the Muslim majority areas of India, furnishes a good illustration of Jinnah's hold over a mass audience. *The Times of India* commented on his presidential address in these words

> Mr Jinnah decided to speak extempore, and no one knew what to expect. Prolonged shouts of 'Zindabad' greeted the slim figure in a black *achkan* as the President stepped before the microphone. Mr Jinnah's sallow face reflected the triumph of his reception. He spoke for nearly two hours, his voice now deep and trenchant, now light and ironic. Such was the dominance of his personality that, despite the improbability of more than a fraction of his audience understanding English, he held his hearers and played with palpable effect on their emotions.[46]

Jinnah's genius as an advocate is better described in the words of those who were best qualified to judge it.

The All-India Reporter (1948)

> Although Mr Jinnah's career as a political leader and as the representative of the successful Muslim Movement for separation in India overshadows all other aspects of his life, a legal journal like this has to take note of the fact that he was a lawyer of outstanding eminence and in his death our country has lost one of its greatest lawyers. As a brilliant advocate, he had few rivals. He was also universally recognized as a man of unimpeachable integrity, and honoured by friend and foe alike for his incorruptibility.[47]

M. C. Chagla

> I joined his chamber and remained with him for about six years. I read his briefs, went with him to court, and listened to his arguments. What impressed me most was the lucidity of his thought and expression. There were no obscure spots or ambiguities about what Jinnah had to tell the court. He was straight and forthright, and always left a strong impression whether his case was intrinsically good or bad. I remember sometimes at a conference he would tell the solicitor that his case was hopeless, but when he went to court he fought like a tiger, and almost made me believe that he had changed his opinion. Whenever I talked to him afterwards about it, he would say that it was the duty of an advocate, however bad the case might be, to do his best for his client.[48]

A 'veteran Muslim barrister' of Bombay recalled in an interview with Hector Bolitho

> One must realize that when he began to practise, he was the solitary Muslim barrister of the time: there may have been one or two others, but they did not amount to a row of pins. This was in a profession made up mostly of Hindus and Parsees. Perhaps they were over-critical of a Muslim—who came from business stock—setting up such a standard of industry. There was no pleasure in Jinnah's life: there were no interests beyond his work. He laboured at his briefs, day and night. I can see him, now, slim as a reed, always frowning, always in a hurry. There was never a whisper of gossip about his private habits. He was a hard-working, celibate, and not very gracious young man. Much too serious to attract friends. A figure like that invites criticism, especially in the lazy East, where we find it easier to forgive a man for his faults than for his virtues.[49]

Another advocate said, 'When he [Jinnah] stood up in courts, slowly looking towards the judge, placing his monocle in his eye—with the sense of timing you would expect from an actor—he became omnipotent. Yes, that is the word—omnipotent'.[50]

Jinnah's integrity was also legendary. The 'veteran Muslim Barrister' already quoted above related also the following story to Bolitho

> There was a well-known businessman, Haji Abdul Karim, who had to appear in Court on a serious charge. He went to Jinnah and asked him how much it would cost to take up the case. Jinnah answered bluntly, 'Five hundred rupees a day.'
>
> The businessman was cautious and he asked, 'How long will the case go on? I have five thousand rupees with me. Will you accept this to cover the whole of your fees?'
>
> Jinnah answered, 'I am not prepared to accept this amount. Five hundred rupees day is my fee, and you must engage me on these terms or find another lawyer.'
>
> Abdul Karim accepted the terms, and Jinnah won the case, in three days. He accepted his fee of fifteen hundred rupees with good grace.[51]

Yet another advocate recalled

> Always, with Jinnah, one comes back to his honesty. Once when a client was referred to him, the solicitor mentioned that the man had limited money with which to fight the suit. Nevertheless, Jinnah took it up. He lost—but he still had faith in the case and he said that it should be taken to the Appeal Court. The solicitor again mentioned that his client had no money. Jinnah pressed him to defray certain of the appeal expenses out of his own pocket, and promised to fight the case without any fee for himself. This time, he won; but when the solicitor offered him a fee Jinnah refused—arguing that he had accepted the case on the condition that there was no fee.[52]

With financial worries behind him, Jinnah moved into a better apartment, began to support his family and in particular bore the educational expenses of his brothers and sisters. He got Fatima admitted to the Bandra Convent School in Bombay. Thereafter, she moved to the Dental School of the Bombay University. Jinnah visited her on Sundays and took her for carriage drives. He also gave up his membership in the Khoja Ismaili Sect of Shiahs into which he had been born and which accepts the Aga Khan as their spiritual leader and joined instead the Khoja sect of Asna Asharis who too are Shiahs but recognize no religious head.

Entrance into Politics

One of Jinnah's own statements tell us when he embarked upon a political career. On 13 August 1919 he appeared as a representative of the Muslim League before the Joint Select Committee constituted to suggest how to bring about progressive realization of a responsible government in India. Montagu, one of the members, asked him, 'How long have you been in public life, Mr Jinnah?' He replied, 'Since I was twenty-one'.[53]

That takes us back to 1897 when he had freshly arrived in Bombay from London. Though Montagu used the broad term 'public life', the Joint Select Committee was considering a purely political question and Jinnah was speaking as the representative of a political party. There can, therefore, be no doubt but that what Montagu was asking Jinnah was how long he had been in politics.

But the Muslim League leader also made a second statement on the subject. At the Annual Dinner of the Old Boys' Association of the Osmania University on 28 September 1939, he informed the gathering, 'I have been in practical politics for over a quarter of a century,'[54] which means since about 1914.

Why did he give 1897 as the commencing date in one case and 1914 in the other?

What Jinnah meant by the first statement was that he had entered into politics as a beginner as soon as he returned to Bombay from London. Having taken a keen interest in politics as a student abroad, it was but natural that directly on returning home he should have begun personally to play the game. He could not very well start at the top; he had to graduate from the civic and provincial level.

His second statement that he had been in 'practical politics' since 1914 meant that from that time he had begun to play a constructive role at the highest level. He had been an increasingly important member of the Congress Party since his first appearance at its annual session in 1906. In October 1913 he was warmly welcomed into the ranks of the Muslim League as well. This unique position of being a respected member of both the principal political parties of the country launched him on his celebrated role of ambassador of Hindu-Muslim unity.

To get back to 1897. From that year he began to attend the meetings of the Anjuman-i-Islam of Bombay of which Badruddin Tyabji[55] was the president. He was elected as a member of the Bombay Corporation in March 1904 but resigned two years later.

In May 1905, he was nominated by the Bombay Presidency Association to be a member of the delegation to plead the Indian case before the British electorate. His name was endorsed by the Provincial Congress but it was blocked by Tilak on the ground that he was too young and inexperienced.

Notes

1. This name is taken from Fatima Jinnah's article 'A Sister's Recollections', in *Pakistan, Past and Present*, published in 1976 in commemoration of the centenary of the birth of the Founder of Pakistan.
2. Fatima Jinnah, 'A Sister's Recollections', op.cit., p. 42.
3. A very pure gelatine prepared from the air bladders of sturgeons and other fishes and used specially in jellies and glue.
4. A water-soluble gum obtained from several acacias and used specially in the manufacture of adhesives and in pharmacy.
5. Fatima Jinnah, 'A Sister's Recollections', op.cit., p. 43.
6. Ibid., p. 43.
7. Ibid., 'My father wanted him to be good at mathematics, as accounts were the back-bone of business'. Fatima Jinnah, *My Brother*, p. 57.
8. Riaz Ahmad, *Quaid-i-Azam Mohammad Ali Jinnah, The Formative Years*, p. 26.
9. Fatima Jinnah, 'A Sister's Recollections', op.cit., p. 43.
10. Ibid., p. 44.
11. Riaz Ahmad, *The Formative Years*, op.cit., pp. 28-29.
12. Fatima Jinnah, 'A Sister's Recollections', op.cit., p. 44.
13. In stating that Jinnah left Karachi for London in the first week of November 1892, we have followed Riaz Ahmad, *The Formative Years*, op.cit., p. 32.
14. Syed Sharifuddin Pirzada, *Some Aspects of Quaid-i-Azam's Life*, p. 9.
15. This story is related by Fatima Jinnah but she does not mention the name of the Englishman who befriended her brother.
16. Popularly called 'Pea-soupers'.
17. Fatima Jinnah, 'A Sister's Recollections', op.cit., p. 45.
18. Riaz Ahmad, *The Formative Years*, op.cit., p. 35.
19. Fatima Jinnah, 'A Sister's Recollections', op.cit., p. 46.

20. Ibid., p. 45.
21. Pirzada, *Some Aspects of Quaid-i-Azam's Life*, op.cit., p. 9.
22. In an address to the Karachi Bar Association in 1947, Jinnah recalled, 'I joined Lincoln's Inn because there, on the main entrance, the name of the Prophet was included in the list of the great lawgivers of the world'. Bolitho, *Jinnah*, op.cit., p. 9. His memory had obviously tricked him into believing that it was the name of the Prophet and not a fresco depicting his image that he had seen.
23. Jamil-UD-Din Ahmad, *Quaid-i-Azam as Seen by his Contemporaries*, p. 81.
24. Fatima Jinnah, 'A Sister's Recollections', op.cit., p. 45.
25. Riaz Ahmad, *The Formative Years*, op.cit., p. 44.
26. R. P. Masani, *Dadabahi Naoroji*, p. 7.
27. Ibid., p. 284.
28. Riaz Ahmad is quite right in pointing out that 'Jinnah had not taken part in Naoroji's election', *The Formative Years*, op.cit., p. 36. As already stated, Jinnah found London cold and wet and depressing when he first arrived there. This is consistent with weather in November. Naoroji had been elected in July.
29. Hector Bolitho, *Jinnah*, op.cit., p. 9.
30. Fatima Jinnah, 'A Sister's Recollections', op.cit., p. 46.
31. A writer and for some time a member of the Indian diplomatic service.
32. Pirzada, *Some Aspects of Quaid-i-Azam's Life*, op.cit., p. 11.
33. Fatima Jinnah, 'A Sister's Recollections', op.cit., p. 47.
34. Sarojini Naidu, *Mohomed Ali Jinnah, An Ambassador of Unity*, p. 3.
35. Fatima Jinnah, 'A Sister's Recollections', op.cit., p. 46.
36. Riaz Ahmad, *The Formative Years*, op.cit., pp. 32-33.
37. Quaid-i-Azam, Mahomed Ali Jinnah, *Speeches as Governor-General of Pakistan*, p. 4.
38. Even in his maturer years, Jinnah was strikingly handsome. 'Lady Wavell said of him, "Mr Jinnah was one of the handsomest men I have ever seen; he combined the clear-cut almost Grecian, features of the West with Oriental grace and movement".' H. Bolitho, *Jinnah*, op.cit., p. 213.
39. Fatima Jinnah, 'A Sister's Recollections', op.cit., p. 47.
40. This account has been taken from M. H. Saiyid, *Mohammad Ali Jinnah*, 1965, pp. 6-7. Saiyid was Jinnah's private secretary from 1940-44.
41. Ibid., p. 8.
42. Waheed Ahmad ed., *Quaid-i-Azam Mohammad Ali Jinnah, The Nation's Voice (March 1935-March 1940)* p. 188.
43. Sarojini Naidu, *An Ambassador of Unity*, op.cit., p. 16.
44. Fatima Jinnah, 'A Sister's Recollections', op.cit., p. 46.
45. M. K. Gandhi, *An Autobiography*, p. 72.
46. Pirzada, *Foundations of Pakistan* II, p. 327.
47. Pirzada, *Some Aspects of Quaid-i-Azam's Life*, op.cit., p. 41.
48. M. C. Chagla, *Roses in December*, op.cit., p. 54.
49. H. Bolitho, *Jinnah*, op.cit., p. 19. Bolitho wrote his book in 1954 when many persons who knew Jinnah personally in his working years were still alive and the biographer could interview them.
50. Ibid., p. 18.

51. Ibid., pp. 20-21.
52. Ibid., pp. 18-19.
53. Pirzada, *Collected Works*, Vol. I, op.cit., p. 326.
54. Waheed Ahmad, *Quaid-i-Azam Mohammad Ali Jinnah,* op.cit., p. 390.
55. Tyabji was a leading barrister of Bombay and became a judge of the Bombay High Court. He presided over the annual session of the Indian National Congress in 1887.

CHAPTER 3

The Quaid-i-Azam's Character and Political Style[1]

The Quaid-i-Azam appeared on the all-India political stage for the first time in December 1906[2] when he attended the annual session of the Indian National Congress at Calcutta. Before we discuss his role from that landmark onwards, it would be helpful to describe the salient features of his character and political style which moulded his course.

Integrity

His sartorial fastidiousness which everyone noticed immediately was nothing but an apparent symbol of the fastidiousness of his entire make-up. Nanji Jafar, who had been at school with Jinnah recalled that one morning when he was playing in the street, Jinnah then about fourteen, came up to him and said, 'Don't play marbles in the dust; it spoils your clothes and dirties your hands. We must stand up and play cricket.'[3]

The governing feature of his character was utter integrity. This was recognized by opponent and friend alike. After the failure of their historic September 1944 talks for a settlement, Gandhi said that 'he had the highest regard for Jinnah's single-mindedness, his great ability and integrity which nothing could buy'.[4]

When standing for election to the Central Legislative Assembly as an independent candidate in 1923, he said in his election manifesto

> Of one thing I can assure you, that the popular cause and the welfare of India will be my keynote and the guiding principle in the future as, I hope, it has been in the past. I have no desire to seek any post or position or title from the Government. My sole object is to serve the cause of the country as best as I can.[5]

During the First Session of the Round Table Conference in London (November 1930-January 1931), Prime Minister Ramsay MacDonald tried to influence Jinnah. He

> ...sent for Jinnah and told him that in the new order of things that would come in India, the British Prime Minister would have to look for prominent Indians to take up the governorships of provinces, obviously implying that Jinnah would have an excellent chance if he proved to be a good boy. Jinnah asked MacDonald if this was an attempt to bribe him to get his support on the British Government's compromise suggestion, particularly Commercial safeguards.[6]

One of his unusual practices was that he did not give large parties for his followers. His own explanation for this was

> I do not like to approach people through their stomachs. I only want to be judged on my merits and actions. Tea and dinner parties are given to dissuade the people from looking at the shortcomings of their leaders but view them only from behind the screen of social charm. This puts difficulties in the way of work. Some people including my loyal colleagues complain of this attitude on my part. They do not say anything openly to my face but think in their heart of hearts that I am unsocial. Some even think that I am stingy and do not like to spend money on my friends and colleagues. But the truth is as I have told you, that the giving of parties is a kind of bribery in return for which people's support is obtained. I thoroughly detest it.[7]

Indeed, he would firmly tell his followers that he preferred defeat to winning elections by adopting dishonest and corrupt methods.[8]

Most politicians go out of their way to curry favour with the Press; Jinnah was apt to go out of his way to tell the Press in so many words that he was indifferent to its opinion of him. This was illustrated by his letter published in *The Times of India* on 10 June 1915. It related to the difference of opinion between the members of the Muslim League on the question whether to hold the next annual session of the League at Bombay at the same time as the annual session of the Indian National Congress. Jinnah was the moving spirit behind those who favoured the proposal. *The Times* had sided with those who had opposed the idea. In his letter to the newspaper, Jinnah pointed out 'a series of misrepresentations' in its columns and also protested against its attitude towards the proposal. And at the end he made clear that 'I for one, Sir, whatever may have been my ambition in life, never aspired to get your increased respect for myself'.[9]

Independence of India, His Lifelong Passion

Jinnah could truthfully claim that he had 'never accepted the idea in the whole of my life that we should be under any foreign domination in this country'.[10] This was, of course, sharply different from the history of Gandhi's attitude toward British imperialism.

Gandhi assisted the British in the Boer War and the Zulu Rebellion in South Africa and worked as a recruiting officer during World War I. At a dinner in April 1915 he explained his conduct in these words, 'I discovered that the British Empire had certain ideals with which I have fallen in love and one of these ideals is that every subject of the British Empire has the freest scope possible for his energy and honour and whatever he thinks is due to his conscience'.[11]

Recalling Gandhi's South African days, his biographer tells us that Gandhi 'vied with Englishmen in...loyalty to the throne, taught his children to sing with him the National Anthem in the correct English style and never missed an opportunity to give public expression to his loyalty to the throne'.[12]

Adopting the Khilafat and the Punjab atrocities as his causes, the erstwhile ultra-loyalist Mahatma in 1920 suddenly turned into a non-cooperating revolutionary and promised to turn out the British within one year.[13] And during World War II he staged an open rebellion under the slogan 'Quit India'.

Such extreme swings of policy were alien to the Quaid's even temperament. He sympathized with the allies in both World Wars and never hindered the flow of India's tremendous help in men and material. At the same time he made his enthusiastic support conditional on his country being treated as an equal member of the family of nations comprising the British Empire.

His Sang-froid

Beverley Nichols commented on the Quaid-i-Azam's sang-froid in these words: 'He had a mind as subtle as Gandhi's but whereas

Gandhi met the sweltering heat of Bombay in a cotton shift, Jinnah was invariably dressed in a lounge suit with a stiff white collar and monocle dangling over his waist-coat. And of the two men he looked considerably cooler.'[14] Two encounters, one of Gandhi with Viceroy Wavell, and the other of Jinnah with Viceroy Mountbatten, will illustrate the point.

The Gandhi-Wavell interview took place on 27 August 1946. Wavell wished Congress to state clearly that the grouping of provinces in the constitution-making body proposed by the Cabinet Mission was compulsory. In the course of the argument Gandhi thumped the table and said, 'If India wants her blood bath she shall have it'. Wavell told him that he was shocked to hear such words from him.[15]

Mountbatten's verbal onslaught on Jinnah took place in July 1947 after Jinnah had informed him that he himself would be the first governor-general of Pakistan. India had already nominated Mountbatten as her governor-general and Mountbatten had taken it for granted that Pakistan would follow suit. 'Mountbatten was wounded in his tenderest spot: his vanity was hurt and his pride affronted'. One day when the Quaid was working on the Indian Independence Bill with Liaquat Ali Khan and Chaudhri Muhammed Ali in a room in the Viceroy's House, Mountbatten burst into the room and 'belaboured the Quaid-i-Azam with arguments, appeals and bluster... The responsibility for the immeasurable loss to Pakistan would rest on the shoulders of Jinnah... He was sure that the verdict of history would uphold him and go against Jinnah... Jinnah bore this onslaught with great dignity and patience' and did not lose his cool. He explained that in assuming the governor-generalship of his newly independent country 'he had not been moved by any personal considerations but had objectively taken only the interest of his people into account'.[16]

His Constitutionalism

Given his orderly disposition, it is not surprising that Jinnah wished to win independence for his motherland by constitutional means. In the course of his presidential address at the Ninth Session of the All-India Muslim League at Lucknow on 30-31 December 1916 he said

If we turn to history, we find that in the past, only such people have been declared fit for freedom who fought for it and attained it. We are living in different times. Peace has its victories. We are fighting and can only fight constitutional battles.[17] Even if a man did take part in agitation, it did not mean that he wanted to pull down the government.[18]

What the situation demanded was that Hindus and Muslims should 'stand united and use every constitutional and legitimate means' to effect the 'transfer of power from the bureaucracy to democracy...the voice of the three hundred million people vibrating throughout the length and breadth of the country, will produce a force which no power on earth can resist'.[19]

He was all for carrying the constitutional battle into the legislature. When there was a difference of opinion in the country in 1923 on the question of Council entry, Jinnah said, 'I, for one am more than ever convinced that the proper course for us is to send our representatives to the Assembly'.[20]

Though by force of argument and personality the Quaid usually was able to get his way in Muslim League meetings, he never departed from the procedure of obtaining the approval of the League Working Committee or Council before committing himself on matters of importance. He explained at a Council meeting that the Working Committee corresponded to a Cabinet and the Council to a Parliament. If the Council disapproved the decision of the Working Committee the members of the latter would have to resign.[21] He was against being elected president of the Muslim League for life. At the Muslim Council meeting at New Delhi on 24 February 1941 he was re-elected president for another year. When one member suggested that the Quaid be elected president for life, the latter said, 'Let me come to you at the end of every year and seek your vote and your confidence. Let your president be on his good behaviour. I am definitely opposed to your electing a life president.'[22]

At another time he told the Muslim League Workers, 'My power is derived from you—the masses... Leaders are made by you. If they do not act honestly, do not make them the leaders. You can do that to me as well.' And he cited the example of Churchill who had been 'thrown into the wilderness' by the electorate despite having been the most successful war leader.[23]

He also believed that 'an opposition party or parties are good correctives for any party which is in power'.²⁴

He emphasized that pure majority rule after the fashion of the British Parliamentary System was not suitable for India because it would mean unbroken Hindu domination. It was necessary for the rights of the minorities to be constitutionally safeguarded. But he disfavoured communal electorates as one of the safeguards. However, he accepted the overwhelming support of fellow Muslims for separate electorates as a mandate and as their representative successfully pleaded for their acceptance by the Hindus in the Lucknow Pact.

He also recognized the right of others to oppose and criticize him. A well-known example of this was the intemperate tirade against him at the Allahabad session of the Muslim League in April 1942. A resolution giving full power to Jinnah to take any action he might consider necessary in furtherance of the objects of the Muslims was carried in the open session with the single dissenting vote of Maulana Hasrat Mohani. During his speech Mohani

> ...went to the extent of casting reflections on Mr Jinnah's judgement and even intentions. He even expressed the suspicion that Mr Jinnah would not uphold the Muslim League ideal and would accept something less than an independent Pakistan. The whole gathering was soon up on its feet... Pandemonium raged all round.

But Jinnah repeatedly called for order and asked the audience to give a patient hearing to the Maulana and 'kept smiling all the time'.²⁵

It is unthinkable that the circumspect Quaid would ever make a martial proclamation like that made by the professedly pacific Mahatma when the Ramgarh Congress in the spring of 1940 authorized him to initiate a civil disobedience campaign. Though Gandhi had not been even an ordinary member of the Congress party since 1934, he accepted the post of 'General' and said, 'When we march as an army, we are no longer a democracy. As soldiers we have got to take orders from the General and obey him implicitly. His word must be law. I am your General.'²⁶

While the Congress 'General' and his lieutenants got themselves locked up in jail for their rebellious conduct during the war, Jinnah reaped the benefit of his constitutionalism and remained free to consolidate the power of the Muslim League unhindered by the formidable Congress machine.

His Secular Politics

By purposely introducing religion into politics, Gandhi, the apostle of non-violence, inflamed religious feelings which intensified violent clashes between the two major communities of the country. Ambedkar summed up the record of Hindu-Muslim relationship from 1920[27] to 1940 as, 'twenty years of civil war between the Hindus and the Muslims in India, interrupted by brief intervals of armed peace'.[28]

Jinnah, on the other hand, tried to build up Hindu-Muslim amity by political give and take and kept religion out of politics till the experience of Hindu rule in the Congress provinces (1937-39) drove him to the conclusion that if the Muslims wished to practice their religion and culture freely they would have to achieve an independent homeland of their own.

During his speech in the Central Legislative Assembly on 7 February 1935 he said that 'religion should not be allowed to come into politics... Religion is merely a matter between man and God.'[29]

Addressing the Jamiat-ul-Ulema Conference at Delhi in April 1936 he argued that the question of constitutional safeguards for the Muslims 'was not a religious question, but was purely a political problem'.[30] Later the same year at the All-India Muslim League Session at Bombay in December 1936 he pointed out that in a system of government by majority rule in India the Muslims would be a minority community. Therefore, 'it was not a religious question. It was a question whether they should not have sufficient safeguards which would inspire confidence in them, so that they too could wholeheartedly join with the sister communities in the march for freedom.'[31]

That Jinnah considered safeguards for minorities a basic political question and not a concession due only to the Muslims on religious grounds is further illustrated by his attitude to the Hindu Scheduled Castes (also called Untouchables or Depressed Classes).

He told the Legislative Assembly on 7 February 1935 that at the Round Table Conference he had 'pleaded more for Depressed Classes before Mahatma Gandhi than I did for the Mussulmans'.[32]

During his presidential address at the All-India Muslim League session at Delhi in 1943 he said, 'in the name of humanity I care more for them [the Untouchables] than for Mussulmans'.[33] And at the Lahore Muslim League Conference on 31 July 1944 he could truthfully claim that at no time had he neglected the interests of the Scheduled Castes and promised that he would 'always stand for their protection and safeguard in any future scheme of constitution'.[34]

Interestingly, in a statement issued on 25 February 1942, Ambedkar, the Scheduled Caste leader complained that, 'The Congress choose to forget that Hinduism is a political ideology of the same character as the Fascist or Nazi ideology... This is not the point of view of Muslims alone. It is also the point of view of the Depressed Classes.'[35]

By following secular politics for as long as he possibly could, Jinnah proved himself a much more faithful disciple of Naoroji and Gokhale than Gandhi who too professed to be a disciple of theirs.

Reserved but Correct

In personal relations, Jinnah was reserved. His sad home-coming from England and first briefless years had stung his proud and self-respecting nature. The failure of his marriage and the early death of his wife created a further inner sadness.

But he was always courteous and correct. He had no time for idle gossip and empty pleasantries but was always willing to engage in meaningful conversation with young and old. Jamil-UD-Din who knew the Quaid well from his student days states that he was able to interview him freely. 'It is difficult and sometimes impossible to seek interviews with lesser men, but never so with him'. It was at private meetings 'that one discovered another aspect of this greatness—as a conversationalist':

> He started slowly at first. You were at once bewitched by the musical ring of his cultured voice, the beauty of his intonation, and the easy flow of his expression. Words fell from his lips like beautifully-formed pearls and rubies and one found it difficult to gather them all in one's lap. As he got into stride you were moved by the intensity of his

intellectual passion; the emotional fervour was not much in evidence as he always kept his emotions in check. While hearing the Quaid-i-Azam one could realize what it was to be 'possessed' of a great 'idea'. Every fibre of his being seemed to vibrate with the 'Pakistan idea'. His passion was infectious. Whether you agreed with him or not you could not escape this infection. If you agreed you were filled with zeal to contribute your mite towards its realization; if you did not, you were haunted by it.[36]

Dr Sir C. R. Reddy, a prominent non-Brahmin leader of South India, depicted Jinnah's no-nonsense personality in these terms

He is the pride of India and not the private possession of the Muslims... A straight thinker, straight fighter and strong hitter, he is anything but a subtlety shop and in fact suspicious of subtle politicians whose texts read one way and whose oft-repeated commentaries in other and different ways according to exigencies. In dignity, racial and personal, he is an example and standard-bearer. He abhors the oily pose of mock modesty and ultra-humility... The spiritual drive of the political missionary is his, for he wants nothing for himself and everything for his country on an equitable basis of distribution as between its component elements... The great root good he has done to India is saving our politics from being clouded over, confused and confounded by metaphysics and moonshine.[37]

The Quaid did not wear his heart on his sleeve but he was not lacking in inner sensitiveness. He was seen to be moved to tears at least on three occasions.

The first occasion was after his amendments to the Nehru Report had been rejected at Calcutta in December 1928 by the All-Parties Conference. Jamshed Nusserwanjee, a Parsee, who saw him off at the railway station on the following morning stated that 'he had tears in his eyes'.[38]

The next occasion was the burial of his wife Ruttie on 22 February 1929: 'As Ruttie's body was being lowered into the grave' wrote eye witness Kanji Dwarkadas, 'Jinnah, as the nearest relative was the first to throw the earth on the grave and he broke down suddenly and sobbed and wept like a child for minutes together'.[39]

The last occasion was January 1948, after Partition, when he went to see an encampment of Hindus who had stayed on in

Pakistan. 'When he saw their misery, he wept. I [Nusserwanjee] saw tears on his cheeks.'[40]

Sarojini Naidu painted the following eloquent pen-portrait of Jinnah

> Never was there a nature whose outer qualities provided so complete an antithesis of its inner worth. Tall and stately, but thin to the point of emaciation, languid and luxurious of habit, Mohomed Ali Jinnah's attenuated form is the deceptive sheathe of a spirit of exceptional vitality and endurance. Somewhat formal and fastidious, and a little aloof and imperious of manner, the calm hauteur of his accustomed reserve but masks for those who know him, a naive and eager humanity, an intuition quick and tender as a woman's, a humour gay and winning as a child's—pre-eminently rational and practical, discreet and dispassionate in his estimate and acceptance of life, the obvious sanity and serenity of his worldly wisdom effectually disguise a shy and splendid idealism which is of the very essence of the man.[41]

The Quaid-i-Azam was always deeply admired and respected for his outstanding integrity and competence. After the movement for the Muslim homeland promised by him intensified and became charged with emotion, he became Pakistan personified and everyone who loved Pakistan loved Jinnah too.

Notes

1. For Jinnah's genius in advocacy *see*, Chapter 2.
2. Speculation that he may have attended any annual session of the Congress prior to 1906 is beside the point. He himself said quite clearly that he 'first attended the annual session of the Congress' in 1906. Pirzada, *Collected Works*, II, op. cit., p. 28.
3. H. Bolitho, *Jinnah*, op. cit., p. 5.
4. Pyarelal, *Mahatma Gandhi, The Last Phase*, I, p. 100. His integrity as a barrister has been noted in Chapter 2. Here we describe his integrity as a politician.
5. Pirzada, *Collected Works*, II, op. cit., p. 28.
6. Kanji Dwarkadas, *India's Fight for Freedom*, p. 385. Dwarkadas met Jinnah in 1916 and remained his friend till Jinnah's death. He also knew Gandhi well.
7. Jamil-UD-Din Ahmad, *Quaid-i-Azam as Seen by his Contemporaries*, op.cit., p. 122.
8. Ibid, p. 119.
9. Pirzada, *Collected Works*, II, op. cit., pp. 133-5.
10. Jamil-UD-Din Ahmad, *Speeches and Writings of Mr Jinnah*, I, op. cit., p. 380.

11. Louis Fischer, *The Life of Mahatma Gandhi*, op. cit., p. 145.
12. Pyarelal, *Mahatma Gandhi, The Early Phase*, I, op.cit., p. 721.
13. *See*, Chapter 7.
14. Jamil-UD-Din Ahmad, *Quaid-i-Azam as Seen by His Contemporaries*, op.cit., p. 181.
15. Wavell, *The Viceroy's Journal*, p. 341 (f.n.).
16. Chaudhri Muhammad Ali, *The Emergence of Pakistan*, pp. 176-7.
17. Pirzada, *Collected Works*, Vol. I, op. cit., p. 195.
18. Ibid., p. 125.
19. Ibid., p. 160.
20. Pirzada, *Collected Works*, II, op. cit., p. 28.
21. Jamil-UD-Din Ahmad, *Speeches and Writings of Mr Jinnah*, II, op. cit., pp. 298-9.
22. Waheed Ahmad, *The Nation's Voice*, II, op. cit., p. 150.
23. Jamil-UD-Din Ahmad, *Speeches and Writings of Mr Jinnah*, II, op. cit., p. 273.
24. Ibid., p. 232.
25. Jamil-UD-Din Ahmad, *Quaid-i-Azam as Seen by His Contemporaries*, op.cit., p. 211.
26. R. Coupland, *Indian Politics, 1936-1942*, op. cit., p. 92.
27. Gandhi assumed supreme leadership of the Congress Party with effect from the Amritsar Congress session of December 1919. Jawaharlal Nehru called it 'the first Gandhi Congress'. (*Autobiography*, op. cit., p. 44.)
28. B. R. Ambedkar, *Pakistan*, p. 175.
29. Jamil-UD-Din Ahmad, *Speeches and Writings of Mr Jinnah*, I, op. cit., p. 5.
30. M. H. Saiyid, *Jinnah*, 1945 edition, op. cit., p. 538.
31. Ibid., p. 545.
32. Jamil-UD Din Ahmad, *Speeches and Writings of Mr Jinnah*, I, op. cit., p. 6.
33. Ibid., p. 504.
34. Jamil-UD-Din Ahmad, *Speeches and Writings of Mr Jinnah*, II, op. cit., p. 82.
35. Ibid., Vol. I, p. 376.
36. Jamil-UD-Din Ahmad, *Quaid-i-Azam As Seen by His Contemporaries*, op. cit., pp. 208-9.
37. Ibid., p. 244.
38. H. Bolitho, *Jinnah*, op. cit., p. 95.
39. Kanji Dwarkadas, *Ruttie Jinnah*, p. 58.
40. H. Bolitho, *Jinnah*, op. cit., p. 95.
41. Sarojini Naidu, *Mohomed Ali Jinnah, An Ambassador of Unity*, op. cit., p. 2.

CHAPTER 4

The Birth of Indian Nationalism and Muslim Nationalism

India in 1906

1906 was a landmark in the political career of Jinnah. In that year he stepped up from local to all-India politics by attending and actively participating in the annual session of the Indian National Congress. But 1906 was also a highly important year in the history of Indian nationalsim. Because of its unhappiness with the partition of Bengal, the predominantly Hindu Congress party displayed the first signs of wavering in its hitherto docile acceptance of British rule and of its movement toward agitational politics. Moreover the Muslims founded the Muslim League, a political party of their own, which eventually won Pakistan.

The Birth of Indian Nationalism

We have already pointed out that the feeling that the peoples and regions of the Indian subcontinent formed a single nation was the creation of the twin forces of administrative unity and Western conceptions of democracy and nationalism provided by the British rule in India.[1]

The Indian National Congress claiming to stand for all-India nationalism[2] was founded in 1885 by Allan Octavian Hume (1829-1912), a Scotsman, who had retired from the Indian Civil Service to devote his life to Indian political regeneration.

Hume at first intended to call the proposed organization 'The Indian National Union'. It held a preliminary meeting in March 1885 and decided to convene a conference at the end of that year. A circular invitation stated:

> A conference of the Indian National Union will be held at Poona from the 25th to the 31st December 1885... composed of Delegates—leading politicians well acquainted with the English language—from all parts of the Bengal, Bombay and Madras Presidencies. The direct objects of the conference will be: (1) To enable all the most earnest labourers in the cause of national progress to become personally known to each other; (2) to discuss and decide upon the political operations to be undertaken during the year. Indirectly this conference will form the germ of a native Parliament and, if properly conducted, will constitute in a few years an unanswerable reply to the assertion that India is still wholly unfit for any form of representative institutions...

In the event the venue of the conference had to be changed from Poona to Bombay because of an outbreak of cholera at Poona a few days before it was due to meet. The word 'Congress' was also substituted for 'Conference' in the description of the assembly on the eve of its meeting.

That the invitation was confined to 'leading politicians well acquainted with the English language' immediately qualified a larger number of Hindus than Muslims as delegates because the Hindus had taken more readily to Western education than the Muslims who had been too stunned by the loss of their empire to be able to adjust to the new conditions to the same extent. The Congress attachment to the English language was re-affirmed by a resolution passed at the twenty-seventh session (1912) which laid down that, 'A person ignorant of English should be held ineligible for membership' of the Imperial Legislative Council (Resolution VIII clause 8).

The first Congress warmly affirmed its loyalty to Queen Victoria by concluding the proceedings with vociferous cheers for her. According to the official report

> Mr Hume, after acknowledging the honour done him, said that as the giving of cheers had been entrusted to him, he must be allowed to propose—on the principle of better late than never—giving of cheers, and that not only three but three times three, and if possible thrice that, for one, the latchet of whose shoes he was unworthy to loose, one to whom they were all dear, to whom they were all as children—need he say, Her Most Gracious Majesty The Queen-Empress.
>
> The rest of the speaker's remarks, the report adds, was lost in the storm of applause that instantly burst out, and the asked-for cheers were given over and over.³

It was the partition of Bengal which shook the loyalty of the Congress. That Bengal was an unwieldy province is undeniable. The boundary of the Presidency of Bengal had reached the river Sutlej in 1803. The North-West Provinces were detached from it in 1835 and Assam in 1874. Nevertheless, Bengal still consisted of Bengal proper, plus Bihar and Orissa. It had a population of 78,000,000 and an area of 190,000 square miles. Its terrain was covered with numerous forests and streams which made it difficult to travel from one part to another. The eastern part of Bengal was backward and distant from Calcutta, the capital. Plans for the partition of the unwieldy province had been mooted before Curzon's time, but in the end it was he who had the courage to grasp the nettle. Despite protests voiced after the proposal became known, partition took effect on the appointed day— 16 October 1905.

Bengali Hindus had every reason to be alarmed at the consequences of the partition. From being a majority in the undivided province, they became a minority in both the new provinces. The new province of East Bengal and Assam, with a population of thirty-one million, with Dhaka as its capital, was preponderantly Muslim. In the residuary province of forty-seven million, the Bengalis were outnumbered by Biharis and Oriyas.

Curzon called partition 'a mere readjustment of administrative boundaries', but the Bengali Hindus believed that Curzon had resorted to partition to curb their rising nationalism. By cutting the language area into two and separating Muslims from Hindus, he had split the 'Bengali nation'. It was nothing but the age-old device of divide and rule. At first, some Muslims joined in the agitation against partition, but before long most of them came out in its favour because they realized that in the new province of East Bengal and Assam they would enjoy a majority of more than sixty per cent and would therefore have a much greater say in their own affairs than they could ever have had in a united Bengal.

The Hindus enlisted the help of religion to make the agitation against partition a mass movement. During the festival of Durga Puja in 1905, a crowd of almost 50,000 collected at a temple of Kali near Culcutta. On 16 October 1905, the day on which partition took effect, all the shops in Calcutta were closed and all business activity came to a halt. Parties paraded the streets singing 'Bande Mataram' and throngs of people bathed in the holy water of the Ganges. Thousands performed the *rakhi-bandhan* ceremony which henceforth was performed on every sixteenth of October. The ritual entailed the tying of a woollen thread by a sister round her brother's wrist and his taking the vow to undo the partition of Bengal. These religious outpourings further emphasized the Hindu character of the agitation.

The Twenty-second Congress in December 1906 at Calcutta was presided over by Naoroji who, now eighty-two years of age, gave his speech to Gokhale to read. Among the resolutions passed by the Congress two were of special importance. One recorded 'the emphatic protest of the Congress against the partition of Bengal' and asked for a reversal 'in such a manner as to keep the entire Bengali-speaking community under one undivided administration'. The other demanded that 'the system of government obtaining in the Self-Governing British Colonies should be extended to India' and indicated steps which should be immediately taken toward that goal.

But these demands were not unexpected. A special feature of the occasion was the terms in which he couched the demand for self-government. Indians 'are British citizens, and are entitled to and claim all British citizen's rights', he argued. He emphasized that Indians must have full control over their own affairs just as the people in the United Kingdom had and concluded, 'The whole matter can be comprised in one word, Self-Government or Swaraj, like that of the United Kingdom or the Colonies'.

Though the demand for self-government for India was not new

> ...it was for the first time, in such a place, that the form and nature of India's demand was expressed by an Indian word, Swaraj, the meaning of which could be easily understood throughout the length and breadth of India by the simplest villager as well as by the educated classes. The old spell had been broken at last and men now spoke out their minds freely. This brought with it a psychological change that worked miracles in the succeeding years.[4]

In his presidential address, Naoroji had called upon his countrymen to agitate for self-government but he had advised them to do so 'peacefully'. His definition of 'agitate' was: 'Agitate means inform. Inform the Indian people what their rights are and why and how they should obtain them, and inform the British people of the rights of the Indian people and why they should grant them.'[5]

This represented the view of the Moderates in the Congress party who were led by Gokhale who believed that Indian aspirations could be realized within the British family of nations.

The Extremists led by Tilak, on the other hand, were not enamoured of the British connection; they believed that constitutional agitation would not bring the desired result. Tilak wished to use boycott as a political weapon and described the scope of boycott as follows

> Boycott is a political weapon. We shall not give them assistance to collect revenue and keep peace. We shall not assist them in fighting beyond the frontiers or outside India with Indian blood and money. We shall not assist them in carrying on the administration of justice. We shall have our own courts, and when the time comes we shall not pay taxes.[6]

This programme strikingly resembled that which Gandhi adopted some years later under the caption 'non-co-operation'.

The Extremists left the Congress in the hands of the Moderates some months after the acrimonious Surat session of December 1907. The Moderates controlled Congress till Tilak returned to its ranks in 1916.

Tilak had been sentenced to deportation for six years in July 1908 for sedition and was released from Mandalay (Burma) jail on 17 June 1914. He returned to freedom a mellower politician. He had realized that 'the bureaucracy is more shrewd than either of us and if we do not adopt their shrewdness we should be perhaps perpetuating our disunion'.[7]

Gokhale passed away on 19 February 1915 and Tilak generously acknowledged his greatness, 'This diamond of India, this jewel of Maharashtra, this prince of workers, is taking eternal rest on the funeral grounds. Look at him and try to emulate him'.[8]

Tilak rejoined the Congress at the Lucknow session of the Congress in December 1916 and gave powerful support to Jinnah in forging the Lucknow Pact. He and Jinnah were both practical politicians. They got on well at a personal level as well. Jinnah acted as his counsel in sedition cases in 1908 and again in 1916.

Sir Syed Ahmed Khan, the Father of Muslim Nationalism

Never since Muhammad bin Qasim conquered Sind in 712 AD had Muslim fortunes in India fallen so low as in the years immediately following the Great Rebellion of 1857. Not only had the Muslims lost an empire but the Hindus, over whom they had ruled for several hundred years, were poised to overwhelm them under the new conditions.

The British authorities held the Muslims chiefly responsible for the Rebellion and the Hindus, who had readily taken to Western education, occupied the bulk of the administrative posts available to Indians. Economically, too the Muslims were in a miserable state. As the ruling class they had, in their heyday, preferred to occupy government positions and had left trade and commerce mostly in Hindu hands.

In the field of education the Muslims were shocked when their British rulers decreed in 1837 that English would replace Persian as the court language. The *ulema* believed that this was a step toward weaning the Muslims from their own religion and culture and converting them to Christianity. They tried to prevent their flock from learning English and castigated the few Muslims who had dared to learn the language of their Christian rulers as *kafirs*. Indeed, Western education on secular lines ran counter to the Muslim tradition of educating children either at home or in *madrassahs* where religious education was a compulsory part of the curriculum. Recalling the attitude of the Muslim community toward English education during the early phase of British rule, Sir Syed Ahmed said

> [The Muslims] could never be brought to admit that sound and useful learning existed in any language except Arabic and Persian... I still remember the days when, in respectable families, the study of English, with the object of obtaining a post in Government service or of securing any other lucrative employment, was considered highly discreditable.[9]

To reconcile the Muslims of India with their angry foreign rulers, to inspire them with hope and to give them a new sense of direction was a herculean task and called for a leader of heroic proportions. They were lucky at this dark hour of their history to find just such a man to uplift them—Syed (afterwards Sir Syed) Ahmed Khan.

Syed Ahmed was born on 17 October 1817 in an aristocratic family of Delhi who had migrated to India from Herat some generations previously. From his immediate ancestors he inherited a mixture of attributes which fitted him admirably for the task he was destined to undertake. His father was deeply religious and utterly unconcerned with worldly rewards while both his grandfathers were distinguished men of the world.

His paternal grandfather was a titled courtier and Commander of 1,000 foot and 300 horsemen in the reign of Alamgir II. Upon his death his titles were offered to Syed Ahmed's father, Syed Muhammad Takki, but he modestly declined the honour. Syed Ahmed's maternal grandfather held several official positions including that of prime minister to the Emperor Akbar II.

Syed Ahmed entered service under the British Government much against the wishes of his family and at the time of the Great Rebellion was posted as sub-judge at Bijnor.

After the failure of the Rebellion, Syed Ahmed decided to enter public life for the express purpose of rehabilitating his downcast community. The outline of his programme as it evolved over the years was to eradicate the antagonism between the Muslims and the British; to modernize the outlook of the Muslims chiefly through the Western system of education so that they could compete on equal terms with the Hindus; and to oppose such demands of the Indian National Congress Party as would enable the Hindus to dominate the Muslims by virtue of their numbers and literary proficiency. His chief concern for his people, as he explained in one of his public speeches, was 'not...to become subjects of the Hindus instead of the subjects of the "people of the Book [Christians]".'[10]

Syed Ahmed believed that the most effective means of reviving the fortune of his people was to educate them. He adopted as his motto the slogan 'educate, educate, educate' and argued that

> If the condition of Mahommedans be mean and miserable, then I think Islam herself will be degraded...each time has its own colour, and unless you adapt yourselves to the circumstances of the time your work cannot prosper... I believe that without high education it is impossible now to acquire honour... My desire is not only to

spread education among Mahommedans, but to spread two other things. The first of these is training in character... The second thing I wish to see established in our people is national feeling and sympathy; and this cannot be created unless boys of our nation read together...the reason why our Prophet ordered all the dwellers in one neighbourhood to meet five times a day for prayers in the mosque, and why the whole had to meet together on Fridays in the city mosque and in Eid all the people of the district had to assemble. The reason was that the effect of the gathering should influence all, and create a national feeling...[11]

Syed Ahmed's most monumental achievement in the field of education was the foundation of the Mohammadan Anglo-Oriental College at Aligarh of which the opening ceremony was performed by the viceroy on 8 January 1877. For the first time Muslims of good families from distant parts of India lived and studied together under the same roof and cultivated a spirit of comradeship. The college at Aligarh attained the status of university in 1920. 'Alig' attained the same status in India as 'Oxon' or 'Cantab' in England.

In the political field it was chiefly the introduction of the Western representative system that worried the Muslims because decisions by the majority of elected representatives spelled Hindu domination. The task before the Muslims was to obtain safeguards in the constitution which would enable them to practice their own way of life unhindered.

The British statesmen themselves were fully aware that the parliamentary system was not suitable for India. In 1892 as well as in 1909 the authors of the constitutional reforms, 'Liberals as well as Conservatives, declared as categorically, as Macaulay had in 1833 that India was not qualified for a parliamentary system'.[12] Prime Minister Lord Salisbury

> pointed out that elective or representative government was 'not an Eastern idea', that its introduction into India would be the gravest possible 'parting of the ways', that it only works well when 'all those who are represented desire much the same thing' and that it puts 'an intolerable strain' on a society divided into hostile sections'.[13]

A. J. Balfour argued that representative government is

> only suitable...when you are dealing with a population in the main homogeneous...in a community where the minority are prepared to

accept the decisions of the majority, where they are all alike in the tradition they are brought up, in their general outlook upon the world and their broad view of national aspirations.[14]

And Morley told the House of Lords in 1909 that, 'If it could be said that this chapter of reforms led directly or necessarily to the establishment of a parliamentary system in India, I for one would have nothing at all to do with it'.[15]

In 1878 Lord Lytton nominated Syed Ahmed as a member of the Viceroy's Council. After two years he was appointed for a second term of the same duration by Lord Ripon. Syed Ahmed's political philosophy started the trend which ultimately convinced the Muslims that they and the Hindus constituted two irreconcilable nations.

His first weighty political speech was made in the Imperial Council on 15 January 1883 on Lord Ripon's Local Self-Government Bill. That measure established Municipal Councils and Rural District Boards whose members—in some cases a majority of them—were directly elected, but it reserved to Government the right to nominate one-third of the members.

It is important to note that Syed Ahmed supported the first step toward self-government that the bill represented and also highly approved the representative institutions which had made England 'great among the nations of the world'. In fact, 'The principle of self-government by means of representative institutions is perhaps the greatest and noblest lesson which the beneficience of England will teach India'. But he asserted that

> ...no part of India has yet arrived at the stage when the system of representation can be adopted, in its fullest scope, even in regard to local affairs...in borrowing from England the system of representative institutions, it is of the greatest importance to remember those socio-political matters in which India is distinguishable from England... India, a continent in itself, is inhabited by vast populations of different races and different creeds; the rigour of religious institutions has kept even neighbours apart; the system of caste is still dominant and powerful. In one and the same district the population may consist of various creeds and various nationalities... The system of representation means the representation of the views and interests of the majority of the population... So long as differences of race and creed and the distinction of caste form an important element in the socio-political life of India, and influences her inhabitants in matters

connected with the administration and welfare of the country at large, the system of election, pure and simple, cannot be safely adopted. The larger community would totally override the interests of the smaller community.

He welcomed the fact that government was reserving to itself the power of nominating one-third of the members of the local bodies as it would ensure a just balance in the representation of the various sections of the Indian population.[16]

As we have said, with the birth of the Indian National Congress at Bombay in December 1885, India entered a new political era. At its first session, out of 72 delegates only 2 were Muslims and they both hailed from Bombay itself and were men of ordinary standing. The second session in Calcutta was attended by 435 delegates out of whom 31 were Muslims. Again, none of the Muslims was a notable person. To improve its communal image, the conveners of the Third Session invited Badruddin Tyabjee, a prominent Muslim from Bombay, to preside over its deliberations at Madras in December 1887. They also made special efforts to attract a larger number of Muslim delegates. The overt moves to entice Muslims into its fold, and some of its demands which were likely to injure Muslim interests, provoked Syed Ahmed openly to oppose the Congress.

On 28 December 1887, at the same time as the Congress was in session at Madras, Syed Ahmed addressed a large audience of Muslims at Lucknow.[17] He criticized the Congress demand that posts in the administrative services be filled by competitive examination. He said

> Think for a moment what would be the result if all appointments were given by competitive examination. Over all races, not only over Mahommedans but over Rajas of high position and the brave Rajputs who have not forgotten the swords of their ancestors, would be placed as ruler a Bengali who at the sight of a table knife would crawl under his chair.

He also opposed the Congress demand that a section of the Viceroy's Council be elected by the people. He emphasized that the Hindus would have four times the number of votes as compared to the Muslims and added, 'It would be like a game of dice, in which one man had four dice and the other only one'.

In another speech at Meerut[18] in March 1888, he complained that the Hindus were bringing undue pressure on the Muslims to join the Congress 'to give a false impression that the Mahommedans have joined them, this is a most unwarranted interference with our nation'. As to what would happen if the British left India, he said, 'Is it possible that...two nations—the Mahommedans and the Hindus—could sit on the same throne? Most certainly not. It is necessary that one of them should conquer the other and thrust it down.' He believed that it was necessary for peace and progress in India that 'the English Government should remain for many years. In fact forever.' He argued that the English being 'people of the Book, our nation cannot expect friendship and affection from any other people'.

In 1896, Syed Ahmed prepared a remarkable memorandum on behalf of the Muhammadan Anglo-Oriental Defence Association in which he advanced the following principles:

(1) equal representation for the Muslims and the Hindus in the North-Western Provinces Legislative Council because, on account of their past historical role, the political importance of the Muslims was not inferior to that of the Hindus, although the latter constituted a vast majority of the population;

(2) separate communal electorates, with Muslims voting for Muslims only; and

(3) weightage in representation for the Muslims on the municipal councils, district boards, etc.[19]

Though not perceptible at the time, Syed Ahmed's proposals contained the seed of Pakistan. They formed the blueprint for the demands put forward by the Aga Khan delegation to the viceroy in 1906. The achievement of the concessions by the delegation put the Muslims of India on the road to a separate homeland of their own.

In his *Causes of the Indian Revolt* Syed Ahmed had stated that the basic cause of the Great Rebellion was lack of proper communication between the rulers and the ruled. This had an interesting and far-reaching consequence. H. O. Hume, who founded the Indian National Congress, told Aftab Ahmad Khan in London in 1892 that it was Syed Ahmed's book that had caused him to feel the need for a forum of public opinion in India and led him to establish the Indian National Congress.[20]

Syed Ahmed was knighted in 1888. He passed away on 27 March 1898.

It was Quaid-i-Azam Mohammad Ali Jinnah who led his people to victory in the struggle for Pakistan. He is, therefore, rightly revered as the Father of the Nation. But to omit Sir Syed's role in any story of Muslim nationalism in India is like surveying a house without examining its foundation. As Hector Bolitho has pointed out in his book *Jinnah, Creator of Pakistan*, Syed Ahmed Khan 'was the father of all that was to happen, ultimately in Mohammed Ali Jinnah's mind'.[21]

During Sir Syed's burial, a lifelong friend of his said, 'Other men have written books and founded colleges; but to arrest, as with a wall, the degeneration of a whole people—that is work of a prophet'.[22]

The Aga Khan Delegation

It was the vigorous agitation against the partition of Bengal inside the Congress and in the streets that galvanized the Muslim community into action. In the words of Nawab Salimullah of Dhaka it had 'roused us from inaction and directed our attention to activities and struggle'.

Muslim fears were further increased when Secretary of State Morley stated in the House of Commons on 20 July 1906 that the governor-general would soon appoint a committee to consider what reforms in the direction of 'the extension of the representative element in the Legislative Council...can be expeditiously carried forward'.

Since the Muslims had no political organization of their own to press their demands, they arranged for an influential delegation of thirty-five led by Aga Khan III to wait on Lord Minto, the viceroy, at Simla on 1 October 1906.

In their address the delegation pleaded that the position accorded to the Muslims 'in any kind of representation...should be commensurate not merely with their numerical strength, but also with their political importance and the value of the contribution which they make to the defence of the Empire' and expressed the hope that due consideration would be given in that connection 'to the position [of rulers] which they occupied in India a little more than a hundred years ago, and of which the traditions have naturally not faded from their minds'. More specifically they demanded first, that the Muslims should be allotted a definite number of seats in the Municipal and District Boards, in the Provincial Councils and in the Imperial Legislature ('reserved seats'); secondly, that in fixing the number of seats for the Muslims, factors other than their numerical strength should also be considered in their favour ('weightage', i.e., a larger number of seats than warranted by their proportion in population); and thirdly, that only Muslims should vote for candidates for the Muslim seats ('separate electorates'). The Aga Khan explained at a later date that his deputation, in effect, had 'asked that the Muslims of India should not be regarded as a mere minority, but as a nation within a nation whose rights and obligations should be guaranteed by statute'.

The viceroy conceded that the position of the Muslims should be estimated not merely on their numerical strength but also with respect to their 'political importance'. He further agreed that in any electoral system the Muslims 'should be represented as a community'.[23]

The Indian Councils Act of 1909 and the regulations framed under it conceded all the three main concessions which the Aga Khan delegation had asked.

It is obvious that the Aga Khan delegation had simply adopted the line propounded by Sir Syed Ahmed Khan in 1896 in his memorandum on behalf of the Anglo-Oriental Defence Association which we have quoted in the preceding section. Nevertheless, some Indian writers have contended that the delegation was a put-up show. In the main they advance two arguments in support of their contention.

In the first place they quote from the speech delivered by Maulana Muhammad Ali as president of the thirty-eighth session of the Indian National Congress at Cocanada,[24] in the course of which he referred to the Aga Khan delegation as a 'command performance'. Secondly, they refer to an entry in Lady Minto's diary dated 1 October 1906 which reads

> This evening I have received the following letter from an official: 'I must send Your Excellency a line to say that a very big thing has happened today. A work of statesmanship that will affect India and Indian history for many a long year. It is nothing less than the pulling

back of sixty-two millions of people from joining the ranks of the seditious opposition.

The extract from Muhammad Ali's speech which the critics of the Aga Khan delegation quote runs as follows

> To follow the fashion of British journalists during the War, 'there is no harm now in saying' that the Deputation's was a 'command' performance! It was clear that Government could no longer resist the demands of educated Indians, and, as usual, it was about to dole out to them a morsel that would keep them gagged for some years. Hitherto the Mussulmans had acted very much like the Irish prisoner in the dock who, in reply to the judge's inquiry whether he had any counsel to represent him in the trial, had frankly replied that he had certainly not engaged counsel, but that he had 'friends in the jury'! But now the Muslims' 'friends in the jury' had themselves privately urged that the accused should engage duly qualified counsel like all others.

Muhammad Ali does not reinforce his witty and cryptic observations with any hard facts and names. In fact his speech read as a whole justifies the appearance of the Aga Khan delegation before the viceroy to convey the Muslim requirements to him. In the very next lines to those quoted above he says

> From whatever source the inspiration may have come, there is no doubt that the Muslim cause was this time properly advocated. In the common territorial electorates the Mussulmans had certainly not succeeded in securing anything like adequate or real representation, and those who denounced and deplored the creation of separate electorates for which the Mussulmans had pleaded should have remembered that separate electorates were the consequence, and not the cause, of the separation between Mussulmans and their more numerous Hindu brethren.

He argued that in fact

> ...the creation of separate electorates was hastening the advent of Hindu-Muslim unity. For the first time a real franchise, however restricted, was being offered to Indians, and if Hindus and Mussulmans remained just as divided as they had hitherto been since the commencement of British rule, and often hostile to one another, mixed electorates would have provided the best battle-ground for

inter-communal strife, and would have still further widened the gulf separating the two communities.

He paid high tribute to Sir Syed who was the father of Muslim nationalism

> Reviewing the actions of a bygone generation today, when it is easier to be wise after the event, I must confess I still think the attitude of Syed Ahmed Khan was eminently wise, and much as I wish that some things which he had said should have been left unsaid, I am constrained to admit that no well-wisher of Mussulmans, nor of India as a whole, could have followed a very different course in leading the Mussulmans...and it is my firm belief that his advocacy succeeded mainly because of the soundness of the policy advocated.

There is also nothing sinister in the observation in Lady Minto's diary that the rapport between the Aga Khan delegation and her husband had pulled back the Muslims from joining the ranks of the seditious elements. No one at that stage could tell whether the Moderates or the Extremists in Congress would gain control of that organization, and the agitation against the partition of Bengal was supported by disorder and terrorism. If the milder Hindus could make things so difficult for the government, there was no knowing what the more warlike Muslims would do if their pleas were turned down. Lady Minto's diary does not say that the Muslim delegation had been inspired by the British officials; it simply expresses the relief felt in official circles that the Muslims had been propitiated and their loyalty had been retained. The British had already greatly pleased Congress by the promise of constitutional reform. But the expected nature of the changes had deeply alarmed the Muslims. It is not surprising that the British should have striven to appease them as well.

The Foundation of the Muslim League[25]

Though the idea of the Muslims having a political party of their own had been in the air for some time, the Muslim League was the child of the Aga Khan delegation. The members realized that it was not sufficient to plead the Muslim case before the viceroy at a single meeting. It was essential for the community to have a standing political organization, constantly to propagate and press their claims at all levels. Three days after they had waited on the viceroy they conferred at the local Nabha House and agreed in principle to give practical shape to the idea.

Influential Muslim delegates from all parts of India were due to gather at Dhaka during the forthcoming Christmas holidays to attend the twentieth session of the Mohammedan Educational Conference[26] and it was decided to make use of that occasion to finalize the question of setting up a political body. After the Conference, a meeting was called on 30 December 1906 under the presidency of Viqar-ul-Malik. It discussed the scheme for 'The Mohammedan All-India Confederacy' which Nawab Salimullah of Dhaka had framed and circulated some time previously. Ultimately, at the motion of Salimullah, it was decided that a political association be formed, styled All-India Muslim League, to:

(1) promote, among the Mussulmans of India, feelings of loyalty to the British Government, and to remove any misconception that may arise as to the intention of Government with regard to any of its measures;

(2) protect and advance the political rights and interests of the Mussulmans of India, and to respectfully represent their needs and aspirations to the Government; and

(3) prevent the rise, among the Mussulmans of India, of any feeling of hostility towards other communities, without prejudice to the other aforementioned objects of the League.

While moving the above resolution, Salimullah said

> Had the party now in power in England been familiar with the position and rights of the Mohammedans of India, and had those among our countrymen who have hitherto been taking a prominent part in the public life of this country been consistently just in asking for the allotment of their respective shares to the various communities in India, it is not improbable that the League which it is now proposed to form would not have been heard of for a long time, if at all; and that we would have gone on pursuing the traditional policy of our people and attending solely to our educational needs... It is only now that I, for one, have been forced, by the practical needs of our community during the crisis through which we in Eastern Bengal are passing, to believe in the urgent necessity of a separate political organization for the Mohammedans of India...only after a central

League like the one proposed to be formed today comes into existence, can the Government find a representative body to which to turn for ascertaining the views of the Mussulmans of India, and to which the Mussulmans themselves can turn for consistent and firm support, sensible and sincere advice, and a true interpretation of the wishes of the Government.

The inaugural session at Dhaka welcomed the partition of Bengal in these words

Resolved: that this meeting, in view of the clear interest of the Mussulmans of Eastern Bengal, considers that the Partition is sure to prove beneficial to the Mohammedan community which constitutes the vast majority of that Province, and that all such methods of agitation as boycotting should be strongly condemned and discouraged.

In March 1908 the Aga Khan was elected 'permanent' president of the Muslim League, and in May of that year the London branch of the League was founded with Syed Ameer Ali as President. The Aga Khan served as president till his resignation in 1913.

Notes

1. *See*, Chapter 1.
2. 'The history of Indian nationalism may be said to have formally begun when in 1885 seventy-two Indians, from most parts of India, assembled at Bombay to attend the first session of the Indian National Congress.' (R. Coupland, *The Indian Problem 1833-1935*, op. cit., p. 23.)
3. C. F. Andrews and Girija Mookerjee, *The Rise and Growth of the Congress in India*, p. 138.
4. Ibid., p. 211.
5. A. M. Zaidi, *The Encyclopaedia of Indian National Congress*, V, p. 135.
6. Stanley A. Wolpert, *Tilak and Gokhale*, p. 197.
7. Ibid., p. 276.
8. Ibid., p. 272.
9. G. F. I. Graham, *The Life of Sir Syed Ahmed Khan*, p. 320.
10. Hafeez Malik, *Political Profile of Sir Sayyid Ahmad Khan, A Documentary Record*, Islamabad, 1982, p. 371.
11. Ibid., pp. 381-4.
12. R. Coupland, *The Indian Problem, 1933-1935*, op. cit., p. 25.
13. Ibid.
14. Ibid., p. 26.

15. Ibid.
16. For text of Syed Ahmed's speech *see*, R. Coupland, *The India Problem, 1833-1935*, op. cit., London, 1942, p. 154.
17. For text of Syed Ahmed's Lucknow speech *see*, Hafiz Malik, pp. 342-55.
18. For the text of Syed Ahmed's Meerut speech *see*, ibid., pp. 359-73. In his pamphlet, 'The Causes of the Indian Revolt', Syed Ahmed had already referred to Hindus and Muslims as 'two antagonistic races'. The pamphlet was published in Urdu in 1858 and in English in 1873.
19. Syed Sharifuddin Pirzada, *Foundations of Pakistan*, 1, p. xxviii.
20. S. M. Ikram, *Modern Muslim India and the Birth of Pakistan*, Lahore, 1977, p. 26.
21. Ibid., p. 38.
22. C. F. Andrews and Girija Mookerjee, *The Rise and Growth of the Congress in India*, op. cit., p. 52.
23. For the texts of the Aga Khan delegation's address and of the viceroy's reply *see*, G. Allana, *Pakistan Movement, Historic Documents*, pp. 5-21.
24. The Cocanada session was held from 28 December 1923 until 1 January 1924.
25. For a documentary account of the foundation of the Muslim League *see*, A. M. Zaidi, *Evolution of Muslim Political Thought in India*, I, pp. 71-91.
26. The Mohammedan Education Conference had been founded by Sir Syed in 1886. It met annually at different places to rouse nation-wide interest in Muslim education. It also led to stimulating exchange of views for the advancement of the community in different fields including social reforms and politics.

CHAPTER 5

On the Ladder to Leadership 1906-1913

Idealists Versus Realists

When the Quaid entered all-India politics in 1906, the Muslims were divided in their attitude toward the Congress Party. Some of them who may appropriately be called the Idealists, joined the Congress. They believed that it was possible for the Hindus and the Muslims to work unitedly for their own good and for the good of their common motherland under the banner of the Congress. Others, who may be described as the Realists, believed that the Congress was a predominantly Hindu organization and merging with it would render them politically ineffective and result in permanent Hindu rule.

The Idealists mainly hailed from the Bombay and Madras presidencies and they usually belonged to the mercantile communities. Of the first twelve annual sessions of Congress two were presided over by Muslims: Badruddin Tyabji presided over the third session (1887) and Rehmatulla M. Sayani over the twelfth (1896). They both represented Bombay and belonged to mercantile communities. Tyabji was by caste a Sulaimani Bohra and Sayani a Khoja.

The strongholds of the Realists were in those areas which had been the seats of Muslim imperialism and culture, such as Delhi, Lucknow and Bengal. They belonged to what previously had been the ruling class and were now landed aristocrats, soldiers, agriculturists and government servants. They also included scholars, writers and poets who carried on the classical forms of bygone days. The Realists were more orthodox in religion than their down-country brethren.

The Realists followed Sir Syed Ahmed Khan's line and out-numbered the Idealists by far.

At the First Congress in 1885 only two Muslims registered themselves as delegates. They both belonged to Bombay where the session was held. Neither of them had a following in his own community. The Reception Committee of the Second Congress invited the two leading Muslim organizations in India to send delegates. These were the Central National Muhammadan Association, of which the secretary was Ameer Ali, and the Muhammadan Literary Society, whose secretary was Nawab Abdul Latif. They both declined the invitation.[1] That Congress session was attended by 435 delegates of whom only thirty-one were Muslims.

To meet the charge of being mainly a Hindu organization, the Third Congress successfully invited Badruddin Tyabji, a well-known Bombay Muslim to preside over it. That session was attended by seventy-six Muslims out of a total of 607 delegates.

At the 1889 Congress the number of Muslim delegates rose to 229 out of 1889 but in 1898 it fell to only ten out of 614. At the Bombay Congress in 1904, which protested against the proposed partition of Bengal, and the 1905 Benares Congress which deplored the partition, the number of Muslims was thirty-six out of 1010 and twenty out of 757 respectively.[2]

Even Tyabji, whose presidentship of the Congress in 1887 was much publicized by the Hindus, recognized the widespread Muslim antagonism toward Congress and declined to attend the session of 1888.[3] His exchanges with Sir Syed and Hume, the founder of the Congress, make interesting reading.

On 28 January 1888 Sir Syed wrote to Tyabji

> The fact that you took a leading part in the Congress at Madras has pleased our Hindu fellow-subjects no doubt, but as to ourselves it has grieved us much... I do not understand what the words 'National Congress' mean. Is it supposed that the different castes and creeds living in India belong to one nation, or can become a nation, and their aims and aspirations be one and the same? I think it is quite impossible and when it is impossible there can be no such thing as a National Congress, nor can it be of equal benefit to all peoples.[4]

Tyabji responded on 18 February 1888

> I am not aware of anyone regarding the whole of India as one nation and if you read my inaugural address, you will find it distinctly stated

that there are numerous communities or nations in India which had peculiar problems of their own to solve, but that there were some questions which touched all those communities and that it was for the discussion of these latter questions only that the Congress was assembled... My policy, therefore, would be to act from within rather than from without. I would say to all Mussulmans 'act with your Hindu fellow-subjects in all matters in which you are agreed, but oppose them as strongly as you can if they bring forward any propositions that you may deem prejudicial to yourselves'. We should thus advance the general progress of India, and at the same time safeguard our own interests.[5]

Tyabji proposed to Hume on 27 October 1888

We must base our proceedings upon the fact that an overwhelming majority of Mahomedans is against the movement. Against this array it is useless saying that the intelligent and educated Mahomedans are in favour of the Congress. If, then, the Mussulman community as a whole is against the Congress—rightly or wrongly does not matter—it follows that the movement *ipso facto* ceases to be a general or National Congress. If this is so, it is deprived of a great deal of its power to do good... It is time to cease to hold Congress every year...I should...like the Congress to be prorogued say for at least five years... If at the end of the 5 years our prospects improve, we can renew our Congress. If not, we can drop it with dignity.[6]

In order to reassure the Muslims, Tyabji during his presidency successfully induced the Congress to pass a resolution which disallowed the discussion of a subject or the passing of a resolution to which either the Hindu or the Muslim delegates were unanimously or nearly unanimously opposed.[7] This constitutional safeguard became a standing demand of Muslim nationalists and was embodied in the Lucknow Pact.

Tyabji passed away on 19 August 1906.

The Quaid's First Congress, 1906

It is not surprising that Jinnah should have joined the ranks of the Idealists and become a member of the Congress party. After absorbing British liberalism in London, he had taken up residence in Bombay which was India's most cosmopolitan city where the mores of social life were set by the highly westernized Parsee community. Jinnah found their way of life congenial to his own refined tastes and he made many Parsee friends. He later married a Parsee socialite.

But the decisive reason why Jinnah became a member of the Congress party was that the three persons who dominated Congress at that time were his political mentors. The three in question were the Parsees Naoroji and Sir Pherozeshah Mehta and Chitpavan Brahman Gokhale.

We have already explained that Jinnah revered Naoroji and Gokhale and acknowledged them as his political gurus.

For Mehta, too, Jinnah entertained the highest respect. He had worked in Mehta's chambers and regarded him as one of the 'greatest politicians and statesmen' of the British Empire.[8] Mehta 'had been associated with the Congress from its very inception and played a leading part in moulding its policy and programme...[he] was really the power behind the Congress for a number of years'.[9] He was popularly called the Lion of Bombay.

The ascendancy of Parsees, a tiny minority in India, was presented as a visible refutation of the allegation that Congress basically was a Hindu organization.

Jinnah attended his first Congress in 1906 as a delegate of Mehta's Bombay Presidency Association. He was a mature gentleman of thirty[10] who had already reached the top layer of legal practitioners by sheer merit and had earned universal respect for his public spirit and integrity. The president of that year's Congress, Naoroji, recognized his worth by choosing him as his private secretary for the session.

That Jinnah should have been an articulate member of the Congress party from the very beginning is, therefore, not surprising. During his first Congress he participated in the discussion on two resolutions.

He supported Resolution V which prayed that a Government Commission be appointed to enquire whether a decision of the Privy Council had violated the Muslim law on *Wakf-i-ala-aulad* and if it had done so, to take legal steps to rectify the situation.

Evidently, conscious of the allegation that the Congress was primarily a Hindu body he said

...it must be a matter of great gratification to the whole of the Mahomedan community that, we have got on the programme of the Indian National Congress, a question which purely affects the Mahomedan community. That shows one thing, gentlemen, that we Mahomedans can equally stand on this common platform and pray for our grievances being remedied through the programme of the National Congress.[11]

The resolution was unanimously carried.

Jinnah made the *Wakf-i-ala-aulad* issue his special concern and earned the warm approbation of the entire Muslim community for his successful efforts to get the desired legislation enacted. This was one of the reasons for the Muslim League first to invite him to attend some of its deliberations as a guest and then to request him to join it as a regular member.

He introduced the Mussulman Wakf Validating Bill in the Legislative Council on 17 March 1911 'to define the rights of the Muslim subjects of His Majesty to make settlements of property by way of "wakf" in favour of their families and descendants'. He explained that the decision of the Privy Council in 1894 had 'paralyzed the Mussulman law, so far as the power of a Mussulman is concerned to make trusts for his family, his children and his descendants.'[12] He piloted the bill through all its stages till it was passed in March 1913. His term as a member of the Legislative Council had expired in January of that year but the governor-general (Lord Hardinge), in response to pleas by the Muslim community nominated him as an additional member to see the bill through. This was the first occasion on which a bill sponsored by a private member had become law.

Jinnah's second intervention during the proceedings of his first Congress was made during the discussion on clause (a) of Resolution IX which ran

> That all examinations held in England only should be simultaneously held in India and England and that all higher appointments which are made in India should be by competitive examination only with due reservation for safeguarding the rights of educationally backward classes.

Jinnah proposed an amendment to the above clause in the following words

I understand that by backward classes is meant the Mahomedan community... I wish to draw your attention to the fact that the Mahomedan community should be treated in the same way as the Hindu community. The foundation upon which the Indian National Congress is based is that we are all equal, that there should be no reservation for any class or community.[13]

The amendment was passed.

He expressed similar views on 11 March 1913 when he appeared before the Royal Commission which had come to India to investigate the question of public services in India. He said he regarded an increase of Indians in the Indian Civil Service as of great political importance and protested that though the promise of equal opportunities for the British and the Indians was given more than half a century ago, the result so far was that out of 1,200 civilians only sixty-five were Indians. He believed if an examination was held in India in addition to the one in London a larger number of Indians would get in. He favoured selection by open competition not qualified by any form of nomination. In his opinion the question of community, class or province should not be considered: 'What we want is the best adminstrators and not necessarily a Hindu, a Muhammadan or a European.'[14]

This was the voice of self-respect and idealism and commendable as such; but it did not take note of the disadvantage under which the Muslim candidates would be placed if recruitment was made purely by an academic contest. The Muslims were proven administrators. They had ruled the country efficiently for several centuries. The Moguls, who were the immediate imperial predecessors of the British, had in the words of the British historian Alexander Dow 'rendered Hindostan the most flourishing empire in the world during two complete centuries'.[15] But under British rule the Hindus, specially the Bengalis, had taken to Western education far more readily than the Muslims. In a system of selection by competitive examination, therefore, the Muslims were no match for the Hindus.

The real situation was described by Sir Syed in his famous Lucknow speech in December 1887. He posed the question, 'What would be the result if all appointments were given by competitive examination?' and answered it in his characteristically robust fashion, 'Over all races, not only over Mahomedans but over Rajas of high position and the brave Rajputs who have not forgotten the swords of their ancestors, would be placed as ruler a Bengali who at the sight of a table knife would crawl under his chair'.

The idealism which inspired Jinnah to propose an amendment to Resolution IX of the 1906 Congress had caused him in October of the same year to question the representative status of the Aga Khan delegation to the viceroy.[16] He evidently believed that the Congress party represented the Muslims no less than the Hindus and was the only true political voice in the country.

He was also a signatory to a Memorandum which the Bombay Presidency Association forwarded to Lord Minto opposing separate electorates.[17] His view, expressed on 31 December 1913, was that by demanding separate electorates the Muslims would 'only get two watertight compartments'.[18] In other words separate electorates would pull Hindus and Muslims further apart and make his dream of Hindu-Muslim unity more difficult to achieve. Here again it was the view of an idealist which offered no solution to the conditions prevailing in India.

On the face of it communal electorates no doubt were

> ...a flagrant breach of the democratic principle...but there was force in the argument stressed by the Moslem leaders that, in the present state of Indian feeling, to make Moslem seats dependent on Hindu votes, so far from tending to make both communities conscious of a common citizenship, would embitter the existing antagonism and convert every election into a dangerous battleground. Nor, as they pointed out, would the mere 'reservation' of seats for Moslems secure their faithful representation unless only Moslems voted for them, since the Hindu votes would go to the candidate who identified himself least wholeheartedly with the interests of his own community. It was a strong case, and the weight of Moslem opinion behind it could not be ignored.[19]

Lord Zetland, who as governor of Bengal (1917-1922) and secretary of state for India (1935-1940) had direct experience of the complexity of Indian politics, summed up the dilemma in similar terms

> That two great peoples [the Hindus and the Muslims] should have lived side by side for so long and yet not intermixed constitutes a state of affairs surely unparalleled in the annals of the human race.

All this being so, it was inevitable that an artificial, though in the circumstances a necessary, system such as that of separate communal electorates, should encourage the fissiparous tendencies already existing. And looking back from the advantage point offered by the passage of time, it is easy to see in it the seeds of the separatism which ended by blossoming into the two sovereign States of India and Pakistan. Yet no alternative means presented itself whereby the end in view, namely the protection of the interests of a people in a permanent minority under a Parliamentary form of government, could be secured.[20]

Jinnah in those years was optimistic that Hindus and Muslims would unite as one nation and in any case, the Hindus would not and, indeed, could not dominate the Muslims.

In a letter to Syed Wazir Hasan on 21 May 1913 he wrote, 'I am one of those who firmly believe in the union of the two great communities in India, and also that sooner or later these communities will be united'.[21]

At the tenth session of the Muslim League (30 December 1917-1 January 1918) he referred to the fear that the Muslims were in a minority and the government of the country might become a Hindu government and reassured fellow-Muslims in the following words

> If 70 million Mussulmans do not approve of the measure which is carried by a ballot box, do you think that it could be enforced or administered in this country? [Cries of 'Never'.] Do you think that the Hindu statesmen with their intellect, with their past history, will ever think of enforcing measures by the ballot box when you get Self-Government? [Cries of 'No'.] Then what is there to fear? [Cries of 'Nothing'.] Therefore I say to my Mussulman friends: Fear not. This is a bogey, which is put before you by your enemies ['Hear, hear'] to frighten you, to scare you away from co-operation and unity which are essential for the establishment of Self-Government [Cheers].[22]

1907-1913

The main feature of these years was the growth of the Quaid's stature as a leader. He became a respected figure not only in the Congress party but in the Muslim League as well. This equipped him with the credentials to play his cherished role of ambassador of Hindu-Muslim unity.

His task was facilitated by certain national and international developments which created the climate for Hindu-Muslim *rapprochement*. When the safeguards requested by the Aga Khan delegation became law under the Act of 1909, the Muslims began to feel sufficiently protected constitutionally no longer to fear Hindu domination. The annulment of the partition of Bengal shocked the Muslims and made them wonder whether they would, after all, not be better off by gaining the friendship of their Hindu countrymen than by continuing to rely solely on the goodwill of their foreign masters. British foreign policy toward the Muslim countries also increasingly disenchanted them from the British Government.

In his inaugural address at the Third Session of the Muslim League at Bombay (29-30 January 1910), the Aga Khan said that separate electorates for the Muslims were 'deemed to be an absolute necessity. Now that we have secured it, I hope it will result in a permanent political *entente cordiale* between the members of the two great sister communities'.[23]

The Aga Khan's initiative was endorsed by Syed Nabiullah in the course of his presidential address at the Fourth Session of the Muslim League at Nagpur in December of the same year: 'The scheme of separate electorates has happily put us in a position effectively to look after our interests...and above all put us in the proper frame of mind to co-operate cordially with our Hindu brethren for the advancement and glory of our common country'.

He said that the cry of unity being in danger because of separate electorates was 'a spurious cry'. Had their 'Hindu friends' not got 'a permanent standing majority?' What more did they want? Being secure in their overwhelming majority it seems as if 'under the plausible plea of unity', they wanted to 'lord over' the Muslims, to 'have it all their own way' and to 'stifle' the 'feeble voice' of the Muslims.

He suggested that Hindu and Muslim leaders, especially legislators, should meet each other from time to time for holding friendly discussions on all questions affecting the general well-being of the country. Accordingly he welcomed Sir William Wedderburn's 'wise proposal' to convene a conference of influential leaders of all communities.[24]

With regard to British foreign policy toward Muslim countries the Muslims of India believed that the Christian powers were determined to subdue the world of Islam. Afghanistan was dominated by Britain and the conclusion of the Anglo-Russian Entente in 1907 had made Iran a dependency of the two contracting powers.

By a coincidence, the year 1911 in which the partition of Bengal was revoked was also the year in which Italy invaded Tripoli. This was followed by the war between Turkey and the Balkan League (1912). At the Sixth Session of the Muslim League at Nagpur (March 1913) even the moderate Mian (afterwards Sir) Muhammad Shafi noted with concern in his presidential address that 'the victories of the Balkan States were acclaimed by some of the European races as triumphs of the Cross over the Crescent'. The fate of Turkey was of great concern to the Muslims of India because the Sultan was the Caliph of Islam.

The partition of Bengal was revoked in December 1911 by an announcement made by King George V during his durbar at Delhi. In *My Indian Years* Lord Hardinge, the viceroy who was principally responsible for the annulment of partition, explains the considerations which had moved him,

> I was most anxious for a policy of conciliation in view of the impending visit of the King and Queen to India...it was brought home to me that if there was to be peace in the two Bengals it was absolutely necessary to do something to remove what was regarded by all Bengalis as an act of flagrant injustice without justification.[25]

The Muslims felt betrayed by the sudden annulment because they had been repeatedly assured by the highest authorities that partition was a settled fact. Their confidence that their interests were safe in British hands was shaken. It was not their loyalty but Hindu subversion that had paid off.

Meanwhile, Jinnah had been steadily climbing the ladder to leadership. In January 1910 he was elected by the Bombay Muslims to represent them in the Imperial Legislative Council, defeating Maulvi Rafiuddin who was the president of the Bombay Muslim League. In the following month he had a heated exchange with no less a person than the governor-general, Lord Minto, who was the president of the Council.

The subject was a resolution on Indentured Labour for Natal. Jinnah said that the question had 'aroused the feelings of all classes in this country to the highest pitch of indignation and horror at the harsh and cruel treatment that is meted out to Indians in South Africa'. Lord Minto objected that 'cruelty' was 'rather a strong word'. Jinnah stood his ground and responded

> I should feel inclined to use much stronger language, but I am fully aware of the constitution of this Council and I do not wish to trespass for a single moment, but I do say this that the treatment that is meted out to Indians is the harshest which can possibly be imagined, and, as I said before, the feeling in this country is unanimous.

The Press reported the incident in headlines and Jinnah won much public acclaim for his refusal to be overawed by the governor-general.[26]

The Quaid took little time to establish himself as an enlightened and effective legislator. The gifts of integrity, idealism and advocacy which had won him a place in the upper echelons of the bar also went to make him a top parliamentarian. Two of his speeches in the early years of his legislative career will serve to illustrate his style.

On 19 March 1912, Jinnah supported Gokhale's motion that the bill to make better provision for the extension of elementary education be referred to a select committee and dispelled the objections raised by some of the speakers.

He pointed out that 'the cardinal principle of this bill is the introduction of compulsion in selected areas' and noted that the government view was that the best way forward was the gradual extension of the existing principle of voluntary expansion. He refuted the government view in these words

> We have been trying this system...for the last fifty or sixty years seriously, and we know what has been the result. In one word...you are going at a jog-trot pace, and that jog-trot pace we object to... By this method...it will take 175 years in order to get all the school-going age children to school... In no country has elementary education become universal without compulsion.

To the objection that there were not enough school buildings and not enough teachers he replied that the real question was whether 'you have got money or not'. He said this was 'not an insurmountable difficulty'. It was simply 'a very very old story'. His exhortation was, 'Find money! Find money! Find money'. He emphasized that 'It is the duty of every civilized government to educate masses'.

Finally, he referred to the objection that there was 'the political danger and the social danger' that education would turn people into 'agitators' and said

> I honestly and sincerely appeal to the government: do you really think that education means sedition? ...let me tell you that you have no better friends in this country...than the educated classes...surely, fair, free and independent criticisms of the acts of government, of the measures of government do not constitute sedition...are you going to keep millions and millions of people trodden under your feet for fear that they demand more rights?[27]

That he was a stickler for constitutional methods was well brought during the debate in April 1913 on the Indian Criminal Law (Amendment) Bill which dealt with offences against the State. He said he was 'not in a position to resist' the principle of the bill because he believed that

> ...every attempt on the part of my countrymen to undermine the authority of the Government and to disturb the law and order, in my opinion, deserves the strongest condemnation and the highest punishment. Those men who have a desire to undermine the authority of the Government, those men who have a desire to disturb the law and order, are, in my opinion, the biggest enemies of my country and my people. They are today doing the greatest harm to the cause of India. Sir, why is this measure brought before this Council today? It is brought because of the doings of some of my countrymen. Repressive measures that have been brought in, in this Council have been brought because of the misdeeds of some of our countrymen... I believe in criticizing the Government, I believe in criticizing Government freely and frankly, but, at the same time, that it is the duty of every educated man to support and help the Government when the Government is right.[28]

Not long after being elected to the Imperial Legislative Council he had written to a friend that 'the problem of all problems that the statesmen in India' had to solve was to 'combine' Hindus and Muslims 'in the common good' because 'we have to live together in every district, town and hamlet, where our daily life is interwoven with each other in every square mile of one common country'. He warned that this problem has to be solved 'before any true advance or real progress can be achieved'.[29]

It must have been a matter of great satisfaction to him that he was invited to attend the Muslim League Council Meeting at Bankipur on 31 December 1912 though he was at that time a member of the Congress Party only. The meeting under the presidency of the Aga Khan adopted a resolution laying down the aims of the Muslim League. Clause 4 of the resolution enacted that one of the aims should be 'the attainment of a system of self-government suitable to India'. One of the members, Mazhar-ul-Haque, objected to the words 'self-government suitable to India' because he thought they were meaningless. Jinnah defended the resolution as framed and praised the League for having placed the 'right ideal' before the community. Though he was a member of the Congress he knew that the Congress was wrong in this matter and thought that the League should be congratulated for going ahead even of the Congress in the formation of the ideal.

The incident is clear proof that Jinnah believed that the Westminster type of parliamentary system would have to be modified to suit the conditions prevailing in India.

Another 'aim' adopted at the same League Council meeting which echoed Jinnah's own dream was 'To promote friendship and union between the Mussulmans and other communities of India'.[30]

1913 was an important year in the Quaid-i-Azam's political career. Early in March he had the satisfaction of having his Wakf Validating Bill passed into law and later in the same month (22-23) he was invited to attend the Sixth Session of the All-India Muslim League at Lucknow as a guest. The very first resolution congratulated Jinnah 'for his skilful piloting of the measure through the Imperial Legislative Council'.

The session also confirmed the 'aims' which the Council had adopted in December and on the question of Hindu-Muslim friendship took a significant step forward by passing the following resolution

> The All-India Muslim League places on record its firm belief that the future development and progress of the people of India depend exclusively on the harmonious working and co-operation of the various communities; deprecates all mischievous attempts to widen the unfortunate breach between the Hindus and Mussulmans; and hopes that the leaders on both sides will periodically meet together to restore the amicable relations prevailing between them in the past and find a *modus operandi* for joint and concerted action in questions of the public good.[31]

In the summer Jinnah went for a holiday to England along with Gokhale. At a public meeting at Caxton Hall, London on 28 June 1913 he moved a resolution for the formation of a Central Association of Indian students in London. He said while they had set up a dozen societies they lacked 'a central organization where they could meet together and form friendships'. He did not ask them to 'eschew political discussion' but 'to take part in politics would simply be to injure their position as students'.[32]

On 10 October while still in London he enrolled himself as a member of the All-India Muslim League at the express desire of his friends Muhammad Ali and Wazir Hasan.

> Typical of his exquisite if somewhat exigent sense of honour is it to find that even so simple an incident partook of something like a sacrament. His two sponsors were required to make a solemn preliminary covenant that loyalty to the Muslim League and the Muslim interest would in no way and at no time imply even the shadow of disloyalty to the larger national cause to which his life was dedicated.[33]

After returning to India he first attended the Twenty-eighth Session of the Congress at Karachi (26-28 December) and then hurried to Agra and attended the Seventh Session of the Muslim League (31 December 1913).

At his instance the Congress passed a resolution demanding a change in the structure and functions of the Council of the Secretary of State in London. In the main the resolution required that the Council should be partly nominated and partly elected instead of being wholly nominated and also that its 'character' should be advisory and not administrative.

The Congress also made a positive response to the League's repeated overtures for communal co-operation

Resolved—That this Congress places on record its warm appreciation of the adoption by the All-India Muslim League of the ideal of Self-Government for India within the British Empire, and expresses its complete accord with the belief that the League has so emphatically declared at its last sessions that the political future of the country depends on the harmonious working and co-operation of the various communities in the country which has been the cherished ideal of the Congress. This Congress most heartily welcomes the hope expressed by the League that the leaders of the different communities will make every endeavour to find a *modus operandi* for joint and concerted action on all questions of national good and earnestly appeals to all the sections of the people to help the object we all have at heart.[34]

At the Muslim League Session Resolution V the question of communal representation led to a heated debate. It was moved by Maulvi Rafi-ud-Din who asked for it to be passed 'without much discussion'. He pointed out that 'for the last six years it had been unanimously passed at every sitting of the League'. The resolution ran

> ...that in the interests of the Mussulman community, it is absolutely necessary that the principle of communal representation be extended to all self-governing public bodies, and respectfully urges that a provision for the adequate and effective representation of Mussulmans on municipal and district boards is a necessary corollary of the application of the principle to the Imperial and Provincial Legislative Councils, and at the same time essential to the successful working of those public bodies.

Evidently, feeling that the resolution would set back the increasing prospects of Hindu-Muslim friendship, Muhammad Ali proposed that the consideration of the question of communal representation in self-governing bodies should be postponed for a year. He argued that 'it would be to the ultimate interest of India' for the Hindus and the Muslims 'to merge together'. He pointed out that in the past the 'Hindus had always opposed separate representation in the Congress but this year out of regard for Muslim feeling, they had not passed the resolution'. The Muslims must show that they were prepared to meet the Hindus halfway.

Muhammad Ali was strongly supported by Jinnah. He urged the Muslims 'to consider the question dispassionately, not from the point of view of present gain, but of lasting advantage in the future. He assured his co-religionists that by demanding special representation they would get only two watertight compartments'.

The Aga Khan also supported the stand of Muhammad Ali and Jinnah but to no purpose. Muhammad Ali's proposal was lost and the resolution as originally worded was passed.[35]

It is clear from the foregoing discussion that at the end of 1913 the stage was set for the Quaid-i-Azam to play the role of ambassador of Hindu-Muslim unity.

The Congress party and the Muslim League had both adopted the common goal of self-government and had declared that they would like to join hands to achieve the common end. The next step obviously was to negotiate a mutually acceptable concord. And who could be better qualified to bring that about than Jinnah, the only leader of high calibre who was a member of both the organizations and was respected by both?

But there was one major hurdle. The Muslims overwhelmingly supported the system of separate electorates and the Hindus equally strongly wished to get rid of it. The impasse could be broken only if one or the other party could be persuaded to back down from its stand. How Jinnah achieved this will be related in the next chapter but it would be relevant first to sum up his own views on the subject.

We have already mentioned that as early as in October 1906 he was a signatory to a memorandum forwarded by the Bombay Presidency Association to Lord Minto opposing separate electorates.

In a letter to the editor of the *Times of India* dated 20 February 1909, he granted that the Muslims were 'entitled to a real and substantial representation in the new reforms' but the difficult question was 'how to do it'. The problem before them broadly was 'whether the demand of separate electorates at all stages from rural board to the Viceregal Council should be granted'. On a population basis the Muslims were entitled to representation to the extent of one to four. If their share could be raised to one to three (weightage), the system of communal representation could be dispensed with, if not, it must be retained.[36]

At a meeting of the Muslims of Bombay held on 13 August 1909, Jinnah successfully proposed that if the alternatives available for Muslim representation in the Bombay Legislative Council were election by separate electorates or selection by nomination, preference should be given to the former.

Jinnah's demeanour during the Twenty-fifth Session of the Congress at Allahabad on 26-29 December 1910 plainly shows that he was already feeling uneasy that his personal views on the issue of separate electorates were at variance with those of the majority of his fellow-Muslims. Under pressure from 'a great many leaders of the Congress' he agreed to move the following resolution which was carried unanimously: 'This Congress strongly deprecates the extension or application of the principle of separate communal electorates to municipalities, district boards or other local bodies.'

Though normally forthright, Jinnah on this occasion was uncharacteristically hesitant and brief

> I am not prepared to make a long speech on this resolution as I did not intend to speak at all, but in response to the wishes of a great many leaders of the Congress I have agreed to move this resolution before you. Gentlemen, I wish it to be made quite clear that I do not represent the Mohammedan community here nor have I any mandate from the Mohammedan community. I only express my personal views here and nothing more. As far as my personal views are concerned, they are well-known to many of you, and these are embodied in this resolution.[37]

The last sentence makes it quite evident that he personally was against separate electorates. This was further emphasized by his observation at the Agra Session of the Muslim League in 1913 that special representation would only get them 'two water-tight compartments'.

This by no means meant that he was opposed to constitutional safeguards to protect the interest of the Muslims as a minority otherwise he would not have insisted at the Muslim League Council Meeting at Bankipur (December 1912) that the aim of the Muslim League should be the attainment of a system of self-government which was 'suitable to India'. Nor would he have suggested weightage for Muslim representation in his letter to the *Times of India* in February 1909.

Notes

1. Rafiq Zakaria, *Rise of Muslims in Indian Politics*, p. 51.
2. We have gleaned the figures of the total number of delegates and of the Muslim delegates in the Congress sessions mentioned above from the Annual Reports of the Indian National Congress.
3. A. G. Noorani, *Badruddin Tyabji*, p. 94.
4. Ibid., pp. 175-6.
5. Ibid., pp. 178-9.
6. Ibid., pp. 187-8.
7. Ibid., p. 167.
8. Pirzada, *Collected Works*, I, op. cit., p. 147.
9. B. P. Sitaramayya, *History of the Indian National Congress*, I, pp. 103-4.
10. His thirtieth birthday fell on 25 December 1906. The Calcutta session of the Congress was held from 26-29 December 1906.
11. Report of the Twenty-Second Congress, p. 69.
12. For the full text of Jinnah's speech introducing the bill *see*, M. Rafique Afzal, *Speeches and Statements of the Quaid-i-Azam Mohammad Ali Jinnah*, pp. 1-11.
13. Report of the Twenty-Second Indian National Congress, p. 120.
14. Pirzada, *Collected Works*, I, op. cit., pp. 56, 58.
15. Alexander Dow, *The History of Hindostan*, xxiii.
16. For the text of Jinnah's letter in the *Gujrati* of 7 October 1906 *see*, Pirzada, *Collected Works*, I, op. cit., p.1.
17. Sharif AL Mujahid, *Quaid-i-Azam, His Times*, p. 7.
18. Ibid., p. 108.
19. R. Coupland, *The Indian Problem 1833-1935*, op. cit., p. 34.
20. 'Essayez', *The Memoirs of Lawrence, Second Marquess of Zetland*, pp. 120-1.
21. Pirzada, *Collected Works*, I, op. cit., p. 94.
22. Ibid., p. 252.
23. Pirzada, *Foundations of Pakistan*, I, op. cit., p. 94.
24. Ibid., pp. 164-5. A conference under Wedderburn's chairmanship took place at Allahabad on 1 January 1911. It was attended by a large number of Hindu and Muslim leaders including the Aga Khan and Jinnah but led to no lasting result. At the close of the conference Jinnah proposed a vote of thanks to the chair.
25. Lord Hardinge of Penhurst, *My Indian Years*, pp. 14-36.
26. M. H. Saiyid, *Mohammad Ali Jinnah*, op.cit., 1962, pp. 39-40.
27. For full text of this speech *see*, Pirzada, *Collected Works*, I, op. cit., pp. 41-46.
28. Ibid., pp. 88-89.
29. For text of Jinnah's letter of January 1910 *see*, Pirzada, *Collected Works*, I, op. cit., p. 15.
30. For an account of the Muslim League Council Meeting on 31 December 1912 *see*, Pirzada, *Foundations of Pakistan*, I, op. cip., 258-9.
31. Ibid., p. 281.
32. For a report of Jinnah's speech *see*, Pirzada, *Collected Works*, I, op. cit., pp. 97-8.

33. Sarojini Naidu, *Mohomed Ali Jinnah, An Ambassador of Unity,* op. cit., p. 11.
34. Annie Besant, *How India Wrought for Freedom,* p. 564.
35. Pirzada, *Foundations of Pakistan,* I, op. cit., pp. 315-7.
36. Pirzada, *Collected Works,* I, op. cit., pp. 9-11.
37. A. M. Zaidi, *The Encyclopaedia of the India National Congress,* V, p. 647.

CHAPTER 6

Ambassador of Hindu-Muslim Unity, 1914-1918

World War I

The most momentous occurrence of this period was the outbreak of World War I on 4 August 1914. The Allies—Britain, France and Russia—were joined by Japan. At the end of October, Turkey threw in its lot with the Central Powers—Germany and Austria. In 1915 Italy decided to side with the Allies and Bulgaria with the Central Powers. Allied victory was assured after the United States declared war on Germany on 6 April 1917. Germany surrendered on 11 November 1918. Soon after Turkey had entered the war, a British Army consisting mainly of Indian soldiers, including Muslims, was despatched to Mesopotamia and Palestine. Indian troops also fought in Europe, Egypt, East Africa and other theatres of war.

The Indian people and princes co-operated wholeheartedly in the war effort. Indian troops arrived in France in September 1914, waging a desperate struggle to stem the German sweep toward the English Channel. In Governor-General Hardinge's words,

> These fine divisions arrived in France just in time to fill a gap in the British line that could not otherwise have been filled... In spite of the severity of the weather and their unfamiliar surroundings they behaved with great gallantry but suffered terrible losses in the trenches. I had previously succeeded in obtaining the right of Indian soldiers to receive the Victoria Cross for bravery and they won two Victoria Crosses within their first month in France. Very few survived to return to India.

During the war, 1,161,789 Indians were recruited, 1,215,338 were sent overseas, and they suffered 101,439 casualties. In September 1914 the Central Legislative Assembly on the motion of non-official members resolved that 'in addition to giving military assistance, the people of India would wish to share in the heavy financial burden of the war'. This resulted in generous monetary donations.

A tremendous amount of material aid was also rendered. For example, Calcutta alone supplied 80,000,000 sandbags a month 'for as long as they were required'.[1]

It is not surprising that Indians of all shades should have expected a generous step forward toward self-government. At the Twenty-ninth National Congress (28-30 December 1914) Bhupendranath Basue said from the presidential chair, 'The war of nations now in progress will knock off the last weights of medieval domination of one man over many, of one race over another; it is not possible to roll back the tide of wider life which is flowing like a warm Gulf Stream through the waterways of the West into the still waters of the East.'[2]

Jinnah who at the Bankipur Muslim Council meeting on 31 December 1912 had said that the ideal of self-government 'might be attained say a century hence'[3] reflected the revolution in expectations brought about by the war in his speech as the President of the Ninth Session of the Muslim League (30-31 December 1916), 'After such colossal upheavals as this war, the world cannot slip back into its old grooves of life and thought...when the terrible ordeal has passed, the liberated soul will feel almost primeval ease and power to plan, build and to create afresh ampler and freer conditions of life for the future.'[4]

The Lucknow Pact

The Muslim League did not hold any regular sessions during 1914. No doubt in retaliation for the League resolution in favour of separate electorates at the Agra session, the Congress reverted to its practice of condemning separate electorates at its Madras Session on 28-30 December (Resolution XVIII). This underscored the point that either the League or the Congress would have to change its stand on the issue of separate electorates if the two organizations were to implement their resolutions to join forces for the achievement of their common goal of self-government.

The Congress had decided to hold its next regular session at Bombay in December 1915. Jinnah believed that if the League were to hold its own session at Bombay at the same time it would provide a good opportunity for them to confer together as to the future of their country. But when he spearheaded the proposal, it was resisted by some *'johookams'*[5] (those who said 'whatever you order', i.e., stooges of the British Government who did whatever they were ordered to do) on the ground that it was inadvisable for 'political reasons' to hold a meeting at a time 'when the war with Turkey was still in progress and when the question of the future of the Caliphate and other matters of the utmost importance to Islam may as yet be undecided'.[6] It was also alleged by some that the 'object in holding the League contemporaneously with the Congress at the same city is...to merge its individuality with that of the Congress'.[7]

In the end Jinnah succeeded in having the Eighth Session of the League convened at Bombay (30 December 1915-1 January 1916). The president of the session, Mazhar-ul-Haque acknowledged that without Jinnah's 'exertions' they could not have met in Bombay. He 'knew what Mr Jinnah had undergone in the matter' and turning to Jinnah said, 'Mr Jinnah, we the Mussulmans of India thank you' [loud cheers].[8]

But the three-day session did not run smoothly. The meeting on 30 December passed peacefully but on the next day those who had opposed the holding of the session at Bombay occupied the visitors seats and created such pandemonium that it was impossible to conduct any business. Jinnah went to Edwards, the Commissioner of Police who was present at the spot with some fifty policemen, and requested him to clear the *pandal* of persons who were not members of the Muslim League. The Commissioner replied that if trouble was apprehended he was prepared to clear the *pandal* of everyone. At a later date Jinnah stated that the 'meeting was broken up under the very nose of the police' because the British Government did not want the Congress and the Muslim League to meet in the same city.[9]

Under the circumstances the president had to adjourn the session on 31 December. At an informal meeting later it was decided to reconvene at the Taj Mahal Hotel on the next day. At the resumed sitting the following resolution was moved by Jinnah and carried unanimously

The All-India Muslim League resolves that a committee...be appointed to formulate and frame a scheme of reforms, and that the said Committee is authorized to confer with political and other organizations or committees if any, appointed by such organizations as they may deem fit, provided always that due regard is paid to the needs and interests of the Mussulmans of India in the formation of the aforesaid scheme of reforms.

It was explained by Jinnah that the objective of the resolution was that Congress and the League 'the two representative political organizations of India' should formulate a scheme of reforms after which 'they could go to the authorities and say these were the reforms which they demanded in the name of United India'.

The next resolution moved by Syed Alay Nabi stated that 'it is absolutely necessary that the principle of communal representation be extended to all self-government public bodies'.

It was opposed by Hasrat Mohani on the main ground that it 'might prove a stumbling block' to the proposed Congress and League committees in their efforts to formulate an agreed scheme of reforms.

Another member moved that the question be deferred till the Congress and League committee had deliberated together.

Jinnah requested that the two amendments be withdrawn because they were bound to be lost if a vote was taken. The amendments were accordingly withdrawn and the resolution was carried by a large majority.[10]

Jinnah's conduct in letting the League pass the resolution in favour of separate electorates clearly shows that he had by now accepted the fact that the majority of Muslims were irrevocably in favour of that system and it would be futile to try to change their minds. Henceforth, he devoted his energy toward persuading the Congress that as the stronger party they should generously let the Muslims have the constitutional safeguard which they considered essential for their political safety.

Jinnah attended the Congress Bombay session (27-29 December 1915) as well. Congress authorized the All-India Congress Committed to frame a scheme of reforms in consultation with the committee appointed by the League. It must have pleased the Quaid that Congress refrained from passing any resolution opposing separate electorates. This augured well for the outcome of the joint efforts of the Congress and the League to frame an agreed framework for constitutional advance.

1916 was a busy and important year in Jinnah's life. In the summer of that year he spent a two-month holiday at Darjeeling with Sir Dinshaw and Lady Petit. During this period their beautiful sixteen-year old daughter Ruttie and the thirty-nine-year old Jinnah fell in love with each other. But when Jinnah asked Sir Dinshaw for the hand of his daughter the latter indignantly refused to give his consent and took out a High Court injunction against the minor girl marrying or having any contacts with Jinnah. Time and separation, however, made no difference to the feelings of Jinnah and Ruttie towards each other. On attaining her majority at eighteen, she forsook her parental home, embraced Islam and married the man of her choice.

Jinnah was elected to the Imperial Legislative Council on 21 June 1916, once more defeating Rafiuddin.

In September he was a signatory to a Memorandum submitted to the viceroy by nineteen Hindu and Muslim additional members of the Imperial Legislative Council saying that India having borne her part in the allied struggle 'in defence of the liberties of weak and small Nationalities' could not 'remain unaffected by the new spirit of change for a better state of things'. What was wanted was 'not merely good government or efficient administration, but government that is acceptable to the people because it is responsible to them'.[11]

While presiding over the Bombay Provincial Conference at Ahmedabad on 21 October 1916 the Quaid spelled out his political philosophy in some detail. He posed the question as to what measures should be adopted 'to attain, as soon as possible, our most cherished goals, namely, self-government under the aegis of the British Crown and the Provincial Autonomy foreshadowed in the Delhi Despatch of Government of India, dated 25th August 1911'? He stated that among the 'burning questions' were the following

> ...the question of admission of the Indians to Commissioned ranks of the Army and Navy; the removal of the most irritating and humiliating disabilities created by statutes which have raised a bar against the people of India in joining Volunteer Corps, no matter what their rank or position in life may be; the unjust application of the Arms Act to the people of India from which the Europeans are exempted; the Press Act and its arbitrary provisions and, still more,

its arbitrary enforcement by the Executive which is subject to no judicial check, so far as the decisions of the High Court at the present moment go; the Defence of India Act, which was purely a war measure and to which the representatives of the people of India assented when it came before the Imperial Council, is worked in a manner in some cases which is highly undesirable; the undue and unjustifiable delay in making elementary education free and compulsory in the selected areas, which is the cause of the greatest dissatisfaction and disappointment to the people.

On the question of separate electorates he said, 'rightly or wrongly' the Muslims were 'absolutely determined' for the 'present to insist' upon them. Consequently, 'to most of us the question is no more open to further discussion or argument, as it has become a mandate of the community'. He appealed to his Hindu brethren that 'in the present state of position, they should try to win the confidence and trust of the Mohammedans who are, after all, in a minority in the country'.

The real question, he summed up, was not of a few more seats going to the Muslims or the Hindus; it was a transfer of power from bureaucracy to democracy. If Hindus and Muslims stood united and firm 'the voice of three hundred millions of people vibrating throughout the length and breadth of the country, will produce a force which no power on earth can resist'.[12]

At the end of December 1916, the Congress and the Muslim League again held their regular sessions at the same place—Lucknow—and during the same week and accepted the unanimously agreed reforms scheme presented by their respective committees. The Congress-League scheme, popularly known as the Lucknow Pact spelled out the steps which needed to be taken towards self-government for India. They also sought to safeguard the interests of the Muslims in four main ways.

Firstly, Muslims were granted separate electorates in elections to the Provincial as well as to the Imperial Legislative Councils. Secondly, provincial autonomy was assured by the recommendations that 'the Provincial autonomy should have full authority to deal with all matters affecting the internal administration of the province' and that 'the authority of the Government of India will ordinarily be limited to general supervision and superintendence over the Provincial Governments'. Thirdly, '...no bill...affecting one or the other community, which question is to be determined by the members of that community in the Legislative Council concerned, shall be proceeded with if three-fourths of the members of that community in that Council, Imperial or Provincial, oppose the bill...'

Fourthly, Muslims were granted weightage in the provinces in which they were in a minority. They could not very well object to non-Muslims being similarly granted weightage in provinces in which they were in a minority. The net result was that the Muslims were to be represented on the Provincial Legislative Councils in the following proportions:
Of the elected Indian Members,

Punjab	one-half
United Provinces	30 per cent
Bengal	40 "
Bihar	25 "
Central Provinces	15 "
Madras	15 "
Bombay	one-third[13]

The acts of 1919 and 1935 granted weightage on the lines of the Lucknow Pact. On balance this worked to the detriment of Muslim interests. Despite weightage the Muslims remained an ineffective minority in Hindu majority provinces. On the other hand they lost the advantage of their majority in the important Muslim provinces of the Punjab and Bengal. After the elections of 1935 and 1937 they were never able to form a Muslim League ministry in the Punjab and in Bengal the League's fortunes fluctuated.

By negotiating on an equal footing with the League, the Congress tacitly conceded that it did not speak for all the communities in India and that it was in fact the Muslim League who really represented the Muslims.

In 1938 when the Congress President, Subhas Chandra Bose, questioned the claim of the Muslim League as the only authoritative political organization of the Muslims of India, Jinnah reminded him that the said status was accepted by the Congress when the Lucknow Pact was arrived at in 1916.[14]

The accord was ratified by the Muslim League by Resolution II of its Ninth Session at Lucknow (30-31 December 1916). Syed

Alay Nabi who seconded the resolution commended the Hindus and the Muslims for their joint efforts but the really interesting though little noticed feature of his remarks was that he referred to the two communities as 'the two great nations of India'.[15]

When the Quaid presided over the Ninth Session he was naturally full of hope that his success in bringing the League and the Congress on the same platform would bring the desired results: 'The united Indian demand, based on the actual needs of the country and framed with due regard to time and circumstances must eventually prove irresistible'.

His address clearly indicated that he now identified himself more closely with the League though he was still a member of the Congress as well. He could scarcely fail to have been moved by the fact that he had been a member of the Congress since 1906 but that party had never elected him as president while the League had done so only three years after he had joined it. In his view the presidentship of the League session was 'the highest gift of the Muslim community' and he referred to the League as 'the chosen leaders and representatives of 70 million of Indian Mussulmans'. The All-India Muslim League, he recalled, had been founded because the Muslims 'were moved by the loud and insistent demand for constitutional and administrative reforms which Hindu politicians were pressing on the Indian Government. They felt—and rightly—the need for organizing themselves for political action, lest the impending changes...should swamp them altogether as a community.' Gone were the days when he looked upon the Congress as representing all the communities in India.

'A minority', he argued, 'must, above everything else, have a complete sense of security before its broader political sense can be evoked for cooperation... To the Mussulmans...that security can only come through adequate and effective safeguards'. And he declared, 'Whatever my individual opinion may be, I am here to interpret and express the sense of the overwhelming body of Muslim opinion, of which the All-India Muslim League is the political organ.'[16]

Clearly, the realities of Indian politics had tempered his logical mind. He had moved away from his stance in 1906 when he had taken a poor view of the Aga Khan delegation and had subscribed to a petition to the viceroy opposing separate electorates. But his idealism in respect of his country's future was undimmed.

He still believed in a united India in which the Hindus and the Muslims would live happily together and he still believed that the key to a smooth and quick attainment of independence from foreign rule was Hindu-Muslim unity. He held on to his mission as ambassador of Hindu-Muslim unity.

The War Conferences

In a sharp exchange with Lord Chelmsford the viceroy in the Indian Legislative Council, Jinnah had demanded that Indians 'should be put on the same footing as the European British subjects' before they were asked to fight. When Chelmsford criticized the demand as 'bargaining', Jinnah retorted, 'My Lord, to say that in my own country I should be put on the same footing as the European British subjects? Is it bargaining?'[17]

A manifesto signed, among others, by Annie Besant, Tilak and Jinnah appeared in the *Bombay Chronicle* on 24 April 1918. It said that the signatories detested 'German tyranny and German methods' and did not wish to see England 'broken by the war'. They 'shall try to help Britain in any case' but 'if Britain welcomes us as a nation whose freedom depends upon the issue of war, the popular enthusiasm will rise to fighting point'. More specifically, if Britain accepted the Congress and League (Lucknow) Pact, 'we will work heart and soul to save Britain, India and the Empire'.[18]

At the War Conference convened by the viceroy at Delhi (27-29 April) Jinnah wished to introduce a resolution on constitutional reform for India but the viceroy ruled it out of order.[19] Gandhi who was also one of the participants confined his contribution to seconding the viceroy's resolution on recruiting in the following words: 'With a full sense of my responsibility I beg to support the resolution'.[20]

The Mahatma reinforced his loyalty by sending a letter to the viceroy in which he wrote, 'If I could make my countrymen retrace their steps, I would make them withdraw all Congress resolutions and not whisper "Home Rule" or "Responsible Government" during the pendency of the war. I would make India offer all her able-bodied sons as a sacrifice to the Empire at this critical moment'.[21]

Acting on the resolution he had supported, Gandhi undertook a recruiting campaign but 'by perseverance he managed in the end to register very few recruits'.[22]

Another war conference was called on 10 June 1918 at Bombay by Lord Willingdon, the governor of the presidency. It got off to a controversial start when Willingdon alleged that the Home Rule League instead of helping in the war effort had 'increased the difficulties and embarrassment of Government'.

The Home Rule League had been founded by Annie Besant in September 1916 and upon her internment on 16 June 1917 Jinnah had taken over the presidency of its Bombay branch. He took strong exception to the governor's criticism. He said he was 'very much pained' at the governor's remarks and claimed that

> ...the Home Rule Party was as sincere and as anxious as any one else to help the defence of The Motherland...but I say that if you wish to enable us to help you, to facilitate and stimulate the recruiting, you must make the educated people feel that they are the citizens of the Empire and King's equal subjects. But the Government does not do so. You say that we shall be trusted and made real partners in the Empire. When? We do not want words. We do not want the consideration of the matter indefinitely put off. We want action and immediate deeds. I will only give one instance of the dilatoriness. At the Delhi War Conference we passed a resolution recommending that a substantial number of King's Commissions should be granted to the people of India and that the training colleges should be thrown open to them. It is nearly two months now. And what has been done? We have heard nothing yet.

He said they would not succeed in preparing the real defence of India 'much less help the Empire, unless India is made a partner of the Empire and you trust her—at once'.[23]

Willingdon's criticism of the Home Rule League had cut Jinnah to the quick. At two public meetings convened to protest against the governor's remarks, Jinnah took the governor to task. The first of these was held on 17 June 1918. Jinnah called Willingdon's 'speech and conduct' at the War Conference 'the greatest possible blunder'. He said Indian young men studying at Oxford and Cambridge had come forward to enlist but their offer was rejected. The conclusion he had reached was that 'they do not trust us and therefore are not prepared to allow us to take arms for the defence of our motherland and Empire. They want us to continue an organization which they call an army, which is a sepoy army and nothing else'.[24]

At the second meeting on 18 June 1918, Jinnah said Lord Willingdon had called the support of the Home Rule Party half-hearted. 'My answer is this: that your policy is more than half-hearted to get the fullest manpower of India'.[25]

The Jinnah People's Memorial Hall

It is not surprising that when it was proposed to build a memorial to Lord Willingdon in the name of the citizens of Bombay Jinnah should have opposed it on the ground that it would imply that the citizens of Bombay approved of his administration. But few could have anticipated that by an irony of fate a public memorial would instead be built in honour of Jinnah. Let us explain.

The pro-Willingdon elements had called a meeting at the Town Hall on 11 December 1918. Jinnah and other Home Rule Leaguers decided to attend the meeting and oppose the proposal to honour Willingdon.

This time Jinnah had the support of his beautiful and talented wife Ruttie. They had married on 19 April 1918 and had spent only a brief honeymoon at Nainital because of Jinnah's multifarious legal and political commitments. She was a cultured, well-read young lady, every inch as patriotic and self-respecting as her husband. She had figured in an unpleasant incident under the Willingdon's roof. At a dinner party at Government House she happened to be wearing a low-cut dress. This did not please Lady Willingdon who asked an ADC to bring a wrap in case Mrs Jinnah felt cold. Jinnah, thereupon, stood up and said, 'When Mrs Jinnah feels cold, she will say so and ask for a wrap'. And he led his wife out of the dining room.[26]

At the Town Hall on 11 December, the Home Rule Leaguers had arrived early in large numbers and taken up front positions in the queue. When the doors opened at 10 a.m. the Home Rule League leaders including Jinnah, immediately walked into places in the queue which their followers had kept for them. The confusion made it impossible for the meeting to be conducted in an orderly fashion though it was claimed that a resolution proposing a memorial to Lord Willingdon had been carried. The police were present in great force and roughly cleared the hall late in the afternoon assaulting the protesters including Jinnah. Ruttie 'made herself conspicuous in the afternoon by appearing in the gallery of the Town Hall and waving greetings to the crowd outside. She later took up a position inside the Town Hall compound and addressed her husband's supporters advising them to stand by their rights and to resist the police'. The proposal to erect a memorial for Willingdon fizzled out.

> To celebrate the victory of Jinnah and the people of Bombay, a one rupee fund was started...to build a Jinnah Memorial Hall. Within one month, 65,000 citizens of Bombay made a fund of Rs 65,000 and the Jinnah Memorial Hall was built in the Congress House compound. Mrs Besant came down specially to Bombay to declare open the Jinnah Memorial Hall and she paid a handsome and glowing tribute to Jinnah for his services to the country.[27]

This was a period of great political triumph and personal happiness for Jinnah. His marriage was at its early idyllic stage and he had scaled the peak of public popularity. 'In 1919', writes M.C. Chagla, 'Jinnah was the uncrowned king of Bombay. He was the idol of the youth. His personality and his sturdy independence attracted and appealed to the best elements in the city'.[28]

In his criticism of Willingdon, the Quaid was not motivated by racial prejudice. His criterion for appraising British dignatories was whether or not they were sympathetic to Indian aspirations. For statesmen such as Montagu, Hardinge and Irwin, he had nothing but praise.

Gandhi, during this period was still wearing loyalist clothes. Soon after he had finally returned to India from South Africa, he was entertained at a garden party by the members of the Gujar Sabha (14 January 1915). Jinnah who welcomed Mr and Mrs Gandhi on behalf of the Sabha said that it was 'a great privilege and certainly a very great honour' to be welcoming the couple. He praised Gandhi for his services in South Africa 'in the cause of the Indians residing there as well as in the cause of India generally'. He was sure Gandhi in India too 'would not only become a worthy ornament but also a real worker whose equals there were very few'. He drew Gandhi's attention to the 'one problem of all problems of India—namely how to bring about unanimity and cooperation between the two communities so that the demands of India may be made unanimously'.[29]

Mrs Besant requested Gandhi in 1915 to join hands with her in starting the Home Rule League but he refused. 'He did not want', he said, 'to embarrass, harass and annoy the British by a political agitation in India when Great Britain was deeply involved in the war against Germany'. He ignored her plea to 'Strike the iron when the metal is hot'.[30] Nor did Gandhi figure in the making of the Lucknow Pact.

He also refused to join Jinnah in the agitation in December 1918 against the proposal to set up a memorial in honour of Lord Willingdon.[31]

Notes

1. 'Essayez', *The Memoirs of Lawrence Second Marquess of Zetland*, op.cit., p. 70.
2. A. M. Zaidi, *An Encyclopaedia of The Indian National Congress*, VI, op.cit., p. 504.
3. Pirzada, *Foundations of Pakistan*, I, op.cit., p. 259.
4. Pirzada, *Collected Works*, I, op.cit., p. 190.
5. The term used by Jinnah. *See*, Pirzada, *Collected Works*, I, op.cit., p. 135.
6. Ibid., p. 131.
7. Pirzada, *Foundations of Pakistan*, I, op.cit., p. 330.
8. Ibid., p. 361.
9. Pirzada, *Foundations of Pakistan*, II, op.cit., p. 409.
10. For a full account of the Eighth Session of the League *see*, Pirzada, *Foundations of Pakistan*, I, op.cit., p. 324-61.
11. For text of Memorandum of the Nineteen, *see*, Pirzada, *Collected Works*, I, op.cit., pp. 141-5.
12. For the text of the Quaid's Ahmedabad speech *see*, ibid., pp. 147-60.
13. For the text of the Lucknow Pact *see*, Pirzada, *Foundations of Pakistan*, I, op.cit., p. 392-7.
14. Pirzada, *Quaid-i-Azam Jinnah's Correspondence*, p. 50.
15. Pirzada, *Foundations of Pakistan*, I, op.cit., p. 380.
16. For the text of Jinnah's address to the Ninth Session of the League *see*, M.H. Saiyid, *Mohammad Ali Jinnah*, op. cit., 1945 edition, pp. 856-89.
17. Stanley Wolpert, *Jinnah of Pakistan*, p. 53.
18. For the text of the manifesto *see*, M. H. Saiyid, *Mohammad Ali Jinnah*, 1945, op. cit., pp. 179-83.
19. Ibid., p. 183.
20. M. K. Gandhi, *An Autobiography*, op. cit., p. 400.

21. Indulal K. Yajnik, *Gandhi as I Knew Him*, pp. 49-50.
22. H. S. L. Polak, H. N. Brailsford, Lord Pethic-Lawrence, *Mahatma Gandhi*, p. 124.
23. Pirzada, *Collected Works*, I, op.cit., pp. 280-1.
24. Ibid., pp. 282-3.
25. Ibid., pp. 283-4.
26. H. Bolitho, *Jinnah*, op.cit., p. 75.
27. Our account is based on Pirzada, *Collected Works*, I, op.cit., pp. 291. and 296-301 and Kanji Dwarkadas, *India's Fight for Freedom*, op.cit., pp. 78-79.
28. M.C. Chagla, *Roses in December*, op.cit., p. 78.
29. Pirzada, *Collected Works*, I, op. cit., pp. 123-4.
30. Kaji Dwarkadas, *Gandhi Through My Diary Leaves*, op.cit., p. 10.
31. Ibid., p. 14.

CHAPTER 7

India in a Ferment, 1919-1923

Constitutional Developments

The British Government could not very well remain unmoved by the explosion of expectations created by the Great War. On 20 August 1917, Edwin Montagu, Secretary of State for India, made the following historic statement in the House of Commons

> The policy of His Majesty's Government, with which the Government of India are in complete accord, is that of the increasing association of Indians in every branch of administration and the gradual development of self-governing institutions with a view to progressive realization of responsible government in India as an integral part of the British Empire.

It was the first time that the goal of British rule in India was officially defined. In British constitutional parlance 'responsible government' could only mean a government responsible to the elected representatives of the people.

Jinnah stated in a press interview that Indians were sure of Montagu's 'sympathies for our ideals and aspirations'. He welcomed the pronouncement of 20 August and expressed 'great approval' of Montagu's decision to come to India 'and examine and ascertain the present political situation'.[1]

Montagu visited India from November 1917 to the following April. Lord Chelmsford's government in India took 'good care that he did not see anybody important without him'. They also so arranged his tour that he would not be able to attend the Congress session at Calcutta.[2]

He managed to outwit them at least on one occasion. Kanji Dwarkadas relates how Montagu managed to have over an hour's talk alone with Mrs Besant:

Charles Roberts, MP, had come along with Montagu to help him. Charles Roberts asked Mrs Besant to meet him [Roberts]. Hardly had Mrs Besant shaken hands with Roberts and sat down when Montagu dropped in as if by accident. Roberts walked out of the room and Montagu had over an hour's talk with Mrs Besant.[3]

Montagu interviewed Jinnah and Gandhi on 26 November. He found Jinnah

...perfectly mannered, impressive-looking, armed to the teeth with dialectics, and insistent upon the whole of his scheme [the Lucknow Pact]... I was rather tired and funked him. Chelmsford tried to argue with him, and was tied up into knots. Jinnah is a very clever man, and it is, of course, an outrage that such a man should have no chance of running the affairs of his own country.

Of Gandhi, Montagu said, 'He is a social reformer... He dresses like a coolie, forswears all personal advancement, lives practically on air, and is a pure visionary... He wants the millions of India to leap to the assistance of the British throne'.[4]

The Montagu-Chelmsford Report was published on 8 July 1918 and the Act of 1919, based mainly on the recommendations of the Report, came into force on the first day of 1921.

At the centre, the Central Legislative Council of sixty-seven of whom thirty-five were officials was replaced by a legislature of two houses—the Indian Legislative Assembly and the Council of State—in both of which the majority of members were elected. 'Responsible government' was not introduced at the centre. The governor-general's Executive Council continued to be responsible only to the secretary of state but instead of an existing Executive Council of six British members and one Indian, there would be three Indian members out of seven. But the real power still lay with the governor-general. He governed with a wholly nominated Executive Council and could legislate and impose taxes under his power to 'certify' bills.

Separate electorates for the Muslims were retained and the number of seats was allotted according to the Lucknow Pact. Communal representation was extended also to the Sikhs, Europeans, Anglo-Indians and Indian Christians.

By lowering the qualifications of the voters, the size of the electorate for the provinces was increased, but even so it totalled no more than 5.5 million out of a total population in British India at that time of some 250 million.

The most novel feature of the new Constitution was the introduction in the provinces of the system of 'diarchy'. The 'reserved' subjects were to be administered by Executive Councillors who were nominated by the governor entirely at his discretion, and the transferred subjects by ministers to be chosen by the governor from the members of the legislature. In theory, the ministers held office during the governor's pleasure, but in effect, they could continue only while they enjoyed the confidence of the House, which could withhold their salary, or censure their administration, or throw out the budgets of their departments. This was the only concession to the concept of 'responsible government' in the entire scheme. Broadly, the reserved subjects were law and order and revenue, and the transferred subjects (the 'nation-building' departments) were local self-government, education, public health, public works, agriculture and co-operative societies.

The Quaid's Views on the Montagu-Chelmsford Report, the Rowlatt Bill and Khilafat

The recommendations of the Montagu-Chelmsford Report and the provisions of the Act of 1919 fell far below the demands unitedly made by the Congress and the Muslim League under the Lucknow Pact and the expectations raised by Montagu's statement of 20 August 1917. But whatever chances they might have had of winning Indian approval were undermined by the civil upheaval following the passage of the Rowlatt Bill and the treatment meted out to the defeated Sultan of Turkey by the allies.

As explained by Muhammad Ali

> A vast majority of the Muslims of the world recognized the Sultan of Turkey to be the Commander of the Faithful and the Successor and Khalifa of their Prophet. It is an essential part of this doctrine that the Khalifa, the Commander of the Faithful, should have adequate territories, adequate military and naval resources, adequate financial resources.[5]

Jinnah had publicly expressed his concern for the future of the Khalifa in the middle of the war. In the course of his presidential address to the Lucknow Session of the Muslim League in December 1916, he pointed out that the Muslims of India had remained loyal to the British Government from the very beginning of the war and 'therefore' urged that the 'Government should have regard for their dearest and most sacred religious feelings and under no circumstances interfere with the question of the future of the Caliphate'.[6]

The Montagu-Chelmsford Report was published on 8 July 1918 and was followed by the publication of the Rowlatt Report on 18 July. The Rowlatt Report was made by the Sedition Committee (popularly called the Rowlatt Committee after its chairman, Mr Justice Rowlatt) which had been appointed by the Government of India to report on the nature and extent of conspiracies connected with the revolutionary movement in India, and to recommend legislation to deal with them. It was felt that the war was nearing its end and legislation was needed to take the place of the Defence of India Act which would automatically expire six months after the war. Two bills based on the Report were introduced in the Imperial Legislature on 6 February 1919. One of them was dropped but the other was passed on 18 March 1919. The punitive part of the Act provided for a speedy trial of offences by a Special Court presided over by three High Court judges who would sit in camera and could take into consideration evidence inadmissable under the Indian Evidence Act. There was no right of appeal. Under preventive measures the Provincial Government could order any person to reside in a particular place and desist from any specified act. It could also arrest a person without warrant and detain him in confinement. The popular view of the Act was summed up in the slogan *'na appeal, na dalil, na vakeel* [no appeal, no argument, no advocate]'.

The Quaid gave his view of the Montagu-Chelmsford proposals in a press statement on 23 July 1918. He said he knew that great difficulties were put in the way of Montagu in India and he thought Montagu had been unduly influenced by the 'alarmist section'. The consequence was that the Government of India had been left practically as it was and the advancement of the Provincial Governments did not go as far as it should. He thought it must be made clear that after five years there should be no reserved subjects in the provinces. Furthermore, he believed that progressive realization of responsible self-government should not be confined to provinces but must be extended simultaneously to Provincial Governments and the Government of India. However, he urged his countrymen to treat the report with due respect and concentrate their energies in the direction of securing the necessary changes.[7]

With regard to the recommendations of the Rowlatt Committee he said in the Legislative Council on 23 September 1918 that he felt 'quite sure no civilized Government will...ever dream of putting those recommendations in the form of laws.'[8]

Mahatma Gandhi's 'Himalayan Miscalculation'

It was the passage of the Rowlatt Bill that stirred Gandhi to action and opened a new phase in the history of Indian nationalism. He decided to meet the situation not with constitutional methods but with a campaign of Satyagraha. He published a pledge that 'we shall refuse civilly to obey these laws...and we further affirm that in the struggle we will faithfully follow truth and refrain from violence to life, person or property.'[9] The date 6 April 1919 was fixed to be a day of *hartal*, fasting, penance and meetings all over the country.

To ask the Indian populace verbally to refrain from violence was easy enough, but to prevent violence by mobs and punitive action by the authorities in practice was a sheer impossibility. Not surprisingly large-scale violence and bloodshed took pace at several places notably at Delhi, at some towns in the Bombay Presidency, at Amritsar, at Lahore and some other towns in the Punjab.

The most horrible incident took place on 13 April at the Jallianwalla Bagh in Amritsar. There a British general named Dyer ordered his troops to open fire on a meeting consisting of thousands of persons and though they had begun to disperse, continued the attack for about ten minutes till only sufficient ammunition remained to ensure the safe retreat of the force. The number of dead ran into hundreds.

Another much condemned action of Dyer's was the 'crawling order' which he gave orally on 19 April. It related to the 150 yard long street, with houses on both sides, in which a certain Miss Sherwood had been assaulted. Dyer felt 'the street ought to be looked upon as sacred; therefore I posted pickets at both ends and told them, no Indians are to be allowed to pass along here', and he added, 'if they had to pass they must go on all fours'.

Indians were also humiliated under martial law orders in some other towns of the Punjab.

Of course, Indian mobs were not blameless either. Kanji Dwarkadas was an eyewitness to a personal effort by Gandhi to halt rioting by a mob in Bombay on 11 April 1919. Gandhi went to a police station where

> ...the crowds had gone completely out of control and were stoning the police station... He got out of the car, stood on the footboard and screamed nervously and in anguish as loud as he could to the people raising his hand 'keep peaceful'... The crowds responded, shouted back, 'Mahatma Gandhi *ki jai*' and hurled more stones on the mounted police and smashed more glass windows of the Police Station, all the time repeating 'Mahatma Gandhi *ki jai*'... Gandhi returned to the car and he went back to Laburnum Road sad, puzzled, confused and crestfallen.[10]

In the end Gandhi had to concede that he had made a 'Himalayan miscalculation...in calling upon the people...to launch upon civil disobedience prematurely'. And he came to the conclusion that 'before restarting civil disobedience on a mass scale, it would be necessary to create a band of well-tried, pure-hearted volunteers who thoroughly understood the strict conditions of Satyagraha'.[11] He suspended the Satyagraha movement for the moment but did not always heed the lesson he had professed to have learnt.

At this stage the Indians ascribed the martial law excesses to hidebound bureaucrats and military officers in India and hoped that the more liberal democratic elements at Westminster would mete out adequate punishment to the wrongdoers.

The Quaid-i-Azam's Response to the Rowlatt Act

The Quaid felt no less frustrated by the Rowlatt legislation than Gandhi but his style of protest was based on cogent reasoning and constitutional opposition.

During the debate on the Rowlatt Bill in the Legislative Council he opposed the bill on the main grounds that it was against the fundamental principles of law and justice that no man be deprived of his liberty without a judicial trial; that it was a most inopportune moment to pass such legislation because high hopes had been raised among the people by the promise of reforms; and that 'if these measures are passed, you will create in this country from one end to the other a discontent and agitation, the like of which you have not witnessed'.[12]

He ended his speech with an appeal to the government to re-consider the matter emphasizing that he was doing so as a man 'who is a lover of law and order, as a man who believes in discipline and authority'.

After the bill was passed, Jinnah on 28 March 1919 sent a letter to the viceroy tendering his resignation from the Imperial Legislative Council. He wrote

> The passing of the Rowlatt Bill...has severely shaken the trust reposed by them in British justice. Further, it has clearly demonstrated the constitution of the Imperial Legislative Council which is a legislature but in name—a machine propelled by a foreign Executive. Neither the unanimous opinion of the non-official Indian members nor the entire public opinion and feeling outside has met with the least respect.
>
> The Government of India and Your Excellency, however, have thought it fit to place on the Statute-book a measure admittedly obnoxious and decidedly coercive at a time of peace, thereby substituting the executive for the judicial.
>
> Besides, by passing this bill, Your Excellency's Government have actively negatived every argument they advanced but a year ago when they appealed to India for help at the War Conference and have ruthlessly trampled upon the principles for which Great Britain avowedly fought the war...
>
> I, therefore, as a protest against the passing of the bill and the manner in which it was passed, tender my resignation as a member of the Imperial Legislative Council...

In my opinion, a Government that passes or sanctions such a law in times of peace forfeits its claim to be called a civilized Government...[13]

The Royal Proclamation and its Calming Effect

World War I ended on 11 November 1919 and on 23 December the Government of India Act received Royal Assent. The latter was accompanied by a Royal Proclamation which, as a gesture of conciliation, granted amnesty to political prisoners resulting in the release, amongst others, of two brothers named Muhammad Ali and Shaukat Ali often referred to as the Ali Brothers.

As the end of the war had approached, the anxiety of the Indian Muslims about the fate of Turkey had increased. An organization for the support of Turkey, the Khilafat Conference, came into existence in the middle of 1919 and held a public session at Delhi on 23 and 24 November 1919. Gandhi attended the Khilafat Conference and presided over the session on 24 November. On his advice the Conference passed a resolution refusing to co-operate with the government unless the Khilafat and the holy places of Islam, of which the Caliph was the Keeper, were treated in accordance with Muslim wishes.

The failure of the rebellion of 1857 had reduced the influence of the *ulema* in Muslim politics but the Khilafat Movement offered them the opportunity to stage a comeback. A new Muslim organization, the Jamiat-i-Ulema-i-Hind, came into being. At the end of December 1919, no less than four parties held their sessions simultaneously at Amritsar to demonstrate Hindu-Muslim solidarity. These were the Congress, the Muslim League, the Khilafat Conference and the Jamiat.

Why did Gandhi, an orthodox Hindu, decide to champion so wholeheartedly the cause of the Caliphate, which was a purely Muslim question without any direct link with India's own movement for self-government? It is best to seek the answer to this question in Gandhi's own pronouncements on the subject. His approach, as usual, was a mixture of religion and practical politics. He wrote in *Young India* (20 October 1921): 'I claim that with us both the Khilafat is the central fact, with Maulana Mohammad Ali because it is his religion, with me because in laying down my life for the Khilafat I ensure the safety of the cow, that is my religion, from the Mussulman knife. Both hold swaraj equally dear because only by swaraj is the safety of our respective faiths possible'.

At another time he said that the Khilafat Movement offered an opportunity, which would not recur for another hundred years, to prove that the Muslim was the brother of the Hindu. Again, 'We talk of Hindu-Mohammedan unity. It would be an empty phrase if the Hindus held aloof from the Mohammedans when their vital interests are at stake.'

The conciliatory Royal Proclamation, however, created a good impression in India and raised hopes that the twin problems of punishment for the martial law excesses in the Punjab and the fate of Turkey would be solved amicably. The very first resolution passed at the Thirty-fourth Session of the Congress at Amritsar (27-30 December 1919) tendered Congress's 'respectful thanks to His Majesty the King Emperor for his gracious Proclamation dated the 23rd of December 1919'.

With regard to the Punjab martial law atrocities the Congress asked for suitable action against General Dyer and against Sir Michael O'Dwyer, Governor of the Punjab. Another resolution urged 'upon His Majesty's Government to settle the Turkish question in accordance with the just and legitimate sentiments of Indian Mussulmans'. The resolution on 'Responsible Government' described the Reforms Act as 'inadequate, unsatisfactory and disappointing' but stated that Congress would work the Reforms 'to secure an early establishment of full responsible Government.'

The Muslim League also held its Twelfth Session at Amritsar from 29 to 31 December 1919. Its first resolution 'tendered its homage to the person and throne of His Majesty the King Emperor and it also passed resolutions similar to the Congress resolutions on Dyer and O'Dwyer and on Khilafat and the Reforms.

Some notable features of the session were that Gandhi, Motilal Nehru and some other Congress leaders attended it; that the newly released Ali Brothers arrived on 30 December and moved the audience to tears with their addresses; and that Hakim Ajmal Khan in his presidential address lavished high praise on Gandhi as 'an acknowledged leader of our country, whose active sympathy...has won him the grateful and reverential affection of all Mussulmans in India'. Clearly, a new phase in Indian politics was developing in which Gandhi for the time being would be the supreme leader of both the Hindus and the Muslims and the Ali Brothers would infuse new fire in the Khilafat Movement as Gandhi's right-hand men.

Both the Ali Brothers were Oxford graduates. They were devout Muslims and had been interned during the war for carrying out propaganda against the British Government and in support of Turkey. This had made them heroes in the eyes of the Muslim masses and natural leaders of the Khilafat Movement. Muhammad Ali, the younger of the two, had an impressive command of the English language.

The End of the Truce

The uneasy truce between the British Government and the Indian politicians, being conditional on bringing the officials of the martial law excesses to book and leaving the empire of the defeated Caliph intact, came to an end during 1920 when the Indians concluded that neither of the demands was being met.

Jinnah had been the first leader of all-India status who had warned the British Government against the consequences of reducing the status of the Caliph. He had done this from the presidential chair of the Muslim League in December 1916 as we have already stated. At that time he was an equally respected member of the Congress.

In the summer of 1919, Jinnah went to England and on 4 September forwarded a memorandum to Prime Minister Lloyd George as the head of a Muslim League deputation. In it he reminded the addressee of the assurance he had held out in a speech on 5 January 1918

> Nor are we fighting...to deprive Turkey of its capital, or of the rich and renowned lands of Asia Minor and Thrace, which are predominantly Turkish in race... We do not challenge the maintenance of the Turkish Empire in the homelands of the Turkish race with its capital at Constantinople.

He pointed out that

> For generations past the Muslims of India generally have recognized the Khilafat of the House of Osman and Constantinople as Darul-Islam and Khilafat (the seat of Islam and the Khilafat). For many centuries the Sultan of Turkey has been recognized as the Servant of the Holy Places of Islam and their Custodian, by all the Muslims of the world.

Finally, he warned the British Prime Minister that 'if Great Britain becomes a party to reducing H.I.M. the Sultan of Turkey and the Khalifa of the Muslim world to the status of a petty sovereign, the reaction in India will be colossal and abiding'.[14]

Jinnah also requested the British prime minister to grant him a private interview but none was granted. He returned to India disappointed.

On 19 January 1920, a Khilafat delegation of Muslims and Hindus waited on Lord Chelmsford, the viceroy, and presented an address which was read by Dr M. A. Ansari. The delegation included Jinnah, Gandhi and the Ali Brothers. The viceroy replied that the future of the institution of the Khilafat was for the Muslims to decide.

> The contention, however, which you urge in your address that Turkey should preserve in full integrity the sovereignty and dominions which she possessed before the war, is one which I fear we cannot reasonably hope will be recognized by the Allied Powers in Conference. Before Turkey made her fatal mistake, His Majesty's Government had guaranteed that such integrity would be the reward of neutrality but now that she had submitted her fate to the arbitrament of the sword she cannot expect any more than any other power which drew the sword in the cause of Germany wholly to escape the consequences of her action.[15]

The Khilafat Conference decided to take its case to the British Government in London and a deputation headed by Muhammad Ali left for England early in March 1920. The delegation were able to secure an interview with the prime minister on 19 March 1920 but were rebuffed in no uncertain terms. Lloyd George told them plainly that he did not 'want any Mussulman in India to imagine that we are going to abandon, when we come to

Turkey the principles which we have ruthlessly applied to [defeated] Christian countries like Germany and Austria'.[16]

While the Muhammad Ali delegation was still in Europe, the terms of the Treaty of Sevres were published (15 May 1920). The Sultan's empire was to be dismembered: the Arab lands were to become independent; Syria was to become a mandate of France, and Mesopotamia and Palestine of Britain; Smyrna and Thrace were to be made over to Greece. But Turkey was allowed to retain Constantinople.

Twelve days later (28 May 1920) the majority and minority reports of the officially appointed Hunter Committee to investigate the April 1919 disturbances were published. The Committee consisted of Lord Hunter as president, four other British members and three Indian members. It split on racial lines, with the British members submitting a Majority Report and the Indians a Minority Report.

The Majority Report in justifying the declaration of martial law found that the disturbances had developed into 'a state of open rebellion against the authority of the Government'. The Minority Report, on the other hand said, 'We are unable to agree in the view that the riots in the Punjab were in the nature of rebellion', and concluded that the 'introduction of martial law and its continuance for a period for which it was continued were not justified'.

An enquiry committee of the Congress had already issued its own report on 25 March 1920. The Committee had consisted of four members including Gandhi. It had concluded that, 'Most of the measures taken under Martial Law…were unnecessary, cruel, oppressive and in utter disregard of the feelings of the people affected by them' and that 'the Jallianwala Bagh massacre was a calculated piece of inhumanity toward utterly innocent and unarmed men, including children, and unparalleled for its ferocity in the history of British administration'.

After the British Government had accepted the findings of the Hunter Committee Majority Report, the only official who received any punishment was General Dyer and his punishment was no more than compulsory retirement.[17] This punishment was upheld by the House of Commons but the House of Lords on 20 July 1920 passed a resolution deploring the action taken against Dyer as 'unjust to that officer and as establishing a precedent dangerous to the preservation of order in the face of rebellion'.

Immediately after the defeat of the motion in the Commons, the *Morning Post* opened a fund to reward Dyer for his role as 'Saviour of India'. It received more than the target of £26,000. Dyer was also presented with a sword of honour. One third of the purse was subscribed in India. And from Bengal, 6,250 British women sent a petition to the prime minister in London protesting against the treatment meted out to the General. That so many British people regarded Dyer as a national hero deeply shocked public opinion in India. The approval of the General's conduct by the House of Lords, whom the Indian intelligentsia regarded as the mouthpiece of the British ruling classes, was especially shocking. It was the last straw that destroyed Indian hopes of ever receiving racial justice at British hands.

The position was thus reached that there was no visible sign that the reforms enacted under the Act of 1919 would be liberalized in the near future; that Dyer had got off lightly for the terrible massacre he had ordered at Amritsar; and that the Turkish empire was being dismembered. Indian public opinion was furious.

Jinnah and Gandhi's Respective Responses

Jinnah presided over a mass protest meeting jointly convened by the Bombay branches of the Home Rule League on 27 June 1920. He said that he did not think he had ever presided over a meeting where he had felt greater pain and greater sorrow than he did at that meeting. He recalled that the Rowlatt Act had been passed in the teeth of Indian opposition and when the people protested against it by holding meetings and passing resolutions, Lieutenant-Governor O'Dwyer resorted to 'butchery' in the Punjab. With regard to the fact that General Dyer had been punished only by being relieved of his command, he asked 'everyone who had got any shred of fairness left, is this the redress for nearly 2,000 lives butchered and 3,000 wounded?' He asked, further, what was the guarantee that such an atrocious tragedy would not occur again.

Gandhi's response was to launch a non-cooperation movement on 1 August 1920 as the leader of the Khilafatists. He returned his war medals 'in pursuance of the scheme of non-cooperation inaugurated today in connection with the Khilafat Movement'.

The League as well as the Congress also called special sessions at Calcutta during the same week in September.

The Special Sessions of the Muslim League and the Congress at Calcutta

Presiding over the Special Session of the League at Calcutta on 7 September 1920, the Quaid said

> First came the Rowlatt Bill—accompanied by the Punjab atrocities—and then came the spoilation of the Ottoman Empire and the Khilafat. The one attacks our liberty, the other our faith...Notwithstanding the unanimous opinion of the Mussulmans, and in breach of the Prime Minister's solemn pledges, unchivalrous and outrageous terms have been imposed upon Turkey and the Ottoman Empire has served for plunder and been broken up by the Allies under the guise of Mandates. This, thank God, has at last convinced us, one and all, that we can no longer abide our trust either in the Government of India or in the Government of His Majesty the King of England to represent India in matters international... We shall have to think out some course more effective than passing resolutions of disapproval to be forwarded to the Secretary of State for India... We are not going to rest content until we have attained the fullest political freedom in our own country. Mr Gandhi has placed his programme of non-co-operation, supported by the authority of the Khilafat Conference, before the country. It is now for you to consider whether or not you approve of its principle; and approving of its principle, whether or not you approve of its details. The operations of the scheme will strike at the individual in each of you, and therefore it rests with you alone to measure your strength and to weigh the pros and the cons of the question before you arrive at a decision. But once you have decided to march, let there be no retreat under any circumstances... The majority report of the Hunter Committee is one more flagrant and disgraceful instance that there can be no justice when there is a conflict between an Englishman and an Indian.

In deploring the resolution passed by the House of Lords in support of Dyer, he described the members of that chamber as the 'blue and brainless blood of England'.

In the end he appealed to the British Government 'not to drive the people of India to desperation, or else there is no course left open to the people except to inaugurate the policy of non-cooperation though not necessarily the programme of Mr Gandhi'.[18]

The words 'not necessarily the programme of Mr Gandhi' are important. They presage Jinnah's total and final break with the Mahatma and the Congress. He, no doubt, had in mind Gandhi's 'Himalayan miscalculation' in April 1919 which had led to the Jalianwalla massacre and other tragic events. Gandhi had vowed then that he would not start another political agitation until he could create 'a band of well-tried, pure-hearted volunteers'. Yet, he had already launched a non-cooperation movement on 1 August 1920. In April 1919 it had been a satyagraha movement and the prescribed-action was *hartal*, fasting, penance and meetings. Non-cooperation entailed stronger action. It was aimed at paralyzing the government as we shall describe later. There was no telling what its consequences would be.

Though the Khilafatist Muslims had enthusiastically embraced Gandhi's non-cooperation programme, he still had to obtain the support of the predominantly Hindu Congress party to that end. When Congress met in special session at Calcutta (4-8 September 1990), the only prominent Hindu leader who supported Gandhi was Motilal Nehru, the leading light of the Allahabad bar and Congress leader of the United Provinces. Lajpat Rai, who presided over the sessions, was an avowed opponent of non-cooperation and was strongly supported by other Congress veterans such as Das, Bipin Chandra Pal, Annie Besant, Malaviya and Jinnah. But Gandhi carried the day with the help of Muslims and Hindus at a popular level. Tilak, who with his grass-roots popularity might have made a difference to the outcome, had breathed his last on the very day on which Gandhi had inaugurated the non-cooperation campaign (1 August).

As pointed out by Jawaharlal Nehru in his autobiography, this special session at Calcutta 'began the Gandhi era in Congress politics' which was broken only for a short period in the twenties 'when he kept in the background and allowed the Swaraj Party' under C.R. Das and Motilal Nehru 'to fill the picture'.[19]

The most important resolution was the one which dealt with non-cooperation. It was proposed by the Mahatma and passed by 1886 votes to 884.

It stated that there could be no contentment in India without redress of the Khilafat and Punjab martial law wrongs and that no course was 'left open to the people of India but to approve and adopt the policy of progressive, non-violent non-cooperation inaugurated by Gandhiji until the said wrongs were righted and Swaraj established'.

Non-cooperation was spelled out in the following terms

(1) surrender of titles and honorary offices and resignation from nominated seats in local bodies;
(2) refusal to attend Government levees, durbars, and other official and semi-official functions held by Government officials or in their honour;
(3) gradual withdrawal of children from schools and colleges owned, aided or controlled by Government, and in place of such schools and colleges, establishment of national schools and colleges in the various provinces;
(4) gradual boycott of British courts by lawyers and litigants, and establishment of private arbitration courts by their aid, for the settlement of private disputes;
(5) refusal on the part of the military, clerical and labouring classes to offer themselves as recruits for service in Mesopotamia;
(6) withdrawal by candidates of their candidature for election to the reformed councils, and refusal on the part of the voters to vote for any candidate who may, despite the Congress advice, offer himself for election;
(7) boycott of foreign goods.[20]

Jinnah Resigns from the Home Rule League as well as from the Congress

The fat was now in the fire and an open clash between Gandhi and Jinnah was only a matter of time. It took place on 3 October 1920. Mrs Besant had resigned as president of the Home Rule League and Gandhi, the new President, chaired the meeting. To bring the goal of the League in line with the programme just adopted by Congress, Gandhi wished to change its creed and also to re-name it Swaraj Sabha. Jinnah opposed him without success and in protest resigned along with some others. Gandhi invited him back to share in 'the new life that has opened up before the country'. Jinnah's reply showed how worried he felt over Gandhi's agitational politics

> If by 'new life' you mean your methods and your programme, I am afraid I cannot accept them; for I am fully convinced that it must lead to disaster...your extreme programme has for the moment struck the imagination mostly of the inexperienced youth and the ignorant and the illiterate. All this means complete disorganization and chaos.

On 19 December 1920, Jinnah gave an address to the students of Ferguson College, Poona. Gandhi's non-cooperation movement had by then been in operation for some months and Jinnah was now in a position to comment on the extent of its efficacy in practice. He said that though he was a believer in the policy of non-cooperation, Gandhi's programme could not be put into practice 'today' with a view to paralysing the government because the requisite materials for its enforcement were lacking. The contemplated boycott of foreign goods was impracticable; the Congress decision to boycott the councils was unfortunate because there was no dearth of other candidates; to undermine the existing educational institutions before new ones could be built was going the wrong way about the business; and a few lawyers who had given up their practice could not by themselves paralyse the system. In his opinion, the whole programme was harmful and impracticable in the current state of political consciousness.[21]

The Thirty-fifth Session of the Congress at Nagpur (26-31 December 1920) witnessed some remarkable developments.

Gandhi's non-cooperation resolution which had been passed at the Amritsar Special Session was confirmed and the creed of the Congress was changed to 'the attainment of Swarajya by the people of India by all legitimate and peaceful means'. But the most extraordinary resolution was the one which envisaged the attainment of Swaraj within one year: 'In order that the Khilafat and the Punjab wrongs may be redressed and Swarajya established within one year, this Congress urges upon all the public bodies, whether affiliated to the Congress or otherwise, to devote their exclusive attention to the promotion of non-violence and non-cooperation with the Government'.

Subhas Chandra Bose called this promise of Swaraj within one year 'not only unwise but childish as it made Congress appear so foolish before all reasonable men'.[22] 'The promised Swaraj did not come. A few months earlier, at the conference with the ex-revolutionaries of Bengal, the Mahatma had said that he was so sure of getting Swaraj before the end of the year that he could not conceive of himself as living beyond December 31st without having won Swaraj'.[23]

Of the thousands who attended the Nagpur session, Jinnah alone had the courage to walk to the rostrum and oppose the resolutions relating to the change in creed and non-cooperation. He explained that he did not dispute the fact that 'the government have done us repeated wrongs of an enormous character which have made our blood boil', but that was not the issue before the people. He said that his objection to the new creed was that it did not make it clear whether Swarajya meant severance of all connection with Britain or not. Personally he wanted 'to keep the British connection'. With regard to non-cooperation he said, 'Let me tell you once more, that the weapon will not destroy the British Empire...it is neither logical nor is it politically sound or wise, nor practically capable of being put in execution'. He said that he knew that Gandhi commanded the majority in that gathering but he appealed to him 'to pause, to cry halt before it is too late'.[24]

The crowd had persistently interrupted Jinnah with hostile shouts. At one point, when he referred to Gandhi as 'Mister', the crowd cried 'Mahatma'. At another, when he called Muhammad Ali 'Mister', he evoked shouts of 'Maulana'. This time he remonstrated, 'if you will not allow me the liberty to address you and speak of a man in the language in which I think it is right, I say you are denying me the liberty which you are asking for'. After having his say he left the meeting in protest.

Among the audience during Jinnah's speech was Colonel Wedgood, who had come to attend the session as a fraternal delegate of the British Labour party. He was so deeply impressed with Jinnah's courage that he openly praised him in the meeting: 'I do not know enough about Mr Jinnah's politics to say whether I agree with him or not, but I do know that a man who has the courage to come to this audience and tell you what he has told you is a man for my money. The first thing in every political leader is not brains, but courage.'[25]

The Muslim League session, which was convened at Nagpur immediately after the Congress session there in December 1920, was presided over by the veteran Congress leader M. A. Ansari. He asserted that 'so far as the Mussulmans are concerned the principle of non-cooperation is not a new idea; rather it is a clear and definite injunction of the divine Shariat which the Mussulmans of India had in their forgetfulness consigned to oblivion'. A resolution affirmed the League's support for non-cooperation and expressed satisfaction at the progress of the movement. Another resolution, echoing the Nagpur Congress resolution regarding the change of creed, declared that one of the objects of the League 'shall be the attainment of Swaraj by the people of India by all peaceful and legitimate means'. Jinnah, realizing it was not his day, did not even bother to attend the meeting. He had left Nagpur on the very day he had walked out of the Congress meeting.

So it was not Jinnah's logic that prevailed but the emotional appeal of Gandhi and his disciples, the eloquent Urdu-speaking Muslim 'nationalists' such as the Ali Brothers, Abul Kalam Azad, Ansari, Kitchlew and Hasrat Mohani. For the time being everyone followed Gandhi. Choudhry Khaliquzzaman, afterwards a prominent League leader, recalled in his book, *Pathway to Pakistan*, 'I was wholeheartedly for Gandhiji's policies at the time and knew too well that but for him both the Khilafat and Congress would suffer a reverse'.[26]

Non-Cooperation in Action

Human nature being what it is, when it came to making practical sacrifices, non-cooperation achieved only a limited amount of success.

The boycott of Councils was a success in the sense that Congress candidates withdrew their candidature and most of the voters kept away from the polling booths. On the other hand, all the seats were captured by non-Congress men, most of whom were responsive to government wishes.

Several hundred lawyers at first renounced their practice but most of them drifted back. The functioning of the official courts was not disrupted. The attempt to set up rival arbitration courts was a failure. However, some of the most eminent lawyers who had given up their profession did not resume it and became invaluable full-time stalwarts of Congress. Prominent among them were Das, Motilal Nehru and his son Jawaharlal, and Rajendra Prasad.

Only a negligible number of title holders renounced their honours and only a negligible number of government servants left their posts. Most importantly, the army and the police were not affected. Titles, however, lost most of their glamour. Vigorous picketing led to a decline in the consumption of liquor but sales returned to normal when the pickets were removed.

Though the movement for the boycott of educational institutions created much youthful excitement at first, it had no appreciable effect on the existing system of education. Of the newly started national universities the most notable were those at Ahmadabad, with Gandhi as its Chancellor, and the National Muslim University (Jamia Millia Islamia) at Aligarh, with Muhammad Ali as its principal. The latter was afterwards moved to Delhi and is still flourishing.

There were impressive bonfires of foreign cloth but the boycott of foreign cloth did not achieve much success. Several leaders, including Patel and Tagore, were against the wanton destruction of valuable cloth when it could have been used to clothe some of the poor millions who went half-naked. Nor did the efforts to remove Untouchability make any discernible headway.

The worst set-backs, of course, were the failures to practice non-violence and to achieve Hindu-Muslim solidarity. The Ali Brothers kept up the fiery temper of the Khilafat Movement. While they were touring jointly with Gandhi, Muhammad Ali said at Madras on 2 April 1921 that if the Amir of Afghanistan were to invade India not to subjugate it, but to attack those who wished to subjugate it, those who held the holy places of Islam and who wished to crush Islam and to destroy the Muslim faith, then it would be the duty of Muslims not only to refuse to assist the government but to gird up their loins and fight for Islam. This speech naturally alarmed most Hindus, but some leaders tried to limit the damage it could do to Hindu-Muslim unity. Gandhi said that if Afghanistan invaded India he would tell Indians not to assist the government.

At the Khilafat Conference on 10 July 1921 which was presided over by Muhammad Ali, a resolution declared that 'under present circumstances the Holy Shariat forbids every Mussalman to serve or enlist himself in the British Army or raise recruits for it'. In September the Ali Brothers and some others were prosecuted for their part in the conference and were each sentenced to rigorous imprisonment for two years. To show solidarity with the Khilafat Movement, the Congress High Command endorsed Gandhi's recommendation that 'we must repeat the formula of the [Ali] brothers regarding the duty of soldiers and invite imprisonment'. This was done on 16 October from innumerable platforms as a challenge to the government.

While Gandhi was doing his best to maintain the appearance of Hindu-Muslim solidarity, a grievous blow to Hindu-Muslim relations was struck by the Moplahs, a Muslim community on the Malabar coast of South India. These people, mostly poor ignorant peasants and fishermen, who were the descendants of Arab settlers, were a fanatical and unruly lot and had had fierce clashes in the past with the authorities as well as with their more prosperous Hindu landlords and money-lenders. Inspired by the Khilafat propaganda they rose in revolt in August (1921) as described by the following official report

> During the early months of 1921, excitement spread speedily from mosque to mosque, from village to village. The violent speeches of the Ali Brothers, the early approach of Swaraj as aforetold in the non-cooperating Press, the July resolutions of the Khilafat Conference....all these combined to fire the brain. Throughout July and August innumerable Khilafat meetings were held, in which the resolutions of the Karachi Conference were fervently endorsed. Knives, swords, and spears were secretly manufactured, bands of desperadoes collected, and preparations were made to proclaim the coming of the kingdom of Islam.

One of the leaders of the revolt proclaimed: 'We have extorted Swaraj from the white man and what we have secured we are not going to give up so easily... We shall give Hindus the option of death or Islam... The Jews and Christians, as believers in a revealed book, may be tolerated, but the idolatrous Hindus can only be allowed to live in a Muslim state on sufferance'. The rebels murdered four Europeans but their real victims were the

Hindus. They ruthlessly murdered, converted people forcibly to Islam, raped women, desecrated temples, and pillaged and destroyed property. It was only strong and sustained military action that brought the situation under control at the end of the year. Unaware of the real situation, Gandhi said that the 'brave Moplahs [were] fighting for what they consider as religion, and in a manner which they consider as religious'. But the Moplahs had in fact dealt a heavy blow to Hindu-Muslim accord.

Just as the Moplah rebellion was nearing its close, serious rioting took place in Bombay when the Prince of Wales landed there in the forenoon of 17 November 1921. There was a *hartal* in the city in response to the Congress decision to boycott the visit. This brought large crowds including mill-hands into the streets, and a free-for-all involving all communities started when the mob interfered with peaceful people using public transport, burnt tram cars and liquor shops, assaulted Europeans and generally dislocated the life of the citizens. The rioting continued for four or five days and it was officially estimated that 53 persons had been killed and 400 wounded. All this took place while Gandhi, the apostle of non-violence and communal harmony, was present in the city and had tried his best to restore calm. He undertook a fast for five days to restore order and as a penance for the excesses of the people. 'With non-violence on our lips', he said in disgust, 'we have terrorized those who happened to differ from us. The Swaraj that I have witnessed during the last two days has stunk in my nostrils'.

Kanji Dwarkadas, who visited Gandhi during the disturbances at Bombay found that 'he was lying on a mat, heart broken and weeping like a baby. "I am bankrupt, I am bankrupt", he was screaming, "I asked people to be non-violent and they have taken to stone-throwing and as they throw stones, they keep shouting "Mahatma Gandhi *ki-jai*".'[27]

By the end of 1921, all the principal leaders except Gandhi were in prison.

The non-cooperation movement was suddenly suspended by Gandhi as the result of the Chauri Chaura tragedy. On 5 February 1922 twenty-two policemen were murdered there by a mob. Gandhi's sudden retreat, ahead of the much publicized trial of strength between the government and the non-cooperators shocked all his principal colleagues.

It 'was resented, I think, by almost all the prominent Congress leaders other than Gandhiji of course', recalled Jawaharlal Nehru.

> My father (who was in goal at the time) was much upset by it... If this was the inevitable consequence of a sporadic act of violence, then surely there was something lacking in the philosophy and technique of a non-violent struggle. For it seemed to us to be impossible to guarantee against the occurrence of some such untoward incident. Must we train the three hundred and odd millions of India in the theory and practice of non-violent action before we could go forward?[28]

In April 1921 Lord Chelmsford had been succeeded as viceroy by Lord Reading the cool and calculating ex-Chief Justice of England. He had hitherto given the Mahatma a long rope. Taking advantage of the disarray in the Congress leadership he moved to prosecute Gandhi for sedition on the basis of three articles he had written.

He was tried by an English judge on 18 March 1922 and sentenced to imprisonment for six years. 'As he disappeared behind the gates of his prison, the masses felt once more the loyalty and affection which the events of the previous month had clouded. The Government, by putting him on trial, made a mistake which it never repeated. After this experience it always imprisoned him untried.[29] He was released on 5 February 1924 for reasons of health after an operation for appendicitis.

Was the non-cooperation movement a success or a failure?

It obviously was a failure so far as the achievement of concrete goals was concerned. Swaraj was not achieved; the Punjab and Khilafat wrongs were not redressed. But the campaign had woken the spirit of the people. Though the subscribing members of Congress never exceeded six million, its actual sympathizers began to number many times that figure. It had proved itself to be a country-wide fighting machine. Government repression had succeeded only in making prison and punishment more honourable. There was a greater realization by the people of their rights, and more consciousness that they must rely on their own efforts to win them. Their faith in the bona fides of the foreign government was considerably reduced. The country on the whole became more Swaraj-conscious. In this way it brought India's ultimate independence closer.

But in its objective of bringing about Hindu-Muslim unity it proved to be an unmitigated disaster. As Gandhi himself wrote on 23 February 1922

> The vast majority of Hindus and Mussulmans have joined the struggle believing it to be religious. The masses have come in because they want to save the Khilafat and the cow. Deprive the Mussulman of the hope of helping the Khilafat, and he will shun the Congress; tell the Hindu he cannot save the cow if he joins the Congress he will, to a man, leave it.[30]

By inflaming the respective religious feelings of the Hindus and the Mussulmans, Gandhi's non-cooperation agitation in the end drew the two communities further apart instead of uniting them. The pan-Islamic fervour of the Khilafat movement immediately led to the Moplah rebellion as already described, and Hindu-Muslim riots from that point became an even more regular feature of the Indian scene than before.

> Placed side by side with the frantic efforts made by Mr Gandhi to bring about Hindu-Muslim unity, the record makes most painful and heart-rending reading. It would not be much exaggeration to say that it is a record of twenty years of civil war between the Hindus and the Muslims in India, interrupted by brief intervals of armed peace.[31]

Gandhi's future non-cooperation movements were mainly Hindu efforts.

Of the principal partners in the non-cooperation movement, the Muslims were fighting for a religious cause. They were therefore, far more zealous and made much greater sacrifices than the Hindus.

The fate of the Khalifa and his dominions had always stirred their emotions powerfully. As Muhammad Ali revealed

> My feelings during the disastrous war in the Balkans were so overpowering that I must confess I even contemplated suicide... The latest message of Reuter that had reached me was that the Bulgarians were only twenty-five miles from the walls of Constantinople—from Constantinople, a name that had for five centuries been sacred to every Muslim as the centre of his highest hopes.[32]

During the Khilafat Movement the refrain of the most popular song among the Muslims was

Boli Amma Muhammad Ali *ki*
Jan beta Khilafat *pe de do*
[Thus spake the mother of Muhammad Ali
My son sacrifice your life for Khilafat]

A tragic incident in the summer of 1920 took place in pursuance of the Islamic doctrine that 'if a Muslim finds himself helpless against iniquity and cannot resist it, he should migrate to a place where he is not faced with the same problem'. Some 18,000 Muslims, mostly from Sind and the North-West Frontier Province, sold their land and belongings and sought asylum in Afghanistan, which was the nearest *dar ul-Islam.* They had been encouraged to do so by Amir Amanullah but in the event he refused to admit them. Many of the pilgrims perished by the roadside; others returned broken and destitute.[33]

As Ambedkar has pointed out, 'The effect of its taking up the Khilafat cause upon the dimensions of the Congress was tremendous. The Congress was really made great and powerful not by the Hindus but by the Muslims'.[34]

To the usual taunt that neither Jinnah personally nor the Muslim League had made sacrifices in the national cause, Jinnah pointed out that Gandhi had ascended 'the *gaddi* [throne] of leadership on our [Muslim] skulls'.[35]

Gandhi himself confessed that it was the charisma of the Ali Brothers that had brought the Muslim masses into his fold. In *Young India* of 24 November 1921 when the Ali Brothers were in gaol, the Mahatma wrote, 'I have felt the greatest need of Maulana Shaukat Ali by my side. I can wield no influence over the Mussulmans except thorough a Mussulman.'

Whatever lofty notions the Mahatma might have harboured, to the ordinary Hindu and Muslim the teaming up of the two communities was a matter of convenience. The Hindus needed Muslim support to present a united front to the British; the Muslims, not having a strong organization of their own, needed Gandhi and the Hindu masses to give weight to their effort to preserve the temporal and spiritual status of the Sultan of Turkey. Khilafat was not an Indian issue, and the fact that the Muslims gave it more frenzied support than they had ever given to an

Indian cause clearly showed that they were Muslims first and Indians afterwards. Gandhi accepted this as quite natural. In a statement published on 2 October 1921, he said 'the brave [Ali] brothers are staunch lovers of their country, but they are Mussulmans first and everything else after, and it must be so with every religiously-minded man'.[36]

Their passionate involvement in the Khilafat agitation, therefore, did not inspire in the Indian Muslims the feelings of Indian nationalism which would have strengthened Indian unity; it nourished instead the feelings of Muslim nationalism which in time developed into the demand for Pakistan.

Muslim Politics in the Doldrums

Meanwhile in Turkey, events were following their own course. The helpless government of the Sultan, dominated by an international force of occupation at Constantinople, had signed the Treaty of Sevres on 20 August 1920. But the treaty was not recognized by the Turkish nationalists, who under Mustafa Kemal Pasha's leadership built up a military force which in 1922 mounted an offensive against the Greeks and took Smyrna. On 1 November, Kemal proclaimed the abolition of the Sultanate and Muhammad VI fled from Constantinople on a British ship. Abdul Mejid, cousin of Muhammed VI, was declared Caliph. Kemal's successes enabled him to obtain greatly improved terms through the Treaty of Lausanne in July 1923. On 29 October, Turkey formally became a republic with Kemal Ataturk as President, and on 3 March 1924 the institution of the Khilafat which had agitated the Indian Muslims so much, but whose incumbent had brought defeat and disaster to Turkey herself by getting involved in the World War, was abolished.

The sudden stoppage of the non-cooperation movement followed by the developments in Turkey stunned the Muslims. They had come out of the shadow of Gandhi but they felt bewildered. They had been so wholly occupied with the fate of the Caliph that there was now a void in their political life. During the non-cooperation movement it was to the Khilafat Conference that the Muslims had flocked. The Muslim League was reduced to the status of an adjunct of the Congress and did not meet as an independent body till 1924.

An effort to revive the Muslim League by convening a session at Lucknow on 31 March 1923 failed; the meeting had to be adjourned *sine die* on 1 April because of a procedural wrangle.

At the Fourteenth Session of the League at Ahmedabad (30 December 1921), Abbas Tyabji, chairman of the Reception Committee, had suggested that after the great help from the Hindus on the Khilafat question, and after finding that the League and the Congress had the same object in view, the League should cease to be a separate and distinct body.[37]

Jinnah and Ruttie

When Jinnah went to London in the summer of 1919, he took Ruttie with him. There, on the night intervening between the 14 and 15 August, Ruttie gave birth to their only daughter whom they named Dina. By a coincidence, Jinnah's political child—Pakistan—was also born 28 years later on the same date of the month and hour.

Ruttie was as patriotic and self-respecting as her husband. In 1918 she and Jinnah were invited by Lord Chelmsford to dinner at the Viceregal Lodge at Simla. When presented to the viceroy, she greeted him in the Indian fashion instead of following the British custom of courtesying to him. After dinner an ADC conducted her to Chelmsford who pompously told her, 'Mrs Jinnah, your husband has a great political future, you must not spoil it. In Rome you must do as the Romans do.' Ruttie flashed back, 'That is exactly what I did Your Excellency. In India I greeted you in the Indian way'. That was the first and the last time she met Chelmsford.

On one occasion in 1921 she happened to be seated next to Lord Reading, the then viceroy, at a lunch in New Delhi. Reading moaned that he could not go to Germany though he very much wanted to do so. Ruttie asked him why he could not go to Germany. Reading replied, 'The Germans do not like us, the British, so I can't go.' Ruttie quietly asked, 'How then did you come to India?' Reading quickly changed the subject.

We learn from Kanji Dwarkadas that Ruttie fell ill in May 1922 but he does not tell us the nature and duration of the illness.[38] We learn further from the same source that she went to England in September of that year but here again the details of the trip are lacking. In her letter to Dwarkadas dated 25 September 1922 written during her outward voyage, however, there is an interesting request: 'Go and see Jinnah and tell me how he is—he has a habit of habitually over-working himself, and now that I am not there to bother and tease him he will be worse than ever'.[39] These certainly are the words of a caring and loving wife but is there not also a tinge of sadness that due to Jinnah's professional pre-occupation she was unable to enjoy as much of her beloved husband's company as she would have liked?

Notes

1. Pirzada, *Collected Works*, I, op.cit., p. 239. Montagu had joined Lloyd George's Government in July 1917, 'only on the condition that he should go to the India Office'. Edwin S. Montagu, *An Indian Diary*, V.
2. Montagu, ibid., p. 59.
3. Kanji Dwarkadas, *India's Fight for Freedom*, op.cit., p. 54.
4. Edwin S. Montagu, *An Indian Diary*, op.cit., pp. 57-8.
5. A. B. Rajput, *Muslim League Yesterday and Today*, p. 29.
6. M. Rafique Afzal, *Selected Speeches and Statements of the Quaid-i-Azam*, op.cit., p. 61.
7. Pirzada, *Collected Works*, I, op.cit., p. 286-90.
8. M. Rafique Afzal, *Selected Speeches and Statements of the Quaid-i-Azam*, op. cit., p. 81.
9. B. P. Sitaramayya, *History of the Indian National Congress*, I, op.cit., p. 161.
10. Kanji Dwarkadas, *India's Fight for Freedom*, op.cit., pp. 108-9.
11. M. K. Gandhi, *An Autobiography*, op.cit., pp. 423-4.
12. M. Rafique Afzal, *Selected Speeches and Statements of the Quaid-i-Azam*, op.cit., p. 85.
13. Ibid., pp. 112-3.
14. Pirzada, *Collected Works*, I, op.cit., p. 360-2.
15. Ibid., p. 380.
16. C.H. Philips, *Selected Documents on the History of India and Pakistan*, IV, p. 220. Lloyd George was notoriously unsympathetic to the Turks. While decorating General Allenby with an order for the conquest of Palestine, he had referred to the campaign as a 'crusade' though two-thirds of his troops had been Muslims. In February 1922 he forced Secretary of State Montagu to resign from his Cabinet because Montagu, without obtaining the Cabinet's authority, had acceded to Viceroy Reading's request to publish a telegram which Reading had sent to London pleading the Khalifa's cause. After dismissal, Montagu seemed 'to lose the greater part of his interest

in life; he was never the same man again'. (This quotation is from the preface of Edwin S. Montagu, *An Indian Diary,* op.cit.
17. Many years after retirement, Governor O'Dwyer was shot dead in March 1940 by a Sikh named Udham Singh at a public meeting in Caxton Hall, London.
18. Pirzada, *Collected Works,* I, op.cit., p. 388-90.
19. Jawaharlal Nehru, *An Autobiography,* op.cit., p. 65.
20. A. M. Zaidi, *The Encyclopaedia of the Indian National Congress,* VII, op.cit., pp. 582-3.
21. For the text of address *see,* Pirzada, *Collected Works,* I, op.cit., p. 401.
22. Subhas Chandra Bose, *The Indian Struggle,* op. cit., p. 70.
23. Ibid., p. 69.
24. For the text of Jinnah's speech *see,* Pirzada, *Collected Works,* I, op.cit., pp. 402-6.
25. Report of the Thirty-fifth Session of the Indian National Congress, p. 60.
26. Choudhry Khaliquzzaman, *Pathway to Pakistan,* p. 54.
27. Kanji Dwarkadas, *India's Fight For Freedom,* op.cit., p. 187.
28. Jawaharlal Nehru, *An Autobiography,* op.cit., p. 82.
29. H. S. L. Polak, H. N. Brailsford, Lord Pethic-Lawrence, *Mahatma Gandhi,* op.cit., p. 158.
30. M. H. Saiyid, *Mohammad Ali Jinnah,* 1945, op. cit., p. 290.
31. B. R. Ambedkar, *Pakistan or the Partition of India,* op. cit., p. 175.
32. R. A. J. Nadvi, *Selections from Muhammad Ali's Comrade,* p. 40.
33. Jinnah, Safi, Iqbal and Fazl-i-Husain were opposed to *hijrat.*
34. A. B. Rajput, *Muslim League Today and Yesterday,* op.cit., p. 53.
35. Jamil-UD-Din Ahmad, *Speeches and Writings of Mr Jinnah,* II, op. cit., p. 242.
36. *Independent,* dated Allahabad, 2 October 1921.
37. Pirzada, *Foundations of Pakistan,* I, op.cit., p. 556.
38. Kanji Dwarkadas, *Ruttie Jinnah,* op. cit., p. 24.
39. Ibid., p. 26.

CHAPTER 8

Jinnah Resumes His Efforts to Bring About Hindu-Muslim Unity, 1924-1929

The Nature of Jinnah's Differences with Congress

The Quaid's differences with the Mahatma and the Mahatma-dominated Congress, which were aired at the Nagpur Congress in December 1920, were not over ideals but over the programme of non-cooperation as the means of achieving them.

As we have already stated, speaking at the sixth anniversary of the death of Gokhale on 19 February 1921, Jinnah said that he had great respect for 'Mahatma' Gandhi but the Mahatma's programme was taking them to a wrong channel.

In a letter to the *Times* of London dated 20 June 1921, he wrote that the people of India

> ...have been suffering from a calendar of grievances, but the situation was precipitated by the Punjab tragedy and the Treaty of Sevres and the people think that their deliverance lies in the immediate attainment of Swaraj. The policies of the British Government and the viceroy can either make India a real partner in the British Commonwealth, or bar the door and make her a rebel.[1]

After a meeting with Jinnah on 1 November 1921, Lord Reading, the viceroy, wrote in his report to the secretary of state that Jinnah 'holds strong views about acceleration of Swaraj, redress of Punjab wrongs and is in favour of Khilafat agitation; but he has not joined Gandhi whose policy he regards as destructive and not constructive'.[2]

Towards the end of 1921, the Quaid issued a statement to the Press in the course of which he asked how could even sober people rally round the government when the government had paid no heed to what the sober had been urging upon it.[3]

In January and February 1922 an All-India Conference which was convened at Bombay and of which Jinnah was one of the three secretaries, proposed to the government that a Round Table Conference be convened to settle the differences between the Congress and the government, but the effort failed because Gandhi could not provide preconditions to the satisfaction of the viceroy.

It is amply clear from what has been stated above that Jinnah's heart was still with the patriotic goals of the Congress though his head had rejected Gandhi's disorderly ways of reaching them. Gandhi's campaign of non-cooperation had failed to win the promised Swaraj or indeed any political concessions. Jinnah's logical mind took him back to the pre-Gandhian days when Hindus and Muslims had united on a political platform and forged the Lucknow Pact. Their concerted demands for steps toward self-government at that time had borne fruit in the form of the Act of 1919.

He therefore resumed his mission for Hindu-Muslim unity based on a constitutional programme. And but for the interregnum of his self-imposed exile in London in the early 1930s, he held on to this mission resolutely till the actual experience of Congress rule (1937-1939) finally forced him to the conclusion that the Congress high command under Gandhi stood for an independent India in which the Hindu majority would lord it over all the minorities including the Muslims.

That he had reverted to his old role became evident when he presided over the Muslim League session at Lahore in May 1924.

The All-India Muslim League's Fifteenth Session, Lahore, 24-25 May 1924

The League Session which had been suspended *sine die* at Lucknow on 1 April 1923 re-convened at Lahore under Jinnah's presidency. It was attended by a large number of Congressmen and Khilafatists including Muhammad Ali.

In his presidential address Jinnah said, 'in view of a very powerful volume of public opinion that rallied round Mr Gandhi's policy and programmes', the Muslim League had 'to go into the background'. It was admitted that the boycott movement had been a failure and that mass civil disobedience could not be undertaken successfully in the near future. He however, conceded that the result of the struggle for the last three years had been that there was 'an open movement for the achievement of Swaraj'.

But while the demand for Swaraj was a just one and the sentiment required every encouragement

> We must not forget that one essential requisite condition to achieve Swaraj is political unity between Hindus and the Mahomedans, for the advent of foreign rule and its continuance in India is primarily due to the fact that the people of India, particularly the Hindus and Mahomedans, are not united and do not sufficiently trust each other. The domination by the bureaucracy will continue so long as the Hindus and Mahomedans do not come to a settlement. I am almost inclined to say that India will get Dominion Responsible Government the day the Hindus and Mahomedans are united. Swaraj is almost an interchangeable term with Hindu-Muslim unity.

He had no doubt that 'if the Hindus and Mahomedans make a wholehearted and earnest effort, we shall be able to find a solution once more as we did at Lucknow in 1916'.[4]

Of the resolutions passed at the Lahore session one reaffirmed that the speedy attainment of Swaraj was one of the 'declared objects' of the League; another demanded that the existing provinces of India should be united under a common government on a federal basis so that each province shall have full and complete provincial autonomy; and yet another declared that the system of separate electorates shall continue provided that it shall be open to any community at any time to abandon its separate electorates in favour of joint electorates.

In a newspaper interview in June, Jinnah refuted Muhammad Ali's assertion that the attendance at the Lahore session of the League had been unrepresentative, and said it had been more representative than at any other session except the 1916 meeting at Lucknow. 'As an Indian Nationalist', Jinnah confessed his 'dislike' for communal representation but 'emphasized the Muslim feeling in its favour'.[5]

The Seventeenth Session of the Muslim League at Aligarh (30-31 December 1925) and the Eighteenth Session at Delhi (29-31 December 1926) both passed resolutions calling for the amendment of the Constitution. An interesting feature of both the sessions was the growing realization that the formula adopted for giving weightage to the minorities had done more harm than good to the Muslims. Sheikh Abdul Qadir in his presidential address at Delhi said

> There is now a growing volume of opinion in favour of the view that the small increase in representation which we got in provinces like Bombay, Madras and the UP leave us very much in the minority still and does not prove of much political assistance, while it tends to reduce our majorities in Bengal and the Punjab to the level of minorities.[6]

Both sessions, in proposing the lines on which the Constitution must be amended, therefore demanded in identical terms that 'All legislatures of the country and other elected bodies shall be constituted on the definite principle of adequate and effective representation of minorities in every province without reducing the majority in any province to a minority or even to an equality.[7]

At the Delhi session Jinnah made his oft-repeated appeal 'to the Muslim and Hindu leaders to let the past be forgotten and the hatchet buried, and to meet in a spirit of friendship and fellowship to formulate a common demand'.[8]

Jinnah's Triumphant Return to the Central Legislative Assembly

The fact that despite his differences with Gandhi and the Khilafatists the Quaid had fully retained the respect of the Muslims of Bombay was manifested when on 14 November 1923 he was elected unopposed as an independent candidate to the Bombay Muslim seat in the Legislative Assembly from which he had resigned as a mark of protest against the passage of the Rowlatt Act. The two candidates who ventured into the arena withdrew from the contest.

The manifesto he had issued on 19 September as a candidate was typically straightforward. As a constitutionalist he declared that whatever the Congress and the Khilafatists might decide on the subject of Council entry, he, for one, was 'more than ever convinced that the proper course for us is to send our representatives to the Assembly'.

He said further, 'Of one thing I can assure you, that the popular cause and the welfare of India will be my keynote and the guiding principle in the future as, I hope, has been in the past. I have no desire to seek any post or position or title from the government. My sole object is to serve the cause of the country as best as I can.'[9]

In November 1926 Jinnah was re-elected to the Central Legislative Assembly from the Muslim Constituency in Bombay defeating his two rival candidates by a 'thumping majority'. He had been so confident of victory that he did not bother to canvass for votes personally. Nor was his popularity confined to the Muslims

> Quite unasked, Jinnah's Hindu friends sent him at least 100 cars to enable him to get his Muslim voters to the polling booths. They wrote to him that owing to the communal electorates, they could not cast their votes for him but they would at least do some service to the Motherland by helping him to win the election by giving him their cars.

In fact he retained 'a great hold on the Hindu community of Bombay...right up to the time of partition'.[10]

Jinnah continued to be an effective parliamentarian and figured prominently in the Assembly debates.

The Congress had boycotted the first elections under the Act of 1919 which were held in 1920. Jinnah also had not stood for election at that time. Taking advantage of the temporary eclipse of Gandhi's domination over the Congress, C. R. Das and Motilal Nehru, who favoured council entry, formed the Swarajya Party in defiance of his wishes. The Swarajya Party was 'an integral part of the Congress' but was pledged to take the political fight into the legislatures. C.R. Das had argued that 'an advancing army does not co-operate with the enemy when it marches into the enemy's territory'.

Jinnah had formed a group of twenty-four in the Central Assembly under the title Independents. The Swarajists captured forty-five seats in the autumn 1923 elections. With twenty-five official and fourteen nominated members, the government controlled a block of thirty-nine. Jinnah and Das both being 'practical politicians' decided that the Independents and the Swarajists should join hands and together form the Nationalist

Party. This working of Muslim and Hindu legislators shoulder to shoulder in the national cause must have been a matter of special satisfaction to Jinnah whose favourite dream was unity of the two communities.

Some Nationalist successes in the Assembly were the passing of an amendment which demanded the revision of the Government of India Act with a view to establishing full responsible government in India and for that purpose the convening of a Round Table Conference; the rejection of the demand under Customs in the budget; and the refusal of demands under Income Tax, Salt and Opium. The Assembly also carried an amendment which, among other things, rejected the recommendations of the Lee Commission and demanded the stoppage of recruitment in England for the civil services in India.

On 16 June 1925, Das suddenly passed away. As pointed out by Subhas Bose, he had been 'a powerful cementing factor within the Swaraj Party...[and] in his absence dissensions began to appear within the Party'.[11] Before long the union between the Independents and the Swarajists faded away.

In February 1924, Jinnah successfully introduced a resolution in the National Assembly which resulted in a considerable economic advantage to India. Hitherto tenders for the purchase of stores worth no less than twenty or twenty-one crores of rupees for the use of the government departments in India were invited in London in sterling. Jinnah pointed out that this gave 'a tremendous advantage to the British manufacturers who are on the spot, who get the information first; and invariably it is really for all practical purposes confined to the tenders coming from the British firms in England'. Under the new resolution tenders would be invited in India in rupees which would benefit Indian businessmen and manufacturers.

Because of Jinnah's well-known interest in the increase of Indians in the commissioned ranks of the Indian Army, he was, in February 1925, appointed a member of the committee which was to report on the questions of the Indianization of the army and the establishment of a military training college in India on the lines of Sandhurst.

To assist the committee during their visit to Sandhurst, a deputation had to be organized and the task of doing this was entrusted to Captain Gracey. This resulted in a heated scene at

Sandhurst and in a sequel after the creation of Pakistan illustrative of the Quaid-i-Azam's character.

The whole story is best told in Gracey's own words

> Jinnah's behaviour with the officers who gave evidence before the deputation was so arrogant: it was as if he were dealing with hostile witnesses before a judge. I had to protest and point out that the officers were giving evidence voluntarily, with the object of helping him, and that they had a right to be treated with courtesy and consideration. Of course, he calmed down immediately. That was something I always liked about him in later years: once he was challenged, he became reasonable, and he would never bear malice afterwards. The outcome of the deputation was the establishment of the military college at Dehra Dun, and, for me, a touching insight into Jinnah's character. He might have remembered the episode at Sandhurst with bitterness, for I had stood up to him in no mean fashion. But no! When my name came up before him as Commander-in-Chief of the Army in Pakistan, he accepted me, and welcomed me, with good grace. He remembered me quite well, but never showed resentment.[12]

The Delhi Muslim Proposals, 20 March 1927

Jinnah did not receive any positive response from the Hindu leadership to his overtures for a constitutional pact between the Muslims and the Hindus similar to the Lucknow Pact. In the meantime Hindu-Muslim relations at the popular level were marked by continuing bloody riots. 'From 1922 onwards the number of serious Hindu-Muslim riots rose steeply. There were 11 in 1923, 18 in 1924, 16 in 1925, 35 in 1926, and 31 up to November 1927'.[13]

To achieve a breakthrough, Jinnah invited Muslim leaders from different parts of the country to meet at Delhi under his presidentship on 20 March 1927. After due deliberation the conferees unanimously offered the following terms for a Hindu-Muslim concord

> Muslims should accept a settlement on the basis of the following proposal, so far as representation in the various legislatures in any future scheme of Constitution is concerned:

(1) Sind should be separated from Bombay and constituted into a separate province.
(2) Reforms should be introduced in the NWF Province and in Baluchistan on the same footing as any other province. In that case, Muslims are prepared to accept a joint electorate in all provinces so constituted, and are further willing to make to Hindu minorities in Sind, Baluchistan and the NW Frontier, the same concessions that Hindu majorities in other provinces are prepared to make to Muslim minorities.

In the Punjab and Bengal the proportion of representation should be in accordance with the population. In the Central Legislature, Muslim representation shall not be less than a third, and that also, by a mixed electorate.[14]

The relinquishment of the well-established right to separate electorates was an unprecedented concession and it was a major achievement of Jinnah to have persuaded his colleagues to offer it. But the olive branch was rejected. Chagla ruefully commented

> The Hindu communal parties accepted the proposal with regard to joint electorates, but rejected the other two, incredible though it might seem. It was a folly and a blunder of the first magnitude. This was the first time that Muslims had agreed to have joint electorates. It was the chance of a lifetime, a rare unexpected opportunity for a new start on a real national political life. Today, it seems inconceivable that the separation of Sind and reforms for Baluchistan and the North-West Frontier Province should have come in the way of the acceptance of joint electorates... Never after that did the Muslims agree to joint electorates. As time passed, the communal demands of the Muslims increased day by day, resulting ultimately in a demand for partition.[15]

Appointment of the Simon Commission

Since the calling off of the non-cooperation movement after the Chauri Chaura incident, Indian politics had lacked an all-India theme, but this was unexpectedly provided by the British Government in November 1927. On the eighth day of that month Stanley Baldwin, the prime minister, announced in the House of Commons the appointment of a commission 'to inquire into the working of the Indian Constitution and to consider the desirability of establishing, extending, modifying or restricting the degree of responsible government'. Such a commission had been promised in the Reforms Act of 1919 at the end of the ten years after the passing of that Act, but 'the Government have decided, for various reasons, which I need not now specify, that it is desirable to anticipate the date (December 1929) contemplated by the Act and to appoint this most important Royal Commission forthwith'.

The reason for advancing the date of the appointment of the commission, which Baldwin had chosen not to elaborate, was simply that the trend of the by-election results in the United Kingdom indicated that Baldwin's Conservative government was likely to be defeated by the Labour party in the elections which were due to take place in 1929. That party was considered in Conservative circles to be unduly sympathetic to Indian political aspirations. The Conservative Government, therefore, decided to appoint a commission of its own choice while they had the chance to do so; in hastening the constitutional process, Baldwin was in fact trying to favour Britain, not India.

The chairman of the commission was to be Sir John Simon, a distinguished lawyer, and it had six other members including Clement Attlee, who was to preside over India's independence as prime minister in 1947. The total omission of Indians from the commission was a psychological error of the first order and immediately raised a storm of protest in India. The protesters rejected government assurances that the Indian point of view would be given a full hearing and due consideration. They demanded complete equality with the British members of the commission; they said that they were not prepared to be treated merely as petitioners and witnesses.

Jinnah stood shoulder to shoulder with the Congress and was in the forefront of the protesters. However, the Muslim League as an organization did not present a united front. It was split into two groups: the 'Jinnah Group' and the 'Shafi Group'. The latter decided to cooperate with the Simon Commission as we will describe more fully presently. Nevertheless the boycott of the commission was an overwhelming success and they were greeted everywhere with shouts of 'Simon go back'.

Jinnah in his capacity as president of the All-India Muslim League and leader of the Independent Party in the Assembly, was a signatory to a manifesto issued over the signatures of several Hindu and Muslim leaders on 10 November 1927. The manifesto declared that, 'Unless a commission on which British and Indian statesmen are invited to sit on equal terms is set up, we cannot conscientiously take any part or share in the work of the commission'.[16]

On 28 November Jinnah was elected president of the Bombay Presidency Muslim League and in a statement to the Press said that the 'underlying idea' of the decision to exclude Indians from the commission was 'the arrogant assertion of the principle that Indians cannot be allowed to share in the responsibility or in the decisions that are taken concerning the future Constitution of India'.[17]

He also participated in a large meeting of the citizens of Bombay on 3 December protesting that Indians had been 'denied their legitimate right to participate on equal terms, in framing the future Constitution of the country'.[18]

On 11 December 1927, the Quaid issued a statement warning fellow Muslims that

> ...attempts will be made to beguile and seduce the Mussulmans from the only honourable course open to them by suggestions that Mussulmans stand to benefit if they present their case before the commission in the absence of their Hindu brothers. But in this case I can assure my community that they will not get even the proverbial 30 pieces of silver which Judas got for betraying Christ... They will only go down to history as disloyal to their country at a critical juncture of its political development justly accused by other communities of having played false not only to them but also to their own motherland.[19]

The Muslim League Splits into Two

Despite Jinnah's exhortation to the Muslims to present a united front, the Muslim League split into two as already mentioned. The Jinnah Group met at Calcutta from 30 December 1927 to 1 January 1928 and the Shafi Group convened at Lahore from 31 December 1927 to 1 January 1928. Both meetings claimed to be the Nineteenth Session of the All-India Muslim League. The basic reason for the split was that the Jinnah Group stood for boycotting the Simon Commission and the Shafi Group for cooperating with it.

The Jinnah Group session was attended by some prominent non-Muslims among them Mrs Annie Besant, Mrs Sarojini Naidu, and Pandit Madan Mohan Malaviya. Mrs Besant and Pandit Malaviya figured among those who addressed the meeting.

One of the resolutions enjoined that 'the Mussulmans throughout the country should have nothing to do with the commission at any stage or in any form'.

Another resolution confirmed the Delhi Muslim Proposals.

Yet another resolution 'severely' condemned Sir Muhammad Shafi and his colleagues for holding a session at Lahore 'in contravention of the Constitution of the League'.

Addressing the meeting at the end of the session Jinnah declared

> A constitutional war has been declared on Great Britain. Negotiations for a settlement are not to come from our side. Let the government sue for peace. We are denied equal partnership. We will resist the new doctrine to the best of our power. Jallianwalla Bagh was a physical butchery, the Simon Commission is a butchery of our souls. By appointing an exclusively white commission, Lord Birkenhead has declared our unfitness for self-government. I welcome Pandit Malaviya, and I welcome the hand of fellowship extended to us by Hindu leaders from the platform of the Congress and the Hindu Mahasabha. For, to me, this offer is more valuable than any concession which the British Government can make. Let us then grasp the hand of fellowship. This is indeed a bright day; and for achieving this unity, thanks are due to Lord Birkenhead.[20]

At the session of the Shafi Group, Nawab Zulfiqar Ali Khan, chairman of the Reception Committee, said that 'The Muslims as a minority community must vindicate their rights; the only chance under the circumstances was to approach the Simon Commission with manly composure and seek justice from it'. A resolution invited the leaders of all the non-Muslim communities in India to come to a settlement with the Muslim community and prepare a Draft Constitution for India, adequately safeguarding the legitimate rights and interests of all communities, for presenting the same before the Statutory Commission.

In the course of his presidential address Shafi said joint electorates 'would be certain to furnish a periodical cause of friction' between the Muslims and the Hindus and would 'be in the highest degree injurious to the cause of Indian nationalism'. Reflecting this view a resolution belittled the Delhi Muslim Proposals of 20 March 1927 as having been 'formulated by some Muslims in their individual capacity' and declared that the same were not acceptable to the Muslims of India.[21]

On 16 February 1928 Jinnah supported a resolution proposed by Lala Lajput Rai in the Legislative Assembly expressing the Assembly's entire lack of confidence in the Simon Commission. Jinnah supported the resolution and reiterated that 'the principle for which we are fighting is that we want for the Indian representatives equal status and equal power.'[22]

One can only imagine Jinnah's distress. Not to speak of Hindu-Muslim unity, even the Muslims were divided amongst themselves. Besides the two Groups of the League there were the Jamiat-i-Ulema-i-Hind, the All-India Khilafat Conference and sundry provincial groups. He sought respite from the endless stress by a trip to England and sailed on 5 May 1928 by SS *Rajputana*.

One of his fellow-passengers on the outward voyage, Dewan Chamanlal, wrote an article recording his impressions of Jinnah. 'Today he is, unfortunately, frankly disgusted', he noted. 'The first problem to solve and settle is the problem of Hindu-Muslim unity', Jinnah told him. He also regretted that 'Gandhi is not a politician', and added, 'I wish he had been'.

Giving his own impressions, Chamanlal wrote

> Mr Jinnah is frankly in a despondent mood. He is one of the few men who have no personal motives to nurse or personal aims to advance. His integrity is beyond question. And yet he has been the loneliest of men. He has never belonged to a party unless he himself was the party. Not that he has ever refused to work shoulder to shoulder with others (as for instance, in the case of the Nationalist Party of 1924), but he has never allowed any man to compromise his sense of integrity.[23]

Origin of the Nehru Committee

The Nehru Report was the Congress' alternative to the forthcoming Simon Report. Lord Birkenhead, the Conservative Secretary of State (1924-1928) had never made a secret of his poor opinion of Indian politicians. He believed that 'India would not be capable of supporting Dominion Status for centuries'. In his opinion 'the real obstacle to democratic institutions in India' was 'the age-long hatred between Hindus and Mohammedans. "All the conferences in the world cannot bridge the unbridgeable".'[24] On 7 July 1925, he declared in the House of Lords

> Let them produce a Constitution which carried behind it a fair amount of general agreement among the great peoples of India. Such a contribution to our problems would nowhere be resented. It would, on the contrary, be most carefully examined by the Government of India, by myself, and I am sure, by the commission, whenever that body may be assembled.[25]

Upon the appointment of the commission he repeated the challenge in the House of Lords on 24 November 1927: 'I have twice in the three years during which I have been Secretary of State invited our critics in India to put forward their own suggestions for a Constitution, to indicate to us the form which in their judgement any reform of the Constitution should take. That offer is still open'.[26]

This taunt stung Congress into action.[27] The All-India Congress Committee had previously passed a resolution at Bombay in May 1927 calling upon the Working Committee 'to frame a Swaraj Constitution in consultation with the elected members of the Central and Provincial Legislatures and other leaders of political parties'.[28] After the appointment of the Simon Commission, the Congress at its Madras session in the last week of December 1927 not only resolved to 'boycott the commission at every stage and in every form' but transformed the project relating to the framing of the Swaraj Constitution. The Constitution no longer was to be framed by the Working Committee itself but the Working Committee was given the

> ...power to coopt, to confer with similar Committees to be appointed by other organizations—political, labour, commercial and communal—in the country and to draft a Swaraj Constitution for India on the basis of a Declaration of Rights, and to place the same for consideration and approval before a Special Convention to be convened in Delhi not later than March next, consisting of the All-India Congress Committee and the leaders and representatives of the other

organizations mentioned above and the elected members of the Central and Provincial Legislatures.[29]

In short, it was no longer to be a Constitution framed only by the Congress as originally planned, but was to be a national effort representing the demands of a united India. The Congress also declared 'the goal of the Indian people to be complete national independence'.

The Working Committee issued invitations to twenty-nine organizations including the All-India Muslim League, the Hindu Mahasabha and the Central Sikh League.[30] The resulting All Parties Conference had Dr M.A. Ansari as its chairman. It held its first meeting at Delhi in February 1928. When the conference met for the second time on 8 March, the discussion revealed differences between the Muslim League on the one hand and the Hindu Mahasabha and the Sikhs on the other.[31] At the third meeting of the conference at Bombay on 19 May 1928 it was found that

> ...the situation was not a promising one. The communal organizations had drifted further apart and each of them had hardened in its attitude and was not prepared to change or modify it... There being no likelihood of an agreed and satisfactory solution at that stage, it was thought that a small committee viewing the communal problem as a whole...might succeed in finding a way out.[32]

A committee with Motilal Nehru as chairman was accordingly appointed by the conference 'to consider and determine the principles of the Constitution for India'.[33] Jawaharlal Nehru was not a member of the Committee but as secretary of the Congress 'had much to do with it'.[34] The Report of the Committee came to be popularly called the 'Nehru Report' after the name of the chairman of the Committee.

At the fourth meeting of the conference at Lucknow in August 1928, Motilal Nehru presented the Report of his Committee. The conference approved the Report except that some members of the conference, among them Jawaharlal Nehru and Subhas Bose (who was a member of the Nehru Committee), took exception to the fact that the Report had settled for Dominion Status. They pointed out that at the Madras session the Congress had declared complete national independence as its goal.

On behalf of those who stood for independence, Jawaharlal Nehru read a statement confirming that in their opinion 'the Constitution of India should only be based on full independence'. They had decided, however, 'not to obstruct or hamper the work of this conference' but proposed 'to carry on such activity as we consider proper and necessary in favour of complete independence'.[35]

The Report came up for final consideration before the All-Parties Convention which opened at Calcutta on 22 December 1928.

The Nehru Report

Aware of the difference within their own ranks whether the objective should be Dominion Status or Complete Independence, the Report finally opted for Dominion Status on the ground that it was 'the greatest common factor among the well recognized political parties in India' but added that 'it is not viewed as a remote stage of our evolution but as the next immediate step'.[36] It also stated that those who believe in the goal of Complete Independence 'retain the fullest right to work for it'.[37]

It was recognized that 'the communal problem in India is primarily the Hindu-Muslim problem'.[38] 'If the fullest religious liberty is given, and cultural autonomy provided for, the communal problem is in effect solved'.[39] The Committee embodied this solution by guaranteeing Fundamental Rights.[40]

The Centre was to be a Parliament of two houses, a Senate and a House of Representatives. The Senate would consist of 200 members, with a specific number of seats allotted to each province on the basis of population. The House of Representatives would consist of 500 members. The provinces would be unicameral. Both the House of Representatives and the provincial Legislative Councils would be elected by universal suffrage.[41]

The principle of provincial autonomy was negated by the provision that 'for peace, order and good government' all the powers not specifically assigned to the provinces were vested in the central government.[42]

There was to be no weightage either; 'a minority must remain a minority whether any seats are reserved for it or not'. The Report rejected the Muslim claim to one-third of the total number of seats in the central legislature: 'The Muslims are a little less than one fourth of the total population of British India and they cannot be allowed reservation over and above that proportion in the central legislature'.[43]

It was noted in the Report that 'the Muslims are insistent on the reservation of seats for the Muslim majorities in the Punjab and Bengal'[44] on the ground 'that Mussulmans will not obtain adequate representation and the slight majority they have will be more than counter balanced by their educational and economic backwardness in these provinces'.[45] But this demand too was rejected.

Yet another contentious decision was the abolition of separate electorates, a right cherished by the vast majority of the Muslims as a vital constitutional safeguard. The reason given for this was that, 'Everybody knows that separate electorates are bad for the growth of national spirit'.[46]

The Report referred to the fact that 'The Muslims being a minority in India as a whole fear that the majority may harass them' but it rejected this 'novel suggestion' because 'we cannot have one community domineering over another'.[47] Nevertheless, it declared itself in favour of the NWF Province and Baluchistan having the same constitutional status as other provinces because 'the right of any part of India to participate in responsible government' could not be denied.[48] The Report also favoured the separation of Sind from Bombay despite the opposition to it of the Hindus in Sind. Here the reason given was that the right of self-determination demanded that the wishes of the Muslims who were in a majority should be acceded to.[49]

The Report was presented for final approval to an All-Parties National Convention which opened on 22 December 1928 at Calcutta.

Jinnah and the Nehru Report

The Quaid who had gone to England on 5 May 1928 returned to India on 26 October 1928. In a press statement on the same day he stated that his position as president of the All-India Muslim League did not permit him to anticipate the decisions of the League on the Nehru Report. 'There is only one hope for India,' he said, 'and that is unity between Hindus and Muslims. Hindus should show a more liberal and generous mind and Muslims more trust.'[50]

When the Muslim League convened at Calcutta for its Twentieth Session on 26 to 30 December 1928, a resolution was passed on 27 December on M.C. Chagla's motion that a delegation including Jinnah be appointed to represent the League at the Convention called by the Indian National Congress to consider the Nehru Report.[51]

On 28 December Jinnah appeared before the Convention which was in progress in the same city. He began with his favourite plea

> ...it is absolutely essential to our progress that a Hindu-Muslim settlement should be reached... Majorities are apt to be oppressive and tyrannical and minorities always dread and fear that their interests and rights, unless clearly and definitely safeguarded by statutory provisions, would suffer and be prejudiced, but this apprehension is enhanced all the more when we have to deal with a communal majority.

He proposed four amendments to the Nehru Report. First, that 'there should be no less than one-third Muslim representation in the Central Legislature'. Secondly, 'In the event of the adult suffrage not being established, Punjab and Bengal also should have seats reserved on population basis for the Mussulmans'. Thirdly, that 'The form of the Constitution should be federal with residuary powers vesting in the provinces... This question is by far the most important from the constitutional point of view'. Fourthly, 'With regard to the question of separation of Sind and the North-West Frontier Province, we cannot wait until the Nehru Constitution is established... The Mussulmans feel that it is shelving the issue and postponing their insistent demand till doomsday and they cannot agree to it'.

Sir Tej Bahadur Sapru reminded the audience that they were

> ...faced with an occasion when the first and last question should be to bring about unity... Gentlemen, remember it is not only our countrymen but the whole world is watching you... If he [Jinnah] is a spoilt child, a naughty child, I am prepared to say, give him what be wants and be finished with it... We must, as practical statesmen, try to solve the problem and not be misled by arithmetical figures.

The Hindu Mahasabha leader, M. R. Jayaker opposed Sapru and said that Jinnah came before the Convention 'neither as a naughty boy nor as a spoilt child but as a fearless and lucid advocate of the small minority of Muslims whose claims he has put forward in the course of his speech'. He went on to state 'well-known Muslims like the esteemed patriots Maulana Abul Kalam Azad, Dr Ansari, Sir Ali Imam, Raja Sahib of Mahmudabad and Dr Kitchlew had given their full assent to compromise embodied in the Nehru Committee Report'.[52]

In replying to the debate, Jinnah asked Jayakar

> whether he wants what he calls the greater common measure of agreement to be still greater or not... What we want is that Hindus and Muslims should march together until our object is attained. Therefore, it is essential that you must get not only the Muslim League but the Mussulmans of India and here I am not speaking as a Mussulman but as an Indian... Minorities cannot give anything to the majority... It is up to the majority, and majority alone can give.

When put to the vote, all Jinnah's amendments were lost.[53]

Jinnah was heartbroken. He left Calcutta by train on the following morning. He was seen off by Jamshed Nusserwanjee. He took Nusserwanjee's hand and with tears in his eyes said, 'Jamshed, this is the parting of the ways.'[54]

The Burial of the Nehru Report

Though some Muslims accepted the Nehru Report, by far the larger majority rejected it. This was demonstrated when a large number of highly influential Muslims attended the Muslim All-Parties Conference at Delhi on 31 December 1928 under the presidentship of the Aga Khan.

The conveners of the conference had invited about 600 representatives 'belonging to all schools of thought'. These included all non-official Muslim members of the Provincial Councils and the Central Legislature, and twenty representatives each from the following organizations: the All-India Muslim League, Calcutta (i.e., the Jinnah Group), the All-India Muslim League, Lahore (i.e., the Shafi Group), the All-India Khilafat Conference, and

JINNAH RESUMES EFFORTS FOR UNITY

the All-India Jamiat-ul-Ulema Conference. Twenty Muslim representatives from each of the provinces of India were also invited.

Jinnah declined the invitation to attend on the ground that there was 'at present' no need for such a conference and it was round the All-India Muslim League that everybody should rally.[55]

The attendance at the Conference including visitors was about 3,000. It included both the Ali Brothers, Sir Muhammad Shafi, Sir Muhammad Iqbal and Hakim Ajmal Khan. Fazal Rahmatullah, general secretary of the Conference, informed the Conference that all the invitees except the 'Jinnah League' had responded to the invitation. He pointed out that thirty-eight out of a total of forty-nine members of the Central Legislatures had joined in convening the Conference.

Interestingly, during the course of his presidential address the Aga Khan observed

> The merits and demerits of separate or so-called communal electorates have been discussed so often that it is unnecessary to re-examine them here in detail. In regard to the implications of the term 'communal' I may remark in passing that the Muslims of India are not a community but in a special sense a nation composed of many communities and population outnumbering in the aggregate the total even of the pre-war German Empire.

Muhammad Ali said

> The Mussulmans were blamed for communalism. There was no country in the world where the treatment meted out to the Untouchable was tolerated and with this treatment of theirs to their own kith and kin, how was it possible for Muslims to trust them? The Nehru Report intended that although the universe may belong to God and the country to the British, it was the Mahasabha who should rule.[56]

On the second day the Conference (1 January 1929) unanimously adopted a manifesto of Muslim claims of which the principal points were

> In view of India's vast extent and its ethnological, linguistic, administrative and geographical or territorial divisions, the only form of government suitable to Indian conditions is a federal system with

complete autonomy and residuary powers vested in the constituent States.

The right of Muslims to elect their representatives on the various Indian legislatures through separate electorates is now the law of the land, and Muslims cannot be deprived of that right without their consent.

In the Provinces in which Mussulmans constitute a minority they shall have a representation in no case less than that enjoyed by them under the existing law [i.e. 'weightage'].

It is essential that Mussulmans should have their due share in the Central and Provincial Cabinets.[57]

A few days earlier while presiding over the All-India Khilafat Conference at Calcutta (25 December 1928), Muhammad Ali in the course of his extempore address in Urdu lasting for over four hours, had complained that though he was a member of the Congress and its Working Committee, he was not given a fair hearing during the debate on the Nehru Report at the Convention. He was 'heckled at every moment and stopped during his speech at every step'. He said also that 'Dr Ansari, the President of the Convention, was a mere puppet in the hands of Pandit Motilal'.[58]

The leaders of the Congress party were fully aware of the differences that had marked the making of the Nehru Report from the very beginning of the project and of the fact that on completion the Report had fully satisfied no sector of public opinion in the country; even Congress' own ranks remained divided over the question whether the goal was to be Dominion Status or Complete Independence.

The report was to be considered by Congress at its Forty-third Session at Calcutta commencing on 29 December 1928 immediately after the All-Parties Convention. The president-elect of the session was Motilal Nehru. He was naturally anxious that his Report should be approved by the Congress. But he was well-aware that his own son, Jawaharlal, as well as Subhas Bose and their sympathizers, would reject the goal of Dominion Status which the Report had set and ask for Full Independence.

To resolve the problem, Motilal turned to Mahatma Gandhi for help. Gandhi had gone into political retirement after he had failed to deliver Swaraj within one year and had suspended the non-cooperation movement following the Chauri Chaura massacre in February 1922. 'Motilal pleaded with him to come to the annual Congress session in Calcutta when the Nehru Report would be a major issue. He could envisage the conflicts that might emerge, for as the weeks passed the opposition to the Report even among Congressmen was becoming alarmingly apparent.'[59]

Motilal's strategy paid off. Gandhi returned to the centre stage of politics which he was to occupy till the closing days of the Raj when he left the practicalities of the transfer of power to Jawaharlal Nehru and Vallabhbhai Patel. He saved the Nehru Report, at least temporarily, by successfully sponsoring the following compromise resolution

> This Congress...whilst adhering to the resolution relating to complete independence passed at the Madras Congress approves the Constitution drawn up by the Committee...this Congress will adopt the Constitution in its entirety if it is accepted by the British Parliament on or before December 31st, 1929, but in the event of its non-acceptance by that date or its earlier rejection, Congress will organize a non-violent non-cooperation.[60]

The Nehru Report in effect was buried. The one-year ultimatum to the British Government was a transparent face-saving device. No one could really have expected the British Government to concede Dominion Status 'as the next immediate step' within a year in response to a Report which instead of uniting the Indian communities on one platform had exposed their divisions.

Not surprisingly, at the next session of the Congress at Lahore (19-31 December 1929) one of the resolutions declared that 'the entire scheme of the Nehru Committee's report' had 'lapsed'.[61] At the same time, another resolution practically confessed the real reason for burying the report

> As the Sikhs in particular, and the Muslims and other minorities in general, had expressed dissatisfaction over the solution of communal questions proposed in the Nehru Report, this Congress assures the Sikhs, the Muslims and other minorities, that no solution thereof in any future Constitution will be acceptable to the Congress that does not give full satisfaction to the parties concerned.[62]

The Legacy of the Nehru Report

The Nehru Report was a watershed in the Indian freedom movement. Instead of bringing about Hindu-Muslim unity, it drove the majority of the Muslims away from the Congress for ever. Jinnah and the Ali Brothers had cooperated with Congress till then and the respect they enjoyed among Muslims had made Congress seem a friendly organization in the eyes of a large body of Muslims. The Ali Brothers were passionately religious and powerful orators in Urdu. They were the darlings of the masses. The results of their castigation of the Congress became immediately perceptible. But in the long run it was the parting of Jinnah which had the decisive result; the Nehru Report had unwittingly laid the foundation of Pakistan. As a Hindu author observes, 'the most visible result' of the Nehru Report 'was almost the complete divorce by Muslims of the nationalism as represented by the Congress'.[63] The Congress henceforth became a principally Hindu party.

Quite obviously, the Congress had suffered an unmitigated disaster. It had set out to prove Birkenhead wrong in his assertion that the Indians could never produce an agreed Constitution; it ended up by proving him right. It had tried to demonstrate the existence of an all-India nationalism; it succeeded in exposing the country's political divisions.

The process of producing the Nehru Report had been riven by communal differences from beginning to end. The authors conveniently covered up their own failure to heal these differences: 'We are certain that as soon as India is free and can face her problems unhampered by alien authority and intervention...we shall then find Hindus and Muslims and Sikhs in one party acting together and opposing another party which also consists of Hindus and Muslims and Sikhs'.[64]

These observations started a new trend in Congress policy. Instead of continuing their efforts to bring about Hindu-Muslim accord by a realistic political give and take, the Congress leaders began to bypass the hurdle of communal differences. They said that the said malady was the result of Britain's policy of divide and rule and that its real cure was independence. But to whom was power to be transferred while the Hindus and the Muslims were at daggers drawn with each other? To that they had an equally convenient answer. Hand over power to Congress they insisted, because Congress was not just one of the political parties but was national organization representing all the interests and peoples of India.[65] It was quickly forgotten that the Conference that produced the Nehru Report and the Convention that finally considered it had both been given the title of 'All Parties' thus admitting the obvious fact that Congress was but one of the political parties in India.

This policy of the predominantly Hindu Congress party of ignoring political realities resulted in the Hindus and the Muslims continuing as separate political entities and in the end each receiving a separate homeland of their own from the departing British Government.

The Muslims for some years following the Nehru Report were too divided into groups and parties to face Congress on the political stage on equal terms. The Muslim All-Parties Conference, which had met in Delhi in December 1928 under the chairmanship of the Aga Khan, was a highly impressive protest meeting but it did not develop into a coherent political party. After issuing their manifesto the participants returned to their respective parties. It was only in the 1930s that they rallied behind Quaid-i-Azam Mohammad Ali Jinnah and presented a united front to the Congress under the flag of the Muslim League.

India has now been independent for half a century but the convenient prophecy that freedom from foreign rule would immediately heal communal divisions has yet to be fulfilled. Sir Chimanlal H. Setalvad, an eminent Hindu, has frankly conceded that 'The real parentage of the Pakistan Movement can be traced to the Congress... Congress leaders said that there was no communal problem in India and if there was, it could be settled after India got independence, forgetting that for the very purpose of getting independence, communal unity was essential.[66] And Jawaharlal Nehru points out that, 'Divide and rule has always been the way of empires; and the measure of their success in this policy has been also the measure of their superiority over those whom they exploit. We cannot complain of it or, at any rate, we ought not to be surprised at it. To ignore it and not to provide against it is in itself a mistake in one's thought'.[67]

Jinnah's Fourteen Points

Jinnah presented his famous Fourteen Points at the Muslim League Council session in Delhi on 28 March 1929. At the same time he wrote a history of the Origins of Fourteen Points. In the history he stated that the Nehru Report could 'at best be treated only as Hindu counter proposals' to the Delhi Muslim proposals of 20 March 1927. As the Nehru Report was not acceptable to the Muslim League, he drafted a proposal embodying fourteen points which he called the 'basic principles' to safeguard the 'rights and interests' of Muslims. To make the proposal acceptable to as many Muslim schools of thought as possible, he made the list of safeguards impressively comprehensive. We reproduce it below in full

(1) The form of the future Constitution should be federal, with the residuary powers vested in the provinces.
(2) A uniform measure of autonomy shall be granted to all provinces.
(3) All legislatures in the country and other elected bodies shall be constituted on the definite principle of adequate and effective representation of minorities in every province without reducing the majority in any province to a minority or even equality.
(4) In the Central Legislature, Mussulman representation shall not be less than one-third.
(5) Representation of communal groups shall continue to be by means of separate electorates as at present, provided it shall be open to any community, at any time, to abandon its separate electorate in favour of joint electorate.
(6) Any territorial re-distribution that might at any time be necessary shall not in any way affect the Muslim majority in the Punjab, Bengal and NWF Province.
(7) Full religious liberty i.e., liberty of belief, worship and observance, propaganda, association and education, shall be guaranteed to all communities.
(8) No bill or resolution or any part thereof shall be passed in any legislature or any other elected body if three-fourths of the members of any community in that particular body oppose such a bill, resolution or part thereof on the ground that it would be injurious to the interests of that community or in the alternative, such other method is devised as may be found feasible and practicable to deal with such cases.
(9) Sind should be separated from the Bombay Presidency.

(10) Reforms should be introduced in the NWF Province and Baluchistan on the same footing as in other provinces.
(11) Provision should be made in the Constitution, giving Muslims an adequate share along with the other Indians in all the services of the State and in local self-governing bodies, having due regard to the requirements of efficiency.
(12) The Constitution should embody adequate safeguards for the protection of Muslim culture and for the protection and promotion of Muslim education, language, religion, personal laws and Muslim charitable institutions and for their due share in the grants-in-aid given by the State and by local self-governing bodies.
(13) No Cabinet, either Central or Provincial, should be formed without there being a proportion of at least one-third Muslim ministers.
(14) No change shall be made in the Constitution by the Central Legislature except with the concurrence of the States constituting the Indian Federation.

The resolution also mentioned an alternative to the above provision in the following terms

> That, in the present circumstances, representation of Mussulmans in the different legislatures of the country and other elected bodies through the separate electorate is inevitable and further, the Government being pledged over and over again not to disturb this franchise so granted to the Muslim community since 1909 till such time as the Mussulmans choose to abandon it, the Mussulmans will not consent to joint electorates unless Sind is actually constituted into a separate province and reforms in fact are introduced in the NWF Province and Baluchistan on the same footing as in other provinces.
>
> Further, it is provided that there shall be reservation of seats according to the Muslim population in the various provinces; but where Mussulmans are in a majority, they shall not contest more seats than their population warrants.
>
> The question of excess representation of Mussulmans over and above their population in provinces where they are in a minority is to be considered hereafter.[68]

Death of Ruttie, 20 February 1929

In spite of the differences of age and temperament between Jinnah and Ruttie they did their best to make their marriage happy. After his marriage with Ruttie, Jinnah 'had no separate existence away from his wife. He found in her a great source of inspiration. His personal, political and social life was always with Ruttie. She was always with him and made his life in all its aspects, pleasant, carefree and well worth living'.[69]

Because of his preoccupation as a practicing barrister, a legislator and a political leader, Jinnah could not offer as much companionship and attention to his young wife as he and she both would have liked. Chagla states that Ruttie would walk into Jinnah's chambers, perch herself upon his table, waiting for Jinnah to finish his work so that they could leave together. 'Jinnah never uttered a word of protest and carried on with his work as if she were not there at all'.[70]

In time she took up activities of her own. On 21 November 1924, she wrote to Dwarkadas, 'Of late willy-nilly I have been propelled towards the study of so-called spiritual phenomena and I am too deeply immersed in the matter now to give it up without some personal satisfaction'.[71]

She also kept a large number of cats and dogs and personally took care of them. At the same time she took an active interest in homes for decrepit animals.[72]

Ruttie, moreover, took an interest in Dwarkadas' social and labour work in which Jinnah also encouraged him. 'She was a source of inspiration in my work', acknowledged Dwarkadas, 'and next to Mrs Besant she was a most helpful and healthy influence on me and my work'.[73]

Unfortunately, Ruttie suffered from restlessness and sleeplessness owing to continuous ill health.[74]

In January 1928, Ruttie and Jinnah separated; she moved to the Taj Mahal Hotel. 'I cannot find fault with either for this separation, which was due to temperamental differences and difference in age. Their points of view on various aspects of life were different.'[75] However, they never ceased to respect and love each other as their subsequent conduct showed.

Ruttie sailed for England on 10 April 1928 and Jinnah on 5 May. Ruttie went to Paris and fell ill there and entered a nursing home. This resulted in a *rapprochement* between husband and wife for Jinnah went over to Paris 'stayed with her in the nursing home for over a month and looked after and nursed her and, as Ruttie told me later, he ate the same food as she did at the nursing home'.[76]

They returned to India separately, Ruttie who was with her mother, was still 'very ill'. At Bombay Ruttie stayed with her mother.

'Throughout January and February 1929, Ruttie continued to be ill and this depressed her. She hardly ever went out except for short walks with me. Every evening Jinnah came to see her and Ruttie, Jinnah and I kept on talking as in the old times. They were getting reconciled to each other'.[77] On 20 February evening—her twenty-ninth birthday, Ruttie passed away.

At the time of Ruttie's death, Jinnah was in Delhi attending the Budget Session of the Assembly. He returned to Bombay for the funeral on the 22 February. She was buried according to Islamic rites. As the body was lowered into the grave, Jinnah broke down and sobbed and wept like a child.

Chagla says that 'no husband could have treated his wife more generously than he [Jinnah] did...[he] treated her wonderfully well, and paid without a murmur all the bills which were necessitated by the luxurious life she led. She was for some time in hospital in Paris, and Jinnah saw to her every comfort regardless of cost'.[78]

Kanji Dwarkadas testifies from 'personal knowledge' that Ruttie retained her affection for Jinnah even though they had decided to lead separate lives.[79] 'She was the gentlest, noblest and kindest of mankind.'[80]

For Jinnah 'the death of his wife was not just a sad event, not just something to be grieved over, but he took it, this act of God, as a failure and personal defeat in his life. I am afraid he never recovered right till the end of his life from this terrible shock'.[81]

These years of trauma in Jinnah's personal life were contemporaneous with major disappointments in his public life. Not to speak of the larger question of Hindu-Muslim unity, even the Muslims were a house divided against itself. He had the best of intentions but nothing seemed to go right.

Notes

1. Pirzada, *Collected Works*, I, op.cit., pp. 412-5.
2. Pirzada, *Collected Works*, II, op. cit., p. 7.
3. Ibid., p. 10.
4. Pirzada, *Collected Works*, II, op.cit., pp. 99-100.
5. Ibid., p. 131.
6. Pirzada, *Foundations of Pakistan*, II, op.cit., pp. 83.
7. Ibid., pp. 69, 102.
8. Ibid., p. 104.
9. Pirzada, *Collected Works*, II, op.cit., p. 28.
10. The accounts of Jinnah's 1926 election and his hold on the Hindu community of Bombay have been taken from Kanji Dawarkadas, *India's Fight for Freedom*, op.cit., pp. 323-4.
11. Subhas Chandra Bose, *The Indian Struggle*, op. cit., p. 116.
12. Hector Bolitho, *Jinnah*, op.cit., pp. 89-90.
13. R. Coupland, *The Indian Problem, 1833-1935*, op.cit., p. 75.
14. M. H. Saiyid, *Mohammad Ali Jinnah*, 1945, op. cit., pp. 368-9.
15. M. C. Chagla, *Roses in December*, op.cit., pp. 93-94.
16. Pirzada, *Collected Works*, III, op.cit., p. 211.
17. Ibid., p. 214.
18. Ibid., p. 217.
19. Ibid., pp. 220-2.
20. For an account of the Jinnah Group session *see*, Pirzada, *Foundations of Pakistan*, II, op.cit., p. 127.
21. For an account of the Shafi Group session *see*, ibid., pp. 128-38.
22. Pirzada, *Collected Works*, III, op.cit., p. 285.
23. Ibid., p. 224.
24. The Second Earl of Birkenhead, *The Life of F.E. Smith, The First Earl of Birkenhead*, op.cit., p. 507.
25. Ibid., p. 508.
26. Debates on Indian Affairs, House of Lords Session 1927, p. 181.
27. It was the feeling of solidarity exhibited in the country in the wake of the appointment of the Simon Commission and 'also the resolve to give an effective reply to Lord Birkenhead's challenge in the House of Lords which was responsible for the decision to convene an All-Parties Conference'. Subhas Chandra Bose, *The Indian Struggle*, op.cit., pp. 145-6.
28. A. M. Zaidi, *The Encyclopaedia of the Indian National Congress*, IX, op. cit., p. 263.
29. Ibid., p. 314.
30. For a list of the organizations invited *see*, All-Parties Conference 1928, Report of the Committee Appointed by the Conference to Determine the Principles of the Constitution for India, pp. 20-21, *(The Nehru Report)*.
31. Ibid., p. 22.
32. Ibid., p. 23.
33. Ibid., p. 17.
34. Jawaharlal Nehru, *Autobiography*, op.cit., p. 172.

35. *The Nehru Report*, op. cit., pp. 161-2.
36. Ibid., p. 1.
37. Ibid., p. 25.
38. Ibid., p. 27.
39. Ibid., p. 29.
40. Ibid., p. 101.
41. Ibid., pp. 104, 109-110.
42. Ibid., p. 105.
43. Ibid., p. 54.
44. Ibid., p. 34.
45. Ibid., p. 44.
46. Ibid., p. 30.
47. Ibid., p. 29.
48. Ibid., p. 31.
49. Ibid., p. 32.
50. Pirzada, *Collected Works*, III, op.cit., pp. 304-5.
51. Pirzada, *Foundations of Pakistan*, II, op.cit., p. 145.
52. M. C. Chagla also resigned from the Muslim League because he supported the Nehru Report. *see*, *Roses in December*, op.cit., p. 97.
53. Our account of Jinnah's appearance before the Convention has been taken from M.H. Saiyid, *Mohammad Ali Jinnah*, 1945, op. cit., pp. 418-35.
54. Hector Bolitho, *Jinnah*, op.cit., p. 95.
55. Pirzada, *Collected Works*, III, op.cit., pp. 311-5.
56. For an account of the proceedings of the Conference *see*, A. M. Zaidi, *Evolution of Muslim Political Thought in India*, III, op. cit., pp. 663-81.
57. R. Coupland, *The Indian Problem, 1833-1935*, op.cit., p. 96.
58. A.M. Zaidi, *Evolution of Muslim Political Thought in India*, III, op. cit., pp. 618-20.
59. Judith M. Brown, *Gandhi*, op.cit., p. 219.
60. A. M. Zaidi, *The Encyclopaedia of the Indian National Congress*, IX, p. 376.
61. Ibid., p. 671.
62. Ibid., p. 672.
63. Ram Gopal, *Indian Muslims*, p. 221.
64. *Report*, p. 49.
65. For example, *see*, Mahatma Gandhi's addresses to the Second Session of the Round Table Conference in Chapter 9.
66. Chimanlal H. Setalvad, *Recollections and Reflections*, pp. 414-5.
67. *Autobiography*, p. 136.
68. Pirzada, *Collected Works*, III, op.cit., pp. 352-4.
69. Kanji Dwarkadas, *India's Fight for Freedom*, op. cit., p. 350.
70. M. C. Chagla, *Roses in December*, op.cit., p. 120.
71. Kanji Dwarkadas, *Ruttie Jinnah*, op. cit., p. 28.
72. Pirzada, *Some Aspects of Quaid-i-Azam's Life*, op. cit., p. 51.
73. Kanji Dwarkadas, *Ruttie Jinnah*, op. cit., pp. 52-53.
74. Ibid., p. 52.
75. Ibid., p. 54.
76. The facts in this paragraph have been taken from Kanji Dwarkadas, *India's Fight for Freedom*, op.cit., p. 335 and Ruttie Jinnah, op.cit., p.54.

77. Kanji Dwarkadas, *Ruttie Jinnah,* op. cit., p. 54.
78. M. C. Chagla, *Roses in December,* op.cit., pp. 120-1.
79. Kanji Dwarkadas, *Ruttie Jinnah,* op.cit., p. 54.
80. Ibid., p. 7.
81. Kanji Dwarkadas, *India's Fight for Freedom,* op.cit., p. 350.

CHAPTER 9

The Round Table Conference and Jinnah's Self-Imposed Exile in England, 1930-1933

Lord Irwin's Goodwill for India

Lord Irwin who took over as viceroy in the first week of April 1926 was a true Christian and a genuine well-wisher of India. He sincerely tried to help India move forward towards Dominion Status. The Quaid-i-Azam and Irwin both being statesmen of the highest integrity, developed a close relationship. The Quaid who was not normally given to a display of emotion, wrote to Irwin in one of his letters (31 October 1927): 'I have come to regard you, if I may say so, with sincere respect and affection'.[1]

In a speech at the Chelmsford Club in Simla on 17 July 1926 Irwin appealed to Hindu and Muslim leaders to compose their differences for the good of their country

> Let the leaders and thoughtful men in each community...throw themselves with ardour into struggle and fight for toleration... I refuse to believe that they can make no contribution now to rescue the good name of India from the hurt which their present discords inflict upon it.[2]

On 29 August 1927, he pleaded in his address to the Indian legislature

> I am not exaggerating when I say that, during the seventeen months that I have been in India, the whole landscape has been overshadowed by the lowering clouds of communal tension, which have repeatedly discharged their thunderbolts, spreading far throughout the land their devastating havoc... United must be the effort if it is to gain success; and on the successful issue of such work depends the building of the Indian Nation. Yet the would-be builders must approach their task sorely handicapped and with heavy heart, so long as the forces

to which they would appeal are distracted and torn by present animosities. For nothing wholesome can flourish in unwholesome soil, and no one may hope to build a house to stand against the wind and the rain and the storm of life upon foundations that are rotten and unsound.[3]

But these exhortations fell on deaf ears. Hindu and Muslim politicians continued to assault one another verbally as described in the last chapter. At the same time their followers continued to bash one another's heads in the streets with *lathis* and brickbats.[4]

Communal discord notwithstanding Congress continued to raise its demands. At the Madras session (December 1927) it declared 'the goal of the Indian people to be complete independence'; and at the Calcutta Congress (December 1928) it gave the British Government one year's ultimatum to accept the Nehru Report failing which it would launch a campaign of non-co-operation.

Lord Irwin's Declaration of 31 October 1929

The expected victory of the Labour Party happened in the general election of May 1929. Ramsay MacDonald became prime minister and Wedgwood Benn took over as secretary of state for India. This raised the hope of a new initiative by the British Government to improve the deteriorating political situation in India because the Labour Party had a tradition of friendliness toward India. On 7 October 1927, George Lansbury, the new chairman of the Labour Party, while presiding over a Labour Party Conference moved a resolution which was adopted unanimously. It declared 'that the policy of the British Government should be one of co-operation with the Indian people, with its object of establishing India, at the earliest possible moment and by her consent, as an equal partner with the other members of the British Commonwealth of Nations'.[5]

In June 1929, Lord Irwin went to England for four months leave and on return made an historic statement on 31 October 1929. It contained two important elements. The first assured Indians that 'it is implicit in the declaration of 1917 that the natural issue of India's constitutional progress, as there contemplated, is the attainment of Dominion Status'. The second superseded the report of the much criticized Simon Commission even before it was issued and gave Indians the desired assurance that before proposals for a constitutional advance were finally submitted to Parliament 'representatives of different parties and interests in India and representatives of the Indian States' would be invited to confer with representatives of the British Government.[6] This gave the Indians the Round Table Conference they had agitated for.

The concessions contained in Irwin's declaration were a matter of great satisfaction for the Quaid. Soon after Irwin had left for England to plead India's case, Jinnah had written to Prime Minister Ramsay MacDonald (19 June 1929) to reinforce Irwin's efforts. Jinnah already knew MacDonald personally and had had a discussion with him in his last visit to London in July 1928. In the letter he warned the British prime minister that 'India has lost her faith in the word of Great Britain. The first and foremost thing I would ask you to consider is how best to restore that faith and revive the confidence of India in the "bona fides" of Great Britain'. He proceeded to make two suggestions to that end.

First, 'I would most earnestly urge upon you at this moment to persuade His Majesty's Government without delay to make a declaration that Great Britain is unequivocally pledged to the policy of granting to India full responsible government with Dominion Status'. Secondly, after the receipt of the Simon Report and before they formulate their proposals, His Majesty's Government 'should invite representatives of India, who would be in a position to deliver the goods...to sit in conference with them with a view to reaching a solution which might carry, to use the words of the Viceroy, "the willing assent of political India".'

In reply MacDonald reassured Jinnah on two important points. He stated first that, 'The report of the Simon Commission you need have no hesitation in assuming it [was] never intended to be anything more than advice given for the guidance of the government' and secondly, 'one thing I can say here—because I have said it before repeatedly and it still remains the intention of the government—that we want India to enjoy Dominion Status'.[7]

That the concessions contained in Irwin's declaration of 31 October 1929 had resulted from his personal intercession with the British Government admits of no doubt. Irwin himself explained afterwards: 'By some means or other, contact had to be regained and confidence in British purpose restored. I accordingly suggested to the Labour Government, which had meanwhile come into office, the two ideas of the Round Table Conference and formal declaration of Dominion Status as the goal of British policy in India'.[8]

The Quaid-i-Azam who had joined hands with the viceroy in asking for the said concessions in his letter to the British prime minister, confirmed that 'without Lord Irwin and his influence and clear grasp of the Indian situation and the firmness he has displayed, such a change of policy at this juncture would not have been secured'. At the same time he warned 'good, as the announcement is so far as it goes, there is yet a greater task awaiting us : "Will united India meet united Westminster?" '[9]

India at this juncture had a golden opportunity to wrest substantial political concessions from Britain. The moment called for a closing of the ranks by the Indian political parties and for a positive constitutional policy. Unfortunately, the largest party of all, the Indian National Congress, persisted in its confrontational attitude with the result that the Round Table Conference and the resulting Act of 1935 fell far short of what could have been gained. This will become clear as we proceed with our exposition.

On the eve of the Lahore Congress, Lord Irwin made one more effort to pacify Indian leaders. He invited them to meet him in Delhi on 23 December. Among those whom he saw that day were Gandhi, Motilal, Sapru and Jinnah. The meeting opened with expressions of horror at the explosion of the bomb under the viceroy's train that morning and congratulations upon his escape, but it failed in its real purpose. Gandhi sought the assurance that the Round Table Conference would proceed on the basis of full Dominion Status. Lord Irwin was unable to provide this assurance.

The Lahore Congress (29-31 December 1929)

In his presidential address Jawaharlal Nehru said that the viceroy had meant well in his declaration of 31 October 1929 'but even a viceroy's goodwill and courteous phrases are poor substitutes for hard facts that confront us. We have sufficient experience of the devious ways of British diplomacy to beware of it'. He went on that 'Independence for us means complete freedom from British domination...I do not think any form of Dominion Status applicable to India will give us real power'.[10] The main resolution passed on Gandhi's motion declared that nothing would be gained by the Congress leaders being represented at the Round Table Conference. It expressed the hope that all Congressmen would 'henceforth devote their exclusive attention to the attainment of complete independence for India. And it authorized the All-India Congress Committee 'whenever it deems fit to launch upon a programme of civil disobedience'.[11]

Jinnah, in an interview on 2 January 1930, said that the resolutions passed by the Congress were 'most misleading, unpractical, unsound and unwise'. In his judgement India stood to 'gain by negotiations more than by any other action, violent or non-violent.[12]

The Civil Disobedience Movement

The All-India Congress Committee which had been charged with the duty to launch the civil disobedience movement delegated its authority to Gandhi. To give a start to the campaign and to test the temper of the country, 26 January was designated Independence Day and a pledge was taken on that day all over the country.

To the surprise of everyone, Gandhi decided to start the struggle by manufacturing salt, thus contravening the salt law. 'We were bewildered', recalled Jawaharlal Nehru, 'and could not quite fit in a national struggle with common salt'.[13] But the Mahatma had made a shrewd choice. The tax on salt was especially unpopular among the poor who regarded salt as a bounty from nature.

Equally ingenious was the programme for public salt-making. On 12 March 1930, the Mahatma set out from Sabarmati ashram[14] on foot for Dandi on the sea coast about 240 miles away to manufacture salt by evaporating sea water. He was accompanied by seventy-nine volunteers from the ashram and was seen off by an estimated crowd of seventy-five thousand. He marched for twenty-four days, arriving at Dandi on 5 April, and manufactured salt on the following day, which was the anniversary of the inauguration of the non-co-operation movement, which on 13 April 1919 had suffered the Jallianwala massacre (6-13 April every year had been observed as National Week).

Gandhi's march was a veritable pilgrim's progress. Villagers everywhere thronged to him and reverently listened to his message. More than 300 village headmen renounced their office. Gandhi's picturesque procession was a godsend to the national and international media and illustrated accounts of mass devotion to Gandhi appeared in innumerable papers.

Originally the Working Committee had authorized only Gandhi to start civil disobedience but while Gandhi was on the way to Dandi, it legitimized mass participation in the movement and broadened the scope to cover activities other than salt-making. Civil disobedience thus spread to well-known favourites such as boycotting foreign cloth, British goods, liquor and drugs. Women came out in large numbers and made pickets outside the shops selling these items.

Gandhi was arrested on 5 May 1920 after he had announced his intention to take possession of the salt works at Dharsana and Charsadda. His arrest was followed by a country-wide *hartal*. Violence and repression in several places naturally followed. Over 60,000 persons including Jawaharlal Nehru and Motilal Nehru were arrested and sentenced to various terms of imprisonment.

The movement, however, was mainly a Hindu effort. At a meeting of the All-India Muslim Conference at Bombay in April 1930, Muhammad Ali 'delivered from his presidential chair a long and vigorous attack on Mr Gandhi's policy, "We refuse to join Mr Gandhi, because his movement is not a movement for the complete independence of India but for making the seventy millions of Indian Mussulmans dependents of the Hindu Mahasabha".'[15] He and his brother Shaukat Ali openly appealed to the Muslims not to join the civil disobedience movement.[16]

The Simon Report

The Report of the Simon Commission was published in May 1930 but it had already been overtaken by Lord Irwin's statement of 31 October 1929 promising a Round Table Conference. The Report only served to alienate Indian nationalists further. It did not so much as mention Dominion Status, which Irwin's statement had already promised as India's political destination.

In a nutshell, the Report declared that 'each province should be as far as possible mistress in her own house'.[17] It recommended that diarchy should lapse and the entire administration of the provinces be entrusted to ministers responsible to the legislature, except that the governor would have overriding powers in certain matters such as the safety of the province or protection of the minorities. But no substantial change was recommended at the centre. The central government was to remain an official government not owing responsibility to the legislature. An all-India federation was envisaged which would include the Princely States, but its achievement would have to be a lengthy process because 'a premature endeavour to introduce forms of responsible government at the Centre before the conditions for its actual practice have emerged would in the end result not in advance but in retrogression'.[18]

Nor did the authors of the Report fail to remind the Indians that 'No third party, however friendly and disinterested, can do what the two communities might cooperate in doing for themselves by mutual agreement'.[19]

The First Session of the Round Table Conference, 21 November 1930 to 19 January 1931

The first session of the Indian Round Table Conference was inaugurated by the King in the Royal Gallery of the House of Lords on 12 November 1930. It was attended by eighty-nine members: sixteen from the three British political parties, fifty-seven from British India and sixteen from the Indian Princely States. All the Indian interests except Congress were represented by well-known figures. There were Muslims such as the Aga Khan, Jinnah, Shafi, and Muhammad Ali, and Hindu liberals such as Sapru, Jayakar and Sastri. Sampuran Singh and Ujjal Singh represented the Sikhs, B. S. Moonje the Hindu Mahasabha, Ambedkar the depressed classes, Colonel Gideny the Anglo-Indians,

K.T. Paul the Indian Christians, and Hubert Carr the British business community in India. The States were represented by the rulers of Bikaner, Kashmir, Bhopal and Patiala and by high officials from Hyderabad, Mysore and Gwalior.

The Quaid, who had cooperated with Lord Irwin in the matter of winning the concessions of a promise of Dominion Status and the Round Table Conference, had tried his best to persuade Irwin to be present in London during the sittings of the conference. In a letter to the viceroy dated 6 August 1930 he had written

> May I once more urge you not to forget the suggestion I made in the course of our conversation in Simla that Your Excellency should do your utmost to arrange and be present in London at the time of the Conference? I am more anxious and more convinced than ever that it is absolutely essential to the success of the Conference.

Irwin replied on 11 August. He gave two reasons why it would not be possible for him to leave India. First, 'The provocative attitude' of the Congress Working Committee, and second, that 'during the Conference frequent references would be necessary to the Government of India, and I should wish to have the opportunity of influencing their views'. Jinnah wrote back on 19 August that he recognized the force of what Irwin had said, 'Nevertheless I would have preferred your presence in London'.

Irwin gave Jinnah letters of introduction to several important figures including Baldwin. He also asked Wedgwood Benn, the secretary of state for India, to arrange for Jinnah to see Ramsay MacDonald, the prime minister. In his letter to Wedgwood Benn the viceroy wrote

> I have seen a good deal of Jinnah from time to time, and have met very few Indians with a more acute intellect or more independent outlook—not of course that he always sees eye to eye with government. But he is not lacking in moral courage, and has been very outspoken against civil disobedience and is genuinely anxious to find the way to settlement...I think he is out to help.[20]

The Round Table Conference had no difficulty in concluding in principle that the form of government in India at the Centre had to be federal. The Indian members demanded a quicker realization of Dominion Status than their British colleagues were willing to concede. Jayakar said that many of his English friends had spoken of their fears as follows: 'If we give you the first instalment of Reforms, namely, Dominion Status, you will make it a most powerful lever for severance from the Empire—the cry of independence'. His own view was that 'if you give India Dominion Status today, in the course of a few months the cry of independence will die of itself'.[21]

It was the perennial communal problem that showed no signs of solution. Sub-Committee No. III (Minorities), chaired personally by Ramsay MacDonald, reported that 'The Minorities and Depressed Classes were definite in their assertion that they could not consent to any self-governing constitution for India unless their demands were met in a reasonable manner'.[22]

At the closing session Ramsay MacDonald declared that 'it is the duty of the communities to come to an agreement'.[23] And he expressed the hope that 'those engaged at present in civil disobedience' will respond to the viceroy's appeal and co-operate in the future work of the Conference.[24]

Though the Indian delegates who attended the Conference were leaders of the highest rank, the absence of Congress left a serious gap. It is true that Congress was only one of the several political parties in the country but it is equally true that Congress was the largest, the best-organized and the most active of all the parties. Jinnah's hope that 'United India' would meet 'United Westminster' was not fulfilled.

Jinnah had addressed the 5th Plenary Meeting on 20 November 1930. He complained about the slow pace at which British promises of self-government for India were being implemented and reminded Prime Minister Ramsay MacDonald, who was chairing the meeting, that two years had already passed since he had expressed the hope at the British Labour Party Conference that 'within a period of months, rather than years, there will be a new Dominion added to the Commonwealth of our nations, a Dominion of another race, a Dominion that will find self-respect as an equal within the Commonwealth—I refer to India'.[25]

Lord Peel had stated in the conference earlier that as the result of the non-cooperation movement by Congress, the Conservatives were 'harassed' by the anxiety that if they agree to some Constitution in the conference...

...and if the representatives of India go back to work it, there is a party [Congress], a very strong party and an organized party, in India, which will, as it were, wrest the opportunity from the hands of those who are here, and will merely use those powers that are granted, for furthering their own separatist and independent ends.[26]

Jinnah resented this as a ploy to delay political concessions to his country and made it clear that so far as the goal of self-government was concerned there was no difference between Congress and all the other interests in India

Now, Sir, let us understand the position in India. The position in India is this, and let me tell your here again, without mincing any words, that there is no section, whether they are Hindus or Muhammadans or whether they are Sikhs or Christians or Parsees or depressed classes, or even commercial classes, merchants or traders, there is not one section in India that has not emphatically declared that India must have a full measure of self-government.

He pointed out that 'seventy millions of Mussulmans—all, barring a few individuals here and there—have kept aloof from the non-cooperation movement. Thirty-five or forty millions of depressed classes have set their face against the non-cooperation movement. Sikhs and Christians have not joined it', and he asked bluntly, 'Do you want every one of the parties who have still maintained that their proper place is to go to this Conference, and across the table to negotiate and come to a settlement which will satisfy the aspirations of India, to go back and join the rest? Is that what you want?'[27]

He observed further

...the cardinal principal which will guide us throughout the deliberations of this Conference is that India wants to be mistress in her own house; and I cannot conceive of any Constitution that you may frame which will not transfer responsibility in the Central Government to a Cabinet responsible to the Legislature... Whoever has used the phrase Dominion Status so far at this Table is concerned, has always said, 'with safeguards during the transitional period'. Sir, that is going to be our cardinal principle.[28]

Unlike Gandhi, who was to claim at the second session of the Round Table Conference that Congress represented everyone in India, thus implying that there were only two parties round the table—the Congress and the British—Jinnah pointed out that there were four main parties. These were the British, the Indian Princes, the Hindus and the Muslims.[29]

Jinnah was a member of the Federal Structure Sub-Committee and had warned the members on 13 January 1931 that

> Hindu-Muslim settlement is a condition precedent, nay it is a *sine qua non*. Before any Constitution can be completed for the Government of India and I maintain that unless you provide safeguards for the Mussulmans that will give them a complete sense of security and a feeling of confidence in the future Constitution of the Government of India and unless you secure their cooperation and willing consent, no Constitution you frame for India will work for 24 hours.[30]

In January 1931 Jinnah decided to take up residence in London. We will have more to say on this subject in a later section of this chapter.

Muhammad Ali's address to the Conference's plenary session on 19 November 1930 was typically out of the ordinary. He had attended the Conference despite being seriously ill and had to speak while seated. He said the 'one purpose' for which he had come despite 'ill-health, and ailments and all sorts of things' was that he wanted to go back to his country only 'if I can go back with the substance of freedom in my hand. Otherwise I will not go back to a slave country. I would even prefer to die in a foreign country so long as it is a free country'.[31] He said that the Hindu-Muslim problem was not entirely a British creation. 'It is the old maxim of "divide and rule" but there is a division of labour here. We divide and you rule'.[32] His wish was tragically fulfilled. He passed away in London on 4 January 1931. His body was taken to Jerusalem and buried there.

Presidential Address of Dr Muhammad Iqbal at the Allahabad Session of the All-India Muslim League, 29 December 1930

While the first session of the Round Table Conference was still in session in London, the poet-philosopher Muhammad Iqbal delivered his famous presidential address at the Allahabad session of the Muslim League on 29 December 1930. The most celebrated passage of the address runs as follows

> I would like to see the Punjab, the North-West Frontier Province, Sind and Baluchistan amalgamated into a single State. Self-government within the British Empire, or without the British Empire, the formation of a consolidated North-West Indian Muslim State appears to me to be the final destiny of the Muslims at least of north-west India.[33]

Read as a whole, the text makes it clear that what Iqbal was proposing at that stage was the grouping of Muslim-majority provinces of north-west India into a single province within India in which 'the Central Federal State' would exercise 'only those powers which are expressly vested in it by the free consent of Federal States'.[34] In a letter to Edward Thompson dated 4 March 1934, Iqbal protested that Thompson, in his review of a book by Iqbal, had wrongly called him a 'protagonist of the scheme called "Pakistan" '; he emphasized that the scheme he had suggested in his Allahabad address was 'the creation of a Muslim province—i.e., a province having an overwhelming population of Muslims in the north-west of India. This new province will be, according to my scheme, a part of the proposed Indian Federation'.[35]

Nevertheless the Allahabad address does hint that the Muslims of India could claim to be a nation

> We are 70 millions, and far more homogeneous than any other people in India. Indeed, the Muslims of India are the only Indian people who can fitly be described as a nation in the modern sense of the word. The Hindus, though ahead of us in almost all aspects, have not yet been able to achieve the kind of homogeneity which is necessary for a nation, and which Islam has given you as a free gift.[36]

Also: 'The Prime Minister of England apparently refuses to see that the problem of India is international... Obviously he does not see that the model of British democracy cannot be of any use in a land of many nations.'[37]

Iqbal's Allahabad discourse was a learned one and and contained some striking ideas. It made a strong impact because it had been delivered by Muslim India's acknowledged national poet. There is no question that Iqbal's poetry and ideas powerfully inspired Muslim nationalism which, in its own time, won Pakistan. His basic message as a poet was that the Muslims should derive inspiration from their great past for reviving their fortune. He was a tower of strength to Jinnah in the Punjab when the League there was overshadowed by the Unionists. He inspired the young intelligentsia of that province and they spread his message far and wide and made the Punjab a stronghold of the League and eventually brought down the Unionist Government. Iqbal had the political sense to recognize that it was Jinnah alone among the Muslim leaders who had the capacity to give them a strong lead. On 21 June 1937 he wrote to Jinnah that he was writing to him 'so often' because he was 'the only Muslim in India today to whom the community has a right to look up for safe guidance through the storm which is coming to north-west India, and perhaps to the whole of India'. In the same letter he said 'Why should not the Muslims of north-west India and Bengal be considered as nations entitled to self-determination just as other nations in India and outside are?'[38]

Iqbal passed away on 21 April 1938. At a mammoth public meeting in Calcutta on the same day, the Quaid-i-Azam paid him a rich tribute: he was 'undoubtedly one of the greatest poets, philosophers and seers of humanity of all times... To me he was a personal friend, philosopher and guide and as such the main source of my inspiration and spiritual support'.[39]

The Second Session of the Round Table Conference, 7 September to 1 December 1931

The British prime minister, in his closing address to the first session of the Round Table Conference, had expressed the hope that 'those engaged at present in civil disobedience' would join the Round Table Conference. As a step toward the fulfilment of that hope, Irwin unconditionally ordered the release of Gandhi and the members of the Congress Working Committee and as an additional gesture of goodwill decreed the release to take place on 26 January 1931, the anniversary of 'Independence Day'.

After prolonged talks, the Irwin-Gandhi Agreement was reached on 5 March 1931. Its main provisions were that the Civil

Disobedience Movement would be discontinued and steps would be taken for the participation of the representatives of the Congress in the Round Table Conference.[40]

On the same day Gandhi acknowledged at a press conference that the settlement 'would have been impossible without the viceroy's inexhaustible patience and equally inexhaustible industry and unfailing courtesy'.[41]

Later in the same month the Congress at its Karachi session (29-31 March 1931) appointed Gandhi to represent it at the Round Table Conference 'with the addition of such other delegates as the Working Committee may appoint'.

Before the second session of the Round Table Conference convened, the reactionary forces in the British ruling circles had strengthened visibly. While the Irwin-Gandhi negotiations were still in progress, Winston Churchill had voiced his views in characteristically picturesque fashion. In his address to the West Sussex Conservative Association on 23 February 1931 he had said that it was

> ...alarming and also nauseating to see Mr Gandhi, a seditious Middle Temple lawyer, now posing as a fakir of a type well known in the East, striding half-naked up the steps of the Viceregal Palace, while he is still organizing and conducting a campaign of civil disobedience, to parley on equal terms with the representative of the King Emperor.

On 18 April 1931 the conciliatory Lord Irwin at the end of his term had handed over charge as viceroy to Lord Willingdon who was more bureaucratic and believed in swift and stern measures to curb political agitation. In August the MacDonald Cabinet resigned to make room for a National Coalition Government to cope with the financial crisis. MacDonald was still prime minister but the Cabinet now included members of not only the Labour party but also the Conservatives and the Liberals. Sir Samuel Hoare, a Conservative, took over as secretary of state for India.

Jinnah visited India before the second session of the Round Table Conference. In a speech in Bombay he said he had 'no eye on any party' and 'no mind for popularity'. At another occasion he told the *Times of India* that the success or failure of the Round Table Conference was entirely dependent upon the consideration of the Hindu-Muslim question. He stated also that he was not likely to return to India 'for a considerably long time. Nevertheless India's welfare and her future progress will be constantly nearest to my heart.'[42]

When the Round Table Conference met for its second session, Gandhi was not the only newcomer. There were also others including Madan Mohan Malaviya, a founder member of the Hindu Mahasabha and the poet Iqbal who not long ago had made his memorable address at the Allahabad session of the Muslim League. But Gandhi was the star attraction and all eyes were on him. He was made a member of both the most important committees of the Conference—the Federal Structure Committee and the Minorities Committee which was personally chaired by Prime Minister Ramsay MacDonald. His pronouncements in these committees and at a plenary session of the Conference starkly represented Congress' dictatorial and arrogant attitudes. They warned the minorities and other political parties what to expect from the Congress in years to come.

The Mahatma told the Federal Structure Committee

> As you are all aware, the Congress case is that there should be complete responsibility transferred to India. That means, and it has been stated, that there should be complete control over defence and over external affairs... Hence I am here very respectfully to claim, on behalf of the Congress, complete control over the army, over the defence forces and over external affairs.[43]

This clearly meant that the British should hand over sovereignty to the predominantly Hindu Congress Party and quit India, that a one-party rule would then follow and it would deal with the minorities as it wished.

At the Minorities Committee meeting on 1 October 1931, Gandhi proposed a week's adjournment so that he could call 'representatives of the different groups together and hold consultations with a view to arriving at some final settlement'.[44] When 'the committee reconvened on 8 October, the Mahatma reported, It is with deep sorrow and deeper humiliation that I have to announce utter failure on my part to secure an agreed solution of the communal question through informal conversations among and with the representatives of different groups'. He asserted that the 'causes of failure were inherent in the composition of the Indian delegation. We are almost all not elected representatives of the parties or groups whom we are presumed to represent; we are here by the nomination of the government.'[45] Sir Muhammad Shafi said that he 'entirely' dissented from Gandhi and pointed out that, 'The leaders of all the various political parties in India are members of the Round Table Conference and they were nominated by the Government of India after consultation with the Working Committees and Executives of these various organization'.[46]

Ambedkar the leader of the Untouchable (also called Depressed) Classes too protested that he had not

> ...the slightestest doubt that if the Depressed Classes of India were given the chance of electing their representatives to this Conference, I would, all the same, find a place here... The Mahatma has been always claiming that the Congress stands for the Depressed Classes, and the Congress represents the Depressed Classes more than I or my colleagues can do. To that claim I can only say that it is one of the many false claims which irresponsible people keep on making.[47]

Even the normally suave prime minister could not refrain from rebuking the Mahatma. He appealed to everyone 'not to attribute your common failure to any method by which you have been elected... Be honest and face the facts. The communal problem is a problem of fact. Does the problem exist in India or does it not?'[48]

Gandhi also echoed what the authors of the Nehru Report had conveniently stated when their own efforts to solve the communal problem had failed. 'I have not a shadow of doubt', he said, 'that the iceberg of communal differences will melt under the warmth of freedom'.[49]

Various groups and representatives had handed over representations which were printed as appendices to the Proceedings. One of these (Appendix XIII) was Provisions for a Settlement of the Communal Problem put forward jointly by Muslims, Depressed Classes, Indian Christians, Anglo-Indians and Europeans. It alone 'covered something in the region of 46 per cent of the population of British India'.[50] But this did not prevent Mahatma Gandhi from claiming that Congress represented '85 per cent or 95 per cent of the population not merely of British India but of the whole of India'.[51]

The Mahatma's address to the Plenary Meeting on 30 November 1931 was in tune with what he had said at the Committee meetings. 'Congress alone', he said, 'claims to represent the whole of India', even the princes 'by right of service'. On the subject of independence he explained, 'India must have real liberty. Call it by any name you like.' He said he wanted to become 'a partner with Great Britain...call it complete independence or whatever you like'.[52]

And he repeated the theme that the Hindu-Muslim quarrel was not old but

> ...is coeval with the British advent, and immediately this relationship, the unfortunate, artificial, unnatural relationship between Great Britain and India is transformed into a natural relationship, when it becomes, if it does become, a voluntary partnership to be given up, to be dissolved at the will of either party, when it becomes that you will find that Hindus, Mussulmans, Sikhs, Europeans, Anglo-Indians, Christians, Untouchables, will all live together as one man.[53]

Coupland points out that the Mahatma's extravagant claims 'seemed to suggest that while Congress was the master of India, he was the master of the Congress'.[54]

The second session of the Round Table Conference did produce two important decisions which pleased the Muslims. These were that the North-West Frontier Province would become a Governor's Province and Sind would be given that status if it could be made financially viable.

In his closing address Ramsay MacDonald reminded the Indian delegates that the 'formidable obstacle' that stood in the way of progress was the communal deadlock. 'I have never concealed from you my conviction', he said, 'that this is above all others a problem for you to settle by agreement amongst yourselves'. But he promised that the communal problem would not be permitted to hold up the work of Constitution making. If the Indians did not come up with a solution, 'His Majesty's Government would be compelled to apply a provisional scheme'.[55]

The Third Session of the Round Table Conference, 17 November to 24 December 1932

The last session of the Round Table Conference turned out to be the least important of its three sessions. It was attended by only forty-six delegates. The British delegation contained members of the parties which supported the National Government but the Labour Party, now the opposition, refused to participate. Also missing was the Indian National Congress. Nor did any of the important princes appear personally. No startling decisions were expected and none emerged.

In opening the session the prime minister explained that 'its object was to supplement the work so far accomplished at the Round Table Conference, by filling in, in some detail, the more important gaps left by the discussions at the two previous sessions'. At the conclusion of the session Secretary of State Hoare claimed that 'we have clearly delimited the field upon which the future Constitution is gong to be built'. At the same time Lord Sankey, the Lord Chancellor, reflected the general feeling that the princes had lost their earlier enthusiasm for joining the federation. Addressing the Indian States' Representatives he said, 'I would beg you to convey to Their Highnesses this message, that they should endeavour to make up their minds as soon as possible about their entry into the Federation. You have excited the hopes of India. Hope deferred makes the heart sick.'

The 'Communal Award'

Since the Indian Delegates had not been able to agree on a scheme of communal representation, it was left to the British prime minister to solve the problem. He announced his 'Communal Award' on 16 April 1932. The Lucknow Pact was still the only constitutional agreement which the Hindus and the Muslims had ever reached. Its principles of weightage had been applied in the Act of 1919. They were followed also in the 'Communal Award'. Consequently, the Muslims in the important provinces of Bengal and the Punjab lost their majorities to the following extent

Province	Muslim percentage of population	Total number of seats	Seats reserved for Muslims
Bengal	54.7	250	199
The Punjab	57.0	175	86

Why the Quaid was Not Invited to the Third Session of the Round Table Conference

On 7 February 1935, Jinnah said he had not been invited to the third session of the Conference 'because I was the strongest opponent of the scheme that was being constructed from the commencement'.[56] In March 1936, he said that he was perhaps the most individualist member of the Conference

> I displeased the Muslims. I displeased my Hindu friends because of the famous 14 points. I displeased the princes because I was deadly against their underhand activities and I displeased the British Parliament because I felt right from the beginning and I rebelled against it and said that it was all a fraud. Within a few weeks I did not have a friend left there... My sole and only object has been the welfare of my country. I assure you that India's interest is and will be sacred to me and nothing will make me budge an inch from that position.[57]

Indeed, it was his independence and plain speaking that had displeased the imperialist conveners of the Conference. When the question of membership of the third session was under consideration, Zafrulla Khan was officiating as a member of the viceroy's Executive Council and it fell to him to recommend the list of Muslim delegates. The secretary of state for India, Sir Samuel Hoare, rejected the names of Jinnah and Muhammad Iqbal out of the list. With regard to Jinnah he wrote, 'He vigorously criticizes every proposal but proposes no positive solutions. Now he had taken up permanent residence in London and no longer has any direct concern with Indian affairs'. About Iqbal he said, 'He participated in the second session but did not utter a single word during the proceedings'. Zafrulla insisted that Jinnah and Iqbal must be invited and the viceroy forwarded the recommendation to the secretary of state. In the end the secretary of state agreed that Iqbal be invited but Zafrulla's effort to get Jinnah invited did not succeed.[58]

In a letter dated 5 April 1934 to Viceroy Lord Willingdon, Sir Samuel Hoare revealed his personal animosity for Jinnah in these words: 'Of all the Indians I have met I think I have disliked Jinnah the most. Throughout the Round Table discussions he invariably behaved like a snake, and no one seemed to trust him.'[59]

Resumption and End of Civil Disobedience Movement by Congress and Gandhi's Resignation from the Congress Party

The truce between Congress and the government which had resulted from the Gandhi-Irwin Pact had broken down before Gandhi returned to India after attending the second session of the Round Table Conference. Nehru and some other leaders had been arrested two days before the Mahatma landed at Bombay. Gandhi sought an interview with Willingdon but was informed that the interview could only take place on certain conditions. The Mahatma found the conditions unacceptable.

> It was absolutely clear now that the Government of India had determined to crush the Congress, and would have no dealings with it. The Working Committee had no choice left but resort to civil disobedience...another attempt was made by Gandhiji to see the viceroy, and he sent him a second telegram asking for an unconditional interview. The reply of the government was to arrest Gandhiji... It was clear that whoever else wanted or did not want the struggle, the government was eager and over-ready for it.[60]

Lord Willingdon's government issued numerous Ordinances to suppress the disorder. In 1930 the Ordinances had been promulgated to meet the situation as it developed; now the government took the initiative and passed Ordinances in anticipation of things to come. 'Every conceivable power was given and taken under a batch of all-India and provincial Ordinances,' recalled Nehru, 'organizations were outlawed; buildings, property, automobiles, bank accounts were seized; public gatherings and processions forbidden and newspapers and printing presses fully controlled.' On 26 March 1932, Secretary of State Hoare stated in the House of Commons that drastic and severe Ordinances had been drawn up because 'the government, with the full knowledge at their disposal, sincerely believed that they were threatened with an attack on the whole basis of government and that Ordinances were essential if India was to be prevented from drifting in anarchy'.

Repression had its effect. In January and February, those convicted for political offences numbered 14,800 and 17,800 respectively. In March the figure dropped to 6,900 and continued to fall; in December it came to only 1,540.

As Nehru summed up

> Apart from the severity of Government repression, the first severe blow to it [Civil Disobedience] came in September 1932 when Gandhiji fasted for the first time on the Harijan issue... Civil Disobedience was finally killed for all practical purposes by the suspension of it in May 1933. It continued after that more in theory than in practice...India was numbed by the violence and harshness of repression.[61]

By March 1934 'Civil Disobedience was as dead as a door-nail'.[62]

Gandhi's status as a saint was not openly challenged but his political performance as the dictator of Congress came in for severe criticism. On 9 May 1933, a joint statement by Bose and Vithalbhai Patel declared, 'We are clearly of the opinion that as a political leader Mahatma Gandhi has failed. The time has therefore come for a radical reorganization of the Congress on a new principle and with a new method. For bringing about this reorganization a change of leadership is necessary.'[63] The Mahatma resigned his membership of the Congress at the Bombay session in October 1934. He held out the assurance that his advice and guidance would be available whenever necessary but he never again joined the Congress formally.

Freedom from the party label enabled Gandhi to assume the role of a political conciliator, which enabled him to tell the viceroy and others in subsequent years that he was speaking only for himself and not as the representative of Congress. In this way he could find out, for the benefit of the Congress policy makers, how the other party's mind was working without committing

Congress in any way. But he had no compunction in assuming command of the party whenever the occasion demanded it.

Choudhary Rahmat Ali, 1897-1951

It was Choudhary Rahmat Ali (1897-1951), a Punjabi studying at Emmanuel College, Cambridge, who invented and first used the expression 'Pakistan'[64] in a pamphlet in which he advocated the partition of India into independent Hindu and Muslim states. The title of the pamphlet was 'Now or Never'; it was issued from Cambridge on 28 January 1933. It was principally aimed at the members of the Joint Select Committee which had been appointed after the Round Table Conference to consider the future Constitution of India and was due to commence its sittings in April 1933, but copies were distributed to other influential persons as well. The text had been drafted by Rahmat Ali, but in order to add weight to the representation, he had persuaded three other students to sign it along with himself.

In 'Now or Never' Rahmat Ali expressed his profound disappointment that the Indian Muslim delegation to the Round Table Conference had agreed to the formation of an All-India Federation, thereby 'signing the death warrant of Islam and its future in India'. He claimed that his appeal was being issued 'on behalf of our thirty million Muslim brethren who live in Pakistan—by which we mean the five northern units of India, viz., Punjab, North-West Frontier Province (Afghan Province), Kashmir, Sind and Baluchistan'. He emphasized that the differences between the Hindus and the Muslims in India

> ...are not confined to the broad basic principles—far from it. They extend to the minutest details of our lives. We do not inter-dine; we do not inter-marry. Our national customs and calendars, even our diet and dress are different. It is preposterous to compare, as some superficial observers do, the differences between Muslims and Hindus and those between Roman Catholics and Protestants. Both the Catholics and Protestants are part and parcel of one religious system—Christianity; while the Hindus and Muslims are the followers of two essentially and fundamentally different religious systems.

The Muslims therefore deserved 'and must demand the recognition of a separate national status by the grant of a separate Federal

Constitution from the rest of India'. He contended that constitutional safeguards 'can never be a substitute for the loss of separate nationality' and asked, 'what safeguards can be devised to prevent our minority of one in four in an All-India Federation being sacrificed on every vital issue to the aims and interests of the majority race, which differs from us in every essential of individual and corporate life?'[65]

How did he coin the name Pakistan? In his book *Pakistan* (1947) he explained that he had long agonized over finding a name which would

> ...be charged with an irresistible eternal appeal to the heart and head of all our people, and possessed of elemental power to seize on our being and make us all go out crusading for the *Millat's* mission.[66] I made it the be-all and end-all of my life, and devoted to it every spark of the fire and fervour of my faith, and every particle of what knowledge and enlightenment I possessed. I observed *chillahs* and prayed for Allah's guidance.[67] I did everything that could help the accomplishment of the task, and never lost faith in divine guidance. I carried on till, at last, in His dispensation Allah showed me the light, and led me to the name 'Pakistan' and to the Pak Plan, both of which are now animating the lives of our people.[68]

Rahmat Ali's scheme of Pakistan was discussed by the joint Select Committee. A British member asked whether any of the delegates or witnesses would tell him whether there was a scheme or Federation of Provinces under the name of Pakistan. The comments of three Indian Muslim politicians were: 'As far as I know, it is only a student's scheme; no responsible people have put it forward'; 'So far as we have considered it, we have considered it chimerical and impracticable'; 'Perhaps it will be enough to say that no such scheme has been considered by any representative gentlemen or association so far'.[69]

On 8 March 1940, Rahmat Ali made a statement at Karachi[70] in which he extended his original proposal for only one independent state in the north-west (Pakistan) to three independent Muslim nations in South Asia, the other two being 'Bang-i-Islam' (the Muslim majority area of Bengal and Assam) and 'Usmanistan' (the Princely State of Hyderabad, because it was 'a part of our patrimony' and already enjoyed *de jure* sovereignty based on the Nizam's treaties with the British).

So far so good. He was not yet in conflict with the main stream of Muslim politics. His original idea of Pakistan was largely founded on Iqbal's conception of a large and autonomous Muslim province in the same region. His new demand for three independent states also foreshadowed what actually transpired later. The Muslim League demanded a Pakistan composed of the north-western and north-eastern Muslim-majority areas of India and supported the Nizam's bid for independence.

If Rahmat Ali had confined himself to demanding only three Muslim states and had cooperted with Jinnah and the Muslim League in their struggle for Pakistan, his reputation would have stood much higher today than it does. But driven by his sincere but fanatical notions, he lost his way and proceeded to expand his conception to absurd lengths. Towards the end of 1946 he bitterly castigated Jinnah, calling him 'Quisling-i-Azam' and blaming him for distorting the original conception of Pakistan. He also criticized the Muslim League for striving for a Pakistan which was perverse and puerile. When Jinnah accepted the plan of 3 June 1947, Rahmat Ali likened him to Judas for having 'betrayed, bartered and dismembered the *millat*'. Later in the same month he produced his own alternative to the Pakistan which had been achieved. He called it the 'Pak Plan' and summed it up in the following words

> This is the course of duty, honour, and *mujahidism*. Like all such courses, it is long, it is hard, and it involves struggle, suffering, and sacrifice. But it leads to ultimate triumph. That is to say, it leads among other things to a division, on the basis of population of all the regions of Dinia between the Hindoos and the Muslims—and others; to the unity and recognition of our 100 million Muslims as a single *Millat*, then to their integration in ten nations each in its individual national homeland, i.e., the Muslims of North-West Dinia in Pakistan, of North-East Dinia in Bangistan and the Ashar and Balus Islands, of the Deccan in Osmanistan, of Bundhelkhand and Malwa in Siddiqistan, of Bihar and Orissa in Faruqistan, of Hindoostan in Haidaristan, of Rajistan in Muinistan, of South India in Maplistan and the Alam Islands (to say nothing here of the integration of the Muslims of Western Ceylon and the Ameen Islands in Safistan, and of Eastern Ceylon in Nasaristan); and, finally, to the co-ordination of all these nations in the Pak Commonwealth of Nations.[71]

His contribution to the achievement of Pakistan was in effect limited to providing its name. Nevertheless it was a highly inspirational contribution. The magic word Pakistan which even the illiterate knew meant the Land of the Pure, fired the Muslim masses to demand a separate homeland of their own more than the stock arguments advanced by many professional politicians. His name will remain inscribed on the pages of every book on the history of Pakistan for all time to come. His unfortunate estrangement from the mainstream of Pakistani leadership forced him into political exile. He died of a chill in Cambridge on 20 February 1951 in straitened circumstances.

The Quaid's Self-Imposed Exile in England

In January 1931, Jinnah sent for his daughter Dina and his sister Fatima to take up residence with him in London and began to look round for a suitable residence. He told Reuter in an interview on 2 February that he intended to stay on in England indefinitely to practice in the Privy Council and enter Parliament because he believed that during the coming year India's constitutional battle would be fought in London and he would be more useful there.[72]

Fatima had wound up her clinic upon Ruttie's death in February 1929 and moved into Jinnah's residence and taken charge of its management. From then on she took care of her illustrious brother till his death.

It was only in September 1931 that Jinnah and his family could move into West Heath House which he had purchased from Lady Graham Wood who had found Jinnah 'most charming, a great gentleman, most courteous'.[73] West Heath House was a three-storied villa in West Heath Road. It had a lodge, a drive and eight acres of garden and grounds.

Reuter's report that Jinnah had intended to enter Parliament is not supported by any authoritative evidence; the Quaid personally never mentioned it. His performance at the Round Table Conference did not win him supporters in any of the British political parties. He had demanded Dominion Status for India forthwith and he had displayed too much independence of mind to have fitted into the groove of any established political organization.

At any rate we have two statements of the Quaid himself telling us why he chose to take up residence in London. On 25 March 1931, he wrote to his friend Abdul Matin Chowdhry, 'I have come to the conclusion that I can be more useful here at any rate for the present. The centre of gravity is here and for the next two or three years London will be the most important scene of the Indian drama of constitutional reforms.'[74]

And on 5 February 1938, he explained to the Muslim University Union

> I received the shock of my life at the meetings of the Round Table Conference. In the face of danger the Hindu sentiment, the Hindu mind, the Hindu attitude led me to the conclusion that there was no hope of unity. I felt very pessimistic about my country. The position was most unfortunate. The Mussulmans were like the No Man's Land; they were led by either the flunkeys of the British Government or the camp-followers of the Congress. Whenever attempts were made to organize the Muslims, toadies and flunkeys on the one hand and traitors in the Congress camp on the other frustrated the efforts. I began to feel that neither could I help India, nor change the Hindu mentality, nor could I make the Mussulmans realize their precarious position. I felt so disappointed and so depressed that I decided to settle down in London. Not that I did not love India; but I felt utterly helpless. I kept in touch with India. At the end of four years I found that the Mussulmans were in the greatest danger. I made up my mind to come back to India, as I could not do any good from London.[75]

Meanwhile in India, the Muslims remained divided. With new constitutional reforms in the offing, some of the Muslim politicians began to feel that they must present a united front in order to make the most of the increased opportunities.

In 1933 the Aziz Group and the Hidayat Group held separate sessions both under the caption 'All-India Muslim League, Twenty-third Session'. The Aziz Group convened at Howrah on 21 October and the Hidayat Group at Delhi on 25-26 November. Presiding over his own Group, Mian Aboul Aziz said

> While far-reaching changes in the system of administration in our country, which will produce, in some cases, momentous results, are in the process of accomplishment, the League, which was expressly

brought into being with the object of consolidating Muslim effort in India, is itself passing through a crisis of the first magnitude.[76]

He said in the multiplicity of organizations, 'no matter what their labels, lurks political disaster'. He appealed to the Muslims of India 'to make the League a Parliament of all Muslims in India, so that it may speak with authority in their name'.[77] Hafiz Hidyat Husain in his presidential address similarly stated that 'efforts must be directed towards bringing all Muslims under the banner of the League'.[78] A resolution passed by the Hidayat Group approved of the proposal of 'certain Muslim leaders of the Punjab suggesting that advantage should be taken of the expected presence in this country of H. H. the Aga Khan and Mr M. A. Jinnah to hold a convention in some suitable place for the purpose of bringing unity in the ranks of the League', and expressed readiness 'to accept, at all times and under all circumstances, the guidance and advice of such revered and trusted leaders of the community as the two above-named gentlemen'.[79]

Notes

1. Pirzada, *Collected Works*, III, op.cit., p. 257. For the text of the Jinnah-Irwin correspondence *see,* ibid., pp. 257-82.
2. Quoted in the *Report of the Indian Statutory Commission,* Vol. I, Cmd., 3568, p. 27.
3. Ibid., p. 28.
4. For a full account of the continuing Civil War *see, The British Raj in India,* by the present authors, pp. 245-50.
5. Quoted by Kanji Dwarkadas, *India's Fight for Freedom,* op.cit., p. 327.
6. For the text of Irwin's declaration of 31 October 1929 *see,* Gwyer and Appadori, *Speeches and Documents of the Indian Constitution,* I, pp. 225-7.
7. For the text of Jinnah's letter to MacDonald and of MacDonald's reply *see,* Pirzada, *Collected Works,* III op.cit., pp. 365-71.
8. *The Life of F.E. Smith, First Earl of Birkenhead,* by his son the Second Earl of Birkenhead, p. 522.
9. Pirzada, *Collected Works,* III, op.cit., p. 418-20.
10. For the text of Nehru's address *see,* A. M. Zaidi, *The Encyclopaedia of The Indian National Congress,* IX, op. cit., pp. 601-18.
11. Ibid., p. 569.
12. Pirzada, *Collected Works,* III, op.cit., pp. 421-2.
13. *Autobiography,* p. 210.
14. On the banks of the River Sabarmati near Ahmadabad.
15. *Times of India,* 24 April 1930 quoted by R. Coupland, *The Indian Problem*

(1933-1935), op.cit., p. 111.
16. Subhas Chandra Bose, *The Indian Struggle*, op. cit., p. 179.
17. *Report*, II, p. 16.
18. Ibid., p. 146.
19. Ibid., p. 63.
20. For the text of the correspondence from which we have quoted *see*, Pirzada, *Collected Works*, III, op.cit., pp. 272-81.
21. Indian Round Table Conference, 12 November 1930-19 January 1931, Proceedings Cmd., 3778, p. 41.
22. Ibid., p. 335.
23. Ibid., p. 507.
24. Ibid., p. 508.
25. Ibid., p. 149.
26. Ibid., p. 64.
27. Ibid., p. 147.
28. Ibid., p. 147.
29. Ibid., p. 146.
30. Pirzada, *Collected Works*, III, op.cit., p. 564.
31. Ibid., Cmd., 3778, p. 98.
32. Ibid., p. 102.
33. A. M. Zaidi, *Evolution of Muslim Political Thought in India*, IV, op. cit., p. 67.
34. Ibid., p. 71.
35. S. Hasan Ahmad, *Iqbal, His Political Ideas at Crossroads*, p. 80.
36. A. M. Zaidi, *Evolution of Muslim Political Thought in India*, IV, op. cit., p. 80.
37. Ibid., p. 79.
38. Ibid., pp. 749-51.
39. Waheed Ahmad, *Quaid-i-Azam Mohammad Ali Jinnah, The Nation's Voice (March 1935-March 1940)*, op. cit., p. 250.
40. P. Sitaramayya, *The History of the Indian National Congress*, I, op.cit., pp. 437-8.
41. Ibid., p. 443.
42. M. H. Saiyid, *Mohammad Ali Jinnah*, 1945, op. cit., pp. 504-6.
43. Indian Round Table Conference (Second Session) Proceedings of Federal Structure Committee and Minorities Committee), p. 387.
44. Ibid., p. 528.
45. Ibid., p. 530.
46. Ibid., p. 531.
47. Ibid., p. 534.
48. Ibid., p. 536.
49. Ibid., p. 530.
50. Ibid., p. 537.
51. Ibid., p. 543.
52. Congress officially stood for 'complete independence' but the Mahatma seemed to settle for Dominion Status. In fact he was personally willing to accept Dominion Status at least till 1 January 1937. *See*, Polak, Brailsford, Lord Pethic-Lawrence, *Mahatma Gandhi*, op.cit., p. 75 n. 2.

53. For the text of Gandhi's address to the Plenary Meeting on 30 November 1931 *see*, *Indian Round Table Conference (7 September-1 December 1931)*, pp. 389-99.
54. Sir Reginald Coupland, *India, A Re-statement*, p. 140.
55. Indian Round Table Conference (7 Sept.-1 Dec. 1931) pp. 417-8.
56. Jamil-UD-Din Ahmed, *Speeches and Writings of Mr Jinnah*, I, p. 3.
57. Waheed Ahmad, *Quaid-i-Azam Mohammad Ali Jinnah, The Nation's Voice (March 1935-March 1940)*, pp. 26-27.
58. This account is taken from p. 322 of Zafrulla Khan's reminiscences in Urdu published under the title *Tahdis-i-Nimat* (an Acknowledgement of Blessing). It has been translated into English by the authors.
59. *Sir Samuel Hoare Collection*, MSS Eur 20, Vol. IV. pp. 1027-9.
60. Jawaharlal Nehru, *Autobiography*, op.cit., p. 321.
61. Ibid., pp. 338-9.
62. Subhas Chandra Bose, *The Indian Struggle*, op.cit., p. 265.
63. For the text of the Bose-Patel Manifesto, *see*, ibid., p. 357.
64. The letter 'i' in the name Pakistan was added later. In an interview with Mountbatten on 17 May 1947, Jinnah explained the derivation of the word Pakistan as follows: 'P for Punjab; A for Afghan (i.e., Pathan or NWFP); K for Kashmir; I for nothing because this letter was not in the word in Urdu; S for Sind and TAN for the last syllable in Baluchistan'.
65. For the text of 'Now or Never' *see*, K. K. Aziz, *Complete Works of Rahmat Ali*, I, pp. 5-10.
66. *Millat:* Nation.
67. *Chillah:* A forty-day period of seclusion and prayer for the fulfilment of a wish.
68. Choudhary Rahmat Ali, *Pakistan*, pp. 224-5.
69. *Joint Committee on Indian Constitutional Reform*, Volume 11C, Minutes of Evidence, pp. 1496-7. The last answers was given by Khalifa Shujauddin. The names of the persons who gave the first two answers are not mentioned.
70. Afterwards issued in pamphlet form under the title, 'The Millat of Islam and the Menace of "Indianism".'
71. Choudhary Rahmat Ali, *Pakistan*, op.cit., p. 370.
72. Sharif AL Mujahid, *Quaid-i-Azam and His Times*, p. 143.
73. Hector Bolitho, *Jinnah*, op. cit., p. 101.
74. Syed Sharifuddin Pirzada, *Quaid-e-Azam Jinnah's Correspondence*, p. 21.
75. Jamil-UD-Din Ahmad, *Speeches and Writings of Mr Jinnah*, I, op. cit., pp. 41-42.
76. Pirzada, *Foundations of Pakistan*, II, op. cit., p. 197.
77. Ibid., p. 202.
78. Ibid., p. 211.
79. Ibid., p. 226.

CHAPTER 10

The Quaid-i-Azam at the Helm 1934-1939

The split in the ranks of the Muslim League was at last mended on 4 March 1934 when at a combined meeting of the Hidayat and Aziz groups held in New Delhi under the presidency of Hidayat Husain, a resolution was passed that the cleavage be made up and Jinnah be elected president of the united body.[1]

The Quaid Resumes His Mission of Forging Hindu-Muslim Unity

Jinnah presided over the Council of the All-India Muslim League at New Delhi on 1-2 April 1934. One of the resolutions stated that 'The League should accept the Communal Award as far as it went, until a substitute was agreed upon by the various communities, and on that basis express its readiness for cooperation with other communities and parties to secure such a future Constitution for India as would be acceptable to the country'.[2]

Giving his impression of the Council meeting, Jinnah told the Associated Press that it was the most representative that he had ever seen during his connection with the League extending to over twenty years. He said,

> Nothing will give me greater happiness, than to bring about complete cooperation and friendship between Hindus and Muslims...Muslims are in no way behind any other community in their demand for national self-government. The crux of the whole issue, therefore, is: can we completely assure Muslims that the safeguards to which they attach vital importance will be embodied in the future Constitution of India?[3]

The Himalayan Odds Facing the Quaid

Jinnah's political career from 1934, when he returned to Indian politics, till 1948, when he died, was one of an amazing fight against impossible odds. He first renewed his endeavour to achieve his long-standing dream of a united independent India based on a political Hindu-Muslim concord after the fashion of the Lucknow Pact. In this he failed through no fault of his own, as we shall demonstrate. Then he struggled to win a separate independent homeland for the Muslims of India. Everyone believed this to be an impossible ambition and it was nothing short of a miracle that he succeeded. Before we narrate the events of these tempestuous years, it would be relevant for us to point out the Himalayan difficulties he had to surmount. It is only by bearing these in mind that the reader can appreciate the magnitude of his effort and crowning glory.

A major handicap under which he laboured throughout this period was ill-health. His respiratory system had begun visibly to deteriorate from 1927: 'Delhi winters did not suit him; and he often suffered from severe attacks of cold and flu. In spite of his poor health he attended the Assembly...and devoted most of his time and energy to political activities.[4] In March 1934 not long after his return to India after a self-imposed exile in London, he was taken seriously ill. Kanji Dwarkadas gives the following firsthand account of what had happened

> One evening in March, 1934, Jinnah rang me up and asked me to see him at 10.30 next morning in his High Court Chamber. I went at the appointed time but Jinnah did not turn up. This was quite unlike him as he was always in the High Court punctually at 10.30. I rang up his house and his bearer told me that Jinnah had taken seriously ill late the night before. For five days he was unconscious and hovered between life and death—it was just touch and go, as the attack he had was likely to affect the heart. On the very day that he regained consciousness, I called at his house. He saw me immediately and kept on talking to me for over half an hour, much to the dislike of his medical attendants.[5]

In December 1938 the Quaid was due to preside over the Twenty-sixth Session of the Muslim League at Patna. Before arriving there on 24 December, he telegraphed that plans for the presidential procession be abandoned because of his 'ill health'. When he was driven away from the railway station he looked weak but was cheerful and smiling.[6] In the course of his presidential address he said, 'You will have to forgive me for having made the speech extempore. My health did not permit my writing out my speech.'[7]

His sister, Fatima, who was his constant companion, tells us that nature had gifted her brother 'with a giant's strength in so far as his determination to achieve the tasks that he had set for himself were concerned, but it had clothed his will in a frail body, unable to keep pace with the driving force of his restless mind and will'.[8] When she begged him to give up temporarily his constant and whirlwind tours that carried him from one end of India to another, he would say, 'Have you ever heard of a general take a holiday, when his army is fighting for its very survival on a battlefield?' When she pleaded that his life was precious and he must take good care of it, he would say, with a distant look in his eyes, 'What is the health of one individual, when I am concerned with the very existence of ten crore Muslims of India?' And 'he plunged himself deeper and deeper into the stormy ocean of political struggle to the utter neglect of his health'.[9]

Early in November 1940 brother and sister left Bombay by train for Delhi where he was to attend the Assembly session. During the course of the journey, as he lay on the berth 'he suddenly shouted aloud, as if somebody had pierced him with a red hot iron...the severity of the pain had benumbed his power of speech, and all he could do was to point with his finger to a spot a little below the spinal cord and to the right side of it'. When the train stopped at a station, Fatima procured a hot water bottle with the help of the guard and applied it on the painful spot. This relieved the pain to some extent. On reaching Delhi, his ailment was diagnosed to be pleurisy. The doctor ordered about a fortnight's rest but Jinnah stayed in bed for only two days and went back to work. Fatima believed that the attack of pleurisy 'was the beginning of the sickness that ultimately claimed his life'.[10]

A few months afterwards (April 1941) the brother and sister were travelling together by train to Madras where he was to preside over the Twenty-eighth Session of the Muslim League.

During the journey he got up but after taking a few steps collapsed on the floor of the compartment. He wobbled back to his berth with the help of his sister. Luckily, the train halted at a junction after a few minutes. A doctor was found who examined him and said, 'Sir, you have had a nervous breakdown'. The doctor advised rest for at least one week. At Madras he felt too weak on the first day of the session (12 April) to deliver an address but insisted on doing so on 14 April. His sister tried to dissuade him but to no avail. She then begged him to be brief. He assured her that he would be 'very brief' but he spoke extempore continuously for nearly two hours.[11]

In the course of his presidential address to the Karachi session of the League (December 1943), 'he coughed four or five times which showed he had a cold'.[12]

Wavell recorded in his *Journal* under the date 10 March 1945, 'Jinnah who was to have seen me on March 7 is sick, I am told that he has a touch of pleurisy and may be laid up for some time'.

During his negotiations with the Cabinet Misson, the Quaid was constantly ill. Dr Jal Patel who examined him in May 1946 diagnosed: 'Again it was bronchitis. It is always bronchitis. He had a temperature for ten days. It is possible that he had always had lung trouble: he was completely exhausted, weak and tired.'[13]

On his return from the London Conference in December 1946 Jinnah felt exhausted and suffered from a nervous breakdown for a whole month.'[14]

M. A. H. Ispahani, who was a close associate of Jinnah, told Stanley Wolpert in an interview in 1978 that Jinnah 'was always coughing, smoking and coughing. We thought it just "smoker's cough" or bronchitis. None of us realized how bad it was—until it was too late.'[15] He had always been a heavy smoker, smoking about fifty cigarettes a day. His favourite brand was Craven A.[16]

> The seven years before the establishment of Pakistan were the busiest and stormiest that he encountered in all his life... To me, who was always with him, it was a common sight to see him get up from a sick bed with difficulty, looking worn out and exhausted... As he surveyed the seething mass of humanity that sat in their tens of thousands on bare earth to listen to him, he would speak to them in a voice that showed no trace of age or ill-health... Little did the

people know how tired, worn out, exhausted, and how sick he was. He was their hero and how can one blame a hero for being heroic?[17]

He was 5 feet 11$^1/_2$ inches tall but even normally a mere 112 pounds in weight. He was losing weight 'ounce by ounce but showed supreme indifference to such private matters as his personal health'.[18]

Fortunately, he had the capacity to sleep at will but 'with the approach of dawn came fresh letters, fresh requests, new problems, and weighty decisions to be made'. He kept up this feverish tempo of life in spite of the 'recurring bouts of fever that emaciated his body'.[19] By the time his dream of Pakistan was realized, he was a dying hero. He had truly sacrificed his own life so that the Muslims of India should have an independent homeland of their own.

On his return to Indian politics in 1934 he failed to achieve a political pact with Congress similar to the Lucknow Pact because a lot of water had flowed under the bridge since 1916. At that earlier time the League as well as the Congress were elite bodies with predominantly conciliatory attitudes. The leading figure in Congress was Tilak, the practical politician. Jinnah revealed in 1926 that the Lucknow Pact was not made at the request of the Muslim League: 'The initiative came from the Congress'.[20] Since then the League had gone downhill and became a house divided against itself. It had again come under one flag in 1934 but its membership was still limited. It had no influence comparable to that of Congress which under Gandhi had become a well-organized mass party. Congress no longer felt the need to make a pact with any other party. At the Round Table Conference, the Mahatma had made it abundantly clear that Congress claimed to represent the whole of India, that Congress stood for immediate independence and that Congress demanded that Britain should hand over power solely to Congress. After World War II had broken out, Congress utilized Britain's difficult position as an opportunity for wresting its objectives without further delay.

It was not till the Bombay session of the Muslim League in 1936 that the programme and policy of the rejuvenated League was laid down. The position that obtained in 1936 was described by the Quaid during his presidential address at the Patna Session (26 December 1938) in the following terms:

Of the intelligentsia of the Muslims who were in the forefront of what is called political life, most—I do not say all—were careerists. They chose their place according to their convenience either in the bureaucratic camp or in the other camp, that is, the Congress camp. Those who thought that they could better their position by joining the bureaucratic camp joined the same. The others thought they could get position and power in the Congress camp and joined that camp. Their object was how best to make careers for themselves. So far as the masses were concerned and so far as my dear young friends, the Muslim youths, were concerned, they were all hypnotized by the Congress falsehood. The youth believe in slogans and catchwords. They were caught right in the net that was spread for them by the Congress. They were led into the belief that the Congress was fighting for the freedom of the motherland. Being honest themselves they could not believe that other people could be otherwise.[21]

What is the difference between the Hindus and the Muslims? Jinnah asked in a speech on 5 February 1938. And he answered

If Wardha makes any decision and issues orders tomorrow, millions of Hindus will follow and obey. I ask you, suppose the Muslim League were to issue any order, what will happen to it? We are not sufficiently equipped and trained, and therefore it will be difficult to produce *laks* of Muslims to carry out orders.[22]

He could have added also that the Hindus were far ahead of the Muslims in education, economic power and ownership of newspapers.

Gandhi, moreover, had a team of high calibre leaders to assist or even replace him, while Jinnah carried the burden of the League leadership virtually single-handed. as Beverly Nichols pointed out in his *Verdict on India*, 'If Gandhi goes, there is always Nehru or Rajagopalachari, or Patel or a dozen others. But if Jinnah goes, who is there?'

Amazingly, until December 1943, the Muslim League did not have a central organization or secretariat to assist the Quaid-i-Azam. At the Karachi session of the League that month, he pleaded

Now the work of the Muslim League organization has grown beyond the physical capacity of any single man. If you were to know what I have to attend to all alone, you would be astonished. All over India—today this thing happening in Patna, tomorrow that thing happening in Bengal, day after tomorrow this thing happening in the NWFP, day after that thing happening in Madras. All sorts of questions arise from day to day and from week to week. Now it is not possible for one single man to do justice to all this.

'A committee with a Secretariat', he said was urgently needed. A Committee of six was accordingly appointed to 'undertake immediately the work of organizing, co-ordinating and unifying the Provincial Leagues and the entire Muslim League organization'.[23]

The odds against Jinnah's winning Pakistan were incalculable. The Hindus and the British at first dismissed the demand out of hand. The Lahore Resolution of March 1940, asking for partition, had not mentioned the word Pakistan. It was the Hindu Press that dubbed it Pakistan by way of ridicule, recalling Rahmat Ali's scheme of that name which had been lightly rejected as a 'student's scheme'. Even after Pakistan had been achieved the Congress and the British leaders expressed the hope that the two parts of the Indian subcontinent would be reunited before long. That the Labour Party, which had never made a secret of its friendship for the Congress, had come into power in July 1945 made Jinnah's task impossible. When Viceroy Wavell went to London for consultations in August he found that the Labour leaders were 'obviously bent on handing over India to their Congress friends as soon as possible'.[24]

The Act of 1935

The British Government's proposals arising from the deliberations of the three sessions of the London Round Table Conference were published as a White Paper in March 1933. After Parliament had approved the White Paper, it set up a Joint Select Committee for making the recommendations on which a bill could be drafted. The Committee came into existence on 11 April 1933 and after 159 sittings produced its report on 22 November 1934. On 19 December a bill was introduced on the basis of that report and eventually received the Royal Assent on 4 August 1935, under the title of the Government of India Act 1935. The Act came into force on 1 April 1937.

Constitutionally, only members of Parliament could be members of the Joint Select Committee and sixteen from each House were chosen to serve on it. They were assisted by twenty representatives from British India and seven from princely India. Their status was that of assessors but they were allowed to take part in general discussions and examine witnesses. The Committee was chaired by Lord Linlithgow, who had previously presided over the Royal Commission on Indian Agriculture and was appointed Viceroy of India in April 1936.[25] Die-hard Conservatives led by Winston Churchill in the Commons and Lord Salisbury in the Lords opposed the reforms at every stage and were largely blamed for retarding the legislative process.

The Act separated Burma from India and created two new provinces: Sind by separation from Bombay, and Orissa by separation from Bihar. Both the new provinces were given the same status as the older by making them Governors Provinces.

Diarchy was abolished in the provinces but it was introduced at the Centre. In the provinces the ministers responsible to the legislature were to have control over all provincial subjects except that the governor was to act 'in his discretion' in certain matters and 'exercise his individual judgement' mainly in the discharge of his special responsibilities, the more important of which were: the prevention of any grave menace to the peace and tranquillity of the province; safeguarding the legitimate interests of the minorities; the protection of the rights of civil servants and those of the States and their rulers; and the prevention of discrimination against British commercial interests. The governor was also authorized (under Section 93) to assume all powers of government in the event of a breakdown of the constitutional machinery. While discharging his 'discretionary' functions and 'special responsibilities', he could refuse assent to a bill, promulgate an ordinance which would be valid for six months or enact a Governor's Act which would have the same validity as an Act of the legislature.

The property qualification for the voters electing members of the provincial legislatures was lowered, giving the right to vote to thirty-five million persons. This was five times the number previously entitled to vote and about one-fourth of the number who would have been so entitled had adult suffrage been granted. The communal distribution of seats followed the 'Communal

Award'. The systems of separate electorates and weightage were retained.

Part II of the Act, providing for the establishment of a federal government at the centre, was to come into force only after Princely States whose population would aggregate half the total population of all the States had acceded to the federation. A State was deemed to have acceded to the federation after its ruler had executed an Instrument of Accession. The federal government and legislature could exercise authority over the affairs of a State only within the limitations set out in the instruments of accession. Paramountcy or treaty relationship with the British Government was to be the concern of the Crown Representative (an additional title for the governor-general). This was consonant with the Butler Committee's recommendation that: 'In view of the historical nature of the relationship between the Paramount Power and the princes, the latter should not be transferred without their own agreement to a relationship with a new government in British India responsible to an Indian legislature'.

The Act provided for a bicameral legislature at the Centre, and the Princely States were given weightage in both. The upper house—the Council of State—was to have 156 members from the States; the lower house—the Federal Assembly—was to consist of 250 members from British India and not more than 125 from the States. The States' representatives were to be nominated by the rulers.

Ministers responsible to the legislature were to administer most subjects, but not defence and external affairs, which were to be administered by the governor-general with the help of Councillors responsible only to himself. The governor-general had legislative powers similar to those of the governors. His 'special responsibilities' were also similar to those of the governors except that he had the additional responsibility to safeguard 'the financial stability and credit of the Federal Government'.

Since not even a single State had acceded to the federation by the time the Act of 1935 was superseded by the Indian Independence Act of 1947, the federation in fact never materialized; the Centre continued to be administered under the Act of 1919. Both the British Government and Congress were responsible for this delay.

It was not till 1939 that the viceroy could communicate to the rulers the terms on which the government would regard their accession as acceptable, and negotiations were suspended when World War II broke out. Congress made no secret of the fact that it regarded the princes as a reactionary element whom the British were using to buttress British imperialism; it saw no reason why the people in princely India should not demand the same freedom as the people in British India were striving for. When provincial autonomy under the new Act came into force in 1937, the contrast between the systems of government in the two Indias became even more marked than before, and propaganda against the princes both within their own territories and outside was stepped up. The princes feared that the Crown representative, who would be the same person as the governor-general, responsible to the federal legislature, would not be able to defend their rights effectively. They saw no point in joining such a federation.

The Constitution under the Act of 1935 was a far cry from the promised goal of Dominion Status: the key portfolios of External Affairs and Defence remained under foreign control and the governor-general and the governors, in whose appointments and removals the legislatures had no hand and who were not responsible to the legislatures, could veto laws passed by the legislatures and, under certain circumstances, could themselves promulgate Ordinances or enact Acts.[26] Nor was it lost on anyone that the Centre was so constructed that the conservative elements such as the princes, the Muslims and the Scheduled Castes[27] could thwart the Indian National Congress, which in organization and numbers was the most important political party in the country.

Clement Attlee, the Labour leader who had been a member of the Simon Commission and was to preside over the Transfer of Power to India in August 1947 as prime minister, protested in his speech on the bill in the House of Commons on 4 June 1935

> This bill...is deliberately framed so as to exclude as far as possible the Congress party from effective power in the new Constitution. On many occasions provisions have been deliberately put forward with that end in view...the government have yielded time after time to the States and time after time to the minority communities, but have always stood strongly up against any yielding to Congress or Nationalists... Is the bill going to be worked by the people of India?

I do not think so. The indications are that if it is going to be worked at all it will be in a grudging spirit and that it is only too likely that its provisions will be used not for seeing how far it can be made useful for self-government but as a means of getting something more.[28]

The Attitude of the Congress Toward the Reforms

Congress had declared its own alternative to proposals contained in the White Paper. A Working Committee resolution, passed in June 1934 and confirmed at the full session in October 1934, read

> The White Paper in no way expresses the will of the people of India, has been more or less condemned by almost all the Indian political parties and falls short of the Congress goal if it does not retard the progress towards it. The only satisfactory alternative to the White Paper is a Constitution drawn up by a Constituent Assembly elected on the basis of adult suffrage or as near it was possible, with the power, if necessary, to the important minorities to have their representatives elected exclusively by the electors belonging to such minorities.[29]

After the Act had been passed, Congress totally rejected it in the following terms

> Whereas the Government of India Act, 1935, which is based on the White Paper and Joint Parliamentary Report and which is in many respects even worse than the proposals contained in them, in no way represents the will of the nation, is designed to facilitate and perpetuate the domination and exploitation of the people of India and is imposed on the country to the accompaniment of widespread repression and the suppression of civil liberties, the Congress reiterates its rejection of the new Constitution in its entirety.[30]

The resolution also repeated the demand for a Constituent Assembly.

Jinnah's Attitude Toward the Reforms and His Unceasing Efforts to Achieve Hindu-Muslim Unity

It took the Quaid some time to wind up his establishment in London. After the Muslim League Council meeting in early April

1934, he was due to sail for London on 23 April but had to postpone his departure because of illness. He left on 24 May. In October, while still abroad, he was elected unopposed to the Indian Legislative Assembly from the Bombay Muslim constituency. He returned to Bombay in December and attended the Assembly session in February 1935. In April he left for England once more and stayed there till October. It was while he was in London that the King gave his Assent to the Act of 1935.

The report of the Joint Select Committee had been published in November 1934. It was debated in the Assembly in the first week of February 1935. During the debate Jinnah said, 'Speaking for myself, personally, I am not satisfied with the Communal Award, and, again, speaking as an individual, my self-respect will never be satisfied until we produce our own scheme'. With regard to the Constitution that was being hammered out in London he said, 'It is bad as far as provinces go: and the Central Scheme is totally bad.' His alternative was 'Modify the Provincial Scheme, drop the Central Scheme and review the whole situation in consultation with Indian opinion with a view to establishing complete responsible government in British India'.[31]

Speaking at a Delhi college on 18 February 1935 he reiterated that if he could achieve communal unity 'half the battle of the country's freedom is won... So long as Hindus and Muslims are not united, let me tell you, there is no hope for India and we shall both remain slaves of foreign domination'.[32]

To bring about communal harmony, Jinnah entered into negotiations with Rajendra Prasad, the then president of the Congress. So keen was he for success of these talks that he 'absented himself from the debates of the Assembly so as to be free to take part in these conversations'.[33] But the effort failed to bring about the desired result.

While explaining the political situation to the students of Bombay in April 1935, the Quaid regretted that 'the [Hindu] Mahasabha was dominated by the one consideration—the main consideration—that in India there should be complete supremacy and ascendancy of Hindus'. He expressed the hope that the leaders of the Congress with their wider experience and very good training would overcome that section and assure the Muslims that 'it is not going to be a Hindu Government but an Indian Government in which the Muslims will not only have a fair and just treatment but also that they will be treated as the equals of the Hindus'.[34]

The Quaid Defuses the Shahidganj Crisis

In February 1936, Jinnah's diplomatic talents were tested by a potentially explosive crisis over Shahidganj, a mosque in Lahore which the Sikhs had taken over. The Muslims had resorted to civil disobedience and the Sikhs had organized a counter-movement. The Quaid was requested to mediate and travelled to Lahore for the purpose arriving on 21 February. He announced that he had come as 'a conciliator and peacemaker' and not 'in a partisan spirit'.

The Muslims suspended the civil disobedience movement in deference to his wishes and at his suggestion the Punjab Government released the Muslims who had been interned under criminal law. The Sikh leaders too promised cooperation. Referring to the suspension of the civil disobedience movement by the Muslims, Jinnah said in one of his speeches

> We took this decision, not because we were afraid, nor at anybody's bidding, but because after a careful review of the situation and my consultations with representatives of various sections of Muslims we became convinced that it was in the best interests of our cause to give up civil disobedience. We shall pursue our remedies through constitutional and peaceful methods.

At another meeting Jinnah referred to his continuous efforts to solve communal problems in India and assured the audience, 'I will not and I cannot give it up. It may give me up. I will not.'

He left Lahore on 7 March after nominating a Conciliation Committee consisting of Muslim, Sikh and Hindu leaders to build on the foundation he had laid. The governor of the Punjab said in a speech at a dinner on the same evening that he was 'greatly indebted to the efforts of Mr Jinnah for this improvement [in the situation] and I wish to pay an unqualified tribute to the work he has done and is doing'.[35]

The Twenty-Fourth Session of the All-Indian Muslim League, Bombay, 11-12 April 1936

No regular sessions of the Muslim League were held during 1934 and 1935. Though Jinnah was the president of the League, he invited Syed Wazir Hasan a former judge of the Oudh Chief Court to preside over the proceedings in April 1936.

In his presidential address, Wazir Hasan recited the shortcomings of the Government of India Act. He said that it should 'be borne in mind that the Hindus and the Mussulmans inhabiting this vast continent are not two communities, but should be considered two nations in many respects'; but he did not ask for Pakistan. In conformity with the League's policy under Jinnah at that time, he ended up by suggesting that a letter be issued by the presidents of the Congress and the League to all other political organizations to settle an annual programme of action and draft a Constitution for India.

Upon the Quaid's motion, the following resolution was passed

> The All-India Muslim League enters its emphatic protest against forcing the Constitution as embodied in the Government of India Act of 1935, upon the people of India against their will... The League considers that, having regard to the conditions prevailing at present in the country, the Provincial Scheme of the Constitution be utilized for what it is worth... The League is clearly of the opinion that the All-India Federal Scheme of the Central Government...is fundamentally bad...and is totally unacceptable.

In moving the resolution, Jinnah said that India received two per cent responsibility and ninty-eight per cent safeguards plus special powers to the governor-general. He said there were four major parties in India: the British, the princes, the Hindus and the Muslims. The British wished to maintain their raj in India and the princes did not want any democratic government. The object of the Hindus and the Muslims was common to a certain extent. The Muslims were as ready as any Hindu to struggle for freedom. But the Muslims were a minority community. It was not a religious question. It was a question whether they should or should not have sufficient safeguards which would inspire confidence in them, so that they too could wholeheartedly join with the sister communities in the march for freedom.

Unfortunately, there was no agreement between the Hindus and the Muslims. He said the Muslims should organize themselves and compel the Congress to approach them for cooperation. He believed that if eighty million Muslims could unite, they could arrive at a settlement with Hindus as two nations, if not as partners.

As to compelling the British Government to modify the Constitution, he said armed revolution was an impossibility, while non-cooperation had been tried and found a failure. This only left constitutional agitation. But it could not be done by one community. It required all communities to stand shoulder to shoulder.

Another resolution stated

> ...whereas in order to strengthen the solidarity of the Muslim community and to secure for the Muslims their proper and effective share in the Provincial Governments, it is essential that the Muslims should organize themselves as one party, with an advanced and progressive programme. It is hereby resolved that the All-India Muslim League do take steps to contest the approaching Provincial elections, and for this purpose appoint Mr Jinnah to a Central Election Board under his presidentship, consisting of not less than 35 members, with powers to constitute and affiliate Provincial Election Boards in various provinces.[36]

At a public speech on 8 January 1937, the Quaid said that the Lucknow Pact stood out as a landmark in the political history of India and if the Muslims were able to settle their differences once, he saw no reason why the same could not be achieved again.[37]

The Muslim League Manifesto, 11 June 1937

To fight the elections due in December 1936-January 1937, the Muslim League issued its Election Manifesto in June 1936. Essentially, it reflected the lines already chalked out by Jinnah at various times. It referred to the Lucknow Pact as 'one of the greatest beacon lights in the constitutional history of India'. It went on to say that the League had always stood for full responsible government for India and 'unflinchingly' stood for the same ideal.

It declared that the Federal Scheme of the Act of 1935 was fundamentally bad and totally unacceptable but laid down that the Provincial Scheme should be utilized for what it was worth. It promised that the Muslim League Party would freely cooperate in the various legislatures with any group or groups whose aims and ideals are approximately the same as those of the League Party.

And it concluded by stating that the League stood for the protection of Muslim rights; the repeal of repressive laws; the rejection of measures which encroached upon the fundamental liberties of the people and led to economic exploitation of the country; the nationalization of the army; and the social, educational and economic development of the rural population.[38]

During a public speech at Nagpur on 1 January 1937, the Quaid again stressed that Hindus and Muslims must stand together for the freedom of their motherland and promised that the Muslim League members in the new legislatures would cooperate with other progressive groups for the uplift and freedom of their motherland.[39]

Election Results

Both the Congress and the League had reason to be satisfied with the result. Overall, out of a total of 1,585 seats in the provincial lower houses, the Congress won no less than 711 seats. It scored clear majorities in five provinces—Madras, the United Provinces, the Central Provinces, Bihar and Orissa. It took nearly half the seats in Bombay and enjoyed the support of some friendly groups to give it a majority. In Assam it was the strongest party. In the North-West Frontier Province it secured nineteen out of fifty seats. In Bengal its share was sixty out of 250. In the Punjab it could win only eighteen out of 175 seats and in Sind only eight out of sixty.

Jinnah reviewed the election result in a press interview on 28 February 1937. He pointed out that the League had fought the elections without an effective organization. Even so, the League had captured fifty per cent of the Muslim seats. In the United Provinces twenty-nine out of thirty-five League candidates had been successful and in Madras ten out of eleven. In Bombay two-thirds of the Muslims seats in the Assembly had gone to the League.

In the Punjab the Unionist Party, a Muslim-Hindu-Sikh coalition won no less than ninety-six out of 175 seats. Though most of its members were Muslims, the party was not identified with the League.

It was the Punjab and Bengal that were to cause Jinnah the worst headaches. Under the system of weightage they had lost the majorities which their population gave them. Their prime ministers had to jockey for coalition with non-Muslims. In a letter to Jinnah (21 June 1937), Iqbal pointed out that under the new Constitution 'even in the Muslim majority provinces, the Muslims are made entirely dependent on non-Muslims'.

Interestingly, Jawaharlal Nehru and Sir Stafford Cripps, a leading member of the Labour Party in the United Kingdom who was to play a leading role in the final phase of India's progress toward freedom, had been in friendly touch with each other during this period. On 22 February 1937, Nehru wrote to Cripps on what he considered to be the significance of Congress's successes at the polls: 'the really significant feature of the election campaign has been the shaking up of the masses'. Cripps responded on 3 March. He congratulated Congress on the 'splendid victories' it had won and said, 'we shall all await with the most profound interest...the attitude you propose to take as regards the operation of the India Act. I am certain that you will maintain the most rigid opposition to imperialism in all its forms and also against the many Fascist methods which are being adopted in India today'. Eleven days later Cripps followed up his letter with a cable to Nehru containing his advice on the question of office acceptance

> We trust that the Indian people will not be led into any compromise over the new Constitution and that the elected representatives will use the power entrusted to them by the people to work for the establishment of freedom by refusing to partake of the empty fruits of office which can do nothing but poison the pure and free spirit of Congress. We salute you as brothers and sisters in the common cause of freedom.[40]

Congress Spurns Jinnah's Olive Branch

After the election, Jinnah repeated his offer of cooperation more than once. At a public speech on 13 March 1937, for example, he said that there was no difference between the Congress and the Muslims except that the latter stood for the establishment of the rights of the minority community. He declared that his heart was pulsating for the freedom of the country. Genuine unity between the Muslims and Hindus was only possible when both the communities had 'developed a better mind by an internal organization'.[41]

But Congress was in no mood to budge from its arrogant stand that it represented all the communities of India and was the sole heir to the British empire in India. That Jawaharlal Nehru was the Congress president both in 1936 and in 1937 made the Quaid's task even more hopeless.

Jawaharlal Nehru, who was destined to be independent India's first prime minister, was born in 1889 and had been educated at Harrow and Trinity College, Cambridge. He was also called to the bar but gave up legal practice and joined Gandhi's non-cooperation movement in 1920. His burning patriotism was undoubted. So was his contribution to India's fight for freedom. He supplemented Gandhi admirably. Gandhi was an Indian to the core, while Nehru, in Gandhi's words was 'more English than Indian in his thoughts and make-up'. Gandhi moved the masses, Nehru rallied the Westernized intelligentsia. But he was also divorced from the reality of Indian politics in one important respect. He seemed to be blind to the fact that the Indians, whether Hindus or Muslims, were a deeply religious people and their respective religions governed their political outlook. The Hindu masses followed Nehru's own guru, Gandhi, blindly not because he talked sensible politics but because they regarded him as a saint. And the Mahatma himself openly avowed that religion guided his entire political life. Nehru was also temperamentally a difficult negotiator. In a letter to him on 15 July 1936, Gandhi had complained that Nehru's colleagues 'dreaded you because of your irritability and impatience of them. They have chafed under your rebukes and magisterial manner and above all of your arrogation of what has appeared to them your infallibility and superior knowledge'.[42]

Nehru was quite frankly an agnostic. He wrote

> Religion as I saw it practised and accepted even by thinking minds whether it was Hinduism or Islam or Buddhism or Christianity, did not attract me. It seemed too closely associated with superstitious practices and dogmatic beliefs, and, behind it lay a method of approach to life's problems which was certainly not that of science.[43]

He was, moreover, an ardent socialist and viewed political problems principally in economic terms. He had visited the Soviet Union in 1927 and attended the tenth anniversary celebrations of the Russian Revolution. He returned full of admiration for Communism. During his presidential address to the Forty-ninth Session of the Congress at Lucknow (12-14 April 1936) he said, 'I am convinced that the only key to the solution of the world's problems and of India's problems lies in socialism... Socialism is thus for me not merely an economic doctrine which I favour; it is a vital creed which I hold with all my head and heart'.

In his autobiography Nehru pooh-poohed the 'incompatibility of Hindu and Muslim "cultures"'. And the idea of a 'Muslim nation in India—a nation within a nation' he simply dismissed out of hand as being politically 'absurd', economically 'fantastic' and 'hardly worth considering'.[44]

It was no wonder that Jinnah's offers of an honourable cooperation between the League and the Congress were treated by Nehru with disdain.

While the elections were in progress, Nehru did not deign even to acknowledge the existence of a political party called the Muslim League. He said there were only two parties in India—the government and the Congress. To this Jinnah replied in a speech at Calcutta on 3 January 1937 insisting, 'There is a third party in this country and that is Muslim India'. But the Quaid kept his cool and said at the same time that the Muslims were ready to cooperate with any progressive and independent group provided its policy approximately corresponded with that of their own.[45] But Nehru refused to let the matter rest there. He accused Jinnah of having raised communalism 'to the nth power'. Who are the Muslims? he asked, and replied

> Apparently only those who follow Mr Jinnah and the Muslim League...I am totally unable to think along these or any other communal lines...

May I suggest that such ideas are medieval and out of date? They bear no relation whatever to modern conditions and modern problems which are essentially economic and political. Religion is both a personal matter and a bond of faith, but to stress religion in matters political and economic is obscurantism and leads to avoidance of real issues.[46]

An exasperated Jinnah said in response

I would request him to come to earth and study more the existing conditions and facts facing us and apply his energy and his ability as a practical man to the solution of problems that are facing us and cry a halt and give up his fantastic programme. Is he going to rise or remain as Peter Pan, who never grew up.[47]

But Nehru continued his disparagement of Jinnah. In a speech at Bombay on 9 February 1937, he referred to a press report of a secret pact between the Congress and Jinnah regarding acceptance of office by the Congress and angrily called it 'false and malicious'. And he went on insultingly

How on earth can I sign a pact with Mr Jinnah whom I have seen only once during the last five years and that too only for minutes at a students meeting at Allahabad? After all what does Mr Jinnah know of the national movement when he has not cared to take part in it once? There are Muslims in the Congress who can provide inspiration to a thousand Jinnahs.[48]

Pandit Nehru seemed to have clean forgotten the compliment he had paid to Jinnah in his *Autobiography*. He had noted that Mrs Sarojini Naidu had given Jinnah the title of 'ambassador of Hindu-Muslim unity' and then himself acknowledged that Jinnah 'had been largely responsible in the past for bringing the Muslim League nearer to the Congress'.[49]

In one of his statements criticizing Jinnah, Nehru had boasted, 'May I suggest to Mr Jinnah that I come into greater touch with the Muslim masses than most of the members of the Muslim League?'[50] This soon proved to be an empty boast. After the elections, Congress started a programme of Muslim mass contact but it 'did not meet with any success; on the other hand, it widened the gulf between the Congress and the League'.[51]

Iqbal who had been watching the political scene wrote to Jinnah on 20 March 1937: 'It is absolutely necessary to tell the world both inside and outside India that the economic problem is not the only problem in the country. From the Muslim point of view the cultural problem is of much greater consequence to most Indian Muslims'.[52] In another letter (28 May 1937), he stated that the 'atheistic socialism' of Nehru was not likely to appeal to the Muslims. The problem of poverty was easier to solve for the Muslims than for the Hindus. The solution lay 'in the enforcement of the law of Islam and its further development in the light of modern ideas'. But for this it was necessary to 'redistribute the country and to provide one or more Muslim states with absolute majorities'.[53] On 21 June 1937, he argued that 'a separate federation of Muslim provinces' was the only course by which the Muslims could be saved from the domination of non-Muslims. 'Why should not the Muslims of North-West India and Bengal be considered as nations entitled to self-determination just as other nations in India and outside India are?'[54] The poet-philosopher was already conjuring up visions of Pakistan!

The Muslims Get a Taste of Hindu Rule

After the Congress Working Committee had decided in July 1937 that Congressmen could accept office, Congress ministries were installed in Madras, Bombay, the Central Provinces, Bihar, Orissa and the United Provinces. Not long afterwards the ministry in the North-West Frontier Province was defeated and replaced by a Congress ministry. In October 1938 a Congress ministry also took office in Assam. All these eight ministries remained in place till the autumn of 1939 when they resigned following the outbreak of World War II for reasons which we will discuss in their proper place.

Before we proceed further, it would be pertinent to explain how Congress managed to form a ministry in the North-West Frontier Province which had a Muslim population of over ninety-one per cent. The premier was Khan Sahib but the power behind the throne was his elder brother, Abdul Ghaffar Khan. The latter had started his Redshirt movement in 1920 because of Pathan resentment against the British Government for denying to their province the representative institutions given to other provinces in India under the new reforms. Congress being the only really effective political party in India at the time, the Redshirts joined forces with it against the British. They were popularly called *surkhposhan* (wearers of red clothes) because of the colour of the shirts they wore as a uniform. Their official designation was *Khudai Khidmatgaran* (Servants of God). In the course of a day-long discussion at his village in 1939, Khan Abdul Ghaffar Khan told one of the present authors (Burke) that he had affiliated his movement with the Congress Party mainly to ensure its survival. As a purely local organization the British Government could have easily crushed it without the knowledge of the outside world. The Frontier Muslims wished to be ruled by nobody but to be left alone to practice their own form of traditional tribal democracy. They allied themselves with Congress because Congress seemed to be the only means of getting rid of the British who were dominating them at the time. When Indian independence approached and the spectre of Hindu rule began to loom, they began to desert Congress, as will become apparent as the narrative proceeds.

The Congress ministries which were formed in 1937 consisted purely of members of the Congress party. Jinnah's friendly overtures for coalition were rebuffed. Maulana Abul Kalam Azad, the foremost Muslim Congress leader, who was to be president of the Congress from 1939 to 1946, pointed out that 1937 was the first time 'that Congress was taking the responsibility of administration...and people watched how the organization would live up to its national character'. And he went on to say, 'I have to admit with regret that both in Bihar and Bombay the Congress did not come out fully successful in its test of nationalism'.

In Bombay, Nariman, a Parsee, 'was the acknowledged leader of the local Congress' but Sardar Patel and his colleagues could not reconcile themselves to the idea that a Parsee should be chief minister and 'felt that it would be unfair to the Hindu supporters of the Congress to deprive them of this honour. Accordingly, Mr B. G. Kher was brought into the picture and elected leader of the Congress Assembly Party in Bombay'. In Bihar, Syed Mahmud, a Muslim 'was the top leader of the province...[but] Sir Krishna Sinha and Anugraha Narayan Sinha' were groomed for the chief ministership. 'Dr Rajendra Prasad played the same role in Bihar as Sardar Patel did in Bombay'. Sri Krishna Sinha headed the government and Syed Mahmud was given a place in his Cabinet.[55]

In the United Provinces a Congress-League coalition nearly came off. There Khaliquzzaman, a Muslim League leader, had 'worked in unison with the Congress in the selection of candidates for the Provincial Legislative Elections'.[56] After the election, Khaliquzzaman naturally expected that the League would be invited to form a coalition with the Congress and given a fair share in the Cabinet. When Abul Kalam Azad visited Lucknow to oversee the formation of a ministry, he held out the hope that two Muslim League leaders—Khaliquzzaman and Nawab Ismail Khan—would be appointed ministers. Thereupon they signed a note that the Muslim League party would work in cooperation with Congress and accept the Congress programme. But Azad's efforts were frustrated by Nehru, who was the president of Congress at the time. He wrote to Khaliquzzaman and Ismail Khan that only one of them could be taken into the ministry. This was not acceptable to them. In the end the League was told that the members elected on the League ticket could join the provincial government only on the following terms

> The Muslim League Group in the United Provinces Assembly shall cease to function as a separate group. The existing members of the Muslim League Party in the United Provinces Assembly shall become part of the Congress Party... The Muslim League Parliamentary Board in the United Provinces will be dissolved, and no candidates will thereafter be set up by the said Board at any by-election.

Since this was tantamount to asking the League to sign its own death warrant as a separate political party, the terms were naturally rejected and the proposal for a coalition government fell through. 'This was a most unfortunate development,' lamented Azad, 'if the League's offer of cooperation had been accepted, the Muslim League party would for all practical purposes merge with the Congress... Mr Jinnah took full advantage of the situation and started an offensive which ultimately led to Pakistan'.[57]

The Instrument of Instructions to the Governors, had directed them that in appointing ministers they must include 'so far as practicable, members of important minority communities'. The Muslims were entitled to argue that it could

...have only one meaning, namely, a person having the confidence of the community. The position taken by the Congress is in direct contradiction with the meaning of this clause and is indeed a covert attempt to break all other parties in the country and to make the Congress the only political party in the country. The demand for signing the Congress pledge can have no other intention. This attempt to establish a totalitarian state may be welcome to the Hindus, but it meant the political death of the Muslims as a free people.[58]

The result of the Congress policy was that all Congress ministries were one-party ministries. However, Congress did not hesitate to join coalitions in provinces in which it was in a minority. The Muslims were entitled to ask 'If coalition is bad, how can it be good in one place and bad in another?'[59]

The rebuff on the question of coalition ministries was followed by the galling experience of 'Hindu Rule'. Broadly, the Muslim complaints against Congress ministries, which held office from July 1937 to October 1939, were the hoisting of the Congress tricolour on buildings under the management of local authorities; the singing of *Bande Mataram* at the opening of the proceedings of the legislatures; the encouragement of Hindi at the cost of Urdu; the introduction of Gandhi's scheme of 'Basic Education' in villages; and the behaviour of the members of Congress—as if they were officials with executive powers and not merely members of a political party.

The League countered the flying of the Congress tricolour by hoisting its own Star and Crescent above it. In the end the practice of flying the Congress flag on public buildings was discontinued.

The singing of *Bande Mataram* was also finally dropped after it had been first curtailed by the Working Committee, which issued a statement in October 1937 recognizing 'the validity of the objections raised by Muslim friends to certain parts of the song' and recommending that 'wherever the *Bande Mataram* is sung at national gatherings only the first two stanzas should be sung'.

Interestingly, the Government of India also viewed *Bande Mataram* with great disfavour. The Home Member (Sir Henry Craik) wrote to Lord Baden-Powell, the founder and head of the Boy Scouts movement, on 30 March 1937 to complain that *Bande Mataram* had been included in the national songs in the book *Scouting for Boys in India* and to request that it be dropped 'quietly' in the next edition. Zetland who was secretary of state for India at the time, stated that to expect the Muslims to 'cherish feelings of love and reverence for *Bande Mataram* was like expecting the 'Czechs, or Poles, joyfully to exclaim "Heil Hitler".[60]

Gandhi's scheme of 'Basic Education' was introduced following a conference in October 1937 at Wardha chaired by him and attended by the Education Ministers of the Congress provinces and other interested persons. The 'Wardha Scheme' was introduced in the Congress provinces, notably Bihar, the United Provinces and Bombay. It embodied Gandhi's favourite idea of village uplift. The basic principle was that seven years schooling 'should centre round some form of manual and productive work'. Hand-spinning was an important part of the curriculum; the medium of instruction was to be the mother tongue (which in effect meant Hindi); and there was to be no religious instruction (which to the Muslims is an essential part of education). The Muslims were particularly angry that children were made to do reverence to Gandhi's portraits.

> But the most striking exhibition of totalitarian mentality was afforded by the attitude of the Congress to the public and to the public services. Everywhere they made it clear that they were now the ruling class. Young Congressmen in the villages lorded it over their neighbours...Congress police stations were up in some districts, and Congress police tried to anticipate the regulars in the investigation of crime.[61]

In the United Provinces a beginning was made even to raise a Congress army. The Provincial Committee set up a 'Military Department' and an Officer's Training Camp was opened. It was planned to raise a Provincial force of 500,000 (including 10,000 women) but only some 25,000 volunteers had been raised when the Congress ministry resigned.[62]

A resolution passed by the Congress Working Committee in September 1938 conceded that Congress workers had interfered in the administration undesirably, 'It has come to the notice of Congress that Congress committees interfere with the ordinary administration...by seeking to influence officers and other members of the Services. Congress advises Congressmen not to interfere with the new course of administration'.

The broad impression created in the mind of the Muslims by Congress rule was well summed up by the Pirpur Report, a committee appointed by the All-India Muslim League to inquire into Muslim grievances in Congress provinces. In its report, published at the end of 1938, the committee observed

> The conduct of the Congress Government seems to substantiate the theory that there is something like identity of purpose between Congress and the Hindu Mahasabha... We Muslims feel that, notwithstanding the non-communal professions of Congress and the desire of a few Congressmen to follow a truly national policy, a vast majority of the Congress members are Hindus who look forward, after many centuries of British and Muslim rule, to the re-establishment of a purely Hindu Raj.[63]

On 5 October 1939, Rajendra Prasad, the then president of Congress, wrote to Jinnah that the charges about an anti-Muslim policy by the Congress ministries were 'wholly unfounded' and offered to 'request the highest judicial authority in India, Sir M. Gwyer, Chief Justice of the Federal Court, to enquire into this matter'. Jinnah declined the proposal, stating that he had already placed the whole case before the viceroy who, along with the governors, had been entrusted under the Constitution to protect the rights and interests of the minorities. In a statement issued on 13 December 1929, Jinnah demanded that a Royal Commission consisting of judges from England should be appointed to investigate the charges against the Congress ministries.[64]

The experience of Congress Raj cured the minorities and the princes of any ideas of federation or Constituent Assembly. Provincial autonomy under the Act of 1935 meant that every provincial ministry would be able to formulate and carry out its own programme and it would be responsible to its own legislature. The Congress High Command nullified this arrangement by imposing its own control over all the Congress governments. The Working Committee appointed a parliamentary sub-committee 'to be in close and constant touch with the work of the Congress parties in all the legislatures in the provinces, to advise them in all their activities, and to take necessary action in any case of emergency'. The members of the sub-committee were Abdul Kalam Azad, Rajendra Prasad and Vallabhbhai Patel. Congress further showed its low regard for autonomy by not letting its most prestigious members take office.

The Muslims and the princes, who had accepted federation on the understanding that the provinces and the states would enjoy a large measure of freedom from the centre, were shocked that Congress had nullified the autonomy granted to the provinces under the Constitution and began to wonder whether their interests would be safe under a Congress-dominated federation of free India. Ministers and legislators, according to Nehru, owed responsibility not to the electorate but to the Congress

> The electorate plumped for the Congress candidates, not because of their individual merits, but because they represented Congress and its programme. Nothing could be clearer than this. The vote was for Congress... It is to Congress as a whole that the electorate gave allegiance, and it is Congress that is responsible to the electorate. The Ministers and Congress Parties in the legislatures are responsible to Congress and only through it to the electorate.[65]

The result was that the control of the 'High Command' 'virtually nullified provincial autonomy and so completely undermined the federal system'.[66]

A Constituent Assembly elected 'on the basis of adult suffrage' even if the minorities were represented on their population basis and by separate electorates would certainly be Congress dominated. To the minorities Congress's future plans seemed 'something very like a "Congress Raj". The government of all India—so it seemed to them—would be run on the same lines and controlled in the last resort by the same little group of people as the present government of the Congress Provinces.'[67]

Communal Rioting

While the Muslim League and the Congress were quarrelling politically, the civil war between the Hindus and the Muslims continued in the streets. From the beginning of October 1937 to the end of September 1939, there were fifty-seven serious riots in the Congress provinces resulting in about 1,700 casualties of which more than 130 were fatal. In the non-Congress provinces during the same period, twenty-eight serious riots took place resulting in about 300 casualties and thirty-six deaths.[68]

The Muslim Reaction to Congress Rule

Congress manœuvres did not destroy the Muslim League as Congress had calculated. Though the Muslims did not yet realize it, Congress in fact had set them on the road to Pakistan. If constitutional safeguards and a neutral British Government pledged to enforce them could not protect the rights of the Muslims, the only course left open to them was to seek complete independence.

The Twenty-fifth Session of the Muslim League in October 1937 was marked by unprecedented enthusiasm. It was held at Lucknow which at that time was under a Congress ministry. The organizers of the session feared disruption and knew that the local police could not be expected to render help in case of trouble. Nevertheless, Jinnah's procession was taken through the streets of the city. It took four hours for Jinnah to reach Kaiserbagh where he was due to stay. The expected demonstration against him turned out to be a small affair: 'A few pieces of black cloth were seen at a distance...but the demonstrators took to their heels very soon'. The session began with the unfurling of the Muslim League flag by Jinnah; it was the first time that the flag had figured in a programme of the League.[69] Another first was that the Quaid wore national dress. He appeared in a light brown *sherwani* (long coat buttoned to the neck), *tung* (tight) white trousers and a black astrakhan cap. The last named was immediately given the title of Jinnah Cap and acquired the same status among the Muslims as the Gandhi Cap of white cotton already enjoyed among the nationalist Hindus.

In the course of his presidential address, Jinnah expressed satisfaction at the growing popularity of the League: 'I find that hundreds of District Leagues have been established in almost every province, from the farthest corner of Madras to the North-West Frontier Province'. He said that 'On the very threshold of what little power and responsibility are given, the majority community have clearly shown their hand: that Hindustan is for the Hindus; only the Congress masquerades under the name of nationalism, whereas the Hindu Mahasabha does not mince words'. He believed that the British Government would give Congress a free hand because 'it matters very little to them—nay, it is all to the good' because the Congress party policy would result in 'class bitterness, communal war and a strengthening of the imperialist hold'. No Hindu leader showed any desire for settlement with the Muslims. An honourable settlement could only be achieved between equals. The time had come when the Muslims should devote their energies to self-organization and the full development of their power.

A resolution was passed that the object of the Muslim League should be 'the establishment in India of full independence in the form of a federation of free democratic states in which the rights and interests of the Mussulmans and other minorities are adequately and effectively safeguarded in the Constitution'.

An important event at the Lucknow session was that the premiers of the Muslim majority provinces of the Punjab (Sikander Hayat Khan), Bengal (Fazlul Haq) and Assam (Muhammad Saadulla) joined the Muslim League along with their followers in the legislatures. They had originally believed that the provincial autonomy promised under the 1935 Act would protect them against interference by the central government but Congress rule had demonstrated that after independence the Congress High Command would not hesitate to override constitutional niceties and impose Hindu rule over the whole of India.

A feature of the session was the presence of several ladies including Fatima Jinnah. During the debate on the resolution on full independence the widow of Muhammad Ali appealed to Muslim women to come to the forefront and join the League and fight for the cause of the community.[70] Henceforth a growing number of Muslim ladies were seen at the League sessions, thanks to Jinnah's appeals that Muslim women should come out and join the national movement.

> Within two or three months after the Lucknow Conference over 170 new branches of the League had been established, 90 of them in the United Provinces and 40 in the Punjab. No less than 100,000 new members were said to have been enlisted in the United Provinces alone. Scarcely less important, since nowhere are politics more personal than in India and nowhere is leadership more eagerly desired and loyally respected, was the swift and striking growth of Mr Jinnah's authority. Always in the forefront of Indian politics, he had hitherto failed to command the confidence of his community as a whole. He had been a sectional rather than a communal leader, a man of the Left, the exponent of a forceful anti-British nationalism which had

seemed to conservative-minded Moslems to show that he was dangerously 'Congress-minded'. But now he was no longer one of several Moslem leaders: he was fast becoming *the* leader.[71]

The Quaid, however, did not abandon his plea for Hindu-Muslim unity. At a public speech at Patna on 27 October 1937 he said, 'The Muslim heart is throbbing for the freedom of the country. If you [Congress] want their co-operation...come down to earth and take your proper place. And then we will march with you in the battle for independence'.[72]

On New Year's day (1 January 1938) he arrived to address a public meeting at Gaya. He was greeted by a crowd of 'tens of thousands' at the railway station. His two-mile long procession was led by a 'pilot motor cycle with the League flag waving over his head, volunteers on horseback, volunteers in uniform and volunteers carrying shining swords and League flags'. It took three hours to pass through its route. The meeting was attended by over 50,000 people. The ladies were accommodated behind purdahs.

In replying to the address of welcome, he noted that it was the first public meeting of the Muslims where special arrangements had been made for ladies and said, 'Believe me, gentlemen, this feature has given me utmost pleasure'. He said he was deeply moved by the affection shown to him: 'You have given me a welcome and presented me an address worthy of a king'.

In the past he claimed to have followed secular politics but on this occasion he proclaimed

> Islam gives us a complete code. It is not only a religion but it contains laws, philosophy and politics. In fact, it contains everything that matters to a man from morning to night. When we talk of Islam we take it as an all-embracing word. We do not mean any ill will. The foundation of our Islamic code is that we stand for liberty, equality and fraternity.[73]

Addressing the Aligarh Muslim University on 5 February 1938, he recalled that many efforts had been made to settle the Hindu-Muslim question. 'At that time there was no pride in me,' he recalled, 'and I used to beg from the Congress. I worked so incessantly to bring about a *rapprochement* that a newspaper remarked that Mr Jinnah is never tired of Hindu-Muslim unity.'[74]

He argued that British parliamentary democracy had no application to Indian conditions

The majority and minority parties in Britain are alterable, their complexion and strength often change. Today it is a Conservative Government, tomorrow Liberal and the day after Labour. But such is not the case with India. Here we have a permanent Hindu majority and the rest are minorities which cannot within any conceivable period of time hope to become majorities. The majority can afford to assume a non-communal label, but it remains exclusively Hindu in its spirit and action.[75]

The Congress Press alleged that by saying that the parliamentary system was unsuited to India, Jinnah was guilty of a disservice to Islam because Islam believes in democracy. To this he replied

So far as I have understood Islam, it does not advocate a democracy which would allow the majority of non-Muslims to decide the faith of the Muslims... I say, what have these votaries, these champions of democracy done? They have kept sixty millions of people as Untouchables; they have set up a system which is nothing but a 'Grand Fascist Council'. Their dictator is not even a four-anna member of the Congress.[76]

At the Special Session of the Muslim League at Calcutta on 17 April 1938, Jinnah expressed satisfaction that within six months after the Lucknow session, the Muslims had been organized as they never were at any time during the last century and a half. Before the Lucknow session, the membership of the League ran to several thousands but now there were hundreds of thousands of Muslims under the banner of the League. There were Muslim League Parties functioning inside seven out of the eleven Provincial Legislatures and the Muslim League had contested with great success a number of by-elections to the Provincial Assemblies. The League now claimed the status of complete equality with Congress.[77]

Jinnah, as president of the Muslim League, and Subhas Bose, as president of the Congress party, corresponded from May till October 1931 in an effort to negotiate a settlement between the two parties. But this never got off the ground because Congress declined to accept the League's prerequisite that the League was the only authoritative and representative political organization of the Muslims of India. In vain did Jinnah remind Bose that this position had been accepted by the Congress when the Congress made the Lucknow Pact with the League in 1916.[78]

A Step Toward Pakistan

In the Muslim League proceedings, the idea of the partition of India into two nations was first mooted at the provincial level. When Jinnah was invited to preside over the Sind Provincial Muslim League Conference which opened at Karachi on 8 October 1938, he said the greatest misfortune of India was that the Congress High Command had adopted 'a most brutal, oppressive and inimical attitude' towards the League. The average Congressman 'arrogates to himself the role of a ruler of this country', but not possessing the educational qualifications, training, culture and traditions of the British bureaucrat, 'he behaves and acts towards the Mussulmans in a much worse manner than the British did towards Indians'. He went on ominously to warn that Congress was 'only tumbling into the hands of those who are looking forward to the creation of a serious situation which will break India vertically and horizontally'. He asked the Congress High Command 'to mark, learn and inwardly digest' the developments which were leading to a world war

> ...the Sudeten Germans were forced under the heels of the majority of Czechoslovakia who oppressed them, suppressed them, maltreated them and showed a brutal and callous disregard for their rights and interests for two decades, hence the inevitable result that the Republic of Czechoslovakia is now broken up and a new map will have to be drawn.

The Conference adopted the following resolution

> This conference, in the interests of abiding peace of the vast Indian continent and of unhampered cultural development, economic and social betterment, and *political self-determination* of the Hindus and Muslims, recommends to the All-India Muslim League to review the entire question of what should be a suitable Constitution for India, which will secure an honourable and legitimate status due to the Muslims, and further devise a scheme of constitution under which *the Muslims may attain full independence.*[79]

At the national level, however, Jinnah and the Muslim League were not yet ready to make a formal bid for partition, though their bitterness was growing and they were edging towards it.

At the All-India Muslim Session at Patna (December 1938), the Quaid said that the Congress had killed every hope of Hindu-Muslim settlement 'in the right royal fashion of Fascism'. The Congress leaders 'may shout as much as they like' that the Congress is a national body but in fact it is 'nothing but a Hindu body'. In fact it did not even represent all the Hindus: 'Does the Congress represent the Scheduled Castes? Does the Congress represent the non-Brahmans? ...What about the Hindu Mahasabha? What about the Liberal Federation? The Congress High Command, in the intoxication of power, like persons who are drunk, may make any claims it pleases them to make.' But, 'it remains what it is—mainly a Hindu body'.

He said he had no hesitation in saying that it was Gandhi who was 'destroying the ideal with which the Congress was started. He is the one man responsible for turning the Congress into an instrument for the revival of Hinduism. His ideal is to revive the Hindu religion and establish Hindu Raj in this country, and he is utilizing the Congress to further this object'.

The Congress game with regard to federation, he went on, was very clear. If Congress can gain control of the federal machinery, then, by means of the direct and indirect powers vested in the federal government, the Congress would be able to 'reduce to a non-entity' the government of Fazlul Haq in Bengal and Sikander Hayat in the Punjab.

But the League was still hopeful that the Indian politicians would be able to maintain the subcontinent's unity by finding a suitable alternative to federation proposed under the 1935 Act. Resolution X authorized 'the President of the All-India Muslim League to adopt such a course as may be necessary with a view to exploring the possibility of a suitable alternative which would safeguard the interests of the Mussulmans and other minorities in India'.

Two other resolutions broke new ground. Resolution IV authorized the Working Committee 'to decide and resort to "Direct Action" if and when necessary'. And Resolution VI resolved that an All-India Muslim Women's Sub-committee be formed so that they could participate in the struggle for social, economic and political emancipation of the Muslim nation in India. The sub-committee was directed to organize provincial and district women's sub-committees.

In his concluding remarks Jinnah pointed out that the Direct Action resolution had laid down 'a fundamental principle of a revolutionary nature'. Till then the League 'had been wedded only to a policy of constitutional progress'. He said that the Patna session had been the most successful he had seen since 1913.[80] His assessment was borne out by the unprecedented enthusiasm that pervaded the event. He had been greeted with shouts of 'Quaid-i-Azam' (Supreme Leader),[81] the seven-mile route to the site of the session was lined with people waving green flags, and the meeting itself was so over-crowded that thousands had to stand outside.

Like most of his speeches, the Quaid's address at Patna was delivered extempore. It was carefully reasoned, factually accurate and of considerable length. Only a person gifted with a phenomenal memory could have performed such a feat. That he was blessed also with extraordinary will power was clearly borne out by his endless tours and his numberless speeches and statements in the face of ill-health and physical frailty.

World War II

On 1 September 1939, Hitler invaded Poland. England and France who had committed themselves to defend Polish independence, thereupon declared war on Germany on 3 September. On 10 June 1940, Italy declared war on France and Great Britain. The hitherto European war developed into World War II when the Japanese made a surprise attack on the naval base at Pearl Harbour in Hawaii on 7 December 1941, and brought the United States of America into the conflict. The European war ended on 7 May 1945 when Germany signed the document of surrender and the Pacific war ended on 14 August 1945 when Japan surrendered unconditionally.

Indian Reaction to World War II

The Indian response to the war broadly fell into three categories. The princes and most of the minority parties—such as the Depressed Classes, the Mahasabha, the Liberals and, after

Germany's attack on the Soviet Union, the Communists—all offered wholehearted support. The Congress, which for several years past had stood for complete independence and the transfer of sovereignty to itself alone, saw the war as an opportunity for wresting power from the beleaguered British Government without further delay; it demanded independence as the price for its help. The Muslim League, under Jinnah, expressed sympathy for the allied cause but officially maintained a posture of benevolent neutrality. It did not do anything to impede the war effort.

The attitude of the Congress was a foregone conclusion. Its foreign policy supremo was Jawaharlal Nehru. He had assumed that role after his return from Europe in 1927. In the course of his trip he had visited the Soviet Union and come back full of enthusiasm for socialism and increased hatred for imperialism. Under his influence the Madras Session of the Indian National Congress (December 1927) passed a resolution which declared that 'in the event of the British Government embarking on any warlike adventure and endeavouring to exploit India in it for the furtherance of their imperialist aims, it will be the duty of the people of India to refuse to take any part in such a war or to co-operate with them in any way whatsoever'. At the Lucknow Session (April 1936) which was presided over by Nehru, a resolution warned that in the event of an international war 'an attempt will inevitably be made to drag in and exploit India to her manifest disadvantage and for the benefit of British Imperialism'. And it declared Congress's opposition to the participation of India in any imperialist war.

At the Tripura Session in March 1939, Nehru moved and carried a resolution which declared that it was 'urgently necessary for India to direct her own foreign policy as an independent nation, thereby keeping aloof from both imperialism and Fascism, and pursuing her path of peace and freedom'.[82]

It was by a proclamation on 4 September 1939 by Lord Linlithgow,[83] the viceroy, that India was brought into the war. In all member states of the British Commonwealth except Eire, war was declared on the advice of ministers responsible to their respective legislatures. Congress leaders expressed their resentment that neither they nor the Indian legislature had been consulted or even informed by the viceroy before he made the declaration of war. But Jinnah correctly pointed out that the position of the Government of India was 'totally different from the position of the Dominions'. India was a 'dependency' of Great Britain.[84] The question of declaring war did not rest with India and according to the existing constitutional position the declaration by the viceroy that India was at war was sufficient.[85]

What would have happened if Linlithgow had approached Congress for support in the war effort? Congress's goal since the Lahore Congress (1928) had been complete independence, and the recently passed Tripura resolution had clearly stated that the purpose of attaining independence was to enable India to keep 'aloof from both imperialism and Fascism'.

For Britain to grant independence to India at this critical juncture was unthinkable. However let us suppose for a moment that independence was offered and Nehru out of his love for democracy and hatred for Fascism had tried to persuade his colleagues to help in the war effort. There would still have remained the total opposition to any war by the Congress guru, Gandhi. Moreover, to whom was power to be handed over? Congress claimed that it alone represented the Indian nation and was therefore entitled to receive power. This would certainly have been deeply resented by the Muslims, the princes, and the Scheduled Castes and would have set off an interminable controversy. By adopting the course he did, Linlithgow, while acting correctly under the then Indian Constitution, managed to avoid endless debate and delay. He concentrated on the war effort and was able to obtain in India all the men and material that could be usefully utilized.

At the viceroy's invitation, Gandhi met him on 5 September and stated afterwards

> I knew that I had no instructions from the Working Committee in the matter... Therefore there could be no question of any understanding or negotiation with me...if there is to be any, it would be between Congress and the government. Having, therefore, made my position *vis-à-vis* Congress quite clear, I told His Excellency that my own sympathies were with England and France from the purely humanitarian standpoint. I told him that I could not contemplate without being stirred to the very depth the destruction of London which had hitherto been regarded as impregnable. And as I was picturing before him the Houses of Parliament and Westminster Abbey and their possible destruction, I broke down.

On 11 September, Linlithgow read out to both houses of the Central Legislature the King's message explaining that preparations for implementing the federal part of the Act of 1935 had been suspended because of the war.

Congress's first official reaction to the war came in the form of a resolution drafted by Nehru and passed on 15 September 1939 by the Working Committee at Wardha, after a week's deliberations. It stated that if Great Britain was fighting for the maintenance and extension of democracy, then she must necessarily end imperialism in her possessions, establish full democracy in India, and the Indian people must have the right of self-determination by framing their own Constitution through a Constituent Assembly without external interference, and must guide their own policy. A free democratic India would gladly associate itself with other free nations for mutual defence against aggression and for economic cooperation.

'To allow for the full elucidation of the issues at stake', the Committee refrained from taking any final decision at that stage but 'the decision cannot long be delayed'. The Committee, therefore, invited 'the British Government to declare in unequivocal terms what their aims are in regard to democracy and imperialism and the new order that is envisaged, in particular, how these aims are going to apply to India and to be given effect to in the present'.[86]

After seeing Gandhi on 5 September 1939, Linlithgow received Jinnah. British officialdom had up to that point been wary of Jinnah. They had regarded him as arrogant and unsociable and found his politics disagreeable. He had condemned British imperialism as intensely as any Congress leader. He had never tired of harping on the need for Hindu-Muslim unity, and the British could never forget that he had been the principal architect of the Congress-League Lucknow Pact of 1916. But in recent years, the picture had undergone a change. Congress had made no secret of their opposition to an 'imperialist war', thus forcing the government to lean more on the Muslim League. The League, moreover, had become a popular party. It had begun to claim equality with Congress and had acquired the position of being the sole representative body of the Muslims of India, and Jinnah had openly despaired of reconciliation with Congress. Henceforth, the viceroy displayed no less respect for Jinnah than he did for Gandhi. In Jinnah's own words

After the war was declared, the Viceroy naturally wanted help from the Muslim League. It was only then that he realized that the Muslim League was a power. For it will be remembered that up to the time of the declaration of war, the Viceroy never thought of me, but of Gandhi and Gandhi alone... Therefore, when I got this invitation from the Viceroy along with Mr Gandhi, I wondered within myself why I was so suddenly promoted, and then I concluded that the answer was the 'All-India Muslim League', whose President I happen to be. I believe that was the worst shock that the Congress High Command received, because it challenged their sole authority to speak on behalf of India.[87]

The Muslim League's official response to the situation created by the war was made by the Working Committee in a resolution passed on 18 September 1939. Unlike Congress, the League did not criticize the viceroy for declaring war on India's behalf. The Working Committee resolution appreciated that the federal scheme had been suspended, but urged that it should be abandoned altogether, because the experience of the working of the provincial part of the 1935 Constitution had 'resulted wholly in a permanent communal majority and the domination of the Hindus over the Muslim minorities'. Such a Constitution was 'totally unsuited to the genius of the peoples of the country which is composed of various nationalities and does not constitute a national state'. The Committee expressed its deep sympathy for Poland, England, and France, but felt that 'real and solid' support to Great Britain could not be 'secured successfully' until the governors were called upon to exercise their special powers to protect the rights of the Muslims in the Congress-governed provinces. It further urged the British Government that 'no declaration regarding the question of constitutional advance for India should be made without the consent and approval of the All-India Muslim League, nor any Constitution be framed and finally adopted by His Majesty's Government and the British Parliament without such consent and approval'. If the government desired full cooperation of the Muslims, 'it must create a sense of security and satisfaction amongst the Mussulmans and take into its confidence the Muslim League, which is the only organization that can speak on behalf of Muslim India'.[88]

Lord Linlithgow made a public statement on 17 October 1939, setting out the government's position on war aims and war efforts.

It began with the assurance that the aim of British policy remained that India should attain Dominion Status. At the end of the war the British Government would 'be prepared to regard the scheme of the 1935 Act as open to modification in the light of Indian views'. The minorities were assured that, during the discussion with regard to constitutional modifications, their views and interests would be given due weight as had always been done in the past. As to the immediate problem of securing 'the association of public opinion in India with the conduct of the war', the right solution would be 'the establishment of a consultative group, representing all major political parties in British India and the Indian princes, over which the Governor-General would himself preside'.

The Congress Working Committee considered the viceroy's statement at a meeting held at Wardha on 22 and 23 October and called it 'an unequivocal reiteration of the old imperialist policy'. As a first step toward ending that policy, the Committee called upon 'the Congress ministries [in the provinces] to tender their resignation'. By 15 November, the ministries in all Congress-ruled provinces had resigned and were replaced by the direct rule of the governors under Section 93 of the 1935 Act. Jinnah asked the Muslims to observe Friday 22 December as the 'Day of Deliverance'. He empasized that the observance was simply to express relief from the oppression of the Congress regime. It was 'not in any way directed against our Hindu fellow-countrymen as a community'.

The Working Committee of the Muslim League, which met on 22 October, neither accepted nor rejected the viceroy's statement. It asked for further discussion and clarification. With regard to the viceroy's promise that the federal scheme of the 1935 Act would be modified, the League insisted that the whole scheme must be scrapped and the entire constitutional problem be considered *de novo*. It commended the viceroy's assurance to the minorities that their views and interests would be given due consideration when constitutional changes were discussed.

At the beginning of November the viceroy discussed with Gandhi, Rajendra Prasad (the president of Congress) and Jinnah the question of expanding the Governor-General's Council as an *ad hoc* arrangement during the war, but the Indian leaders could not come up with an agreement between themselves 'as would contribute to the harmonious working in the centre'. Rajendra Prasad had taken the position that it was 'impossible to cooperate with the government unless its policy was made clear in a declaration on the lines suggested by Congress'.

Meeting at Allahabad from 19 to 23 November 1939, the Congress Working Committee criticized the British Government for advancing the rights of minorities 'as a barrier to India's freedom' and declared again that 'the recognition of India's independence and of the right of her people to frame their Constitution through a Constituent Assembly...is the only democratic method of determining the Constitution of a free country... The Constituent Assembly should be elected on the basis of adult suffrage.'

Jinnah wrote to the viceroy on 5 November 1939 seeking the assurance that no constitutional changes would be made without the approval of the two major communities of India, viz., the Muslims and the Hindus; that the entire problem of India's future Constitution would be examined and reconsidered *de novo*; and that no Indian troops would be used outside India against any Muslim country. Lord Linlithgow replied on 23 December that the re-examination of India's constitutional status did 'not exclude examination of any part either of the Act of 1935 or of the policy and plans on which it is based'. He also said that the government was 'not under any misapprehension as to the importance of the contentment of the Muslim community to the stability and success of any constitutional developments in India. You need, therefore, have no fear that the weight which your community's position in India necessarily gives their views will be underrated'. The question of Indian troops being used against a Muslim country, he pointed out, was hypothetical because the British Government was not at war with any Muslim power.

When Congress convened for its regular session at Ramgarh under the presidentship of Abul Kalam Azad (19-20 March 1940), it largely reiterated its past pronouncements that Britain was

> Carrying on the war fundamentally for imperialist ends... Congress therefore strongly disapproves of Indian troops being made to fight for Great Britain and of the drain from India of men and material for the purpose of the war... Congress hereby declares again that

nothing short of complete independence can be accepted by the people of India...no permanent solution [of the communal problem] is possible except through a Constituent Assembly.

Jinnah criticized the setting up of a Constituent Assembly on the lines suggested by Congress. A Constituent Assembly elected by adult suffrage even with separate electorates, he pointed out, would have a Hindu majority and thus be 'a second and larger edition of Congress'. It would be nothing but 'a packed body, manœuvred and managed by a Congress caucus'. With regard to the promise by Congress that if the minorities differed from any majority decision the dispute would be referred to a tribunal, Jinnah said

> Who will appoint the tribunal? And suppose an agreed tribunal is possible, and the award is made and the decision given, who will, may I know, be there to see that this award is implemented or carried out in accordance with the terms of that award? And who will see that it is honoured in practice, because, we are told, the British will have parted with their power, mainly or completely? Then what will be the sanction behind the award which will enforce it? We come back to the same answer; the Hindu majority would do it and will it be with the help of the British bayonet or Mr Gandhi's 'Ahimsa'? Can we trust them any more? Besides, ladies and gentlemen, can you imagine that a question of this character, of a social contract upon which the future Constitution of India would be based, affecting 90 millions of Mussulmans, can be decided by means of a judicial tribunal?[89]

Notes

1. Pirzada, *Foundations of Pakistan*, II, op.cit., p. 229.
2. For the proceedings of the Council meeting *see*, Pirzada, ibid., pp. 229-32.
3. Ibid., pp. 232-3.
4. Stanley Wolpert, *Jinnah of Pakistan*, op.cit., p. 89.
5. Kanji Dwarkadas, *India's Fight for Freedom*, op.cit., pp. 441-2.
6. Waheed Ahmad, *The Nation's Voice (March 1935-March 1940)*, op.cit., p. 320.
7. Ibid., p. 333,
8. Fatima Jinnah, *My Brother*, op.cit., p. 1.
9. Ibid., p. 2. (1 *crore* is 100 million).
10. Ibid., pp. 4-7.

11. Ibid., pp. 7-8
12. Pirzada, *Foundations of Pakistan*, II, op.cit., p. 461.
13. H. Bolitho, *Jinnah*, op.cit., p. 160.
14. Ibid., p. 174.
15. Stanley Wolpert, *Jinnah of Pakistan*, op.cit., p. 150.
16. Fatima Jinnah, *My Brother*, op.cit., p. 33.
17. Ibid., pp. 9-10.
18. Ibid., p. 4 with n. 3.
19. Ibid., p. 10.
20. Pirzada, *Collected Works*, III, op.cit., p. 108.
21. Waheed Ahmad, *The Nation's Voice (March 1935-March 1940)*, op.cit., pp. 327-8.
22. Jamil-UD-Din Ahmad, *Speeches and Writings of Mr Jinnah*, I, p. 47. Wardha, a small town in the Central Provinces was used by Gandhi as a retreat. Another town where the had an ashram was Sabarmati near Ahmedabad. (A *lak* is 100 thousand.)
23. Pirzada, *Foundations of Pakistan*, II, op.cit., pp. 450, 451, 487.
24. Wavell, *The Viceroy's Journal*, op.cit., pp. 169-70.
25. He was appointed viceroy by Baldwin, who had succeeded MacDonald as prime minister in June 1935.
26. The governor-general could enact a 'Governor-General's Act' and the governor a 'Governor's Act'.
27. The Untouchables or the Depressed Classes were given the official name of 'Scheduled Castes'.
28. Parliamentary Debates, H. C., Vol. 302, 1935, Cols. 1824-8.
29. A. M. Zaidi, *The Encyclopaedia of the Indian National Congress*, X, op.cit., pp. 398-9.
30. Ibid., XI., pp. 116-7.
31. M. H. Saiyid, *Mohammad Ali Jinnah*, 1945, pp. 518-9.
32. Ibid., p. 520.
33. Ibid., p. 523.
34. Ibid., pp. 525-6.
35. This account has been taken from M. H. Saiyid, *Mohammad Ali Jinnah*, 1962, pp. 237-40 and Waheed Ahmad, *The Nation's Voice (March 1935-March 1940)*, op.cit., pp. 12-34.
36. Pirzada, *Foundations of Pakistan*, II, op.cit., pp. 234-63; M. H. Saiyid, *Mohammad Ali Jinnah*, 1945, op.cit., pp. 540-9.
37. Waheed Ahmad, *The Nation's Voice (March 1935-March 1940)*, op.cit., p. 111.
38. For the text of manifesto *see*, A. M. Zaidi, *Evolution of Muslim Political Thought in India*, IV, op.cit., pp. 237-42.
39. Waheed Ahmad, *The Nation's Voice (March 1935-March 1936)*, op.cit., p. 103.
40. For texts of letters exchanged by Nehru and Cripps *see*, P. N. Chopra, *Towards Freedom, 1937-47*, I, pp. 161, 191, 231.
41. Waheed Ahmad, *The Nation's Voice (March 1935-March 1936)*, op.cit., p. 131.
42. Jawaharlal Nehru, *A Bunch of Old Letters*, p. 204.

43. Jawarharlal Nehru, *The Discovery of India*, op.cit., pp. 21-22. *See also, Autobiography*, op.cit., p. 374.
44. Ibid., p. 469.
45. P. N. Chopra, *Towards Freedom, 1937-47*, I, p. 14. Jinnah, in fact had already stated at the First Session of the Round Table Conference that there were four parties in India: 'The British party, the Indian princes, the Hindus and the Mussulmans'.
46. Ibid., pp. 24-25.
47. Waheed Ahmad, *The Nation's Voice (March 1935-March 1940)*, op.cit., p. 120. Peter Pan was the principal character in J.M. Barrie's play of that name (1904). He was a little boy who ran away to 'Never-Never Land' and never grew up.
48. P. N. Chopra, *Towards Freedom, 1937-47*, I, op.cit., p. 119.
49. Jawaharlal Nehru, *Autobiography*, op. cit., p. 67.
50. P. N. Chopra, *Towards Freedom, 1937-47*, I, op.cit., p. 26.
51. V. P. Menon, *The Transfer of Power in India*, op.cit., p. 56.
52. A. M. Zaidi, *Evolution of Muslim Political Thought in India*, IV, op.cit., p. 746.
53. Ibid., p. 748.
54. Ibid., pp. 750-1.
55. Maulana Abul Kalam Azad, *India Wins Freedom*, op.cit., pp. 16-18.
56. B. Pattabhi Sitaramayya, *History of the Indian National Congress*, II, op.cit., p. 690.
57. This account is taken from Maulana Abul Kalam Azad, *India Wins Freedom*, op.cit., pp. 170-71 and Choudhry Khaliquzzaman, *Pathway to Pakistan*, pp. 160-1.
58. B .R. Ambedkar, *Pakistan*, p. 27.
59. Ibid., p. 28.
60. 'Essayez', op.cit., p. 272.
61. R. Coupland, *Indian Politics, 1936-1942*, op.cit., p. 103-4.
62. Ibid., pp. 104-5.
63. The Muslim League case against Congress rule is mainly contained in three publications: *The Pirpur Report*; A. K. Fazlul Haq's *Muslim Sufferings Under Congress Rule*; and *The Shareef Report*. They can be found in K. K. Aziz, *Muslims Under Congress Rule*, Part IX, op.cit.
64. Waheed Ahmad, *The Nation's Voice (March 1935-March 1940)*, op.cit., p. 423.
65. R. Coupland, *Indian Politics, 1936-1942*, op.cit., p. 96.
66. Ibid., p. 99.
67. Ibid., p. 107.
68. Ibid., p. 131.
69. This account is taken from M. H. Saiyid, *Mohammad Ali Jinnah*, 1945, op.cit., pp. 573-4. Saiyid was personnally involved in making the arrangments for the session. His account is, therefore, that of an eye witness.
70. For an account of the Lucknow Session *see*, Pirzada, *Foundations of Pakistan*, II, pp. 264-81.
71. R. Coupland, *Indian Politics, 1936-1942*, op.cit., p. 183.
72. Waheed Ahmad, *The Nation's Voice (March 1935-March 1940)*, op.cit., p. 193.

73. Ibid., pp. 220-1.
74. Ibid., p. 233.
75. Ibid., p. 235.
76. Ibid., p. 470.
77. For text of speech *see*, ibid., pp. 241-6.
78. For text of letters exchanged by Jinnah and Bose *see*, Pirzada, *Quaid-i-Azam Jinnah's Correspondence*, op.cit., pp. 46-52.
79. R. Coupland, *Indian Politics, 1936-1942*, op.cit., p. 197.
80. For an account of the Patna Session *see*, Pirzada, *Foundations of Pakistan*, II, op.cit., pp. 300-24. It will be recalled that it was in 1913 that he had joined the League as a regular member.
81. Sharif AL Mujahid, at p. 433 of his *Quaid-i-Azam Jinnah, Studies in Interpretation*, states that Jinnah was referred to as Quaid-i-Azam for the first time in a League session at Lucknow in 1937.
82. R. Coupland, *Indian Politics, 1936-1942*, op.cit., p. 208.
83. Linlithgow had taken over as viceroy on 18 April 1936.
84. Jamil-UD-Din Ahmad, *Speeches and Writings of Mr Jinnah*, I, pp. 197-8.
85. Waheed Ahmad, *The Nation's Voice*, II, op.cit., p. 109.
86. A. M. Zaidi, *The Encyclopaedia of the Indian National Congress*, XII, pp. 193-8.
87. Jamil-UD-Din Ahmad, *Speeches and Writings of Mr Jinnah*, I, op.cit., p. 154.
88. For the text of the resolution *see*, Waheed Ahmad, *The Nation's Voice (March 1935-March 1940)*, op.cit., pp. 644-6.
89. Pirzada, *Foundations of Pakistan*, II, op.cit., p. 331.

CHAPTER 11

The Struggle for Pakistan 1940-1946

The Pakistan Resolution

On 19 January 1940, *Time and Tide* of London published an article by Jinnah under the caption 'The Constitutional Future of India'. He maintained that the 'root cause of all India's constitutional ills' was that 'democratic systems based on the concept of a homogeneous nation such as England are very definitely not applicable to heterogeneous countries such as India'. He argued that Hindus and Muslims 'are in fact two different nations' because their respective religions have 'definite social codes which govern not so much man's relation with God, as man's relation with his neighbour'. The Muslim League stood for a free India but 'it is irrevocably opposed to any federal objective which must necessarily result in a majority community rule under the guise of democracy and a parliamentary system of government'. His remedy was that

> ...a Constitution must be evolved that recognizes that there are in India two nations, who both must share the governance of their common motherland. In evolving such a Constitution, the Muslims are ready to cooperate with the British Government, the Congress or any party, so that the present enmities may cease and India may take its place amongst the great countries of the world.[1]

It is clear that by calling Hindus and Muslims two nations, Jinnah had reached the threshold of partition, but he was still reluctant to abandon his lifelong dream that Hindus and Muslims would come to an understanding and unitedly make 'their common motherland' one of 'the great countries of the world'.

The Quaid-i-Azam crossed the Rubicon at the Lahore session of the Muslim League in March 1940. On arrival he was enthusiastically received at the railway station by a huge crowd and a number of bands. One hundred and one crackers were fired. On the opening day of the session (22 March) he sat on an ornamental chair dressed in a white *achkan* and *churidar* trousers. Miss Fatima Jinnah sat at his right.

It was on 24 March that the resolution demanding Pakistan was passed. The political bombshell was embodied in a resolution moved on 23 March by Fazlul Haq, premier of Bengal. It was passed unanimously amid great enthusiasm on 24 March. The League circles first called it the Lahore Resolution but it later received the name Pakistan Resolution under circumstances which will be explained later. Its most important part ran

> Resolved: that it is the considered view of this Session of the All-India Muslim League that no constitutional plan would be workable in this country or acceptable to the Muslims unless it is designed on the following basic principles, viz., that geographically contiguous units are demarcated into regions which should be so constituted, with such territorial readjustments as may be necessary, that the areas in which the Muslims are numerically in a majority, as in the North-Western and Eastern zones of India, should be grouped to constitute Independent States in which the constituent units shall be autonomous and sovereign.

On the opening day, Jinnah had expounded the rationale of the resolution in his extempore presidential address lasting for a hundred minutes and frequently punctuated by thunderous applause. Though most of his audience of over 100,000 did not know English, he held their attention and visibly touched their emotion. He began by saying that since the last session at Patna fifteen months earlier, the League had established a provincial League in every province and 'there was not a single by-election in which our opponents won against Muslim League candidates'. He asserted that the Muslims were 'a nation by any definition'

> The Hindus and the Muslims belong to two different religious philosophies, social customs, and literature. They neither inter-marry, nor inter-dine together, and indeed they belong to two different civilizations which are based mainly on conflicting ideas and conceptions. Their aspects on life are different. It is quite clear that Hindus and Mussulmans derive their inspiration from different sources of history. They have different epics, their heroes are different, and

they have different episodes. Very often the hero of one is a foe of the other, and likewise, their victories and defeats overlap. To yoke together two such nations under a single state, one as a numerical minority and the other as a majority, must lead to growing discontent and the final destruction of any fabric that may be so built up for the government of such a state.

The only course 'open to us all', he went on, 'is to allow the major nations separate homelands by dividing India into autonomous national states'. It was futile to expect that the nationalities which had remained as divergent as ever despite 1,000 years of close contact, would 'transform themselves into one nation merely by means of subjecting them to a democratic Constitution and holding them forcibly together by unnatural and artificial methods of British parliamentary statutes'.[2] The Lahore Resolution was loosely worded and was variously interpreted. It was only at the Muslim League Legislators' Convention in Delhi in April 1946 that Pakistan was clearly defined as a single sovereign state comprising six provinces, namely Bengal, Assam, the Punjab, the North-West Frontier Province, Sind and Baluchistan.

The word Pakistan had not been used in the Lahore Resolution and the League hierarchy continued to use the description 'Lahore Resolution' until it was compelled to accept the word Pakistan because of its spontaneous adoption by the Muslim masses. To start with, however, it was the Hindus who derisively dubbed the resolution 'Pakistan'. But the move recoiled upon them.

Remembering how the Muslim leaders of the day themselves had rejected Rahmat Ali's Pakistan out of hand as chimerical, the Hindu Press and community by way of ridicule immediately nicknamed the Lahore Resolution 'the Pakistan Resolution'. Khaliquzzaman recalled

> The next morning the Hindu Press came out with big headlines: 'Pakistan Resolution Passed', although the word was not used by anyone in the speeches nor in the body of the Resolution. The Nationalist Press supplied to the Muslim masses a concentrated slogan which immediately conveyed to them the idea of a state. It would have taken long for the Muslim leaders to explain the Lahore Resolution and convey its real meaning and significance to them. Years of labour of the Muslim leaders to propagate its full import amongst the masses was shortened by the Hindu Press in naming the resolution the 'Pakistan Resolution'.[3]

The League leaders would have been hard put to it to coin a more magical name for their goal than Pakistan, which every Muslim, literate or not, immediately interpreted as 'the Land of the Pure'. Carrying a clear meaning and an immediate appeal, the word itself became a factor in adding weight and vigour to the movement for a separate homeland for the Muslims in the subcontinent.

At first, the idea of Pakistan had but few friends. The Hindu reaction was predictably hostile. The British whose attitude mattered the most, were also dismissive. Linlithgow wrote to Secretary of State Zetland on 24 March 1940 that he did not 'attach too much importance' to Jinnah's demand, which was as preposterous and incapable of acceptance as that which Congress were putting forward. In the House of Lords, Zetland said on 18 April 1940 that the acceptance of the Lahore Resolution

> ... would be equivalent to admitting the failure of the devoted efforts of Englishmen and Indians over a long period of concentrated effort: for those labours have been based upon the assumption that even in the admitted diversity of India, a measure of political unity could be achieved sufficiently to enable India as a whole to take its place as an integral unit in the British Commonwealth of Nations.

Moreover

> if separate Muslim States did indeed come into existence in India, as now contemplated by the All-India Muslims League, the day would come when they might find the temptation to join an Islamic Commonwealth of nations well nigh irresistable. More particularly would this be the case with the North-West of India, which would, in these circumstances, be a Muslim state coterminous with the vast block of territory dominated by Islam which runs from North Africa and Turkey in the West to Afghanistan in the East.

Whatever the Hindus and the British may have thought of the demand for Pakistan, the Muslims immediately welcomed it with their whole heart. the Muslims at last had found the key to the problem that had baffled them for so long. They had wanted India to be free but they did not wish to exchange British rule for Hindu rule. British rule at least had the merit of being neutral between the Hindus and the Muslims. Hindu rule they feared would inflict upon them infinitely more humiliation and hardship than British rule. They had ruled India for several hundred years before the British and could with Pakistan revive Muslim glory at least in parts where they constituted a majority. No longer could the Congress leaders chide them that they merely followed the negative policy of opposing the Congress programme for independence without defining a comparable positive alternative of their own.

That the Muslims of India looked upon the Quaid as their outstanding leader was demonstrated by the fact that it was to him that they had turned in 1934 to reunite the Muslim League which had become divided into the Aziz Group and the Hidayat Group. They respected him for his utter integrity and for his brilliant and fearless advocacy of the causes he believed in. Nevertheless many had been disconcerted by this incessant hankering after friendship with the Hindus.

This reservation now disappeared; he was instantly hailed as the champion of Islam. He could, moreover, at last fight Gandhi on an equal footing. Gandhi had been promising *Ramrajya* to the Hindu masses; Jinnah now promised Pakistan to the Muslim masses. If the Mahatma reminded the Hindus of Buddha and Mahavira, the Quaid-i-Azam reminded the Muslims of Moses who had led his people to the promised land. The masses instinctively came to his assistance first; the intelligentsia came last.[4] In the end he was able to defeat Gandhi because he was a practical politician.

The claim that the Muslims constituted a nation and not merely a minority also brought two other immediate advantages. Firstly, as a minority the Muslims hitherto had been entitled to a share in government proportionate to their numerical strength. As a nation they could, under International Law, claim complete equality of representation with the Hindus in all governmental agencies. Secondly, the Muslims of the Muslim majority provinces now flocked to the banner of the League with greater zest. The achievement of Pakistan would rid them of the menace of a predominantly Hindu central government.

The Quaid Defuses the Khaksar Crisis

On 19 March 1940, three days before the Lahore session of the League was due to open, about 150 to 200 Khaksars[5] took out a procession in Lahore in military formation in defiance of government orders. This resulted in a dangerous armed clash with the police leading to the death of twenty-four Khaksars and two policemen. Jinnah was advised to postpone the League session because of the prevailing tension but refused to do so. He arrived in Lahore according to programme on 21 March, and went straight to the hospital to visit the wounded Khaksars. The Khaksars were threatening to disrupt the proceedings of the League session. Despite the danger to his personal safety, Jinnah made so bold as to announce that he would address an open meeting of Khaksars and the Muslim public. At the meeting he said he would do everything in his power to see that justice was meted out to the Khaksars. Under his guidance the League passed a resolution calling upon the government to appoint an impartial committee of enquiry and urged that orders declaring the Khaksar organization unlawful be removed as soon as possible. The Working Committee was authorized to take appropriate action after publication of the report of the Committee. In explaining the resolution Jinnah stated that as the matter was *sub judice* it would 'not be in the fitness of things that, on the one hand, we ask for an enquiry, and on the other, we pronounce our judgement'. He managed to defuse the crisis by diverting the action from agitational to constitutional channels, just as he had done previously in case of Shahidganj.

The Quaid-i-Azam's Further Advocacy of the Demand for Pakistan

Jinnah did not hesitate candidly to admit that he had been over-optimistic in his zealous pursuit of Hindu-Muslim unity. At the Lahore session he referred to what had happened in the Congress-governed provinces and confessed, 'I never dreamt that they would ever come down so low'.[6] During an address on 3 March 1941 he said 'it was good' that Providence had frustrated his efforts for twenty-five years to bring about an adjustment between Hindus and Muslims. 'For, if some kind of patchwork would have been done on the basis of oneness of India, it would have resulted in terrible disaster'. If Hindu Raj was established 'the last vestige of Islamic spirit will be destroyed. We got ample proof of it during the short-lived Congress regimes in the seven provinces of India'.[7]

He now recognized that Pakistan in fact had existed for ages. The Pakistani homelands were in the north-west and east where Muslims were even 'today' in a majority of seventy per cent.[8] On another occasion he explained that

> Pakistan started the moment the first non-Muslim was converted to Islam in India long before the Muslims established their rule. As soon as a Hindu embraced Islam he was an outcast not only religiously but also socially, culturally and economically. As for a Muslim it was a duty imposed on him by Islam not to merge his identity and individuality in any alien society.

In a gathering of high European and American officials he was asked who was the author of Pakistan. Jinnah's reply was 'Every Mussulman'.[9] India had never been a single nation; it was 'the British bayonet that is now holding India together.[10]

With regard to Gandhi's statement that partition would mean 'a vivisection of India' he said it was a device to frighten the Hindus to allege that their motherland 'is vivisected by these wretched Muslims... May I know when was India one?' We are told, he went on, that it is not in the interest of the Muslims themselves and thanked his Hindu friends 'most profusely for pointing out our mistake... We are prepared to take the consequences of our well-considered resolution. Please look after yourselves'. To the argument that Pakistan was not economically a practical scheme, his reply was 'if the worst comes to the worst, like a sensible man we will cut our coat according to our cloth'. Next, what about the Hindu minorities in the Muslim zones, he asked, and answered as follows

> Do you suggest as an argument that because the Hindu minority or minorities in the Muslim zone will be minorities, therefore the 90 million Muslims should remain as a minority in an artificial 'one India' with unitary form of central government so that you can dominate over them all including those zones where they are in a solid majority?[11]

In an interview with the correspondent of the *Daily Worker*, London, Jinnah said that he had stated many times that Pakistan would have friendly relations with India. We will say, 'Hands off India' to all outsiders.[12]

However, he was not prepared to put up with criticism from any one that he had shifted from his original political stance. During a speech in the Legislative Assembly he claimed that the Mussulmans 'always had at their back—and it has never been different during the last 25 years—that they are a separate entity'. M. S. Aney heckled him and alleged, 'At least that was not the view of Mr Jinnah before 1920'. Jinnah rejoined, 'Since 1916, since the Lucknow Pact was passed, on the fundamental principle of two separate entities'. But Aney refused to be silenced and boasted, 'I was there'. Jinnah thereupon suppressed him with sarcasm: 'My friend may have been there, but he was not even heard of at that time'.[13]

The Hindu Exponents of the Two Nation Doctrine

The belief that the Hindus and the Muslims constituted two separate nations of India was not confined to the Muslims. Some notable Hindus subscribed to it with equal conviction.

Lala Lajpat Rai, an eminent Hindu leader who had presided over the Special Session of the Congress at Calcutta in September 1920, stated in a letter to C. R. Das

> There is one point more which has been troubling me very much of late and one which I want you to think about carefully, and that is the question of Hindu-Muslim unity. I have devoted most of my time during the last six months to the study of Muslim history and Muslim law, and I am inclined to think it is neither possible nor practicable.[14]

His suggestion was

> ...that the Punjab should be partitioned into two provinces, the Western Punjab with a large Muslim majority to be a Muslim-governed province; and the Eastern Punjab with a large Hindu-Sikh majority to be a non-Muslim-governed province. I do not discuss Bengal. To me it is unimaginable that the rich and highly progressive and alive Hindus

of Bengal will ever work out the Pact agreed to by Mr Das. I will make the same suggestion in their case, but if Bengal is prepared to accept Mr Das's Pact, I have nothing to say. It is its own lookout.[15]

Savakar, the president of the Hindu Mahasabha plainly admitted that India could not be assumed to be a 'unitarian and homogeneous nation' but on the contrary the Hindus and the Muslims were two nations. However, he conveniently declared that the two nations must dwell in the same country. The Constitution would be such that the Hindu nation would be enabled to occupy a predominant position that was its due and the Muslim nation would be made to live in a position of subordinate cooperation with the Hindu nation. Minority was no justification for privilege and majority was to be no ground for penalty.[16]

Hinduism, with its great genius for assimilation, had reached a degree of compatibility with the pre-Muslim alien cultures but Panikkar, the noted Hindu historian concedes that 'Islam split Indian society into two sections from top to bottom and what has now come to be known in the phraseology of today as "two separate nations" came into being from the very beginning'.[17]

The German Blitzkrieg and its Repercussions in India

India was deeply affected by the German blitzkrieg of 1940. The German forces had taken Belgium, The Netherlands and Luxembourg in May and occupied Paris on 13 June. Many thought that Britain too might fall, which could bring the aggressive Germans to India through the Suez Canal. In the meantime Neville Chamberlain had resigned as British prime minister and a coalition government including Conservatives and Labourites had been formed under Winston Churchill.

Congress saw Britain's desperate situation as an opportunity for making a fresh bid for immediate independence and offered to pay an unusual price for the prize. They decided to divest Gandhi of his leadership of the Congress so that the Mahatma's utter commitment to non-violence would not deter Congress from supporting the war effort wholeheartedly. The interestingly worded resolution of the Working Committee passed on 21 June 1940 at Wardha noted that true to his ideal of non-violence Gandhi 'feels that at this critical phase in the history of man, the Congress should enforce this ideal by itself declaring that it does not want that India should maintain armed forces to defend her freedom against external aggression or internal disorder'. The Committee, however, had 'come to the conclusion that they are unable to go the full length with Gandhiji' and, therefore, absolved him from the responsibility for the policy they wished to pursue. The Committee while still adhering to the policy of non-violence 'in the national struggle for freedom', were 'unable to extend it to the region of national defence'.

Meeting next at Delhi (3-7 July 1940), the Working Committee resolved that it was 'more than ever convinced that the acknowledgment by Great Britain of the complete independence of India' was 'the only solution of the problems facing both India and Great Britain'. The Committee therefore demanded that a declaration to that effect 'should be immediately made and that as an immediate step in giving effect to it, a provisional National Government should be constituted at the Centre without delay'. The Committee declared that 'if these measures are adopted it will enable Congress to throw in its full weight in the efforts for the effective organization of the defence of the country'. The Wardha and Delhi resolutions of the Working Committee were confirmed by the All-India Congress Committee at Poona on 27 and 28 July.[18]

The Working Committee of the All-India Muslim League resolved on 16 June 1940 that in view of the grave world situation a basis for cooperation should be found between the government and the Muslim League and such other parties as were willing to shoulder the defence of the country, and authorized Jinnah to get in touch with the viceroy to explore the possibilities in that direction.

Jinnah interviewed the viceroy on 27 June and on 1 July also submitted in writing the League's terms for cooperation. These were: that no pronouncement should be made by the government which would militate against the principle of the division of India laid down in the Lahore Resolution; that no interim or final scheme of Constitution should be adopted without the previous consent of Muslim India; that to mobilize the full resources of the country for the war effect 'Muslim India leadership must be fully trusted as equals and have an equal share in the authority and control of the governments, central or provincial'; that the Executive Council of the viceroy should be enlarged within the framework of the present Constitution and Muslim representation must be equal to that of the Hindus if Congress came in, otherwise they should have the majority of the additional members; that in the provinces which were under the direct rule of the governor under Section 93, non-official advisers should be appointed, the majority of whom should be Muslims, and where coalition ministries could be formed it would be for the parties concerned to come to an agreement amongst themselves; that there should be a War Council to be presided over by the viceroy and which the princes should be invited to join to advise the government with regard to matters connected with the prosecution of the war; and finally, that the representatives of the Muslims on the War Council, on the Executive Council and among the non-official advisers of the governors in Section 93 provinces should be chosen by the Muslim League.[19]

Lord Linlithgow issued a statement on behalf of the British Government on 8 August 1940 which popularly became known as the 'August Offer'. It revived the offer to expand the Governor-General's Council by inviting representative Indians to join it and promised to establish a War Advisory Council consisting of representatives of Indian States and of other interests in the country. It also sought to placate both the Muslim League and Congress. It assured the minorities that the government 'could not contemplate the transfer of their present responsibilities for the peace and welfare of India to any system of government whose authority is directly denied by large and powerful elements in India's national life'. It stated that 'a moment when the Commonwealth is engaged in a struggle for existence is not one in which fundamental constitutional issues can be decisively resolved', but promised that after the war a representative body would be set up 'in order to devise the framework of the new Constitution'. The words 'Constituent Assembly' were not used, but in effect the Congress demand that it would be the Indians themselves who would frame their new Constitution (and not the British Parliament) was conceded.

In a meeting held at Bombay on 15-16 September 1940, the All-India Congress committee said that the British Government 'had no intention to recognize India's independence and would, if they could, continue to hold this country indefinitely in bondage for British exploitation'. The British Government had 'created an intolerable situation' and imposed upon Congress 'a struggle for the preservation of the honour and the elementary rights of the people'. Realizing that a 'struggle' with the government without Gandhi's magnetic leadership would be ineffective, the Committee proceeded to rehabilitate the Mahatma. It requested him to guide Congress in the action that should be taken, adding that the Delhi resolution confirmed by the All-India Congress Committee at Patna, which prevented him from so doing, had lapsed.[20]

A resolution passed by the Working Committee of the Muslim League meeting at the Quaid's residence in Bombay from 31 August to 2 September 1940, noted 'with satisfaction' that the 8 August 1940 offer of the British Government 'practically met the demands of the League for a clear assurance to the effect that no future Constitution, interim or final should be adopted by the British Government without their approval and consent'.[21]

At a Muslim Students Conference in New Delhi in November 1940, Jinnah spelled out his attitude toward the war

> We do not want Nazis to win this war. We want Great Britain to win this war. There is no question of our changing the masters. We want to take our freedom from Great Britain. For that reason, we from the beginning did not place any obstacles in the way of Great Britain. For instance, in spite of the fact that Pakistan is our anchorsheet, we did not demand Pakistan as a condition precedent for our wholehearted support to the British Government. We only asked for an assurance that the British Government would not let us down by entering into an agreement either interim or final with the Congress.[22]

As we have already stated, the All-India Congress Committee by its resolution on 16 September 1940, had authorized Gandhi to guide the Congress as to what action should be taken against the British Government. At the same time it had restricted the extent to which the Mahatma could go. The Congress did not have any ill will against the British nation it had said, and 'the spirit of satyagraha forbids the Congress from doing anything with a view to embarrass them'. In consonance with the spirit of the resolution, Gandhi did not raise the larger issue of independence in the satyagraha he launched on 17 October 1940, but raised only the issue of freedom of speech by which he meant freedom to denounce war as a method of settling international disputes. But the movement did not attract wholehearted support. Gandhi, however, was not perturbed by the criticism that the movement was a failure. He explained that the purpose was not to make an appreciable impression on the war effort but to register a moral protest.

Twenty-Eighth Session of the Muslim League, Madras, 12-15 April 1941

In the course of his extempore presidential address the Quaid recalled that the foundation of the revival of the Muslim League had been laid only in 1936 at the Bombay session. During the five years since then

> We have established a flag of our own, a national flag of Muslim India. We have established a remarkable platform which displays and demonstrates a complete unity of the entire solid body of Muslim India. We have defined in the clearest language our goal about which Muslim India was groping in the dark, and the goal is Pakistan.[23]

He made a survey of political developments in recent years and reiterated that the League did not 'make the demand for Pakistan here and now' because it did not wish to embarrass the British Government when they were 'engaged in a struggle of life and death for their own existence'.

He wound up with 'a note of real warning' to the British Government

> Please stop your policy of appeasement towards those who are bent upon frustrating your war efforts and doing their best to oppose the prosecution of the war and the defence of India at this critical moment... You are not loyal to those who are willing to stand by you and sincerely support you; you desire to placate those who have the greatest nuisance value in the political and economic fields.

As promised in the August Offer, the viceroy in July 1941, enlarged his Executive Council and also set up a National Defence Council.

Of the eight Muslims who had agreed to serve on the National Defence Committee, five were members of the Muslim League. These five were Sikander Hayat, Fazlul Haq and Saadullah—premiers respectively of the Punjab, Bengal and Assam—and the Nawab of Chattari and Begum Shah Nawaz. Since they had accepted the viceroy's invitation without consulting the Muslim League, Jinnah ordered them to resign. Sikander Hayat and Saadullah did so without creating trouble. Fazlul Haq followed suit after some demurral. The Nawab of Chattari had already resigned because he had been appointed as President of the Hyderabad Executive Council. Begum Shah Nawaz refused to resign and was expelled from the League for five years. Sir Sultan Ahmad was similarly punished for joining the Executive Council. He was asked to resign and upon refusal to do so was expelled from the League for five years. These instances clearly demonstrated Jinnah's ascendancy over the Muslim League.

The Cripps Mission, 23 March to 12 April 1942

Sir Stafford Cripps mission to India (23 March-12 April 1942) was the direct result of the spectacular Japanese victories that directly threatened India. After the German setbacks in the Battle of Britain and on the Russian front, the threat to India from the West had receded. But the rapid Japanese advance in the winter of 1941-42 made it seem that the Japanese could invade India from the east. After the disastrous fall of Singapore on 15 February 1942, the Japanese Navy commanded the Bay of Bengal. Rangoon fell on 7 March and the gloom deepened while Cripps was in India. Colombo suffered an air raid on 5 April and on the next day Japanese bombs fell on Indian soil—at Vizagapatam and Cocanada. The Andaman Islands were occupied and there was some panic in Calcutta and Madras.

Apart from the physical threat to India from Japan, Britain was under pressure from the USA and China to break the political deadlock in India and so secure wholehearted Indian participation in the war against Japan. In Churchill's War Cabinet itself, there was a demand from the Labour ministers, notably Attlee and Cripps,[24] that Indian goodwill should be won by generous political concessions.

Generalissimo and Madame Chiang Kai-shek had visited India from 9 to 22 February 1942 as guests of the viceroy and met not only the commander-in-chief and officials, but also the Indian leaders. The couple were already on friendly terms with Nehru and saw much of him during their visit. Chiang conferred with Gandhi, Azad and others, and the viceroy managed to arrange a meeting with Jinnah as well.

Before leaving India on 22 February, the Chinese leader broadcast a message to the Indian people from Calcutta. He said that China and India comprised one-half of the world's population and 'should freedom be denied to either China or India, there could be no real peace in the world'. He expressed the hope that Great Britain 'will as speedily as possible' give the people of India 'real political power'. Jinnah immediately issued a press statement complaining that Chiang Kai-shek was 'saturated with ideas of those who surrounded him most while in India' and stressing that Muslim India 'cannot accept the machinations of those who speak in the name of freedom for Hindu India only...both Hindu and Muslim nations should be free equally in their respective homelands'.

Cripps arrived in Delhi on 23 March, 1942 and made a press statement on the same day. 'My association in the past has been more close with my friends in the Congress than with the members of other parties or communities', he confessed, but held out the assurance that 'I am fully impressed with the need in any scheme for the future of India to meet the deep anxieties which undoubtedly exist among the Muslims and other communities. I shall therefore embark upon my task with a mind equally open to all points of view'.[25]

During the Pakistan Day celebrations in Delhi on the same day, the Quaid said in a public speech that there was the fear that Cripps 'is a friend of the Congress but pointed out that Cripps had not come to India in his personal capacity but as a representative of the British Government. He assured the audience that if Cripps's proposal turned out to be detrimental to Muslim interests, they would never be accepted.[26]

On 25 March, Cripps privately disclosed to Jinnah, as president of the Muslim League, and Azad, as president of the Congress, the proposals he intended to make public in the form of a Declaration. He recorded an account of his interview with Jinnah in the following terms

> Directly Mr Jinnah arrived I broached the question of my past attitude towards the Muslim League and told him that the views I took two and a half years ago were sincerely taken and represented my judgement of the situation as it then was and that I had regarded the Pakistan propaganda as pure political pressure. He responded very amiably to this, recognizing the sincerity of my views, which I told him the last two years had changed in view of the change in the communal feeling in India and the growth of the Pakistan Movement...I then gave him the documents to read...which I think rather surprised him in the distance it went to meet the Pakistan case.[27]

A press report stated that Jinnah was beaming with pleasure when Cripps escorted him out after the interview and said the proposals would be placed before the League Working Committee.[28]

It was on 29 March that Cripps publicly disclosed the contents of the Declaration by reading it out at a press conference.[29] The object was 'the creation of a new Indian Union which shall constitute a Dominion, associated with the United Kingdom and other Dominions by a common allegiance to the Crown, but equal to them in every respect'. The said goal would be achieved in the following manner. Immediately after the war an elected body would be set up to frame a new Constitution for India. It would be elected by the members of the Lower Houses of the Provincial Legislatures and representatives of the Princely States. His Majesty's Government would implement forthwith the Constitution so framed. Any province of British India not prepared to accept the new Constitution would have the right to retain its present constitutional position. To such non-acceding provinces, his Majesty's Government would be prepared to give the same full status as to the Indian Union.

Since negotiations with the Congress party broke down because of the scope of clause (e) of the Declaration, we quote it below in full

> During the critical period which now faces India and until the new Constitution can be framed, His Majesty's Government must inevitably

bear the responsibility for and retain control and direction of the defence of India as part of their world war effort, but the task of organizing to the full the military, moral and material resources of India must be the responsibility of the Government of India with the cooperation of the peoples of India. His Majesty's Government desire and invite the immediate and effective participation of the leaders of the principal sections of the Indian people in the counsels of their country, of the Commonwealth and of the United Nations.

Gandhi, the most influential figure in the Congress, was against India joining the war under any circumstances because it would violate the principle of non-violence. He was also 'inclined more and more to the view that the Allies could not win the war. He feared that it might end in the triumph of Germany and Japan or at best there might be a stalemate'.[30] During his meeting with Cripps on 27 March 1942, Gandhi gave his opinion that Congress would not accept the Declaration, firstly because of the provisions relating to the states, and secondly, because of the non-accession option given to the provinces. Gandhi later related to his biographer, Louis Fischer, that after reading the Declaration he had told Cripps, 'if this is your entire proposal to India, I would advise you to take the next plane home'.[31] Cripps's own view, expressed after the unsuccessful termination of his mission, was that it was Gandhi's advice to the Congress Working Committee that had finally caused that body to reject the Declaration.[32]

In his presidential address to the Allahabad session of the League (4 April 1942), the Quaid-i-Azam analysed the Cripps proposals and expressed disappointment that their main objective was the creation of a new Indian Union and Pakistan was treated only 'as a remote possibility'.

Azad in his *India Wins Freedom* has given a full account of the Congress negotiations with Cripps and has included in it the text of the letters he exchanged with him. The crux of the matter was that Congress made their cooperation conditional on the assurance that the proposed National Government 'must be a Cabinet government with full power, and must not merely be a continuation of the viceroy's Executive Council'.[33] Cripps replied that this would not be possible because it required constitutional changes of a most complicated character and on a very large scale.[34] In his last letter to Cripps dated 11 April 1942, Azad alleged that Cripps had gone back on his earlier assurance that the National Government 'would function as a Cabinet and that the position of the viceroy should be analogous to that of the King of England *vis-à-vis* his Cabinet'.[35]

The formal rejection of Cripps's proposals took the form of a Congress Working Committee Resolution dated 11 April 1942. It stated that Congress had always made it clear that its cooperation in the war effort was conditional on the grant of freedom to India 'for only the realization of present freedom could light the flame which would illuminate millions of hearts and move them to action'. The new proposals related principally to the future.[36] Azad says plainly that 'the war had given India an opportunity for achieving her freedom. We must not lose it by depending upon a mere promise'.[37]

The Muslim League too rejected Cripps's proposals by a Working Committee resolution of the same date. It expressed gratification that the possibility of Pakistan was 'recognized by implication' but stated that 'the only solution of India's constitutional problem is the partition of India into independent zones; and it will therefore be unfair to Moslems to compel them to enter such a constitution-making body whose main object is the creation of a new Indian Union'. The Committee concluded that as 'the proposals for the future are unacceptable, it will serve no useful purpose to deal further with the question of the immediate arrangements'.[38]

Cripps believed that 'the League would have been ready to accept the proposals if Congress had been prepared to do so'.[39]

In the course of his correspondence with Cripps, Azad could not refrain from harping on the Congress theme that 'if the British Government did not pursue a policy of encouraging disruption, all of us, to whatever party or group we belonged, would be able to come together and find a common line of action'.[40] But Secretary of State Amery realistically pointed out in the House of Commons that Sir Stafford Cripps 'flew many thousands of miles to meet the Indian leaders in order to arrive at an agreement with them. The Indian leaders in Delhi moved not one step to meet each other'.[41]

The Muslim League and the British Government benefited from the Cripps mission while the Congress suffered a setback. Only two years previously the birth of the Pakistan idea had been greeted with derision. The British Government had now officially declared it to be an acceptable possibility. Jawaharlal Nehru complained that his old friend, Cripps, had 'allowed himself to become the devil's advocate'.[42] The British Government had valued the Muslims as a counterpoise against the hostile Congress from the very beginning of the war. They now looked upon the Muslims even more benignly than before. And by soon staging the Quit India revolt and courting internment, Gandhi and his colleagues left the field clear for Jinnah to boost the already growing strength of the Pakistan Movement.

By Congress's refusal to accept the proposals, the British Government were saved the headache of having to form an interim central government in which the Congress would have been the largest party. To start with, it would have been difficult to satisfy both the Congress and the League with regard to their respective shares in the membership of the viceroy's Executive Council and their portfolios in it. Once in office, there could be no guarantee that the two would work together smoothly as a team. Most of all there was no knowing how the Congress element in the government would conduct itself having regard to the party's long record of hostility toward the British Government and the presence of a strong pacifist element in its leadership.

C. Rajagopalachari, the Congress leader of Madras was so disappointed at the failure of the Cripps mission that he successfully sponsored two resolutions in a meeting of the Madras Congress legislatures. The first recommended that the 'Muslim League's claim for separation' should be acknowledged so that a National Government could be formed jointly by the Congress and the League. The second sought permission of the All-India Congress for the Madras Congress to enter into a coalition with the Muslim League to form a popular government in Madras. In a letter to Azad the Congress president, dated 30 April 1942, Rajagopalachari offered his regret for having sponsored the resolutions without prior consultation with Azad and his other colleagues of the Working Committee and tendered his resignation from the Working Committee.

Gandhi's Quit India Rebellion

After Cripps had left, Gandhi told Azad that 'if the Japanese Army ever came into India it would come not as our enemy but as the enemy of the British. It was his view that if the British left, the Japanese would not attack India'.[43] The Mahatma told a representative of *The News Chronicle*, London

> It is just likely that the Japanese will not want to invade India, their prey having gone. But it is equally likely that they will want to invade India in order to use her ports for strategic purposes. Then, I would advise the people to do the same thing that I have advised them to do now, viz., offer stubborn non-violent noncooperation.

In the same interview he said, 'under my proposal they [the British] have to leave India in God's hands—but in modern parlance to anarchy'.[44]

'The Quit India Resolution' was passed by the All-India Congress Committee on 8 August 1942. Its operative part ran

> The Committee feels that it is no longer justified in holding the nation back from endeavouring to assert its will against an imperialist and authoritarian government which dominates over it and prevents it from functioning in its own interest and in the interest of humanity. The Committee resolves, therefore, to sanction, for the vindication of India's inalienable right to freedom and independence, the starting of a mass struggle on non-violent lines on the widest possible scale, so that the country might utilize all the non-violent strength it has gathered during the last twenty-two years of peaceful struggle. Such a struggle must inevitably be under the leadership of Gandhiji and the Committee requests him to take the lead and to guide the nation in the steps to be taken.[45]

On 9 August Gandhi, the members of the Working Committee, and other leading Congressmen were arrested.

In the days preceding his arrest he had told the Press that 'this is open rebellion' and wrote in the *Harijan*, 'I can but do or die'.[46]

Though the Working Committee resolution had spoken of 'a mass struggle on non-violent lines' some of Gandhi's own utterances which have been quoted above suggested that the outbreak of violence was unavoidable. At another time he had been asked directly, 'What may be permitted for disorganizing government within the limits of non-violence?' His reply was:

Cutting wires, removing rails, destroying small bridges, cannot be objected to in a struggle like this provided ample precautions are taken to safeguard life. If the Japanese were invading us, there can be no doubt that even on principle of non-violent self-defence, these would have to be carried out. The non-violent revolutionaries have to regard the British Power in the same way as they [the revolutionaries] would the Axis Powers and carry out the same measures.[47]

Of course, the Mahatma omitted to explain how these acts of sabotage were to be perpetrated without provoking a violent confrontation with the forces of law and order. In fact the disorders that inevitably ensued were sufficiently intense and destructive for Linlithgow to call them 'the most serious rebellion since that of 1857'[48] but their duration was short. On 1 September he could report that the situation was 'settling down very rapidly'[49] and on 21 September that 'taken as a whole things are pretty comfortable'.[50] By the end of the year the rebellion had virtually subsided.

The Muslim League Attitude Toward the Quit India Rebellion

Meanwhile, in a statement issued from Bombay, the Quaid said: 'Now we are presented with a new formula and that formula is "Quit India" ...We do not know what this "big move" is going to be... When the time comes the Working Committee of the Muslim League will decide how to face the new situation'.[51]

On 9 August, the day after Congress had passed the Quit India resolution, Jinnah declared in a statement that he deeply regretted that 'Congress had finally declared war and has launched a most dangerous mass movement in spite of numerous warnings from various individuals, parties and organizations in this country'.[52]

During a special interview with the *Daily Herald* of London on 14 August, he endorsed the action of the government in arresting the Congress leaders and taking firm measures to quell the riots because it was 'faced with what is legally high treason'.[53]

The Working Committee of the Muslim League met at Bombay from 16 to 20 August and passed a resolution which claimed that the Muslims were 'not a whit less insistent on freedom for the country', but they were firmly convinced that the Congress movement was 'not directed for securing the independence of all the constituent elements in the life of the country, but for the establishment of a Hindu raj and to deal a death blow to the Muslim goal of Pakistan'.

The resolution called upon the Muslims to abstain from any participation in the Congress movement and to continue to pursue their normal life, and ended with a stern warning

> The Working Committee hope that no attempt shall be made from any quarter to intimidate, coerce, molest or interfere in any manner with the normal life of the Muslims, otherwise the Muslims will be compelled to offer resistance and adopt all such measures as may be necessary for the protection of their life, honour and property.[54]

At a press conference on 13 September the Muslim League President reiterated that the Congress movement was 'unlawful and unconstitutional', and added that an even greater objection was that it was a declaration of 'internecine civil war' because the movement had been launched to force demands which were strenuously opposed not only by the Muslim League but equally by the other minorities and interests in the country.

The warning of the Muslim League Working Committee was heeded. The Quit India insurgents left the Muslims strictly alone and there were no Hindu-Muslim disturbances during the upheaval.

A Murderous Attack on the Quaid-i-Azam

In June and July 1943, Jinnah received several threats of murder from the Khaksars. The Khaksar movement had been founded by Allama Mashriqi in September 1931. Its members dressed and drilled in semi-military style. During 1942 and the first quarter of 1943, Mashriqi corresponded with Gandhi and others. He proposed that a demand for India's independence should be made jointly by the Congress and the Muslim League and that after independence Pakistan should be won by negotiations with the Congress. The Quaid was also all for joining with the Congress to secure independence but his position was that the issue of Pakistan must be settled before the joint fight for independence was launched. After that an alliance would be formed between the Hindu nation and the Muslim nation as equals to confront the foreign imperialists. He argued

> If Muslims had joined the Congress movement in the name of freedom and independence, Mr Gandhi would have represented to England and America and the world that he alone represented the whole of India and that his demand was also supported by Muslim India. A greater folly and more serious blunder could not have been committed if they had fallen into this trap.[55]

The threat to Jinnah's life materialized on the afternoon of 26 July 1943. A Khaksar named Rafiq Sabir Maznavi walked up to the Quaid's residence in Bombay and told the watchman that he wanted to see his master. He was taken to the office of Jinnah's secretary and was there informed that Jinnah was very busy. Just at that moment, Jinnah happened to walk into the room. As Jinnah was leaving, Sabir sprang upon him and hit him on the jaw with a clenched fist. When Jinnah reeled back, the assailant attacked him with a large knife. Jinnah defended himself by catching hold of the assailant's hand. This softened the blow and Jinnah escaped with no more than a wound on his chin and some cuts on his hand. In the meantime Jinnah's chauffeur and others arrived at the scene and overpowered Sabir. He was subsequently sentenced to five years rigorous imprisonment by a British judge.

The Bengal Famine

In the autumn and winter (1942-3), Bengal suffered a dreadful famine. The official estimate was that one and a half million died of starvation or its after-effects, but Nehru wrote feelingly, 'a million had died, or two million, or three; no one knows how many starved to death or died of disease during these months of horror. No one knows of the many millions of emaciated boys and girls and little children who just escaped death then, but are stunted and broken in body and spirit'.

The shortage of the rice crop was small and ordinarily would have been met by purchases from Burma and Thailand, but these sources were at this time under Japanese control. Prices had been rising sharply for some time because of panic-buying, but the provincial government was inefficient and imprudent and allowed the situation to get out of hand, while the central government under Linglithgow did not assert itself effectively. Relief efforts were also hampered by a lack of adequate transport facilities; the railway system was burdened by military supplies for the eastern front and boats had been requisitioned to deny them to the Japanese in case of invasion. It was not until Wavell took over as viceroy on 20 October 1943 and took a vigorous interest in the tragedy that anything worthwhile was done to alleviate the suffering. Within a week of assuming the viceroyalty, he flew to Calcutta and went round the streets by night to see how the destitute were sleeping, and by day to see them fed. He also visited the Contai district of Midnapore, one of the areas worst affected by the famine. He was able to induce the ministry to introduce systematic rationing and take other measures. He also directed the army to assist in the transport and distribution of supplies.

Wavell's Appointment as Viceroy

The Japanese launched an offensive in Arakan in February 1944 and in March they threatened Imphal (in Manipur State, India). But they had stretched themselves too far and had had to divert their aeroplanes to the Pacific. They were forced to withdraw and this proved to be the turning point. By August they had been cleared from Indian soil and had retreated to Burma. The Allied forces mounted a counter-offensive and Rangoon was retaken in May 1945.

In the meantime there was a change of viceroyalty in India. Wavell was in England when his appointment was announced on 19 June 1943 but he did not arrive in India till 17 October to assume office three days later. At a farewell dinner in London held in his honour on 6 October, Wavell said that he was aware that 'some quarters' believed that political progress in India should not be attempted during the war. He agreed that the first aim must be to defeat the enemy but he did not think that that should necessarily bar political progress if progress was possible.[56]

But his directive from the Churchill government was to 'beware above all things lest the achievement of victory and the ending of the miseries of war should be retarded by undue concentration on political issues while the enemy is at the gate'.⁵⁷ Churchill's personal view on the policy to be followed in India was contained in a memorandum he wrote on 6 October 1943

> Gandhi had raised the cry of 'Quit India' and made it clear that he was prepared to cooperate with Japan... We are now preparing very important offensive operations from India against Japan... There could hardly be a less suitable time for raising again the political agitation on its old well-known lines, and for trying to form a responsible government based in the main on Gandhi.

Gandhi's conduct, Churchill noted, had alienated even American public opinion from him: 'In all my visits to America, I have never been asked a single question about India'.⁵⁸

In his address to the Legislature on 17 February 1944 Wavell said, 'On the main problem of Indian unity, the difference between Hindu and Muslim, I can only say this. You cannot alter geography... India is a natural unit'. Jinnah referred to Wavell's 'theory of Geographical Unity of India' in a speech at the Aligarh University Union on 9 March 1944. He said that they in Aligarh stood in no need of any lessons in geography as they had a most efficient department of geography of their own, and they knew very well that India never was and is not a Geographical Unity. Both geographically and historically India had always been divided into several States, and nothing could deter the Mussulmans of India from establishing Pakistan which was their destiny.⁵⁹

The Jinnah-Khizar Rift

Khizar Hayat Khan Tiwana had succeeded Sikandar Hayat Khan as head of the all-party Unionist Ministry in the Punjab in 1942. During the Lucknow session of the Muslim League in October 1937, Sikander had announced that he would advise all the Muslim members of the Unionist Party in the Punjab to join the Muslim League. He had however not dissolved the Unionist Party and had maintained the label Unionist for his ministry. It was not till April 1944 that Jinnah felt confident enough to challenge that position. He personally visited the Punjab for several days for a showdown with Khizar.

Jinnah said no one could owe allegiance to two political parties, and demanded that the name 'Unionist Party' should be discarded and be replaced by the 'Muslim League Coalition Party'. Khizar claimed that under the 'Sikander-Jinnah Pact' it had been agreed that, while the Punjab Muslims would support the Muslim League on all-India issues, the description of the ministry as Unionist would be retained and Jinnah would not interfere in provincial matters. Jinnah denied that there had been any 'pact' between himself and Sikander. 'How could there be a pact between a leader and a follower?' he asked.

Though some of his followers had begun to waver, Khizar himself insisted that he was entitled to be both a Unionist and a Muslim Leaguer. When Jinnah, in a two-and-a-half hour meeting on 20 April, argued that for a Muslim to adhere to the Unionist Party as well as to the Muslim League was like keeping a mistress in addition to a wife, Khizar responded wittily that being a Muslim himself, he was entitled to have two wives.

Not long afterwards, Khizar was expelled from the Muslim League. His defiance of Jinnah cost him dear in the long run. His followers began to desert him in increasing numbers as Jinnah's domination over all Muslim politicians continued to grow with the passage of time.

Gandhi Offers to Trade Non-Violence for a Declaration of Immediate Indian Independence

While Gandhi was still in prison his wife passed away on 22 February 1944. Not long afterwards the Mahatma himself caught malaria and his health began to deteriorate. The Government of India released him on 6 May on medical advice. Things had not gone his way in the recent past. His Quit India rebellion had not achieved independence nor had it appreciably dented the war effort. Jinnah, the Muslim League and the Pakistan Movement had been gathering strength. The tide of war had turned in favour of the Allies and the British Government was no longer under any pressure to offer concessions to the Congress.

Following the German blitzkrieg, Congress in its eagerness to achieve independence immediately, had offered to depose the pacific Mahatma from leadership and co-operate in the war effort. In his own eagerness to achieve the same result, Gandhi now went a step further and offered personally to forget about his dedication to non-violence and assist in the war effort. At the same time he expressed the wish to seek a compromise with Jinnah impliedly relinquishing the claim that the Congress represented the whole of India including the Muslims. 'I was completely taken aback,' recalled Azad 'and knew that both these actions were doomed to failure.'[60]

On 27 July 1944 Gandhi wrote to the viceroy

> I am prepared to advise the Working Committee to declare that in view of changed conditions mass Civil Disobedience envisaged by the resolution of August 1942 cannot be offered and that full co-operation in the war effort should be given by the Congress, if a declaration of immediate Indian Independence is made and a National Government responsible to the Central Assembly be formed.[61]

Wavell replied on 15 August

> I must make it quite clear that until the war is over, responsibility for defence and military operations cannot be divided from the other responsibilities of Government, and that until hostilities cease and the new Constitution is in operation, His Majesty's Government and the Governor-General must retain their responsibility over the entire field... It is clear in these circumstances that no purpose would be served by discussion on the basis which you suggest. If however the leaders of the Hindus, the Muslims and the important minorities were willing to cooperate in a transitional government established and working within the present Constitutions, I believe good progress might be made. For such a transitional government to succeed there must, before it is formed, be agreement in principle between Hindus and Muslims and all important elements as to the method by which the new Constitution should be framed.[62]

Jinnah-Gandhi Negotiations, 9-26 September 1944

In his continuing efforts to bring about a Hindu-Muslim accord, Rajagopalachari had seen Gandhi in jail and obtained his approval to a scheme which came to be known as the Rajaji Formula. It ran:

Subject to the terms set out below as regards the Constitution for Free India, the Muslim League endorses the Indian demand for Independence and will co-operate with Congress in the formation of a provisional interim government for the transitional period.

After the termination of the war, a commission shall be appointed for demarcating contiguous districts in the north-west and east of India, wherein the Muslim population is in absolute majority. In the areas thus demarcated, a plebiscite of all the inhabitants held on the basis of adult suffrage or other practicable franchise shall ultimately decide the issue of separation from Hindustan. If the majority decide in favour of forming a sovereign State separate from Hindustan, such a decision shall be given effect to, without prejudice to the right of districts on the border to choose to join either State.

These terms shall be binding only in case of transfer by British of full power and responsibility of the governance of India.

It was on 17 July 1944 that Gandhi set the ball rolling by writing to Jinnah. 'I have not written to you since my release. Today my heart says that I should write to you. We will meet whenever you choose. Do not disappoint me.' Jinnah, who at the time was in Kashmir, replied that he would be glad to receive Gandhi at his residence in Bombay on his return. They met at Jinnah's house in Bombay on 9 September and thereafter corresponded at some length. They also personally conferred together a number of times up to 26 September, but without arriving at an agreement.[63] They did not keep any minutes of their oral discussions but the texts of their letters are available.

The first letter in the series was written by Jinnah to Gandhi on 10 September, and we learn from it that during their meeting on the previous day Jinnah had tried to persuade Gandhi to accept the Pakistan Resolution of March 1940, while Gandhi had put forward the Rajaji Formula. The main points that emerged during the debate were the following:

Jinnah complained that Gandhi's claim that he had come to discuss Hindu-Muslim settlement in his individual capacity raised 'great difficulty' in his way because he himself could speak only in his capacity as president of the Muslim League. Gandhi characteristically claimed, 'Though I represent nobody but myself, I aspire to represent all the inhabitants of India', to which Jinnah replied, 'I cannot accept that statement of yours. It is quite clear that you represent nobody else but Hindus, and as long as you do not realize your true position and the realities, it is very difficult for me to argue with you'.

For his part, Gandhi questioned the right of the Indian Muslims to call themselves a nation. 'I find no parallel in history', he wrote in one of his letters, 'for a body of converts and their descendants claiming to be a nation apart from the parent stock', to which Jinnah rejoined

> We maintain and hold that Muslims and Hindus are two major nations by any definition or test of a nation. We are a nation of a hundred million, and, what is more, we are a nation with our own distinctive culture and civilization, language and literature, art and architecture, names and nomenclature, sense of value and proportion, legal laws and moral codes, customs and calendar, history and traditions, aptitudes and ambitions. In short, we have our own distinctive outlook on life and of life. By all canons of international law we are a nation.

The two leaders also differed with regard to the boundaries of Pakistan and how the issue of whether India should be divided at all was to be determined. Gandhi said his assumption was that

> ... the Muslims living in the north-west zones, i.e., Baluchistan, Sind, North-West Frontier Province and that part of the Punjab where they are in absolute majority over all the other elements, and in parts of Bengal and Assam where they are in absolute majority, desire to live in separation from India.

Jinnah protested that if this proposal was 'given effect to, the present boundaries of these provinces would be maimed and mutilated beyond redemption and leave us only with the husk'. His position was that Pakistan would comprise the whole of six provinces, viz., Sind, Baluchistan, North-West Frontier Province, the Punjab, Bengal and Assam subject to territorial adjustment that may be agreed upon.

Gandhi also said that the issue of partition should be decided by a vote of the entire adult population of the six provinces concerned. Jinnah, on the other hand, maintained that only Muslims should vote on the question because 'we claim the right of self-determination as a nation, and not as a territorial unit'.[64]

But the immediate reasons why the talks broke down were, firstly, that Gandhi stated, 'we reach by joint effort independence for India as it stands. India, become free, will proceed to demarcation, plebiscite and partition if the people concerned vote for partition'. This to Jinnah meant that Congress wanted to get rid of the British first so that they could then be in a position to deny Pakistan to the Muslims. He therefore insisted that 'we come to a settlement of our own immediately'. Second, Gandhi said that he could be 'no willing party to a division which does not provide for the simultaneous safeguarding of common interests such as defence, foreign affairs and the like'. Denial of complete control over these vital subjects clearly meant denial of sovereignty to Pakistan. It is no wonder that a frustrated Jinnah told Gandhi that, 'as a result of our correspondence and discussions I find that the question of the division of India as Pakistan and Hindustan is only on your lips and it does not come from your heart'.

During a press conference on 4 October 1944, Jinnah said

> My attention has been drawn to Mr Gandhi's press statement which was published on 29 September. It is a pity that he thinks that the presence of a third party hinders a solution, and it was very painful to me when he said, a mind enslaved cannot act as if it was free. No power can enslave the mind and soul of man, and I am sure Mr Gandhi is the last person to allow his mind to be enslaved. I do hope that he will get over this depression from which he is perpetually suffering. We have to reach an agreement of our own and find a solution in spite of that third party.[65]

The Muslim League president also expressed his amazement that Gandhi 'should repeat *ad nauseam* that he has by his offer satisfied the essence of the Lahore Resolution. It would be difficult to conceive of a more disingenuous, tortuous and crooked assertion which he keeps on repeating naïvely'.[66] To the question whether there was any possibility of his meeting Gandhi again in the near future, Jinnah replied, 'Mr Gandhi says that it depends on the inner voice. I have no admission to that place. I cannot say.'[67]

Though the Gandhi-Jinnah negotiations failed to achieve the avowed goal of Hindu-Muslim unity, they brought to Jinnah and the Muslim League two important political gains. Firstly, the supreme leader of Congress had now offered to discuss the question of Pakistan seriously—hitherto Congress and the Mahatma had kept the door to that subject uncompromisingly shut.

Secondly, Congress could no longer justifiably claim that it stood for all the communities in India including the Muslims. That he thought it necessary to approach the president of the Muslim League for a Hindu-Muslim settlement was tacit admission on Gandhi's part that it was the Muslim League that really represented the Muslims and that Jinnah was as much a personification of the League as he himself was of the Congress.

Jinnah explained to Kanji Dwarkadas that his insistence that Gandhi should come to his residence to see him was not due to arrogance as some quarters suggested. It was because experience had taught him that a peaceful discussion with Gandhi was not possible at the latter's residence

> Hardly was he [Jinnah] with Gandhiji that one after one of his secretaries and associates came in and interrupted the conversation on all kinds of flimsy excuses—articles had to be revised, papers were to be corrected immediately, a young daughter-in-law had come to see him complaining against ill-treatment by her mother-in-law, etc., etc., and no proper discussion could take place. Jinnah complained to Gandhiji that if the latter's colleagues did not like Jinnah coming down for frank talks, he would not any more come to Gandhiji's house, and Gandhiji accepting Jinnah's just grievance readily agreed.[68]

In December 1921, Dwarkadas had also personally protested to Gandhi that there had been 'no peace and quiet' during his talk with the Mahatma.[69]

The Simla Conference

As the fortunes of war began to turn in favour of the Allies, Wavell felt that the time had come for him to make proposals for a resolution of the political deadlock in India. During an informal discussion of the political situation in the Governors conference on 31 August 1944, Wavell gave it as his view that in the short-term, India could be kept quiet, but the long-term view was 'less comfortable' because 'as soon as the war with Japan ended, His Majesty's Government's cheque would be presented and would have to be honoured'.[70]

His objective, as stated in a letter to Churchill, was to form 'a provisional government, of the type suggested in the Cripps

Declaration, within the present Constitution, coupled with an earnest but not necessarily simultaneous attempt to devise a means to reach a constitutional settlement'.[71] Wavell told Amery that he attached much importance to his proposals and was prepared to visit London to urge their acceptance, but it was not till 11 January 1945 that he was informed that he could come in late March. He eventually arrived on 23 March.

He had a one-and-a-quarter hour meeting with Churchill on 29 March. The prime minister thought that the problem of India, 'could be kept on ice', but Wavell told him quite firmly that the question of India was very urgent and very important. Wavell's impression was that Churchill seemed 'to favour partition into Pakistan, Hindustan, Princestan, etc'.[72]

During May, while Wavell was still in England, the war in Europe came to an end, the coalition government in England broke up and a Conservative 'caretaker' Government under Churchill took office, with Amery continuing as secretary of state for India. It was on 31 May that the visiting viceroy at last got a go-ahead from the Cabinet largely on the lines he had desired. He left London on 1 June and landed at Karachi on 4 June.

The British Government's new proposals were publicly disclosed on 14 June 1945, on which date the viceroy made a broadcast at New Delhi and the secretary of state made a statement in the House of Commons. In his broadcast, Wavell said that the proposals he was making were not an attempt to impose a constitutional settlement, but the hope that the Indian parties would agree among themselves on a settlement of the communal issue which had not been fulfilled, and in the meantime great problems had to be solved. He therefore invited the Indian leaders to take counsel with him

> ...with a view to the formation of a new Executive Council more representative of organized political opinion. The proposed new Council would represent the main communities and would include equal proportions of Caste Hindus and Muslims. It would work, if formed, under the existing Constitution. But it would be an entirely Indian council except for the Viceroy and the Commander-in-Chief who would retain his position as War Member... Moreover, Members will now be selected by the Governor-General after consultation with political leaders... The Council will work within the framework of the present Constitution; and there can be no question of the

Governor-General agreeing not to exercise his constitutional power of control; but it will of course not be exercised unreasonably.[73]

One of the main tasks of this new Executive Council, he stipulated, would be to prosecute the war against Japan with the utmost energy. He stated further that he had invited the following persons to a conference in Simla on 25 June to advise him in regard to the formation of the new Executive Council

> ...those now holding office as Premier in a provincial Government; or, for provinces now under Section 93 Government, those who last held office of Premier; the Leader of the Congress Party and the Deputy Leader of the Muslim League in the Central Assembly; the leader of the Congress Party and the Muslim League in the Council of State; also the leaders of the Nationalist Party and the European Group in the Assembly; Mr Gandhi and Mr Jinnah as the recognized leaders of the two main political parties; Rao Bahadur N. Siva Raj to represent the Scheduled Classes; Master Tara Singh to represent the Sikhs.

The viceroy concluded the broadcast with the announcement that orders had been given for the immediate release of the members of the Congress Working Committee who were still in detention.[74]

The Congress Working Committee met at Bombay on 21 and 22 June and decided that Congress 'as an organization should participate in the Simla Conference', and authorized the president of the Congress, Abul Kalam Azad, to represent the party. After his usual protestation that he represented 'no institution' and could not attend the conference as he represented 'no institution' and could not attend the conference as a representative of Congress, Gandhi agreed to come to Simla.

On 24 June, Wavell separately interviewed Azad, Gandhi and Jinnah.

Azad appeared to accept the main principles underlying the proposals, including wholehearted support for the war effort. He said Congress would accept equality of Caste Hindus and Muslims but would not compromise on the method of selection. Congress must have a voice in the selection of non-Hindus; the Muslims in particular must not be selected by an exclusively communal body.

Gandhi said he would attend the conference if the viceroy insisted but would simply 'sit in a corner'. He gave a 'general blessing on the proposals' and added that he had recommended them to the Working Committee. In the end he did not attend the formal meetings but remained available at Simla for the duration.

Jinnah expressed the anxiety that the Muslims would be in a minority in the new Executive Council because the other minorities such as the Sikhs and the Scheduled Castes would always vote with the Hindus, and that the viceroy would be most reluctant to exercise his veto. He claimed that the Muslim League had the right to nominate all Muslim members to the Council. Wavell said he could not accept this. Jinnah argued that the League had won all the by-elections in the preceding two years and therefore represented all the Muslims of India. He suggested that the viceroy was thinking of the nomination of Muslims by Congress, to which the latter replied that he also had in mind the nomination of a Muslim by the Punjab Unionist Party. Jinnah protested that the Unionist Party had betrayed Muslim interests.

The Congress had begun to see things in a new light. Evidently they had realized that they had made a mistake in rejecting the Cripps offer and had wasted three years in jail by launching the Quit India rebellion. When Azad and Nehru had visited Commander-in-Chief Wavell during Cripps's visit he had appeared to Azad to speak like a politician rather than like a soldier, but now Azad was impressed by the frankness and sincerity of the viceroy. 'I saw that this attitude was not that of a politician but a soldier'. On the same afternoon (24 June) Azad gave a brief report of his meeting with Wavell to the Congress Working Committee and expressed the opinion that, though Wavell's offer was no different from that of Cripps, it should be accepted. Circumstances had changed. The war in Europe was now over and even Japan could not last long. Once the war was over, the British would have no special reason to seek Congress cooperation. Congress should participate in the conference and accept the terms if these were at all suitable. Azad also says that Gandhi was present at the meeting but did 'not on this occasion raise the question that participation in the war meant that Congress was giving up non-violence'.[75]

On the very first day of the conference (25 June), it became clear that the crux was the composition of the Executive Council; all parties would accept the proposal if they could reach agreement on the method of selection. Jinnah refused to see Azad but agreed to meet Pant as the Congress spokesman, but their talks failed because Congress would not accept the League's demand for the exclusion of Congress Muslims. By 29 June it became clear that the parties would not be able to come up with an agreed list of Executive Councillors and the conference was adjourned until 14 July to enable them to file separate lists. In the following days all the parties except the Muslim League sent their respective lists to the viceroy.

At the same time Wavell confidentially prepared a list of his own for the membership of the Executive Council. This consisted of five Caste Hindus (two of whom were not members of Congress); five Muslims (four of whom were members of the Muslim League and the fifth a nominee of Khizar Hayat Khan, leader of the Unionist party of the Punjab); one Sikh; two Scheduled Castes; and one Indian Christian. Including the viceroy himself and the commander-in-chief, this would make an Executive Council of sixteen.

In a meeting with the viceroy on 27 June, Jinnah had said that he wanted a council of fourteen, including the viceroy and commander-in-chief with five Hindus, five Muslims, one Sikh and one Scheduled Caste. He said this was the only council in which the Muslims would stand a chance of not being out-voted on every issue. It was after seeing Jinnah on 11 July that the viceroy accepted that the conference had failed because he had been unable to accede to Jinnah's demands. He give Jinnah the names of the four Muslim League members and of the non-League Muslim member from the Punjab on his own list. But Jinnah said that it was impossible for him to co-operate unless (1) all Muslim members were drawn from the League, and (2) no decision objected to by the Muslims should be taken in council except by a clear two-thirds majority or some similar provision.[76]

After the failure of the conference Jinnah explained that

> ... if we accept this arrangement the Pakistan issue will be shelved and put into cold storage indefinitely, whereas Congress will have secured under this arrangement what they want, namely, a clear road for their advance towards securing Hindu national independence of India, because the future Executive will work as unitary Government of India, and we know that this interim or provisional arrangement will have a way of settling down for an unlimited period, and all

the forces in the proposed Executive, plus the known policy of the British Government and Lord Wavell's strong inclination for a united India, would completely jeopardize us.[77]

When the conference met on 15 July, Wavell formally announced its failure and sportingly blamed himself for the result: 'I wish to make it clear that the responsibility for the failure is mine. The main idea underlying the conference was mine. It if had succeeded, its success would have been attributed to me, and I cannot place the blame for its failure upon any of the parties.' In fact the viceroy deserved the greatest praise. With resolution and persistence he had succeeded in winning the consent of Churchill and others to open the Indian question and give the Indian leaders another chance to install a national government.

It was the two principal political parties, Congress and the Muslim League, that were really responsible for the failure. They had taken up positions which admitted of no compromise. If Congress had allowed the Muslim League to have a monopoly of Muslims, it would have been tantamount to accepting that it was itself purely a Hindu body. And if the League had permitted Congress to nominate Muslims, it would have thereby accepted the Congress claim that it represented all the communities in India. In his final report to Amery on the Simla Conference, Wavell correctly diagnosed that

> The immediate cause of the failure of the conference was Jinnah's intransigence about Muslim representation and Muslim safeguards. The deeper cause was the real distrust of the Muslims other than Nationalist Muslims, for Congress and the Hindus. Their fear that Congress, by parading its national character and using Muslim dummies, will permeate the entire administration of any united India is real, and cannot be dismissed as an obsession of Jinnah and his immediate entourage.[78]

Congress leaders blamed Jinnah for the lost opportunity and said that the viceroy should have gone ahead without the League. But in fact that entire plan had been based on the idea that the Executive Council would be an all-party body. During Wavell's discussion with the India Committee on 26 March 1945, Attlee had raised the possibility that the members of the proposed Executive Council might walk out if they were overridden by a viceregal veto, to which the viceroy had replied that the real safeguard was the communal balance; unless Hindus and Muslims were united, they could not out-vote him.[79]

Jinnah was under great stress during the Simla Conference. Wavell recorded in his journal: 'I had one and a half hours with Jinnah yesterday (8 July). He was obviously in a high state of nervous tension, and said to me more than once, "I am at the end of my tether", he also said, "I ask you not to wreck the [Muslim] League'. After the failure of the conference the impression gained ground that Jinnah would be able to veto any constitutional advance of which he did not approve, and that it was necessary to win his favour if one aspired to be accepted as a representative Muslim. On 12 July 1945, Amery wrote to Wavell that Congress 'must now either acquiesce in Pakistan, or realize that they have somehow or other to win over Muslim support against Jinnah, and that a mere facade of tame Congress Muslims does not help them'.[80]

Some days after the conference, the Quaid-i-Azam, at a public meeting, referred to Gandhi's presence at Simla during the Simla Conference in scathing terms: 'The first question is why did Mr Gandhi as one of the leaders of the recognized parties go to Simla? Having gone there, why did Mr Gandhi not attend the conference? The reason is simple. It was to play the role of wire-puller.'[81]

On 31 August 1945, Churchill told Wavell that the only reason he had agreed to his political move resulting in the Simla Conference was that the India Committee had told him it was bound to fail.[82] Churchill's view as already expressed to Amery on 29 July 1941 was that if the British Government had refused self-government, Hindus and Muslims would have united in demanding it and that the more the British Government said that they meant to give it, the more violently they disagreed and prevented the British Government from doing anything.[83]

The Labour Party takes Office in the United Kingdom

Two important events, not long after the Simla Conference, further enlivened the political scene in India. On 26 July 1945 the results of the national election in the United Kingdom were announced. Labour under Attlee won a sweeping victory by winning 388 seats out of 640. Pethick-Lawrence[84] replaced Amery as secretary of state for India. And on 14 August, Japan under the impact of the two atom bombs, surrendered earlier than had been expected.

Congress circles, counting on the traditional sympathy of the Labour Party with Indian aspirations for freedom, expected some quick new moves. The *Hindustan Times* hailed the defeat of the Conservatives as the 'downfall of India's oppressors' and the Congress president and his colleagues sent messages of congratulations to the Labour prime minister. For the Muslim League, however, the change of government in Britain created fresh worries.

On 21 August it was announced in New Delhi that central and provincial elections would be held in the coming winter, and on 24 August Wavell, in response to a summons from the new government, left for London for consultations. There he found that, unlike the Churchill government whom he had to prod for action, the Attlee Cabinet were all for quick action irrespective of the problems that had to be faced. Wavell told the India and Burma Committee on 29 August the scheme represented by the Cripps offer was no longer acceptable in India. If a constituent assembly as contemplated by that offer were set up, it would be boycotted by one or other or possibly by both the major communities. The Muslims would boycott it unless the Pakistan issue was conceded, and to concede that would certainly lead to a boycott by the Hindus. He thought it most unlikely that Jinnah would now enter into discussions without a prior guarantee of acceptance in principle of Pakistan. His own judgement was that Jinnah spoke for ninety-nine per cent of the Muslim population of India in their apprehension about Hindu domination. Before further progress could be made, the problem of Pakistan had to be faced, perhaps by a declaration by the British Government that an examination of the Pakistan issue was necessary.[85]

The Attlee Cabinet's view that urgent action was necessary to tackle India's constitutional problem was underlined by developments inside India. The announcement in October 1945 that three officers of the so-called Indian National Army, a Hindu, a Muslim and a Sikh would be tried by court-martial immediately raised a storm of protest. The INA had been founded by Captain Mohan Singh of the Indian Army who had surrendered to the Japanese in Malaya. After the fall of Singapore, Mohan Singh raised a force of some 40,000 volunteers from the Indian prisoners of war to fight alongside the Japanese and drive the British out of India. In July 1943, Subhas Bose arrived in Singapore and took over command of the INA from Mohan Singh. When the Allies recaptured Rangoon from the Japanese, the INA were taken prisoner by the Allied forces and sent to India. Prima facie they were guilty of having waged war against the King Emperor, a crime punishable by death. But the issue was not straightforward. India was striving for freedom and these men had fought for that cause. The All-India Congress Committee had already declared in a resolution passed in the third week of September that 'it would be a tragedy if these officers, men and women, were punished for the offence of having laboured, however mistakenly, for the freedom of India'.

It soon became clear that the public trial of the three INA officers and the choice of the historic Red Fort in Delhi as its stage, had been a political blunder. In Bose's home town of Calcutta, a students procession in favour of the INA developed into a serious riot which raged from 21 to 23 November. It resulted in substantial casualties and damage: thirty-three (including an American) killed; nearly 200 police, fire brigade and soldiers (seventy British and thirty-seven American) and about 200 civilians injured; 150 military or police vehicles and a large number of civilian cars destroyed or damaged.

The trial of the three officers already in the dock concluded on 31 December. Each one of them was sentenced to transportation for life, cashiering and forfeiture of pay and allowances. The commander-in-chief confirmed the finding of the court but remitted the sentences of transportation for life while confirming the sentences of cashiering and forfeiture of pay and allowances. Fifteen other officers and men of the INA were tried and sentenced before Auchinleck, the commander-in-chief, decided at the end of April 1946, to discontinue all further proceedings.

Azad has written that there was no longer anything secret about the upsurge for freedom. All sections of the services—civil and military—were moved by the same spirit. Men and officers of the defence forces declared openly that they had poured out their blood during the war on the assurance that India would be free. They demanded that this assurance must now be honoured. 'Wherever I went during this period,' he relates, 'young men of the defence forces came out to welcome me and expressed their sympathy and admiration without any regard for the reaction of their European officers.'

The unrest among the Indian armed forces manifested itself in minor incidents in the army and the air force, and on 18 February 1946 the ratings of the Royal Indian Navy mutinied at Bombay, the principal naval base in the country. Officers were thrown out of the ships, British soldiers were attacked in the streets and the mutineers roamed the city in naval lorries. Congress and Muslim League flags were hoisted to give a political slant to the uprising. On 21 February there was fighting between the mutineers and the soldiers who tried to control them. On 22 February the mutineers, who had seized the majority of the ships in the harbour, trained their guns on the city and ignored the demand that they should surrender. More than 200 persons were killed during the disturbances.

The rioting and violence alarmed the Congress leadership. Azad thought that it was not the appropriate time for direct action: 'We must now watch the course of events and carry on negotiations with the British Government'.[86] He sought an interview with Commander-in-Chief Auchinleck and was able to obtain the assurances that there would be no victimization if the mutineers returned to duty unconditionally and that their grievances would be sympathetically considered. Through the personal efforts of Patel, who had the support of Jinnah and Nehru, the mutineers surrendered on 23 February 1946.

There had been, at the same time, minor outbreaks in Calcutta and Madras and a serious uprising at Karachi which was suppressed with considerable loss of life and casualties among the mutineers.

Wavell's Breakdown Plan

On 27 December 1945, Wavell sent the secretary of state a Breakdown Plan. In his forwarding letter he stated that if the Congress and the Muslim League were unable to come to any agreement on the Pakistan issue, the British Government should be ready to make their own award to break the deadlock. The Breakdown Plan would be based on two points of principle: (1) that if the Muslims insist on self-determination in genuinely Muslim areas this must be conceded; (2) on the other hand there can be no question of compelling large non-Muslim population to remain in Pakistan against their will.

If these principles were followed, the effect would be 'that at least two divisions of the Punjab and almost the whole of western Bengal including Calcutta would have to be allowed to join the Union. The attractiveness of Pakistan to the Muslims would largely disappear. Only "the husk", in Jinnah's own words, would remain'. Wavell believed that, faced with the situation thus created, 'there would be at least a chance' that Jinnah would forgo Pakistan and 'set to work to secure the best possible terms for the Muslims inside the Union of India'.[87]

The Parliamentary Delegation

On 4 December 1945 it was announced in London that His Majesty's Government would send a Parliamentary Delegation to India. The move had resulted from Pethick-Lawrence's feeling that there was an unfortunate lack of first-hand knowledge of Indian conditions among the back-benchers in Parliament. A ten-member all-party Parliamentary Delegation arrived in India on 5 January 1946 under the leadership of Professor Robert Richards, a member of the Labour Party, and stayed in the country for about a month. Wavell found that their knowledge of India was 'not very comprehensive' but they were 'keen and interested'. They toured India and met the various leaders. They were politely received but aroused little enthusiasm because they had brought no new political proposals and had no negotiating powers.

The delegates conveyed their individual impressions orally to Attlee on 13 February 1946. Mrs Nichol said that she had begun her visit to India impressed by the strong necessity of maintaining the unity of India but as time went on she began to feel that some form of Pakistan must be conceded. R.W. Sorensen regarded Pakistan as wholly irrational but, in his view, necessary. In his individual written report of 13 March to the secretary of state for India, Sorensen said that all the members were agreed that the Indian situation was one of 'almost explosive urgency'.

Election Results

The results of the elections to the Central Legislative Assembly were declared towards the end of December 1945 and the outcome of the elections to the provincial legislatures became known in the early part of 1946. The Muslim League had fought these elections on the issue of Pakistan versus United India, and its claim had been amply vindicated.

In the Central Assembly the Muslim League won every Muslim seat; the Nationalist (Congress) Muslims forfeited their deposits in many cases. Congress achieved overwhelming success in the general constituencies; the Hindu Mahasabha and other candidates in most cases had withdrawn their candidature to avoid the ignominy of defeat. The Muslim League polled 86.6 per cent of the votes cast in Muslim constituencies. In a total of 102 seats the breakdown was: Congress fifty-seven, Muslim League thirty, Independents five, Akali Sikhs two and Europeans eight.

The provincial elections were held early in 1946. Their results further emphasized that Congress and the Muslim League were the two main parties in the country. Congress won an absolute majority in eight provinces and formed ministries there.

Of the five provinces which the Muslim League wished to include in Pakistan, the key provinces were the Punjab and Bengal. Out of the total of eighty-six Muslim seats in the Punjab, the Muslim League captured seventy-five. Congress won fifty-one seats, the Akali Sikhs twenty-two, the Unionists twenty, and the Independents seven. After political manœuvring the position became: Muslim League seventy-nine, Congress fifty-one, Akali Sikhs twenty-two, Unionists ten and Independents ten. The League was the largest single party but did not enjoy an overall majority. Premier Khizar Hayat's Unionist Party, which was anti-Muslim League, had fared miserably in the elections but Khizar was able to continue as premier in the new ministry because Congress and the Akalis joined hands with him.

The Bengal Assembly consisted of 250 members. The Muslim League took 113 (out of a total of 119 Muslim seats). Congress captured eighty-seven. A League ministry under H. S. Suhrawardy was formed.

In Sind, the League won twenty-seven seats; one independent Muslim joined the party later. Nationalist Muslims secured three seats, the Syed group four and Congress twenty-one. A League ministry under G. H. Hidayatullah was installed by the governor. In Assam Congress had a clear majority and formed a ministry under Gopinath Bardoloi which included one Nationalist Muslim.

The League fared badly in the North-West Frontier Province, where it captured seventeen seats as compared to thirty (including nineteen Muslim seats) won by Congress. Other Muslims secured two seats and Akali Sikhs one. Congress formed a ministry under Khan Sahib.

The Cabinet Mission

On 19 February 1946, Lord Pethick-Lawrence Secretary of State for India announced in Parliament that a special mission consisting of three Cabinet ministers would proceed to India in order, in association with the viceroy, to hold discussions with leaders of Indian opinion. The three Cabinet ministers would be Pethick-Lawrence, Sir Stafford Cripps and A. V. Alexander. In a debate in the Commons on 15 March, Prime Minister Attlee said: 'India must choose what will be her future Constitution'. He expressed the hope that India would decide by her own free will to remain within the British Commonwealth. If, on the other hand she elects for independence, she has a right to do so

> I am well aware, when I speak of India, that I speak of a country containing a congeries of races, religions and languages... We are very mindful of the rights of the minorities, and minorities should be able to live free from fear. On the other hand we cannot allow a minority to place a veto on the advance of the majority.

On landing at Karachi on 23 March, Cripps told a press conference that the purposes of the mission were 'to get machinery set up for framing the constitutional structure in which the Indians will have full control of their destiny and the formation of a new interim government'. The Mission arrived in Delhi on 24 March and left on 29 June.

For a fair appraisal of the Quaid-i-Azam's three-month long gruelling negotiations with the Cabinet Mission it is necessary first to describe the awesome difficulties under which he laboured. The first of these was the continued delicate state of his health. He was constantly indisposed and in May, at a critical stage in the negotiations, he went down with bronchitis and ran a temperature for ten days. But he never gave up the fight and battled on till the end of the negotiations. Only a person who placed the call of duty higher than his own life could have striven in this fashion.

Secondly, the Congress was still by far stronger than the Muslim League as a party. 'They have the best organized—in fact the only well organized—political machine; and they command almost unlimited financial support...they can always raise mob passion and mob support...and could undoubtedly bring about a very serious revolt against British rule'.[88]

Thirdly, the Congress had several powerful spokesmen, while for the League Jinnah had to carry the entire burden of advocacy single-handedly.

Fourthly, the bias of the Mission was heavily in favour of the Congress. Secretary of State Pethick-Lawrence, the leader, and Cripps, the sharpest brain amongst them, made no secret of their personal friendship for the Congress leaders.

In 1949 Pethick-Lawrence, jointly with H. S. L. Polak and H. N. Brailsford, wrote a biography of Gandhi under the title *Mahatma Gandhi*. In it Pethick-Lawrence dealt with the last years of Gandhi's life (1939-48). While describing the work of the 'Cabinet Mission of 1946' he wrote (page 268)

> Cripps was, of course well acquainted with Gandhi and other Indian leaders. My friendship with Gandhi was of long standing. Some thirty years previously he had lunched with my wife and myself in our flat in London, and had described to us his South African experiences and the active and important part he had played there in fighting for the status of his fellow Indians. In the cold weather of 1926-27 my wife and I had met him again in India, when we attended the annual meeting of Congress in Gauhati. In 1931 I had sat with him on the Round Table Conference and on its Federal Structure Committee, held in St James's Palace. Since then we had some personal correspondence, and he had had my good wishes on his birthday, which happened to be the same day of the year as my wedding day.

Gandhi, true to form, made it clear at the outset that he was speaking entirely for himself and not expressing the opinions of the Congress. All the same he remained in touch with the Mission and with the Congress leaders during the entire period of the negotiations.

Wavell was much perturbed by Pethick-Lawrence's and Cripps's private contacts with the Congress leaders and the deference they showed to Gandhi. This is borne out by numerous entries in his journal. For instance

> It has, I think been the bane of the Mission that it has been unable to keep away from continual personal contacts with Congress, and so have been unable to remain really impartial.[89]
>
> I knew he [Cripps] had been in private correspondence with Nehru about the objectives before the Mission came out—a proceeding which I should not call strictly honest, though to a politician it seems quite normal.[90]
>
> I was frankly horrified at the deference shown to Gandhi, when he expressed the wish for a glass of water, the secretary was sent to fetch it himself, instead of sending a *chaprassi;* and when it didn't come at once Cripps hustled off himself to see about it.[91]

Under the date 23 June 1946, Wavell wrote in his *Journal* that Pethick-Lawrence had gone to Gandhi's prayers, 'a most unnecessary and undignified excursion to my mind, but I think it happens often, and had talked with Gandhi'.[92]

Wavell also felt 'sure' that it was under Cripps's advice that Congress eventually accepted the Mission's May 16 statement thus preventing Paragraph 8 of the June 16 statement being operated in Jinnah's favour.[93]

Finally, Jinnah suffered from the disadvantage that it was the Muslim League, a minority party, which alone demanded Pakistan. The Congress, the smaller minorities and the British Government including the comparatively fair-minded Wavell with whom the final decision lay, were all strongly opposed to the partition of British India.

As if all these daunting odds were not enough, the senior Indian officials who assisted the Mission were two high calibre Hindus—Sir Benegal Rau, on Special Duty in the Governor-General's Secretariat (Reforms) and V. P. Menon, Reforms Commissioner and Secretary to the Governor-General (Public).

The basic draft of the Mission's Statement of 16 May—which was their final 'award', was consequently drawn up by Cripps 'with Rau and Menon'.⁹⁴

Menon and Rau, in fact, had already done the future independent India a good turn before the Cabinet Mission had even set foot in India. Though the appointment of the Cabinet Mission was officially announced in Parliament on 19 February 1946, Pethick-Lawrence had privately informed Wavell of this by a telegram on 22 January. He had added that the Mission would probably arrive towards the end of March and meanwhile they proposed to study 'problems in the light of your proposals and other relevant material'.⁹⁵ In response to a request from the viceroy's private secretary, Menon on 23 January 1946 forwarded his own and Rau's 'joint suggestions' for demarcation of the Pakistan areas. These suggestions recommended the exclusion of the districts of Amritsar and Gurdaspur from Pakistan. It was argued that Amritsar was sacred to the Sikhs and Gurdaspur must go with Amritsar because 'these two form a compact block'. With regard to the East Zone the recommendation was that 'the vital port of Calcutta' must be excluded from Pakistan'.⁹⁶ On 29 January, the secretary of state telegraphed the viceroy asking him to send as soon as possible 'your definition of genuine Moslem areas if we are compelled to give a decision on this'. The viceroy telegraphed his recommendations on 6 February 1946. These included that Amritsar and Gurdaspur districts as well as Calcutta should be excluded from Pakistan.⁹⁷ Menon's note did not explain in what way the Muslim majority district of Gurdaspur formed an inseparable 'compact block' with Amritsar and neither the viceroy nor the other members of the Cabinet Mission ever bothered to question the assertion.

Jinnah's comment on Attlee's statement in Parliament on 15 March, that a minority could not be allowed to place a veto on the advance of the majority, was that 'the Muslims of India are not a minority but a nation and self-determination is their birthright.⁹⁸ With respect to his forthcoming negotiations with the Cabinet Mission he said, 'One thing is certain—there will be no compromise on the subject of Pakistan because that means our very existence is at stake'.⁹⁹

The constitutionalist Quaid-i-Azam took appropriate steps to strengthen his hand as the spokesman of the Muslim League.

He convened a meeting of the Muslim League Working Committee at Delhi (4-6 April 1946) which passed a resolution that 'the President alone should meet the Cabinet Delegation and the viceroy'. This was immediately followed by an All-India Muslim Legislator's Convention (Delhi 7-9 April). It was attended by nearly 500 members of the Provincial and Central Legislatures who had recently been elected on the Muslim League ticket from all parts of India. It was the first gathering of its kind in the history of Indian politics and was called by some 'the Muslim Constituent Assembly'. In his presidential address, Jinnah said that the Convention would lay down 'once and for all in unequivocal terms what we stand for'. He said that Congress desired that the British Government should first grant independence and then hand over the government to Congress by setting up a national government of Congress's conception. When Congress was saddled in power it would proceed to form a constitution-making body with sovereign authority to decide the fate of the 400 million inhabitants of the subcontinent. The League must not accept a single constitution-making body which would only register the decree of Congress, because the Muslims would be in a hopeless minority in it. If any interim Constitution was forced on the Muslims they must resist it in every possible way.

A resolution passed unanimously by the Convention (the 'Delhi Resolution') stated that no formula devised by the British Government for transferring power to the peoples of India would be acceptable to the Muslim nation unless it conformed to the following principles

> That the zones comprising Bengal and Assam in the North-East and the Punjab, North-West Frontier Province, Sind and Baluchistan in the North-West of India, namely Pakistan zones where the Muslims are in a dominant majority, be constituted into a sovereign independent State and that an unequivocal undertaking be given to implement the establishment of Pakistan without delay;
>
> That two separate constitution-making bodies be set up by the people of Pakistan and Hindustan for the purpose of framing their respective Constitutions;
>
> That the acceptance of the Muslim League demand of Pakistan and its implementation without delay are the *sine qua non* for Muslim League cooperation and participation in the formation of an Interim Government at the Centre;

That any attempt to impose a Constitution on a united-India basis or to force any interim arrangement at the Centre contrary to the Muslim League demand will leave the Muslims no alternative but to resist such imposition by all possible means for their survival and national existence.[100]

This impressive show of strength, staged in the very city where the members of the Cabinet Mission were quartered, demonstrated to the Mission and to all others that the 100 million Muslims of India were solidly behind the demand for Pakistan and further that Quaid-i-Azam Mohammad Ali Jinnah was their undisputed supreme leader.

The Mission began their talks by first informing themselves of the views of the different leaders and parties. Finding the view-points of the League and Congress irreconcilable, they next gave a chance to the parties to come to an agreement between themselves. This phase included a Conference at Simla (5-12 May) to which Congress and the League were each asked to nominate four delegates for discussions with one another as well as with the Mission. This popularly came to be called the Second Simla Conference, the first being that convened by Wavell in June 1945. When it became clear that the parties would not be able to reach a concord, the Mission on 16 May 1946, put forward their own proposals in the form of a Statement.

Azad, the president of the Congress, conferred with the Mission on 3 April. He stated that the picture that the Congress had of the future of India was that of a Federal Government with fully autonomous provinces with residuary powers vested in the units. The compulsory federal subjects might be defence, communications, foreign affairs and such others as may be absolutely necessary for the administration of India as a whole. The future Constitution will have to be determined by a Constitution-making Body.[101]

Gandhi appeared before the Mission later on the same day. He called Jinnah's Pakistan 'a sin' which he, Gandhi, would not commit. He also proposed that Jinnah may be allowed to form the interim government. If he does not do so, the offer to form a government should be made to Congress. The interim government he stipulated, 'would be subject to the vote of the Assembly from which they were drawn'. This made it plain that the Mahatma in fact was asking for a Congress government and the offer to Jinnah was mere eyewash; the vote of the assembly meant the vote of the Congress which would be the majority party in the central assembly.[102]

At the outset of his interview with the Mission on 4 April, the Quaid was asked by them to give his reason why he thought it better for the future of India that India should have a Pakistan. He replied that never in her long history did India ever have 'any Government of India in the sense of a single government'. He went on to explain the irreconcilable social and cultural differences between the Hindus and the Muslims and argued, 'You cannot make a nation unless there are essential uniting forces. How are you to put 100 millions of Muslims together with 250 millions whose way of life is so different. No government can ever work on such a basis and if this is forced upon India it must lead us on to disaster.' He said there could be agreements between the completely sovereign states of Pakistan and Hindustan on matters of common interest such as defence, foreign policy and communications but he 'could not agree to anything which would derogate from the sovereignty of Pakistan'. He claimed five provinces for Pakistan but was 'quite willing to consider mutual adjustment'. But he 'wanted a viable Pakistan which could not be carved up or mutilated...Pakistan must be a live State economically'. He insisted that Pakistan must have Calcutta. Hindustan would have Bombay and Madras and she could have a new port in Orissa. 'Pakistan without Calcutta would be like asking a man to live without his heart.'[103]

When Jinnah next met the Mission (16 April 1946) he was informed that 'the Delegation had come to the conclusion that the full and complete demand for Pakistan in the form in which Mr Jinnah had put forward had little chance of acceptance'. In particular the Delegation said that of the Muslim majority districts which were claimed for Pakistan 'perhaps Gurdaspur' would have to be excluded. About Calcutta the Delegation 'did not think agreement could be reached on the basis that Calcutta was included in Pakistan'. Jinnah replied he could not in any event accept the exclusion of Calcutta.

The Second Simla Conference having failed to produce an agreed solution, the Mission on 16 May issued their own Statement.

Statement by the Cabinet Delegates and the Viceroy Issued in New Delhi on 16 May 1946

The Statement began by explaining that the Mission had done their 'utmost' to assist the Congress and the Muslim League to come to an agreement 'upon the fundamental issue of the unity or division of India' but it had proved impossible to close the gap between the parties. The Mission, therefore, felt that it was their duty to put forward arrangements whereby Indians may decide the future Constitution of India and an Interim Government may be set up to carry on the administration of British India until such time as a new Constitution can be brought into being.

Being 'greatly impressed by the very genuine and acute anxiety of the Muslims lest they should find themselves subjected to a perpetual Hindu-majority rule', the Mission in the first instance had examined the question of a sovereign state of Pakistan consisting of the six provinces claimed by the Muslim League, and had rejected it mainly on the ground that it would not solve the communal minority problem, because the size of the non-Muslim minorities in such a Pakistan would be 'very considerable': 37.93 per cent in the North-Western area and 48.31 per cent in the North-Eastern area. Also, there would be Muslim minorities numbering some 20 million in the remainder of British India, dispersed among a total population of 188 million. Every argument that could be used in favour of Pakistan could also be used in favour of the exclusion of the non-Muslim areas from Pakistan.

The Statement also rejected the idea of a smaller Pakistan confined to the Muslim-majority areas, because such a Pakistan was regarded by the Muslim League as quite impracticable. The Mission themselves also felt convinced that any solution which involved a partition of Bengal and the Punjab would be contrary to the wishes and interests of a very large portion of the inhabitants of these provinces, each of which had its own common language and a long history and tradition. Moreover, a division of the Punjab would leave substantial bodies of Sikhs on both sides of the boundary.

The Mission then indicated the nature of a solution which in their view 'would be just to the essential claims of all parties, and would at the same time be more likely to bring about a stable and practical form of Constitution for all-India'. The outline sketched by them envisaged three tiers.

At the top would be the Union of India, comprising both British India and the Princely States. The bottom tier would comprise provinces and states. The provinces would be free to unite together in groups, and such groups, if formed, would constitute the middle tier.

To bring the contemplated Constitution into being, a Constituent Assembly would be set up. Its numbers would be elected by the members of the provincial legislatures, each province contributing numbers proportionate to its population. The voting would be by communities, Muslims, Sikhs and 'general'—'general' would include everyone who was not either Muslim or Sikh. For each one million of the population there would be one representative. The States would contribute members to the constitution-making proportionate to their total population.

After a preliminary meeting of the Constituent Assembly, the provincial representatives would divide themselves into three sections: Section A would consist of Madras, Bombay, United Provinces, Bihar, Central Provinces and Orissa; B of the Punjab, North-West Frontier Province and Sind; and C of Bengal and Assam (Sections B and C would have Muslim majorities). Each section would frame the Constitutions of the provinces belonging to it and would also decide whether a group should be formed and with what subjects it should deal. Lastly, the Constituent Assembly would reassemble to decide the Constitution of the Union. The Mission recommended that this Constitution for All-India should take the following basic form:

(1) There should be a Union of India, embracing both British India and the States, which should deal with the following subjects: Foreign Affairs, Defence, and Communications; and should have the powers necessary to raise the finances required for the above subjects.

(2) The Union should have an Executive and a Legislature constituted from British Indian and States' representatives. Any question raising a major communal issue in the Legislature should require for its decision a majority of the representatives present and voting of each of the two major communities as well as a majority of all the members present and voting.

(3) All subjects other than the Union subjects and all residuary powers should vest in the Provinces.

(4) The States will retain all subjects and powers other than those ceded to the Union.

(5) Provinces should be free to form groups with Executives and Legislatures, and each group could determine the provincial subjects to be taken in common.

(6) The Constitution of the Union and of the groups should contain a provision whereby any Province could by a majority vote of its Legislative Assembly call for a reconsideration of the terms of the Constitution after an initial period of ten years and at ten-yearly intervals thereafter.

The Statement also made made further recommendations to allay the fears of the Muslims and other minorities:

(1) Resolutions altering the basic form of the Constitution as recommended by the Mission or involving a major communal issue should not be passed by the constitution-making body unless accepted by each of the major communities.

(2) After the inauguration of the Constitution, it should be open to any province to elect to come out of the group in which it had been placed. Such a decision should be taken by the new legislature of the province after the first general election under the new Constitution.

(3) An Advisory Committee would be set up at the preliminary meeting of the Constituent Assembly to report on the rights of citizens, minorities and tribal and excluded areas.

The Statement declared that it would be necessary to negotiate a treaty between the Union Constituent Assembly and the United Kingdom to provide for certain matters arising out of the transfer of power.

Finally, the Statement emphasized that, while the constitution-making proceeded, it was of the 'greatest importance' to set up 'at once' an interim government in which all the portfolios, including that of War Member, would be held by Indian leaders having the confidence of the people.[104]

At a press conference on the same day, Cripps made it clear that a departure from the basic form of the Constitution as laid down in paragraph fifteen of the Statement could only be made if a majority of both communities agreed to it.

On the afternoon of 16 May, Wavell and Alexander interviewed Azad and Nehru. 'It turned out that what Nehru was thinking about was immediate independence, in the interim period, in fact he disclosed almost nakedly, the real Congress objective—immediate control of the Centre, so that they can deal with Muslims and princes and then make at leisure a Constitution to suit themselves'.[105]

In an article in *Harijan* dated 17 May 1946 Gandhi wrote that in their Statement the Cabinet Mission had recommended

> what in their opinion was worthy of acceptance by the Constituent Assembly. It was open to that body to vary them, reject them or improve upon them... There was no 'take it or leave it' business about their recommendations... Similarly about grouping. The provinces were free to reject the very idea of grouping.

Subject to the above interpretation 'the Mission had brought forth something of which they have every reason to be proud'.[106]

On 21 May, Gandhi sent to Cripps the draft of an article which was published in *Harijan* on 26 May. He asserted in it that 'there was nothing in it [the Mission's Statement] binding in law... What is binding is that part of it which commits the British Government'.[107]

The Quaid gave his initial reaction to the Mission's Statement in a statement issued on 22 May. He regretted that 'the Mission should have thought fit to advance commonplace and exploded arguments against Pakistan and resorted to special pleading couched in deplorable language which is calculated to hurt the feelings of Muslim India'. The Muslims still held that 'a complete Sovereign State of Pakistan' was the only solution which could secure a stable government and lead to the welfare not only of the Hindus and the Muslims but of all the peoples of the Indian subcontinent.[108]

A resolution passed by the Congress Working Committee on 24 May 1946 contained the following main points: the Committee read the Mission's Statement to mean that 'in the first instance, the respective provinces will make their choice whether or not to belong to the section in which they are placed'; that 'the governor-general may continue as the head of the government during the interim period, but the government should function as a Cabinet responsible to the Central Legislature'; and finally, that 'in the absence of a full picture, the Committee are unable to give a final opinion at this stage'.[109]

The Mission responded to Jinnah's statement of 22 May and the resolution of the Congress Working Committee of 24 May with a statement of their own issued on 25 May. They made it clear that the interpretation of the Congress 'to the effect that the Provinces can in the first instance make the choice whether or not to belong to the section in which they are placed does not accord with the Delegation's intentions...this is an essential feature of the scheme and can only be modified by agreement between the parties'. The Mission declared also that the interim government could not be made legally responsible to Central Government because the existing Constitution must continue during the interim period.[110]

In their Statement of 16 May, the Mission had mentioned that the viceroy had already started discussions for the formation of an interim government and hoped soon to form one. In an interview with Wavell at 10 a.m. on 3 June 1946, Jinnah said that the question of absence of parity at the Centre in a Union Government was a very difficult point for the Muslim League to accept. He asked also what would happen if Congress rejected the proposals and the Muslim League accepted them. Wavell said speaking personally be thought that if the Muslim League accepted them they would not lose by it. Jinnah enquired whether in these circumstances the Muslim League would be invited to join the interim government and be given their due proportion of portfolios. Wavell replied that he could guarantee that the Muslim League would have a share in it. Jinnah thereupon asked whether he could have an assurance to that effect in writing. Wavell discussed the matter with the Cabinet Delegation at 11 a.m. and it was agreed that the viceroy 'should draft a letter to Mr Jinnah'. Wavell then invited Jinnah to see him on the same afternoon at 4 p.m. He showed Jinnah two written assurances the first of which Wavell himself had drafted. It read,

> The Delegation cannot give you a written assurance of what its action will be in the event of the breakdown of the present negotiations; but I can give you, on behalf of the Delegation, my personal assurance that...we shall go ahead with the plan laid down in our Statement so far as circumstances permit, if either party accepts.

The second, which had been drafted by Cripps, ran, 'It is our intention to stick to the scheme as far a possible if either party are prepared to come in and work it'.[111]

On 7 June 1946 Jinnah forwarded to Wavell a copy of the resolution which the Council of the Muslim League had passed on the previous day. The resolution severely criticized the Statement of the Mission for rejecting the demand for Pakistan but

> ... having regard to the grave issues involved, and prompted by its earnest desire for a peaceful solution, if possible, of the Indian constitutional problem, and inasmuch as the basis and the foundation of Pakistan are inherent in the Mission's plan by virtue of the compulsory grouping of the six Muslim Provinces in Sections B and C, is willing to co-operate with the constitution-making machinery proposed in the scheme outlined by the Mission, in the hope that it would ultimately result in the establishment of complete sovereign Pakistan, and in the consummation of the goal of independence for the major nations, Muslims and Hindus, and all the other people inhabiting the vast subcontinent.[112]

He also saw the viceroy personally on the same day and informed him that the only basis on which the League would join the interim government was on the ratio of five Congress, five League and two others. As regards portfolios the League was interested in Defence, External Affairs, and Planning and Development, with the last of which Commerce should go. The only portfolio he would consider taking personally was Defence (this was the first and only time that he expressed an interest in holding any office during British rule).[113]

After some tortuous negotiations during the immediately following days it became evident that the parity of five to five was wholly unacceptable to the Congress. To break the deadlock, the Mission issued a statement on 16 June 1946. In it they directly invited fourteen persons to serve on the interim government. Of these six were Hindu members of the Congress party, five were members of the Muslim League and three represented the minority communities of Sikhs, Indian Christians and Parsees. Paragraph eight of the statement ran

> In the event of the two major parties or either of them proving unwilling to join in the setting up of a coalition government on the above lines, it is the intention of the viceroy to proceed with the formation of an interim government which will be as representative as possible of those willing to accept the Statement of May 16th.[114]

'But once again,' explained Pethick-Lawrence, 'the hopes of an agreed settlement were shipwrecked. The rock on which they foundered was the desire of Gandhi and the Congress Working Committee to substitute for one of the proposed Hindu members of the interim government a Muslim not a member of the Muslim League.'[115] This, of course, was a repetition of the issue which had been responsible for the failure of Wavell's Simla Conference in 1945.

The position was thus reached that the League had accepted the Mission's Statement of 16 May but the Congress had not. So under paragraph eight of the Mission's Statement of 16 June, the League was entitled to come into the proposed interim government but the Congress was not. This evidently was not an acceptable prospect for Congress' friends in the Mission. Cripps, as we have already mentioned, therefore, privately advised the Congress to accept the 16 May Statement. Accordingly, Azad wrote a letter to Wavell on 25 June enclosing the text of a resolution that had been passed that day by the Congress Working Committee. In his letter, Azad said that the Committee had

> ... reluctantly come to the conclusion that they are unable to assist you in forming a provisional government as proposed in your statement of 16 June 1946. With regard to the proposals made in the statement of 16th May, 196...we have pointed out what in our opinion were the defects in the proposals. We also gave our interpretation of some of the provisions of the Statement. While adhering to our views, we accept your proposals and are prepared to work them with a view to achieve our objective.[116]

The Mission decided that, 'although cleverly worded', the Congress president's reply must be regarded as an acceptance of the long-term proposals[117] and invited Jinnah on the same afternoon to confer with them. The secretary of state told the Muslim League president that the delegation were satisfied that the Congress letter constituted an acceptance. It was not in any way a provisional acceptance. The Muslim League, in accepting the Statement, had also adhered to their own point of view and had made statements maintaining their goal of complete sovereign Pakistan, and others which went quite as far as any reservations made by the Congress. Jinnah complained that the reservations made by Congress were most vital and broke the whole thing.[118]

Jinnah issued an angry statement on 27 June criticizing the decision to postpone the setting up of an interim government and saying that it was very difficult to see what were the mysterious causes behind it. Clause eight of the statement of 16 June had made it quite clear that the delegation and the viceroy were 'in honour bound to go ahead with the formation of the interim government immediately with those who were willing to come into the interim government'. Any attempt to whittle down the assurances given to the Muslim League would be 'regarded by Muslim India as a going back on the part of the Cabinet Delegation and the viceroy on their pledged word in writing and as a breach of faith'.[119]

When the Mission finally left Delhi on 29 June 1946 the situation, thus, was that both Congress and the League had accepted the Statement of 16 May for a long-term settlement and were taking part in the elections of members of the constitution-making body. But no representative central government had been set up.

Jinnah was feeling despondent at the outcome of the Cabinet Delegation's visit but was rescued from his predicament by Jawaharlal Nehru who had succeeded Azad as the president of the Congress. At a press conference on 10 July 1946, Nehru asserted that Congress had 'agreed to go into the Constituent Assembly and we have agreed to nothing else... What we do there, we are entirely and absolutely free to determine. We have committed ourselves on no single matter to anybody'. Referring to grouping he said, 'The big probability is that there will be no grouping'. He also visualized a far stronger central government than the one outlined by the Cabinet Mission: among other matters 'there must be some overall power to intervene in grave crisis, breakdown of the administration, or economic breakdown or famine. The scope of the Centre, even though limited, inevitably grows.'[120] Azad frankly admitted that Nehru's 'unfortunate statement that the Congress would be free to modify the Cabinet Mission Plan re-opened the whole question of political and communal settlement. Mr Jinnah took full advantage of his mistake'.[121] Louis Fischer, who attended the conference, said to Nehru, 'You have changed the entire basis of the agreement with England'. Nehru smiled and relied, 'I am fully aware of that'.[122]

Nehru's re-writing of the Cabinet Mission scheme was a godsend to Jinnah. It furnished him a legitimate excuse for withdrawing the League's acceptance of the scheme. He called a meeting of the Council of the Muslim League to reconsider the League's attitude toward the Cabinet Mission's proposals. The Council met at Bombay from 27 to 29 July 1946 and passed a resolution withdrawing the League's acceptance of the Cabinet Mission's proposals.

In the course of his addresses to the session the Quaid said that in accepting the Mission's Statement of 16 May the Muslim League was

> ... moved by higher and greater considerations then the rest of India... We, therefore, sacrificed our full sovereignty of Pakistan on the altar of securing independence and freedom for all. We voluntarily delegated three subjects to the Union to work for ten years...I do not think any responsible man could have allowed the situation to give rise to bloodshed and civil war.

He claimed that the League was the only party that emerged from the negotiations with the Cabinet Mission with clean hands.

Jinnah felt that the League had exhausted all reason and there was no use looking to any other source for help. A resolution stated that the League was 'convinced that now the time has come for the Muslim nation to resort to Direct Action to achieve Pakistan' and directed the Working Committee to prepare a programme of Direct Action. 'Today we have said goodbye to constitutions and constitutional methods', declared the Quaid. 'Throughout the painful negotiations, the two parties with whom we bargained held a pistol at us... We also have a pistol'.[123] Jinnah's claim that the League was the only party which had negotiated with the Mission with clean hands was endorsed by Wavell in his review of the Mission's visit: Jinnah 'is straight compared with Congress, and does not constantly shift his ground, though he too drives a hard bargain'.[124]

The results of the elections to the Constituent Assembly became known in the second part of July. The Muslim League won seventy-three seats, that is, all but five allotted to Muslims, and the Congress won all but nine general seats.

The Interim Government

On 22 July 1946, Wavell wrote identical letters to Nehru and Jinnah asking them whether the Congress and the Muslim League would be prepared to enter an interim government on the basis that six members (including one Scheduled Caste representative) would be nominated by Congress and five by the Muslim League. Three representatives of minorities including a Sikh would be nominated by the viceroy.[125] On 31 July, Jinnah replied that the proposal was not acceptable to the Muslim League because it destroyed the principal of parity.[126] At Nehru's invitation he and Jinnah conferred together on 15 August but could not come to an agreement on the question of joining Congress in an interim government. The stumbling block evidently was the insistence by Congress on its right to nominate a Nationalist (i.e., a Congress) Muslim as a part of its quota.[127]

In the meantime the Working Committee of the Muslim League had decided that Friday 16 August 1946 would be observed as the Direct Action Day. From that day there was serious trouble in Calcutta and some rioting in Sylhet. According to a Written Answer to a Parliamentary Question in the British Parliament on 18 November, the casualty figures for Calcutta for the period 16-19 August were 4,000 dead and 10,000 injured. In his letter of 21 August to Pethick-Lawrence, Wavell had reported that appreciably more Muslims than Hindus had been killed.[128] The 'Great Calcutta Killing' marked the start of the bloodiest phase of the 'war of succession' between Hindus and Muslims and it became increasingly difficult for the British to maintain control. Previously they had to cope with Congress civil disobedience movements. Now, furious Muslims had also come out in the streets in their thousands.

The negotiations with the League having reached a deadlock, the viceroy decided to form an interim government with Congress alone, leaving the door open for the League to come in later. A communiqué issued on 24 August announced that the existing members of the Governor-General's Executive Council had resigned and that in their places the following persons had been appointed: Pandit Jawaharlal Nehru, Sardar Vallabhbhai Patel, Dr Rajendra Prasad, M. Asaf Ali, C. Rajagopalachari, Sarat Chandra Bose, Dr John Matthai, Sardar Baldev Singh, Sir Shafaat Ahmad Khan,[129]

Jagjivan Ram, Syed Ali Zaheer and Cooverji Hormusji Bhabha. Two more Muslim members were to be appointed later. It was stated that the interim government would be installed on 2 September.

The communiqué was supplemented by a broadcast by Wavell on the same day. He said no one was sorrier than he was that it had not been possible to secure a coalition by including the Muslim League in the interim government and no one could be more sure that it was a coalition government that was needed in the interest of all the communities in India. He stated that it was still open to the Muslim League to propose five names for places in a government of fourteen, of which six would be nominees of Congress and three would be representatives of the minorities.[130]

Two days later, Jinnah declared that the viceroy had struck a severe blow to Muslim India and had added insult to injury by nominating three Muslims who did not command the confidence of Muslim India. He reiterated that the only solution to India's problems was the division of India into Pakistan and Hindustan.[131]

That the viceroy had formed an interim government consisting only of the Congress nominees added further fuel to the communal fire. On 31 August, Sir Evan Jenkins (Governor of the Punjab), reported to Wavell that the Muslims were frightened and angry. They thought that the refusal of the British Government to put the Muslim League in power when Congress was non-cooperating, and the apparent eagerness to bring in Congress as soon as the party positions were reversed, could be explained only as a deep-laid plot between the British and Congress. The Muslims regarded the formation of the interim government as an unconditional surrender of power to the Hindus, and feared that the governor-general would be unable to prevent the Hindus from using their newly-acquired power for the suppression of the Muslims all over India.

After Congress had taken the reins at the Centre on 2 September, Jinnah faced a desperate situation. The armed forces were predominantly Hindu and Sikh and the Indian members of the other services were predominantly Hindu. The British were preparing to concede independence to India and if they withdrew leaving Congress in undisputed control, Congress would be free to deal with the Muslims as it wished. Wavell too felt unhappy at the purely Congress interim government. He genuinely desired a Hindu-Muslim settlement and a united India, and had worked hard to that end. More immediately, he needed the Muslim League in the government to act as a counterpoise to Congress.

At his prayer meeting on the day Congress took office Gandhi said 'the door to *purna* [complete] swaraj has opened', and told his listeners that full freedom would be achieved only when their 'uncrowned king, Jawaharlal', and his colleagues had rendered true service.[132] On 26 September, Wavell pleaded with Nehru and Gandhi, in separate interviews, that it would help him to persuade Jinnah to cooperate if he could give him an assurance that Congress would not insist on nominating a Nationalist Muslim. Nehru replied that Congress had recently decided that it would not give way on that issue. Gandhi said if it had been merely a Congress 'right' they could have made concessions on it but since it was a 'duty', it was a different matter.[133]

Two days later, Wavell informed Jinnah that he had not succeeded in persuading the Congress leaders to make a gesture by not appointing a Nationalist Muslim. The Muslim League president realized that Congress would not give up the right to nominate a Nationalist Muslim and that he would have to accept that position if he did not wish to leave the interim government solely in the hands of Congress. When he saw Wavell on 2 October he therefore said nothing at all on the issue of a Nationalist Muslim. Wavell rightly inferred from this that the Muslim League wanted to come into the interim government.[134] On 13 October Jinnah wrote to Wavell that, though the Muslim League did not agree with much that had happened, 'in the interests of the Mussulmans and other communities it will be fatal to leave the entire field of administration of the Central Government in the hands of Congress', and the League had therefore decided to nominate five members for the interim government. On 15 October he gave the viceroy the following five names: Liaquat Ali Khan, I. I. Chundrigar, Abdur Rab Nisthar, Ghazanfar Ali Khan and Jogindar Nath Mandal. The last named was a Scheduled Caste Hindu and was obviously a tit-for-tat for the Congress insistence upon including a Nationalist Muslim in its own quota. To accommodate the five League nominees, Congress obtained the resignations of Sarat Chandra Bose, Shafaat Ahmad Khan and Syed Ali Zaheer (there were already two vacancies).

Addressing the students of Islamia College, Lahore, on 19 October, Ghazanfar Ali Khan declared, 'We are going into the interim government to get a foothold [in the] fight for our cherished goal of Pakistan'.[135] At a later date (15 November 1946) Jinnah said that the Muslim League members of the Interim Government were there 'as sentinels who would watch Muslim interests in the day-to-day administration of Government'.[136]

Of the important portfolios, the League wished to secure either External Affairs or Defence but in the end had to settle for Finance. The reconstituted interim government as installed on 26 October 1946 consisted of the following:

External Affairs and Commonwealth Relations	: Jawaharlal Nehru
Defence	: Baldev Singh
Home (including Information and Broadcasting)	: Vallabhbhai Patel
Finance	: Liaquat Ali Khan
Posts and Air	: Abdur Rab Nishtar
Food and Agriculture	: Rajendra Prasad
Labour	: Jagjivan Ram
Transport and Railways	: M. Asaf Ali
Industries and Supplies	: John Matthai
Education and Arts	: C. Rajagopalachari
Works, Mines and Power	: C. H. Babha
Commerce	: I. I. Chundrigar
Law	: Jogindar Nath Mandal
Health	: Ghazanfar Ali Khan

Azad has revealed that Congress had offered Finance to the League at the suggestion of Rafi Ahmad Kidwai, a Nationalist Muslim of the United Provinces. Kidwai argued that Finance was a highly technical subject and the League had no member who could handle it effectively. His view was that the League would therefore refuse it. If this happened Congress would lose nothing. If on the other hand a League nominee accepted the Finance portfolio he would soon make a fool of himself. Either way Congress would stand to gain. Patel jumped at the proposal and gave it his strongest support.[137]

The Muslim League side of the story is related by Chaudhri Muhammad Ali. He states that he had advised Jinnah in June 1946, when the formation of an interim government was first under consideration, that if the League wished to influence the policies of government in every department it should take charge of Finance. He had not been able to convince Jinnah of the strategic importance of Finance at that time but now that events had 'practically forced the Finance portfolio upon the League', he was sent for again and repeated his advice even more forcefully. His recommendation was accepted and he became an unofficial adviser to the Muslim League bloc in the government. This was nothing unusual 'since many of the senior Hindu officials were acting in a similar capacity for the Congress bloc'.[138]

Azad states that Patel soon

> ... realized that he had played into the hands of the League by offering it Finance. Any proposal he made was either rejected or modified beyond recognition by Liaquat Ali. His persistent interference made it difficult for any Congress member to function effectively. Internal dissensions broke out within the government and went on increasing.[139]

Intensification of the Civil War

On the eve of the installation of the purely Congress interim government in September, a serious communal riot erupted in Bombay. Wavell noted in his *Journal* on 20 October 1946 that since 1 September there had been 1,500 casualties of which more than 360 had been fatal. In the second week of October communal clashes took place in the Noakali and Tippera districts of East Bengal. The Hindu population panicked and a large number fled and became refugees. The most serious rioting took place at the end of October in Bihar and continued for several days.

> Six districts out of sixteen were affected...the government's final figure of the Muslims killed was in the neighbourhood of 5,400. The Friends Service Unit estimated that the number killed could not exceed 10,000...the Hindus of Bihar, to their shame, had tarred themselves with the same brush as the Muslims in Bengal... The Bihar disturbances of 1946 finally shattered the dream of an undivided India.[140]

In the second half of October Nehru had visited the North-West Frontier Province in his capacity as Member for External Affairs in the interim government. The governor had advised against the visit. So had Gandhi and Azad. In Azad's view, 'His tour in the Frontier at this stage would give dissident elements an opportunity of organizing their opposition to Congress'.[141] When Nehru landed at the airport, he found thousands of Pathans massed there with black flags shouting hostile slogans. Khan Sahib, the Congress premier and others who had come to receive him were helpless and themselves needed police protection. On the next day during his tour of the tribal area he encountered hostile demonstrations everywhere. It was a great shock to the tribesmen to find a Hindu coming down to talk to them from a position of authority. As the party were leaving Malakand, the demonstrators surrounded the car in which Nehru and Khan Sahib and Khan Sahib's brother Ghaffar Khan were travelling. They managed to escape when Khan Sahib brandished a pistol. Nehru suffered bruises on the ear and chin. The Khan brothers too were injured.

The slaughter of Muslims in Bihar was followed by a dreadful massacre of Muslims in Garhmuktesar in the United Provinces during a Hindu festival.

Liaquat told Abell (the viceroy's secretary) on 18 November that the state of the country was one of civil war.[142] In a letter he wrote to the secretary of state on 22 November, Wavell said that the recent disorders had not been sudden outbreaks of excitable people as had often occurred in the past, but were deliberately planned by the worst political elements, and they showed that neither the police nor the Indian officials could now be relied on to act impartially.[143] In a plan for withdrawal from India in the event of a political breakdown which Wavell had submitted to London in September 1946, he had already concluded that Britain could not hold India longer than the spring of 1948.[144]

The London Conference, 3-6 December 1946

On 14 October 1946, while the question of the Muslim League joining the interim government was still pending, Wavell had an interview with Liaquat and Jinnah. In it the viceroy had said that he 'hoped Jinnah understood that the presence of the League in the interim government would be conditional on their reconsideration of the Bombay resolution' by which the League had withdrawn its acceptance of the Cabinet Mission's Statement of May regarding the setting up of the Constituent Assembly. Jinnah replied that he realized that but 'it would be necessary to secure certain guarantees from the Congress'.[145]

Congress's position, as spelled out by Nehru in a letter to Wavell dated 23 October 1946, was that 'We have made our position perfectly clear in this respect [i.e., in respect of the Cabinet Mission's Statement of 16 May] on many occasions both to the Cabinet Delegation and subsequently. The Delegation's interpretation was not our interpretation of the Statement of May 16th.'[146]

On 19 November 1946, when Wavell interviewed Jinnah and Nehru one after the other he advised Jinnah that the right policy for the Muslim League was to come into the Constituent Assembly and negotiate with the Congress. Jinnah replied that a settlement between Hindus and Muslims was 'quite impossible'. He also said that to call the Constituent Assembly would be the greatest possible mistake and would lead to terrible disaster. Nehru, however recommended that invitations to the Constituent Assembly should be 'issued at once'.[147]

Two days later the viceroy issued invitations for the meeting of the Constituent Assembly on 9 December and on the following day the Quaid issued a statement that the summoning of the Constituent Assembly was 'one more blunder of very grave and serious character' and that no representative of the League would attend it.[148]

In an equally outspoken speech on the same day, Nehru complained that the Muslim League had been endeavouring to establish itself as the King's Party in the interim government, and the British Government for its part had been exploiting that position for its own purposes. He alleged that there was a mental alliance between the League and senior British officials. He felt that Congress should remain in the interim government, but for how long that would be he could not say. What form their struggle should take would have to be considered when the occasion arose. He warned the viceroy that their patience was 'fast reaching the limit'.[149]

These threats from both the major parties, together with the deteriorating law and order situation and the viceroy's warning that the growing crisis called for a definite policy on the part of the British Government, caused the British Government to invite the Indian leaders for discussions to find a way of preventing a breakdown.

The Conference met in London from 3 to 6 December. Nehru represented Congress, Jinnah and Liaquat the League, and Baldev Singh the Sikhs. The last meeting, attended by all of those who had taken part in the discussions, took place on 6 December under the chairmanship of Prime Minister Attlee, who said that the British Government had asked the Indian leaders to come to London in the hope that they might be able to assist in settling the differences which had arisen between the parties in regard to the Constituent Assembly. The British Government had done their part but they had been unable to get acceptance by either side of the view held by the other. He then read out the Statement which was to be issued by the British Government that night

> The Cabinet Mission have throughout maintained the view that the decisions of the Sections should, in the absence of agreements to the contrary, be taken by simple majority vote of the representatives in the sections. This view has been accepted by the Muslim League, but Congress have put forward a different view. They have asserted that the true meaning of the Statement, read as a whole, is that the provinces have a right to decide both as to grouping and as to their own Constitutions. His Majesty's Government have had legal advice which confirms that the Statement of 16th May means what the Cabinet Mission have always stated was their intention... On the matter immediately in dispute, His Majesty's Government urge Congress to accept the view of the Cabinet Mission in order that the way may be open for the Muslim League to reconsider their attitude.

As an obvious warning to Congress if it remained intransigent, the Statement concluded as follows

> There has never been any prospect of success for the Constituent Assembly, except upon the basis of an agreed procedure. Should a Constitution come to be framed by a Constituent Assembly in which a large section of the Indian population had not been represented, his Majesty's Government could not of course contemplate—as the Congress have stated they would contemplate—forcing such a Constitution upon any unwilling parts of the country.[150]

When the Constituent Assembly met on 9 December, not a single member of the Muslim League attended it.

Notes

1. For the text of Jinnah's article *see*, Waheed Ahmad, *The Nation's Voice (March 1935 March 1940)*, op. cit., pp. 473-9.
2. For an account of the proceeding of the Lahore Session *see*, Pirzada, *Foundation of Pakistan*, II, op. cit., pp. 325-49.
3. Choudhry Khaliquzzaman, *Pathway to Pakistan*, op.cit., p. 237.
4. This was stated by Jinnah himself after the achievement of Pakistan. *See, Speeches as Governor-General of Pakistan*, p. 4.
5. For a description of the Khaksar Movement *see*, the section on 'A Muderous Attack on the Quaid-i-Azam' in this chapter.
6. Pirzada, *Foundations of Pakistan*, II, op. cit., pp. 330.
7. Waheed Ahmad, *The Nation's Voice*, II, op. cit., p. 178.
8. Ibid., p. 115.
9. Jamil-UD-Din Ahmad, *Speeches and Writings of Mr Jinnah*, II, op. cit., p. 2.
10. Waheed Ahmad, *The Nation's Voice*, II, p. 257.
11. Ibid., pp. 169-71.
12. Jamil-UD-Din Ahmad, *Speeches and Writings of Mr Jinnah*, II, op. cit., p. 141.
13. Ibid., pp. 210-11.
14. Pirzada, *Foundations of Pakistan*, II, op. cit., p. 335.
15. Pirzada, *Evolution of Pakistan*, p. 100.
16. B. R. Ambedkar, *Pakistan*, op. cit., pp. 131-2.
17. K. M. Panikkar, *A Survey of Indian History*, p. 143.
18. A. M. Zaidi, *The Encyclopaedia of the Indian National Congress*, XII, op. cit., pp. 427, 429, 374.
19. For the text of the letter *see*, Pirzada, *Quaid-i-Azam Jinnah's Correspondence*, op. cit., pp. 204-5.
20. A. M. Zaidi, *The Encyclopaedia of the Indian National Congress*, XII, op. cit., pp. 375-6.
21. Waheed Ahmad, *The Nation's Voice*, II, op. cit., p. 495.
22. Jamil-UD-Din Ahmad, *Speeches and Writings of Mr Jinnah*, I, op. cit., p. 193.
23. For the text of Jinnah's address at the Madras session *see*, Pirzada, *Foundations of Pakistan*, II, op., cit., 359-71.
24. Clement Attlee was Lord Privy Seal till 19 February 1942. From that date he became Deputy Prime Minister and Stafford Cripps joined the War Cabinet as Lord Privy Seal and Leader of the House of Commons.
25. *The Transfer for Power*, I, p. 463. Henceforth *TOP*.
26. Waheed Ahmad, *The Nation's Voice*, I, op. cit., p. 406.
27. *TOP*, I, op. cit., p. 380.
28. Waheed Ahmad, *The Nation's Voice*, II, op. cit., p. 412.

29. For the text of the Declaration which was published on 30 March 1942, see, TOP, I, op. cit., pp. 565-6.
30. Azad, *India Wins Freedom*, op. cit., p. 40.
31. Louis Fischer, *The Life of Mahatma Gandhi*, op. cit., p. 386.
32. TOP, II, op. cit., pp. 342.
33. Azad, *India Wins Freedom*, op. cit., p. 260.
34. Ibid., p. 262.
35. Ibid., p. 264.
36. For text of resolution see, TOP, I, op. cit., p. 745.
37. Azad, *India Wins Freedom*, op. cit., p. 67.
38. TOP, I, op. cit., p. 748.
39. TOP, II, op. cit., p. 342.
40. Azad, *India Wins Freedom*, op. cit., p. 265.
41. *Hansard*, 28 April 1942, H. of C. ccclxxix, 910 (Part II).
42. Quoted by Sir Reginald Coupland, *India, a Re-Statement*, op. cit., p. 218.
43. Azad, *India Wins Freedom*, op. cit., p. 74.
44. P. N. Chopra, *Quit India Movement*, p. 394.
45. For the text of the resolution see, Azad's *India Wins Freedom*, op. cit., pp. 266-70.
46. Coupland, *India, a Re-Statement*, op. cit., p. 222.
47. P. N. Chopra, *Quit India Movement*, op. cit., p. 396.
48. TOP, II, op. cit., p. 853.
49. Ibid., p. 868.
50. Ibid., p. 1003.
51. Jamil-UD-Din Ahmad, *Speeches and Writings of Mr Jinnah*, I, op. cit., pp. 401-3.
52. Ibid., p. 421.
53. Ibid., p. 424.
54. Pirzada, *Foundations of Pakistan*, II, op. cit., pp. 395-8.
55. Jamil-UD-Din Ahmad, *Speeches and Writings of Mr Jinnah*, I, op. cit., p. 456.
56. TOP, IV, op. cit., p. 378.
57. Ibid., p. 388.
58. Ibid., p. 379.
59. Jamil-UD-Din Ahmad, *Speeches and Writings of Mr Jinnah*, II, op. cit., p. 3.
60. Azad, *India Wins Freedom*, op. cit., p. 96.
61. TOP, IV, op. cit., p. 1136.
62. Ibid., p. 1198.
63. For the texts of the letters exchanged by Jinnah and Gandhi see, Pirzada, *Quaid-i-Azam Jinnah's Correspondence*, op. cit., pp. 99-129.
64. Jinnah's insistence that only the Muslims in the Muslim-majority provinces should be asked to vote on the issue of Pakistan was understandable. In the two biggest provinces, Bengal and the Punjab, the Muslims were only in a small numerical majority which the non-Muslims—who were more affluent, better organized and who controlled most of the Press—might have overturned.

65. Jamil-UD-Din Ahmad, *Speeches and Writings of Mr Jinnah*, II, op. cit., p. 129.
66. Ibid., p. 132.
67. Ibid., p. 135.
68. Kanji Dwarkadas, *India's Fight for Freedom*, op. cit., p. 353.
69. Ibid., p. 190.
70. *TOP*, V, op. cit., p. 1.
71. Ibid., p. 132.
72. Wavell, *The Viceroy's Journal*, op. cit., p. 120.
73. Ibid., V, p. 1122.
74. Ibid., p. 1122-4.
75. Azad, *India Wins Freedom*, op. cit., p. 114.
76. *TOP*, V, op. cit., p. 1225.
77. Jamil-UD-Din Ahmad, *Speeches and Writings of Mr Jinnah*, II, op. cit., p. 186.
78. *TOP*, V, op. cit., p. 1263.
79. Ibid., p. 742.
80. Ibid., p. 1237.
81. Jamil-UD-Din Ahmad, *Speeches and Writings of Mr Jinnah*, II, op. cit., p. 192.
82. Wavell, *The Viceroy's Journal*, op. cit., p. 168.
83. Waheed Ahmad, *The Nation's Voice*,II, op. cit., p. xxxviii.
84. Created Baron on 16 August 1945.
85. *TOP*, VI, op. cit., pp. 174-5.
86. Azad, *India Wins Freedom*, op. cit., 140.
87. *TOP*, VI, op. cit., p. 700.
88. Wavell, *The Viceroy's Journal*, op. cit., p. 197.
89. Ibid., p. 287.
90. Ibid., p. 311.
91. Ibid., p. 236.
92. Ibid., p. 300.
93. Ibid., p. 313. The significance of Congress's acceptance of the Mission's 16 May Statement will become clear when we discuss the point at a later stage.
94. Ibid., p. 257.
95. *TOP*, VI, op. cit., p. 834.
96. R/3/1/105. For a facsimile of this 'most secret' note *see*, S. M. Burke and Salim AL-Din Quraishi, *The British Raj in India*, op. cit., appendix A.
97. For facsimiles of the secretary of state's telegram and the viceroy's reply *see*, ibid., appendices C and D.
98. Jamil-UD-Din Ahmad, *Speeches and Writings of Mr Jinnah*, II, op. cit., p. 277.
99. Ibid., p. 278.
100. For proceedings of the League Legislators' Convention *see*, Pirzada, *Foundations of Pakistan*, II, op. cit., pp. 505-24.
101. *TOP*, VII, op. cit., p. 110.
102. Ibid., p. 116. Referring to Gandhi's offer that Jinnah be allowed to form a government, Wavell commented in his *Journal*, op. cit., (p. 236) 'the catch

being that he would be subject to the Hindu majority in the Central Assembly'.
103. *TOP*, VII, p.p. 118-24.
104. For text of Statement *see*, *TOP*, VII, op. cit., pp. 582-91.
105. Wavell, *The Viceroy's Journal*, op. cit., p. 271.
106. *TOP*, VII, op. cit., p. 613.
107. Ibid., p. 646.
108. Ibid., pp. 663-9.
109. Ibid., pp. 679-82.
110. Ibid., pp. 688-9.
111. This account is taken from ibid., pp. 784-6 read with *The Viceroy's Journal*, op. cit., p. 286. The assurance thus, in effect was verbal. Of course that does not make it less binding.
112. *TOP*, VII, op. cit., p. 837.
113. Ibid., p. 839.
114. Ibid., p. 955.
115. Polak, Brailsford, Pethick-Lawrence, *Mahatma Gandhi*, op. cit., p. 279.
116. *TOP*, VII, op. cit., p. 1036.
117. Ibid., p. 1042.
118. Ibid., pp. 1044-5.
119. Ibid., pp. 1071-3.
120. Gwyer and Appadorai, *Speeches and Documents on the Indian Constitution*, II, p. 612-5.
121. Azad, *India Wins Freedom*, op.cit., p. 170.
122. Louis Fischer in his Introduction to Azad's *India Wins Freedom*, p. xvii. This Introduction will be found in the edition published in New York by Longmans Green but not in the Indian edition.
123. For an account of the proceedings *see*, Pirzada, *Foundations of Pakistan*, II, op. cit., pp. 544-62.
124. Wavell, *The Viceroy's Journal*, op. cit., p. 315.
125. *TOP*, VIII, op. cit., p. 98.
126. Ibid., p. 156. Jinnah feared that some of the minority members specially the Sikhs would side with the Congress and this would add to Congress's initial majority of 6 to 5 against the League.
127. Ibid., pp. 237, 248.
128. Ibid., p. 274.
129. Some days later Shafaat Ahmad Khan was stabbed and wounded by two Muslims in Simla.
130. *TOP*, VIII, op. cit., p. 306.
131. Jamil-UD-Din Ahmad, *Speeches and Writings of Mr Jinnah*, II, op. cit., p. 336-9.
132. *TOP*, VIII, op. cit., p. 386.
133. Ibid., pp. 594-5.
134. Ibid., p. 644.
135. Ibid., p. 756.
136. *TOP*, IX, op. cit., p. 74.
137. Azad, *India Wins Freedom*, op. cit., p. 178.

138. Muhammad Ali at that time was Financial Adviser, War and Supply, in the Government of India. After Independence he became Secretary-General of the Government of Pakistan and was Prime Minister from 1955 to 1956. This account is taken from his book, *The Emergence of Pakistan*.
139. Azad, *India Wins Freedom*, op. cit., p. 179.
140. Pyarelal, *Mahatma Gandhi, The Last Phase*, I, op. cit., p. 641.
141. Azad, *India Wins Freedom* op. cit., p. 181.
142. *TOP*, IX, op. cit., p. 96.
143. Ibid., p. 140.
144. *TOP*, VIII, op. cit., p. 457.
145. Ibid., p. 713.
146. Ibid., p. 781.
147. *TOP*, IX, op. cit., pp 108-12.
148. Ibid., p. 135.
149. Ibid., pp. 131-2.
150. Ibid., pp 295-6.

CHAPTER 12

Pakistan Zindabad

Attlee's Statement on New Indian Policy and Mountbatten's Appointment as Viceroy

The Muslim League's refusal to take part in the Constituent Assembly meant that the plan of the Cabinet Mission for the transfer of power in accordance with a Constitution framed cooperatively by the Indian political parties themselves had come to a deadlock. Clearly a new initiative was called for. Accordingly, Prime Minister Attlee made the following statement on Indian policy in the house of Commons on 20 February 1947

> His Majesty's Government desire to hand over their responsibility to authorities established by a Constitution approved by all parties in India in accordance with the Cabinet Mission's plan, but unfortunately there is at present no clear prospect that such a Constitution and such authorities will emerge. The present state of uncertainty is fraught with danger and cannot be indefinitely prolonged. His Majesty's Government wish to make it clear that it is their definite intention to take the necessary steps to effect the transference of power into responsible Indian hands by a date not later than June 1948...if it should appear that such a Constitution will not have been worked out by a fully representative Assembly before the time mentioned [above], His Majesty's Government will have to consider to whom the powers of the Central Government in British India should be handed over, on the due date, whether as a whole to some form of Central Government for British India or in some areas to the existing Provincial Governments, or in such other way as may seem most reasonable and in the best interests of the Indian people.
>
> In regard to the Indian States, as was explicitly stated by the Cabinet Mission, His Majesty's Government do not intend to hand over their powers and obligation under paramountcy to any government of British India. It is not intended to bring paramountcy, as a system, to a conclusion earlier than the date of the final transfer of power,

but it is contemplated that for the intervening period the relations of the Crown with individual States may be adjusted by agreement.[1]

It was announced at the same time that Rear-Admiral the Viscount Mountbatten would succeed Lord Wavell as viceroy in March.

The directive to Mountbatten took the form of a letter to him from Attlee dated 18 March 1947 which read

> ...it is the definite objective of His Majesty's Government to obtain a unitary Government for British India and the Indian States, if possible within the British Commonwealth, through the medium of Constituent Assembly, set up and run in accordance with the Cabinet Mission's plan, and you should do the utmost in your power to persuade all parties to work together to this end, and advise His Majesty's Government, in the light of developments, as to the steps that will have to be taken.
>
> Since, however, this plan can only become operative in respect of British India by agreement between the major parties, there can be no question of compelling either major party to accept it.[2]

Attlee had first offered the viceroyalty to Mountbatten in an interview on 18 December 1946. He had explained that the crisis in India had reached a stage that

> If we were not very careful, we might well find ourselves handing India over not simply to civil war, but to a political movement of a definitely totalitarian character. Urgent action was needed to break the deadlock, and principal members of the Cabinet had reached the conclusion that a new personal approach was perhaps the only hope.

Mountbatten defended Wavell by saying that 'Wavell had done nothing throughout that time which he would not have done himself'. Attlee

> ...agreed that fundamentally it was not Wavell's general policy in the past that was in question, but its implementation today. The hard fact was that in spite of his unremitting efforts it had largely broken down, and Attlee reiterated that in this new situation the problem was now more one of personality. The need for closer personal contact with the Indian leaders was paramount.[3]

Wavell was first informed by Attlee by telegram on 12 February that he would be succeeded as viceroy by Mountbatten. On the following day he recorded in his *Journal*, 'an unexpected appointment but a clever one from their point of view; and Dickie's personality may perhaps accomplish what I have failed to do'. He evidently shared Attlee's view that Mountbatten was capable of meeting the adroit Indian politicians on their own ground and outsmarting them and would be able to extricate Britain from the shambles in India with the least possible damage to British reputation and material interests.

As a second cousin of King George VI, Mountbatten carried an aura which was expected to impress the pomp-conscious Indians especially the princes. He was a highly gifted person with a fine presence, an intelligent mind, the faculty of quick decision and the resilience to take setbacks in his stride. At the same time he was inordinately vain and ambitious, and had a burning desire to succeed and project himself in the best possible light. The author of his official biography sums up

> A picture of Mountbatten without his warts would indeed be unconvincing, for, like everything else about him, his faults were on the grandest scale. His vanity, though child-like, was monstrous, his ambition unbridled. The truth, in his hands, was swiftly converted from what it was to what it should have been. He sought to rewrite history with a cavalier indifference to the facts to magnify his own achievements.[4]

The new viceroy was ably assisted by his charming wife, Edwina. She became a close friend of Nehru. Nehru's biographer diagnoses:

> As for Lady Mountbatten, it can only be surmised that she helped to fill a void in Nehru's life. He had always suffered from a sense of loneliness. His wife's death at an early age had accentuated this feeling. Especially during the Partition days, when he was more prone to moods of despair, Lady Mountbatten's sympathy was a source of comfort. She, too, was a cultivated Westerner, and a woman of great charm who could understand him as most Indian women whom he knew could not.[5]

Pyarelal describes Lady Mountbatten as 'a "secret weapon" of no small strategic value in Lord Mountbatten's arsenal of personal diplomacy'.[6]

Indeed, the Mountbattens were no strangers to Jawaharlal Nehru. A year earlier (18-26 March 1946) Nehru had visited Singapore at the instance of Lord Wavell,[7] to investigate the condition of the Indian community there as a representative of the Indian National Congress. Mountbatten at that time was in Singapore as the Supreme Allied Commander. Nehru's visit was frowned upon by the local British administration because he had been concerned with sabotaging the war effort under Gandhi's 'Quit India' movement and because Singapore had been the headquarters of the Japanese-inspired Indian National Army. Indeed, the British Military Administration had signalled to New Delhi that they could not provide any transport for the Indian leader.

Nehru had not long before come out of prison, so that the effects of imprisonment on his mind and general outlook had not entirely worn off. Wavell had sent a message to Mountbatten that Singapore presented 'a magnificent opportunity to begin the cure', and had added that Nehru personally was a man of great culture and sincerity and 'very probably' the future prime minister of India, and should be treated accordingly.

The Supreme Allied Commander accordingly placed his own car at Nehru's disposal and he was welcomed by Mountbatten and given tea. Thereafter Mountbatten and Nehru, seated side by side, drove off to the YMCA. This display of cordiality by Mountbatten transformed the temper of the crowds lining the route. Instead of staging an anti-British demonstration they staged one of Anglo-Indian unity. At the YMCA they were warmly greeted by Lady Mountbatten and lustily cheered by a huge disorderly crowd.

In deference to Mountbatten's wish, Nehru abandoned his plan to ceremoniously lay a wreath on the INA monument and contented himself with quietly depositing a personal wreath. When Nehru landed at Rangoon on his way back to India he told Aung San[8] that Mountbatten was 'a very noble specimen of British imperialism'. After the announcement of Mountbatten's appointment, Ismay said that 'there was a danger of an issue being made of Mountbatten's selection as a pro-Hindu and anti-Muslim League appointment.[9] And indeed, the mutual liking between the Mountbattens and Nehru, which was born at Singapore, quickly developed into a genuine friendship. This was of immense political advantage to the viceroy as well as to the Congress leader. In Mountbatten's view Nehru was 'indispensable' for the handing over of power to take place in the most peaceful and dignified manner possible.[10]

As a special case, Mountbatten was allowed to bring with him from the United Kingdom, staff of his own choice to supplement the team he would inherit from Wavell. Those he brought out were Lord Ismay as chief of staff, Sir Eric Mieville as principal secretary and Alan Campbell-Johnson as press attaché.

Attlee's declaration of 20 February saved the interim government from breaking up. On 5 February 1947, Wavell had received a formal demand from the Congress nominees in the interim government for the expulsion of the Muslim League members of the interim government. It was alleged that by a resolution passed on 31 January 1947 the Muslim League had rejected the Cabinet Mission scheme of 16 May 1946.[11] On 13 February Nehru wrote to the viceroy that the delay in expelling the League members from government would 'lead us to reconsider our position in the interim government'.[12] However, when he saw the viceroy on 22 February he praised Attlee's statement of 20 February as 'a courageous document which would have far-reaching effects' and added that Congress would not now press 'for an immediate answer' to the request for the expulsion of the Muslim League members from the interim government.[13] The Quaid did not comment on Attlee's statement but declared that the League would not yield an inch in its demand for Pakistan.[14]

However, in the Punjab, Attlee's statement intensified the Muslim League agitation against the Unionist Government of Khizar Hayat. Khizar told the governor that Attlee's announcement of 20 February was 'the work of lunatics'.[15] He resigned his premiership on 2 March. The governor invited the Nawab of Mamdot, leader of the Muslim League in the Punjab, to form the government but the League could not muster a majority because, as expected, the Hindus and the Sikhs refused to form a coalition with the Muslim League. The governor believed that forming a purely Muslim League ministry would exacerbate the already serious communal tension in the province. In April the Nawab of Mamdot again offered to form a ministry. Thereupon Mountbatten asked Jinnah to see him on 26 April and told him that any attempt to impose a mainly one-community government on the Sikhs would produce immediate armed retaliation. Mountbatten made it clear that nothing would induce him to change his mind and that he would instruct the governor accordingly. Mountbatten asked Jinnah whether he could tell the governor that he (Jinnah) agreed. Jinnah replied, 'Certainly not, I definitely do not agree'. Nevertheless, the Punjab remained under the governor's rule till the transfer of power.

During the same interview the Quaid cleared up for Mountbatten a point of constitutional law. Mountbatten mentioned that Suhrawardy had said that if Bengal remained united and became independent it would wish to 'remain within the Commonwealth'. Jinnah replied, 'Of course, just as I indicated to you that Pakistan would wish to remain within the Commonwealth'. Mountbatten tried to correct him and said, 'No, you told me that if the Pakistan Government was formed, its first act might well be to ask to be admitted to membership of the British Commonwealth'. Jinnah said Mountbatten had completely misunderstood the position; it was not a question of being admitted, it was a question of not being kicked out. And he went on to say that Churchill had told him: 'You have only to stand firm and demand your rights not to be expelled from the British Commonwealth, and you are bound to be accepted. The country would never stand for the expulsion of loyal members of the Empire.' Jinnah pointed out there was no precedent for forcing parts of the empire to leave the Commonwealth against their will.[16]

Congress Requests the British Government to Partition India

The continual denial to the Muslims of governmental office in the Punjab increasingly frustrated them, and communal tension and the number of consequent casualties began to mount apace. On 4 March, Master Tara Singh, the Sikh leader, shouted *'Pakistan murdabad'*,[17] and, brandishing a sword, proclaimed *'raj karega Khalsa, agey rahe na koi'*.[18] Two police officers who interviewed Tara Singh at Amritsar on 10 March reported that he was extremely excited, asserting the civil war and threatening attacks on police stations and a mass Sikh rising had already begun.

On 4 March large-scale rioting broke out in Lahore and on 5 and 6 March also in Multan, Rawalpindi, Amritsar and Jullunder, with smaller disturbances elsewhere. The worst affected parts were the predominantly Muslim districts of Attock, Rawalpindi and Jhelum in the north-west and Multan in the south-west, where trouble rapidly spread to rural areas.

These events in the Punjab had their repercussions in the adjoining North-West Frontier Province, where the Muslim Leaguers organized demonstrations against the Congress Ministry of Dr Khan Sahib. On 21 February a procession in Peshawar broke the police cordons and came right up the road in front of the Governor's House and also into Khan Sahib's garden besieging his house on all sides. Tear-gas was used but when the police were ordered to fire they quietly disobeyed orders. The mob broke all the windows of Khan Sahib's house. Eventually the deputy commissioner was able to get the crowd to move on.[19] There was also trouble in Mardan and elsewhere and League leaders, including members of the provincial legislature, were arrested; the arrest of the Pir of Manki Sharif angered his followers in the tribal areas. On 5 March, Wavell reported to the secretary of state that the Congress ministry in North-West Frontier Province 'may not last long'.[20] At a Muslim League demonstration at the Assembly Hall in Peshawar on 10 March, troops had to open fire, resulting in fifteen casualties, two of whom subsequently died.

The massacres in the Punjab as well as those which had already taken place in Bengal and Bihar, finally persuaded the non-Muslim minorities that their safety lay in the partition of the Punjab and Bengal. This in effect meant the partition of India into Muslim-majority and non-Muslim majority areas. One of the resolutions passed by the Congress Working Committee at Delhi on 8 March 1947 referred to the widespread violence in the Punjab and read

> These tragic events have demonstrated that there can be no settlement of the problem in the Punjab by violence and coercion, and that no arrangement based on coercion can last. Therefore it is necessary to find a way out which involves the least amount of compulsion. This would necessitate a division of the Punjab into two Provinces, so that the predominantly Muslim part may be separated from the predominantly non-Muslim part. The Working Committee commend

this resolution, which should work to the advantage of all the communities concerned.[21]

On 9 March, Nehru forwarded the above resolution of the Congress Working Committee along with two other resolutions passed at the same session with the request that he 'will be good enough to send them to His Majesty's Government'. In the same letter he made clear that the principle that had led Congress to ask for the partition of the Punjab 'applies to Bengal' also.[22] On 19 March Governor Burrows of Bengal wrote to Wavell that the movement for partitioning Bengal was 'gathering momentum'.[23]

On behalf of the Sikhs, Baldev Singh wrote to Wavell on 11 March confirming that the Sikhs too wished the Punjab to be partitioned: 'The only solution is a division of the Punjab and the creation of a new Province embracing the contiguous areas where non-Muslims form a clear majority as a whole'.[24]

The Congress request to the British Government that the Punjab and Bengal be partitioned was a development of the highest importance but for some reason it received less attention from the powers that be than it deserved. It meant that the Congress and the Muslim League were both agreed that dividing the country into Muslim-majority and non-Muslim majority areas was the best constitutional solution of the Indian problem. Previously the League alone had contended that the Muslims and the Hindus could not co-exist peacefully in the subcontinent. Now the Congress too had reached the same conclusion and had asked for partition for the same reason. The British Government had consistently challenged the Indians to put forward an agreed solution. Here at last was an agreed solution. A lot of hassle and extra bloodshed would have been avoided if the British Government had taken the Indians at their word and promptly taken in hand the process of transferring power to the two successor states as they had to do in the end in any case.

The Congress resolution in favour of partition had another important repercussion. It spelled the end of Mahatma Gandhi's dictatorship over the Congress party. The resolution had been passed without consulting or even informing the Mahatma. On 20 March Gandhi wrote to Nehru that he did not know the reason behind the Working Committee resolution and protested that he had not been given the opportunity of even putting forward his view 'which was against any partition based on communal grounds and the two-nation theory'. To Sardar Patel he wrote at the same time, 'Try to explain to me your Punjab resolution if you can. I cannot understand it.'

Patel replied on 24 March that the resolution 'was adopted after deepest deliberation... That you had expressed your view against it, we learnt only from the papers. But you are, of course, entitled to say what you feel right.' Nehru wrote on the following day that he and the Working Committee felt convinced 'that we must press for immediate division so that reality might be brought into the picture'.

Pyrelal's comment on the above exchanges between Gandhi and his two most powerful colleagues was, 'Such a thing would have been inconceivable in olden days. Even when he was ranging over the length and breadth of India, they did not fail to consult him before taking any vital decision.'[25]

The fact, of course, was that the Mahatma's usefulness as a holy man capable of inspiring powerful mass movements to coerce the British Government had lost its purpose. India's independence was assured; a definite time limit for its advent had been fixed. The situation now demanded hard-headed negotiations on the practicalities of the process of partition. Gandhi's image as a spiritual icon remained but his technique as a politician was outmoded. Instead of being a source of inspiration, he became a nuisance for his Congress colleagues. A few days before Independence the Mahatma announced his decision to spend the rest of his life in Pakistan looking after the minorities. This brought forth the following comment from Mountbatten in the Viceroy's Personal Report No. 16 dated 8 August 1947: 'This will infuriate Jinnah, but will be a great relief to Congress for, as I have said before, his influence is largely negative or even destructive and directed against the only man who has his feet firmly on the ground, Vallabhbhai Patel'.[26]

The Opening Phase of Mountbatten's Viceroyalty

Lord and Lady Mountbatten landed at Delhi on 22 March 1947 and he took over as viceroy two days later. He could very well have represented to the British Government that both the Congress and the Muslim League had already asked for the partition of India into Muslim-majority and non-Muslim majority areas and sought their permission to embark upon the process of partition straightaway. But he chose instead to follow the policy laid down in Attlee's pronouncement of 20 February that in the first instance the attempt to transfer power in accordance with the Cabinet Mission plan must continue. It is to that end, therefore, that he first directed his endeavours.

Not surprisingly, Mountbatten's relations with the Congress party had a flying start. We have already explained that the foundation of Nehru's friendship with Lord and Lady Mountbatten had been laid in March 1946 when the Indian leader visited Singapore. The political complexion in India too had changed in favour of the Congress. The Muslims, the princes and the Untouchables who hitherto had served the British interests by acting as a counterbalance to the rebellious Congress, had lost their bargaining power. In post-independent India, it was the Congress party which was expected to rule the country. Consequently it was Congress's friendship which had now to be cultivated. That Mountbatten personally was bitterly opposed to partition made it much easier for him to court the Congress leaders; the new viceroy referred to the demand for Pakistan 'this mad Pakistan'.[27] His enthusiasm for a united India and his hatred for the demand for Pakistan revived Congress's hopes for a united India and caused them to forget all about their own resolution asking for Pakistan.

All these factors greatly increased the already formidable odds facing the Quaid-i-Azam in his fight for Pakistan. However, there was one strong point in his favour and in the end it was that which proved decisive. Attlee's statement of 20 February had fixed the date by which power must be transferred. It had laid down at the same time that, if an agreed all-India Constitution was not forthcoming, power could be transferred to more than one unit. What Jinnah needed to do to win Pakistan, therefore, was to stick to the decision that the Muslim League would not join the Congress in the Constituent Assembly and to refuse to budge from the position that Pakistan was the only solution acceptable to the Muslim League. And this is precisely what he did.

No sooner was Mountbatten sworn in than he got down to business. He had interviews on the same afternoon with Nehru and Liaquat, the seniormost members of the interim government. His bias in favour of the Congress leaders became immediately obvious. His own record of the interview with Nehru begins with the sentence, 'Pandit Nehru struck me as most sincere'.[28] At the end of the meeting Mountbatten said to him, 'Mr Nehru, I want you to regard me not as the last viceroy winding up the British Raj, but as the first to lead the way to new India'. Nehru turned, looked intensely moved, smiled and and then said, 'Now I know what they mean they speak of your charm being so dangerous'.[29]

During the interview Mountbatten had asked Nehru about Jinnah.

> Nehru explained Jinnah's creed, which he admitted had scored enormous success, as always to avoid taking any positive action which might split his followers; to refuse to hold meetings or to answer questions; never to make a progressive statement because it might lead to internal Muslim dissensions. These negative qualities were ones which had a direct appeal to the Muslims—therefore it was not to be hoped that logic would prevail.[30]

About his interview with Liaquat, Mountbatten recorded, 'He gave me his version of how Coalition Government had been formed—a totally different version to that rendered by Nehru—and quite untrue'.[31]

Mountbatten invited Gandhi for interviews on 31 March and 1 April. Pyarelal noted that Gandhi returned from the first meeting 'greatly impressed by the viceroy's sincerity, gentlemanliness and nobility of character'.[32] At their second meeting, Gandhi gave Mountbatten 'the brief summary of the solution' which he wished him to adopt

> Jinnah should forthwith be invited to form the Central Government with members of the Muslim League. This Government to operate under the Viceroy in the way the present Interim Government is operating. Any difficulty experienced through Congress having a majority in the Assembly to be overcome by their able advocacy of the measures they wished to introduce.[33]

Mountbatten mentioned Gandhi's plan to Nehru later on the same day. Nehru was not surprised to hear it since it was the same as Gandhi had put up to the Cabinet Mission and which had been turned down as being quite impracticable.[34]

During the Gandhi-Mountbatten meeting on 2 April, the Mahatma 'came down firmly for his great plan'. If Jinnah should refuse, Gandhi pointed out, the offer would have to be made to the only other great party in India—Congress. When Mountbatten 'twitted him' that he really desired that a government run by Congress should be formed, the Mahatma assured the viceroy 'with burning sincerity that this was far from being the case'.[35]

There can be little doubt but that Gandhi was asking Mountbatten to hand over power to Congress, but instead of saying so straightforwardly, he gave it the moral wrapping of mentioning the Muslim League first. Criticizing Gandhi's plan, V.P. Menon pointed out in a note that if Jinnah formed a government 'composed entirely of Muslim League nominees, that government will find itself facing a predominant Congress majority in the Central Legislature from which Jinnah has to get his essential legislation and supply'.[36] At his Staff Meeting on 5 April, Mountbatten called Gandhi's scheme 'undoubtedly wild'.[37] The problem was finally solved on 11 April when Gandhi wrote to Mountbatten that he had discussed the formula with Nehru and several members of the Congress Working Committee but had failed to carry any of them with him except Badshah Khan.[38]

Mountbatten did not have his first encounter with Jinnah till 5 April. Two days earlier Pethick-Lawrence, who as leader of the Cabinet Mission had considerable experience of negotiating with the Quaid, warned him: 'You still have the toughest customer to come in Mr Jinnah'.[39]

Mountbatten began his report on his first meeting with Jinnah with the observation that when the latter first arrived on 5 April 'he was in a most frigid, haughty and disdainful frame of mind'. Jinnah claimed that there was only one solution—a 'surgical operation' on India, otherwise India would 'perish altogether'. Mountbatten replied that he had not yet made up his mind. Jinnah said that it was easier to deal with the Muslim League because it had only one recognized leader, namely himself but that was not true of the Congress. Gandhi had openly confessed that he represented nobody but he still had enormous authority with no responsibility. Nehru and Patel represented different points of view within the Congress but neither could speak for the party as a whole.[40] Mountbatten's reaction to the first meeting was, 'My God he was cold. It took most of the interview to unfreeze him.' Jinnah and Fatima were due to dine with the Mountbattens that night but the function was postponed till the following night (6 April) because 'Mountbatten felt he could not sustain another session with Jinnah today'.[41] The dinner for the Jinnahs went off better than the Mountbatten-Jinnah interview had gone. The guests stayed until an hour past midnight and Mountbatten was able to record that 'the ice was really broken'.[42]

However, the two opening encounters had proved sufficient to convince Mountbatten that the Quaid-i-Azam 'would not in the end agree to the Cabinet Mission's plan as the final solution. He foresaw that eventually a truncated Pakistan would emerge.'[43] But it would have been unseemly for the proud viceroy openly to acknowledge defeat so soon.

In his third meeting with Jinnah on 7 April, Mountbatten 'tried by every means to bring him up to the point of saying that he would accept the Cabinet Mission plan and enter the Constituent Assembly'. Jinnah responded by arguing at great length that it was quite valueless entering the Constituent Assembly or even trying to go back to the Cabinet Mission plan, since the whole basis of that plan was a spirit of cooperation and it was clear that in no circumstances did Congress intend to work the plan either in accordance with the spirit or the letter. He said that India had passed beyond the stage at which any such compromise solution could possibly work; and he categorically called upon Mountbatten to hand over power as soon as possible, preferably province by province, and let the provinces themselves choose how they formed into groups.[44]

Mountbatten again interviewed Jinnah on the next day and once more tried to bring him back the Cabinet Mission plan but to no avail. When Mountbatten asked Jinnah to put forward his arguments for partition, 'he recited the classical ones'. Mountbatten then pointed out that his remarks applied also to the partition of the Punjab and Bengal. While admitting the logic of the argument, Jinnah 'expressed himself most upset at my trying to give him a "moth-eaten" Pakistan'. He appealed to Mountbatten not to destroy the unity of Bengal and the Punjab.[45]

During their next meeting on 9 April, Jinnah once more appealed to the viceroy not to give him a 'moth-eaten' Pakistan. Mountbatten told Jinnah that he

> ...regarded it as a very great tragedy that he should be trying to force me to give up the idea of a united India. I painted a picture of the greatness that India could achieve—four hundred million people of different races and creeds, all bound together by a central Union Government with all the economic strength that would accrue to them from industrialization, playing a great part in world affairs as the most progressive single entity in the Far East.

Mountbatten even tried to tempt Jinnah to accept a united India by saying that 'it was a day-dream of mine to be able to put the Central Government under the Prime Ministership of Mr Jinnah himself'. Jinnah replied that 'nothing would have given him greater pleasure than to have seen such unity, and he entirely agreed that it was indeed tragic that the behaviour of the Hindus had made it impossible for the Muslims to share in this'.[46]

Jinnah's interview with Mountbatten on 10 April was their sixth gruelling session in a row.[47] Once again Mountbatten tried to bring Jinnah back to the Cabinet Mission plan by citing Jinnah's own complaint that the truncated Pakistan which Mountbatten was visualizing would be economically 'very difficult if not impossible to function'. But all was in vain. That Mountbatten's celebrated charm and powers of persuasion had utterly failed to budge the Quaid-i-Azam from his demand of Pakistan had bruised the former's most vulnerable trait—his vanity. In the Staff Meeting on 11 April he gave vent to his frustration: Jinnah was 'impossible to argue with'; 'Mr Jinnah was a psychopathic case'. At the same time he was compelled to confess that it was now 'quite clear to him, that if any effort was made to try and impose the Cabinet Mission plan, the Muslim League would resort to arms'. Accordingly, he asked Lord Ismay 'to start to work out the details of a plan at present primarily under consideration'.[48]

Plan Balkan

The plan which Mountbatten had asked Ismay to work out was that which the former had outlined at the Staff Meeting on 10 April. Its central feature was that 'There would be demission of power to Provinces, who would be free at their own discretion to join together into one or more groups'. This meant a retreat to the second of the two alternative schemes laid down in Attlee's Statement of 20 February. The plan also stated that 'the Punjab and Bengal would be partitioned'.[49] The plan which had been abandoned was called Plan Union and the new plan was named Plan Balkan.

Plan Balkan was discussed at the Governors Conference on 15 and 16 April. On the first day of the Conference Mountbatten said that the 'dominating impression which he had gathered since his arrival was the necessity for a very early decision on how power was to be transferred. This need had not been fully appreciated before he left London'.[50] He also 'pointed out that a quick decision would also give Pakistan a greater chance to fail on its demerits'.[51] Having failed to prevent the birth of Pakistan, he was evidently determined to do what he could to cause the infant country's collapse so that India could be reunited into one country.

The Quaid meanwhile issued a statement that the proposal of partitioning Bengal and the Punjab was a 'sinister move'. The division of India as proposed by the Muslim League was based on the fundamental fact that there were two nations—Hindus and Muslims—and the underlying principle was that 'we want a National Home and a National State in our homelands which are predominantly Muslim and comprise 6 units of the Punjab, NWFP, Sind, Baluchistan, Bengal and Assam. This will give the Hindus their national home and national state of Hindustan which means three-fourths of British India'. 'The question of partitioning Bengal and the Punjab is...actuated by spite and bitterness...to unnerve the Muslims by...repeatedly emphasizing that the Muslims will get a truncated or mutilated moth-eaten Pakistan'. He emphasized that the States of Pakistan and Hindustan should be made absolutely free, independent and sovereign.[52]

In his Personal Report to London on 1 May, Mountbatten wrote that he would be sending Ismay to London on the following day with the final draft of Plan Balkan and requested that Ismay be released after a week carrying the necessary authority for Mountbatten to go ahead because 'we all feel that every day now counts out here if we are to prevent the communal conflict from spreading to unmanageable proportions'.[53]

Pending the receipt of the approval of the plan by the British Government, Mountbatten went up to Simla for a change of air. He took with him V.P. Menon and Mieville. Nehru and Krishna Menon followed as his guests on 8 May. On 10 May Mountbatten received back from London the plan he had sent through Ismay, as finalized and approved by the British Government. Following a 'hunch', Mountbatten gave Nehru the text of the plan as the latter was going to bed that evening. On the following morning Nehru wrote to Mountbatten that the proposal had 'produced a devastating effect' upon him. They presented 'an entirely new picture—a picture of fragmentation and conflict and disorder and, unhappily also of a worsening of relations between India and Britain'.[54] He promised to follow up the letter with a note on the proposals. In the note on the following day Nehru warned that the announcement of the proposals by HMG would provoke wide and deep resentment all over the country, and no responsible leader outside the Muslim League would be able to persuade the country to accept them.[55]

A revolt by Nehru and Congress was an unthinkable prospect for Mountbatten who had staked everything on winning their goodwill. He thanked his hunch for having shown the plan to Nehru before it was made public. Without that hunch, he told his staff, 'Dickie Mountbatten would have been finished and could have packed his bags'.[56] He telegraphed to Ismay to stay on in London to 'pilot through' his new proposals 'on Dominion Status'. He characterized Nehru's attitude as a 'bombshell'.[57]

On 14 May, Ismay advised Mountbatten that the situation was now so confused that Attlee and his colleagues felt that either a minister or ministers should proceed to India to discuss the situation or Mountbatten should personally fly to London. He added that he had taken it on himself to say that Mountbatten would be opposed to any ministers proceeding to India.[58] Later on the same day Attlee telegraphed to Mountbatten asking him to come to London for consultations.

Developments in the North-West Frontier Province

In the second half of April 1947 developments in the North-West Frontier Province and Bengal came to the fore. During the Governors Conference, Caroe said that his province was liable to 'drop to bits' at any moment and that the only way of relieving tension was to announce a general election straightaway. The question was discussed on 16 April in a meeting at which Mountbatten presided and which was attended by Nehru and Caroe among others. Caroe said there had been a swing against Khan Sahib's Congress government in the preceding twelve months. Nehru believed that elections, if held immediately, would probably cause some disturbances but conceded that it was desirable to obtain the views of the people before the final hand-over of power was effected.

A further meeting convened by the viceroy on 18 April, for which Khan Sahib had flown in, produced only an acrimonious debate between the governor and his premier. Mountbatten thereupon decided to visit the province personally and assess the situation on the spot.

The viceroy, accompanied by Lady Mountbatten and their daughter, touched down at Peshawar soon after midday on 28 April and drove to Government House. There he learnt that a crowd of Muslim League demonstrators estimated at 50,000 had gathered less than a mile away and would angrily march on Government House unless he showed himself to them. After consulting the governor and the premier, Mountbatten decided to show himself to the crowd from the top of a nearby railway embankment. Lady Mountbatten accompanied him as it was reported there were many women in the gathering. The crowd was good-humoured and greeted the viceroy with shouts and flag-waving. He stood for a few minutes in company with the governor and other officials and then withdrew after saluting, but without making any address.

On the same afternoon Mountbatten conferred with Khan Sahib and his Cabinet of four ministers. He said his instructions from the British Government were that India should be handed over in accordance with the will of the people so far as that could be found out. Though he would be telling the Muslim League that he would not yield to violence, he told them 'privately' that he thought elections were necessary. Khan Sahib told Mountbatten that Jinnah had no control over the Muslim League in the Frontier and the League was run by the governor and his officials 'with the object of throwing my government out of power'. Commenting on these allegations in his Personal Report to London on 1 May,[59] Mountbatten wrote, 'I could not suppress my laughter at such a fantastic suggestion'.

The meeting with the ministers on 28 April was followed by one with local Hindu representatives, who complained of a lack of adequate police protection.

Mountbatten next received the Muslim League leaders, who had been released from gaol for the occasion. He ordered that they should all be lodged in the same gaol so that they could consult each other; also that they should be permitted to go to Delhi on parole to see Jinnah.

All the sixteen senior officials, Indian and British, with whom Mountbatten talked during the same day 'were absolutely convinced that fresh elections at the earliest possible moment were absolutely necessary if a great disaster was to be avoided'.

On the following day the viceregal party made a tour of the Khyber and attended a couple of *jirgas* (tribal meetings) in which the tribesmen made clear their bitter opposition to Hindu Raj; they said they would rather make terms with Afghanistan. Some pressed hard for Pakistan. After lunch Mountbatten and his entourage left the Frontier Province.

Proposal for a United Independent Bengal

With regard to Bengal an interesting situation was created when Suhrawardy, the Muslim League premier, told Mountbatten on 26 April that he was confident that he could get Bengal to remain united and independent and could obtain Jinnah's agreement to such a course. Mountbatten replied that this was very good news, for he was against splitting India up into many units and considered it far better to keep Bengal as one economic unit than to have it partitioned. When Mountbatten mentioned the idea to Jinnah later on the same day, he replied without hesitation, 'I should be delighted. What is the use of Bengal without Calcutta? They had much better remain united and independent. I am sure they would be on friendly terms with us.'

The chances of a communal settlement were greater in Bengal than in the Punjab, where racial, cultural, an linguistic differences were deeper. In Bengal, one language was spoken and written by all, and most Muslims were converts from Hinduism and had retained elements of their ancestral culture. Sarat Chandra Bose, brother of the late Subhas Bose, also advocated a united independent Bengal.

Gandhi supported the proposal for a united independent Bengal because it would mean 'repudiation of the two-nation theory' on which the demand for Pakistan was based. But when he discussed the scheme with Nehru and Patel he found them both 'dead against' it.[60]

The proposal for an independent Bengal had to be abandoned because Plan Dominion Status, under which power was eventually transferred in India, envisaged the partition of the country into only the two states of India and Pakistan.

Plan Dominion Status

The new proposals on Dominion Status which Mountbatten had mentioned in his telegram to Ismay on 11 May, were the brainchild of V. P. Menon who was a confidant of Patel. Already in late December 1946 or early January 1947 Menon had had lengthy discussions with Patel and had represented that a united India under the Cabinet Mission Plan was an illusion and that it was better that the country should be divided, rather than that it should gravitate towards civil war. Patel had assured him that if power could be transferred at once on the basis of Dominion Status, he for one would use his influence to see that Congress accepted it.

At Mountbatten's suggestion, Menon discussed Plan Dominion Status with Nehru on 8 and 9 May and found that Nehru was not averse to the transfer of power on the basis of Dominion Status.[61] After Plan Balkan had been abandoned following Nehru's angry rejection of it, Mountbatten at a Staff Meeting on 12 May asked Menon to redraft his plan 'on the basis of no option for independence being given to Bengal or any other Province'.[62]

Menon immediately got to work and produced a draft plan. That night Mountbatten told Menon that he had shown the draft to Nehru who had said that it would not be unacceptable to Congress.[63]

Mountbatten returned to Delhi from Simla on 14 May. Being anxious to avoid further 'bombshells', he was determined to obtain the agreement of the leaders of the principal political parties to the new plan before taking it to London. He asked Menon to draw up a 'Heads of Agreement' which was shown to Nehru, Patel, Baldev Singh, Jinnah and Liaquat. Nehru sent a note on 16 May that Congress accepted the plan but 'strictly subject to a final settlement'. On the following day he sent some further comments to Mountbatten in the form of a letter in which he agreed that the governor-general should be common to both states, if there were to be two states, and that for their part Congress would be happy if Mountbatten could continue in this office.

At a Staff Meeting on 16 May, Mountbatten said that Jinnah and Liaquat had accepted the plan as outlined in the Heads of Agreement but had declined to state this in writing. Mountbatten informed the meeting that

> ...he had already cautiously tried out threatening Mr Jinnah that, unless he met requirements adequately, power would be demitted to the Interim Government on a Dominion Status basis. Mr Jinnah had taken this very calmly and said that he could not stop such a step in any event. The viceroy said that this abnormal reaction, which was typical of Mr Jinnah, was rather disturbing. If Mr Jinnah saw himself betrayed he might derive great satisfaction by going down in history as a martyr for his cause, butchered by the British on the Congress altar.[64]

When, on 15 May, Mountbatten discussed with Liaquat the question of Dominion Status for Pakistan and Hindustan under one governor-general, he found Liaquat 'surprisingly receptive to this idea'.[65] But when the viceroy raised the question in a meeting with Jinnah and Liaquat on 17 May, Jinnah said he felt that it would be better to have two governors-general. Jinnah said further that there should be a representative of the Crown to be responsible for the division of assets between the two states and he expressed his keenness that Mountbatten should fill that post. Mountbatten said he could not consider taking on the post suggested by Jinnah because 'it would be an impossible position if the so-called "Arbitrator" was junior in rank to the governors-general, who would be the king's representative'. Mountbatten suggested that Jinnah should send him a letter giving a full description of his suggestion of a supreme arbitrator. He asked Jinnah to state clearly in the letter that if his scheme was deemed by the government to be unpractical he would accept, as an interim measure, the appointment of a common governor-general between the two countries.[66] The requested letter never arrived, presumably because Jinnah did not wish to state that he would accept a common governor-general if his plan for an arbitrator was turned down.

Mountbatten, accompanied by V.P. Menon, left for London on 18 May and returned to New Delhi on 31 May. The new plan—that power would be transferred to India and Pakistan as Dominions, with the Act of 1935 basically serving as their respective Constitutions for the time being—had a number of obvious advantages: power could be transferred quickly without waiting for the newly independent countries to complete their new Constitutions; India would remain within the Commonwealth, at least to start with. British civil and military officers already in India would readily volunteer to assist the new administrations for the desired period; and above all it was a plan which was being sponsored by the viceroy with the consent of the principal Indian parties. Mountbatten, therefore, had no difficulty in obtaining the approval of the British Government to the new proposals.

He was also able to win Churchill's enthusiastic support and a promise that the Opposition would help to rush the necessary legislation through. Churchill authorized him to give Jinnah a curt message: 'This is a matter of life and death for Pakistan if you do not accept this offer with both hands'.[67]

Mountbatten returned to Delhi on 31 May with the plan as finalized by the British Cabinet. He took the precaution of showing it to the Indian leaders on 2 June for their concurrence before it was released generally. Those invited were Nehru, Patel and Kripalani as representatives of Congress; Jinnah, Liaquat and Nishtar as representatives of the Muslim League; and Baldev Singh as the representative of the Sikhs. He asked the leaders to take the copies to their Working Committees and to let him know by midnight that night what those Committees thought of it.

The Congress leaders prophesied that their Working Committee would be in favour of acceptance and promised to let Mountbatten have their views in writing that night. Jinnah said that the Muslim

League Working Committee would not be able to commit themselves without prior reference to the All-India Muslim League Council. He undertook to convene the Council in a week's time but when pressed, promised verbally to give Mountbatten the reaction of the Working Committee that night. Mountbatten informed the meeting that he intended to make a broadcast over All-India Radio on the following evening and persuaded Nehru, Jinnah and Baldev Singh to do the same after him.

Jinnah called on the viceroy at 11 p.m. on 2 June and said he would support the proposals personally and do his utmost to have them accepted. His Working Committee was hopeful that the plan would be accepted by the All-India Council of the Muslim League. To Mountbatten's question whether he would be justified in advising Attlee to go ahead and make the statement, Jinnah firmly replied, 'Yes'. But, still apprehensive of what Jinnah might say at the leaders meeting on the following day, Mountbatten requested him simply to nod his head in assent when he (Mountbatten) declared that he felt satisfied with the assurances given. Jinnah agreed to do so and duly nodded his head at the proper moment.

The Congress president's letter was received by the viceroy at 0015 hours on 3 June. It stated that the Congress Working Committee was prepared to accept the plan and recommend it to the All-India Congress Committee for acceptance 'in order to achieve a final settlement'.

Baldev Singh's letter arrived on the morning of 3 June. He accepted the principle of division as laid down in the plan but hoped that the Boundary Commission would be instructed to take note not only of the factor of Muslim-majority and non-Muslim-majority geographical areas, but also of 'other factors' such as the amount of property owned by non-Muslims and the amount of land revenue paid them, and the location of Sikh cultural institutions.

During Mountbatten's absence in England, Jinnah had created a sensation (on 22 May) by demanding an eight-hundred mile corridor to link West and East Pakistan. Nehru called the demand 'fantastic and absurd'. On his return to India, Mountbatten was able to prevail upon Jinnah not to pursue it.

The Plan of 3 June 1947

The plan for the transfer of power to which all concerned had agreed, was authoritatively announced by the British Government in the form of a statement on 3 June by Prime Minister Attlee in the Commons and Secretary of State for India the Earl of Listowel in the House of Lords. It stated that the British Government had always desired to transfer power in accordance with the wishes of the Indian peoples themselves. But the Indian political parties had not been able to agree how this could be done. The task of devising a method by which the wishes of the Indian people could be ascertained had therefore devolved on the British Government who had decided to adopt the following plan:

The existing Constituent Assembly would continue to function but any Constitution framed by it could not apply to those parts of the country which were unwilling to accept it. The procedure outlined in the statement was designed to ascertain the wishes of such unwilling parts on the question whether their Constitution was to be framed by the existing Constituent Assembly or by a new and separate Constituent Assembly.[68] After this had been done, it would be possible to determine the authority or authorities to whom power should be transferred.

> The Provincial Legislative Assemblies of Bengal and the Punjab (excluding the European members) will therefore each be asked to meet in two parts, one representing the Muslim majority districts and the other the rest of the Province.
>
> The members of the two parts of each Legislative Assembly sitting separately will be empowered to vote whether or not the Province should be partitioned. If a simple majority of either part decides in favour of partition, division will take place and arrangements will be made accordingly.
>
> For the immediate purpose of deciding on the issue of partition, the members of the Legislative Assemblies of Bengal and the Punjab will sit in two parts according to Muslim majority districts (as laid down in the Appendix) and non-Muslim majority districts. This is only a preliminary step of a purely temporary nature as it is evident that for the purposes of final partition of these Provinces a detailed investigation of boundary questions will be needed; and, as soon as a decision involving partition has been taken for either Province, a

Boundary Commission will be set up by the Governor-General, the membership and terms of reference of which will be settled in consultation with those concerned.

It will be instructed to demarcate the boundaries of two parts of the Punjab on the basis of ascertaining the contiguous majority areas of Muslim and non-Muslims. It will also be instructed to take into account other factors. Similar instructions will be given to the Bengal Boundary Commission. Until the report of a Boundary Commission has been put into effect, the provisional boundaries indicated in the Appendix will be used.

The Legislative Assembly of Sind was similarly authorized to decide at a special meeting whether that province wished to participate in the existing Constituent Assembly or to join a new one. If it was decided to partition the Punjab, a referendum would be held in the North-West Frontier Province 'of electors of the present [provincial] Legislative Assembly' to choose which Constituent Assembly they wished to join. The referendum would be held 'under the aegis of the governor-general and in consultation with the Provincial Government'.

Baluchistan would also be given an opportunity to reconsider its position and the governor-general was examining how this could most appropriately be done.

> Though Assam is predominantly a non-Muslim Province, the district of Sylhet which is contiguous to Bengal is predominantly Muslim. There has been a demand that, in the event of the partition of Bengal, Sylhet should be amalgamated with the Muslim part of Bengal. Accordingly, if it is decided that Bengal should be partitioned, a referendum will be held in the Sylhet district, under the aegis of the Governor-General and in consultation with the Assam Provincial Government, to decide whether the district of Sylhet should continue to form part of the Assam Province or should be amalgamated with the new Province of Eastern Bengal, if that Province agrees. If the referendum results in favour of amalgamation with Eastern Bengal, a Boundary Commission with terms of reference similar to those for the Punjab and Bengal will be set up to demarcate the Muslim majority areas of Sylhet District and contiguous Muslim majority areas of adjoining districts, which will then be transferred to Eastern Bengal.
> Agreements with tribes of the North-West Frontier of India will have to be negotiated by the appropriate successor authority.[69]

With regard to the Princely States the statement made it clear that the policy 'contained in the Cabinet Mission Memorandum of 12th May 1946 remains unchanged'.⁷⁰

Mountbatten had already arranged that he would introduce the plan to the Indian people by a broadcast on the All-India Radio at precisely the same time as Attlee and Listowel were presenting it to Parliament at Westminster (7 p.m. Indian Standard Time). Also that he would be followed at the microphone by the leaders of the three principal Indian political parties to convey their acceptance of the plan.

In his broadcast Mountbatten regretted that it had been impossible to obtain the agreement of Indian leaders either on the Cabinet Mission plan or on any other plan that would have preserved the unity of India. But there could be no question of coercing any large areas in which one community had a majority to live against their will under a government in which another community had a majority. The only alternative to coercion was partition.⁷¹

The Indian leaders broadcast their acceptance in the following terms

> Nehru: It is with no joy in my heart that I commend these proposals to you, though I have no doubt in my mind that this is the right course. For generations we have dreamt and struggled for a free and independent united India. The proposals to allow certain parts to secede, if they so will, is painful for any of us to contemplate. Nevertheless, I am convinced that our present decision is the right one even from the larger viewpoint.
>
> The united India that we have laboured for was not one of compulsion and coercion, but a free and willing association of a free people. It may be that in this way we shall reach that united India sooner than otherwise and then she will have a stronger and more secure foundation. We are little men serving a great cause, but because the cause is great, something of that greatness falls upon us also...
>
> Jinnah: It is for us now to consider whether the plan as presented to us by His Majesty's Government should be accepted by us as a compromise or a settlement. On this point I do not wish to prejudge the decision of the Council of the All-Indian Muslim League which has been summoned to meet on Monday, 9th June; and the final decision can only be taken by that Council according to our Constitution precedents and practice.

> But so far as I have been able to gather on the whole reaction in the Muslim League circles in Delhi has been hopeful...
> Baldev Singh: It [the plan] does not please everybody, not the Sikh community, anyway. But it is certainly worthwhile. Let us take it...

In his broadcast Jinnah also called upon the Provincial Muslim League of the North-West Frontier Province to cease its campaign of civil disobedience because it had been decided to seek the mandate of the people there by a referendum.

On the morning of 4 June, the viceroy held a press conference and in the course of it stated publicly for the first time that transfer of power could take place on 'about 15 August' 1947.

The Council of the All-India Muslim League met at the Imperial Hotel, New Delhi on 9-10 June 1947 and stated in its resolution that, although it could not agree to the partition of Bengal and the Punjab or give its consent to such partition, it had to consider the plan for the transfer of power as a whole. It gave full authority to the Quaid-i-Azam to accept the fundamental principles of the plan as a compromise and left it to him to work out the details.[72]

While the Council of the League was in session on 9 June in the first floor ballroom of the hotel, a party of Khaksars armed with spades came in through the garden at the side of the hotel, and rushed through the lounge shouting 'Get Jinnah'. They were half way up the staircase leading to the ballroom before the Muslim League National Guards could grapple with them and halt their progress. It took the police using tear-gas to quell the disturbance. The Quaid-i-Azam 'behaved with great composure'. Sidney Smith of the *Daily Express* who saw Jinnah afterwards said that Jinnah had no doubt that the assault was an attempt on his life.[73]

The All-India Congress Committee passed a resolution on 15 June accepting the 3 June plan. However, it expressed the hope that India would one day be reunited: 'The AICC earnestly trusts that when the present passions have subsided, India's problems will be viewed in their proper perspective and the false doctrine of two nations in India will be discredited and discarded by all'.[74]

All the main parties had thus accepted the plan. Commented V. P. Menon

> But acceptance was one thing; its implementation was a different matter altogether. Here was a task which normally should have taken years to accomplish but which had to be compressed into the short

space of a few weeks! It was a task before which anybody would have quailed, for it was one which seemed verily to tempt the Gods.[75]

The Constitutional and Legal Formalities of Partition and Independence

The Bengal Legislative Assembly met on 20 June and voted in accordance with the procedure laid down in the 3 June 1947 plan. As a result, the province was divided into West Bengal, which would join India, and East Bengal, which would join Pakistan. The proceeding in the Punjab Assembly on 23 June similarly resulted in the partition of that province into East Punjab and West Punjab, which would join India and Pakistan respectively. On 26 June the Sind Legislative Assembly too, opted for Pakistan.

In the case of Baluchistan, the viceroy decided that the future of the province should be decided by the *Shahi Jirga*, excluding the Sardars of Kalat State but including, for this purpose, the non-official members of Quetta Municipality; they voted to join Pakistan.

In Sylhet, the referendum went in favour of Pakistan: 239,619 persons voted in favour of joining Pakistan and 184,914 against.

The referendum in the North-West Frontier Province was conducted from 6 to 17 July; 289,244 votes were cast for Pakistan and 2,874 for India. The total electorate entitled to vote in the referendum was 572,789; the vote for Pakistan, therefore, was 50.49 per cent. In his Personal Report dated 25 July 1947, Mountbatten commented

> It is particularly satisfactory that over 50 per cent of the total electorate voted for joining Pakistan (and the total votes cast were only 15 per cent less than last time without a boycott), as that disposes of any possible argument on the Congress side that, in spite of the boycott, the Province was not really in favour of joining Pakistan.

In deference to Congress's wishes, Caroe had been replaced as governor by General Rob Lockhart, and the referendum had been conducted by Brigadier J. B. Booth as Referendum Commissioner, assisted by British officers of the Indian Army. Liaquat had represented to Mountbatten on 11 June that the

Khan Sahib ministry should also be dismissed because there was 'a much greater likelihood of the ministers abusing their powers than the governor', but the Congress ministry was allowed to function until it was finally dismissed on 21 August 1947 by Jinnah as Governor-General of Pakistan.

Thus each of the territories which were to comprise Pakistan—East Bengal, Sylhet, West Punjab, Sind, Baluchistan and the North-West Frontier Province—had positively signified its wish to form a part of Pakistan.

His Majesty's Government lost no time in providing the legal framework for giving effect to the political decision that power should be transferred to two independent countries. The Indian Independence Act which received the Royal Assent on 18 July 1947, ordained that as from the fifteenth day of August 1947 'two independent Dominions shall be set up in India, to be known respectively as India and Pakistan'. Each of the new Dominions was to have a governor-general and the same person could be the governor-general of both the new Dominions.

The governor-general was to make provision for the division of the Indian armed forces between the new Dominions and for the command of those forces until the division was completed.

The districts which were 'provisionally' included in the new provinces of East Bengal and West Pakistan were named but the actual demarcation of the boundaries was to conform to the 'Award' of the boundary commissions 'appointed or to be appointed' by the governor-general. The 'Award' was defined as the 'decisions of the chairman contained in his report to the governor-general'.

The suzerainty of His Majesty over the Indian States was to lapse on 15 August 1947.

During the debate on the Indian Independence Bill in Parliament, both the government and the opposition spokesman expressed their unhappiness that India had to be divided. Prime Minister Attlee declared, 'For myself, I earnestly hope that this severance may not endure and that the two new Dominions which we now propose to set up may, in course of time, come together again to form one great member State of the British Commonwealth of Nations'. Opposition leader Harold Macmillan echoed these sentiments: 'We must hope with the prime minister that in this partition are also the seeds of some form of future unity'.

The Quaid-i-Azam's Wisdom in Preventing Mountbatten from Becoming Governor-General of Pakistan

We have already mentioned that it was on 17 May that Mountbatten first raised with Jinnah the question of a common governor-general between Pakistan and India and that Jinnah had said that he would prefer separate governors-general for the two countries and would like Mountbatten to occupy the position of a Crown Representative for the division of assets between the two new dominions.

Mountbatten had left for London on 18 May to obtain the approval of the British Government for his revised plan for the transfer of power, and returned from there on 31 May. Thereafter he tried to get an answer from Jinnah on the matter of the governor-generalship, but the latter always put off giving an answer. Finally, Jinnah said he could not let Mountbatten know until he had seen the Indian Independence Bill. After he had seen the bill, he still did not wish to answer till he had consulted two of his colleagues who were away at the referendums in the North-West Frontier Province and Sylhet.

Nevertheless, Mountbatten and his advisers had convinced themselves that in the end Jinnah would accept a common governor-general. At the staff meeting on 9 June Mountbatten had said, 'Pakistan would be the Dominion which would gain most advantages if he [Mountbatten] stayed behind as Governor-General of both Dominions. In fact, if he has his own separate Governor-General, Mr Jinnah might well wreck his prospects.'[76] During an interview with Mountbatten on 23 June, Jinnah had said that whatever decision he reached would not be taken on grounds of not wanting the viceroy, in whom he had implicit trust and confidence, but the rule of his life was that he must always consider the interests of his people; at various times of his career he had had to pass over those nearest and dearest to him.[77] But Mountbatten's optimistic conviction that Jinnah ultimately would have to accept him as governor-general of Pakistan was not shaken.

For Mountbatten personally, of course, a request from both Dominions to become their governor-general would have been the crowning glory. His name would have been enshrined in history for all time as the statesman with the magic touch who had not only achieved the impossible, by solving the dreaded India-Pakistan problem with the consent of the Congress and the Muslim League, but who, at the same time, had attained the unthinkable by winning in equal measure the trust of both these historical foes.

Mountbatten was utterly taken aback when Jinnah at last told him on 2 July that he himself would be Pakistan's governor-general. The Muslim League leader explained that he wished to have British governors in every province of Pakistan except Sind which, since it would be under his personal supervision in Karachi, could have a Muslim governor. He pointed out, further, that he had also agreed to the three heads of the Pakistani Defence Services being British, and concluded by saying that the only way in which he could sell the idea of all these British officials would be to become the governor-general of Pakistan himself. He pressed Mountbatten to remain as governor-general of India.

All Mountbatten's efforts to move the Quaid-i-Azam from his resolve to become governor-general of Pakistan were in vain. When Mountbatten threatened, 'Do you realize what this will cost you?' Jinnah said sadly, 'It may cost me several crores of rupees in assets', to which Mountbatten replied, 'It may well cost you the whole of your assets and the future of Pakistan', and left the room.[78]

In his telegram to Attlee on the following day, Mountbatten reported that he had spent another four hours trying to make Jinnah realize the advantages that Pakistan would gain from having the same governor-general as India until partition was complete.[79] And the Viceroy's Conference Paper, VCP 115, July recorded

> During the next twenty-fours hours [after Jinnah had stated that he himself would be governor-general of Pakistan] the Viceroy spent much time in pointing out to both Mr Jinnah and Mr Liaquat Ali Khan, and on one occasion to a meeting consisting of Mr Jinnah, Mr Liaquat Ali Khan, Mr Rahman and Mr Muhammad Ali, the enormous advantages that Pakistan would gain from sharing, for a short initial period, the same Governor-General as Hindustan.[80]

In his letter to Attlee dated 5 July, Mountbatten described Jinnah's announcement that he himself would be the governor-general of Pakistan as a 'bombshell', and confessed that he considered 'the whole of this situation to be my fault. I should have foreseen it, and have cleared the position with both Jinnah and Congress one way or the other three or four weeks ago'.[81] To his daughter Patricia on the same day he expressed himself even more dejectedly

> Your poor old Daddy has finally and irretrievably 'boobed' and I've now landed myself in a position from which I cannot conceivably extricate myself with honour. Either I accept to stay with the Dominion of India and be forever accused of taking sides...or I let down the Congress leaders...Mummy feels I should preserve my reputation for impartiality and go on 15th August. The others feel I cannot let down Nehru and must stay. In both cases I'm in the wrong. In fact I've at last made a mess of things through over-confidence and over-tiredness. I'm just whacked and worn out and would really like to go.
>
> I'm so depressed darling, because until this stupid situation I'd done so well. It has certainly taken me down many pegs.[82]

It would appear that Jinnah's proposal for separate governors-general for India and Pakistan and, in addition, a Crown Representative with arbitral jurisdiction over both countries, was never given the consideration it deserved. The common governor-general would have been a constitutional functionary who would have been bound to follow the advice of each one of the two Cabinets. What would he have done when these Cabinets made diametrically opposite recommendations? He could have only mediated between them; he could not have overruled the party he believed to be in the wrong. The arbitrator on the other hand would have had all the opportunity to mediate that the joint governor-general could have had, plus the authority in reserve to impose his decision on the recalcitrant party.

It is stated that 'Jinnah's idea of an "arbitrator" or "stake-holder" was put up verbally to representatives of the India Office for their opinion' and that 'they were unanimous that such a system would be unconstitutional and unworkable'.[83] But Jinnah was not alone in feeling that the situation called for the appointment of some person other than a constitutional governor-general to help India and Pakistan resolve their differences. When

Mountbatten saw Churchill during his visit to London in May, the latter had suggested that if Mountbatten 'were appointed Governor-General of Hindustan and Governor-General of Pakistan...[he] might adopt the title of "Moderator"'.[84] During his visit to London in July, Ismay had reported to Mountbatten that at a meeting at which Attlee met the opposition leaders, the Liberal leader Lord Samuel 'was anxious to revive the idea of a viceroy presiding over the two governors-general, but the rest of the meeting turned this down as impracticable, probably unacceptable to Congress and too late'.[85]

The real reason why Jinnah's proposal was rejected seems to be that Mountbatten personally was averse to taking on the unpleasant task of trying to arbitrate between India and Pakistan. There was only one person at that time who could have dared to act as umpire between the two countries and that person was Mountbatten. Once he had indicated that he was unwilling to volunteer for the role, the matter so far as His Majesty's Government was concerned was at an end. We have Mountbatten's own words showing how thankless the position of an arbitrator seemed to him.

In his Personal Report No. 8 dated 5 June 1947 he had written

> Both sides were still very anxious to obtain my services as arbitrator in all matters of dispute in working out the partition. But I pointed out that since both sides were already approaching the problem from such widely divergent points of view it was clear that I should have to give a decision which one side or the other side would dislike practically every day, and however much they now professed to believe in my impartiality, such a procedure could not fail to undermine their confidence in me within a very short time.[86]

Pakistanis believe that Jinnah's decision against having a common governor-general

> ...had far-reaching effects. The loss that Pakistan would incur in material assets was easy to foresee. But there were other intangible factors, such as the accession of the States, the Kashmir question, and the award of the Boundary Commission, in which the balance was tilted against Pakistan with far more momentous consequences.[87]

But what Jinnah's followers at that time needed most was a sense of security, and their own Qauid-i-Azam's decision personally to become the head of state of the country which he had done so much to create for them provided just that. Even Mountbatten conceded that 'Jinnah had scored an undoubted victory from the psychological point of view over Congress in not having a "foreigner" as the first governor-general of Pakistan'.[88] Chaudhri Muhammad Ali correctly assessed that 'in the struggle for survival that lay ahead, moral factors would count far more than material losses'.

Jinnah's action may well have saved the infant state of Pakistan from an early demise. India and other prophets of doom were predicting that Pakistan was a mistake which history would soon rectify by returning it to Greater India. During the debate on the Indian Independence Act, Attlee as well as the leader of the Opposition had expressed the hope that partition would not endure. Mountbatten himself had never made any secret of his belief that the division of the subcontinent into two separate states was a tragic ending to British rule there. In fact, he had devised a strategy by which he hoped to recapture lost ground.

His instruments for turning defeat into victory were to be the common governor-generalship and the joint Defence Council. This is clear from what H. V. Hodson has written in his book, *The Great Divide*

> ...it was still Lord Mountbatten's hope and resolve that a rudimentary Centre would survive Partition, for defence and all that went with it. Two means were thought to assure this—a common Governor-Generalship for the initial period, an intention frustrated by Mr Jinnah, and the Joint Defence Council, which though operative for six months after the transfer of power was determined in its general and long-term purpose by the enmity between the two Dominions after the Punjab troubles and the Kashmir conflict.[89]

With regard to the Defence Council, Hodson has quoted from a letter which Mountbatten himself wrote to the King

> My original idea had been that the Council should continue in its existing form for at least another year—and I secretly hoped forever. It could carry on under my chairmanship (if both sides so wished) until I left, and then under the chairmanship of the Prime Minister of the Dominion in which each successive meeting took place. It

was in my mind that its scope might indeed expand, to cover financial and economic matters also, and eventually External Affairs and Communications, which would mean the 'virtual accession' of the two Dominions to one another, on the same basis as the States.[90]

It needs little imagination to realize that such an 'accession' by unequals to each would have spelled the end of Pakistan as a sovereign state and assured its absorption by India. This became precisely the fate of all the Princely States, which had been persuaded to surrender only the three specified subjects of Defence, External Affairs and Communications, with unequivocal assurances that the terms of the Instrument of Accession would not be varied without the ruler's consent, and that his sovereignty in all other matters would remain intact.

Of course, the Indian politicians would have desired nothing better than that Mountbatten should have become the governor-general of Pakistan. It would have greatly facilitated their efforts to snuff out Pakistan in her infancy. Nehru in his broadcast of 3 June and the All-India Congress Committee in its resolution of 15 June, from both of which we have already quoted, had expressed the wish and the hope that circumstances would cause Partition to be annulled.

The Quaid-i-Azam wrote to Prime Minister Attlee on 1 October 1947

> every effort is being made to put difficulties in our way by our enemies in order to paralyse or cripple our State and bring about its collapse... It is amazing that the top-most Hindu leaders repeatedly say that Pakistan will have to submit to the Union of India. Pakistan will never surrender. It is an aim which is foolish and impossible of achievement now but unfortunately the danger lies in the fact that it has become an obsession with them and they are not only thinking in these terms but are trying to put this policy into effect, as is evident from every deed, every action and every measure that is adopted and directed against Pakistan by the leaders of the Congress and the Dominion Government.[91]

The reality of the Quaid's fears was fully borne out by a secret report which Supreme Commander Field-Marshal Auchinleck had independently sent from Delhi to London on 28 September 1947: 'I have no hesitation whatever in affirming that the present Indian

Cabinet are implacably determined to do all in their power to prevent the establishment of the Dominion of Pakistan on a firm basis. In this I am supported...by all responsible British officers cognizant of the situation'.[92]

The Radcliffe Boundary Awards[93]

As laid down by the Indian Independence Act, the viceroy set up two Boundary Commissions. One of them was to deal with the detailed partition of Bengal and separation of Sylhet from Assam and the other to deal similarly with the partition of the Punjab. Each of the Commissions would have a chairman and four members, two nominated by the Congress and two by the Muslim League. Sir Cyril (later Viscount) Radcliffe, a leading member of the English Bar, was appointed chairman of both the Commissions. His colleagues were all High Court judges but being nominees of political parties they functioned in the commission as partisans of their respective parties. The Indian Independence Act had realistically anticipated this and had carefully defined the Award of the Commission as 'the decisions of the chairman contained in his report to the governor-general'.

Radcliffe had never visited India and there is no indication that he had any worthwhile knowledge of Indian affairs. He arrived in Delhi on 8 July. Mountbatten disclosed the awards to the Indian leaders on 17 August.

The Awards satisfied no one. Congress criticism of the award relating to Bengal chiefly related to the allotment to Pakistan of the Chittagong Hill Tracts. The reason for this in the words of Mountbatten's Personal Report dated 16 August was that

> ...the whole economic life of the people of the Hill Tracts depends upon East Bengal, that there are only one or two indifferent tracks through the jungle into Assam, and that it would be disastrous for the people themselves to be cut off from East Bengal. The population consists of less than a quarter of a million, nearly all tribesmen who, if they have any religion at all, are Buddhists (and so are technically non-Muslims, under the terms of the Boundary Commission). In a sense Chittagong, the only port of East Bengal, also depends upon the Hill Tracts; for if the jungles of the latter were subjected to unrestricted felling, I am told that Chittagong port would silt up.[94]

The Muslim League catalogue of grievances against the boundary decisions was longer and more serious.

In Bengal, Pakistan had lost some Muslim-majority areas but had also gained some which were non-Muslim. The chief Pakistani criticism was the allotment of Calcutta to India. As an important industrial and commercial centre, Calcutta would have strengthened the economy of East Pakistan, and as a major seaport it would have provided an important sea-link between the two wings of Pakistan.

In the Punjab 'other factors' had worked wholly to Pakistan's detriment. Some Muslim-majority areas, though contiguous to Pakistan, were given to India, while no non-Muslim majority territory was made over to Pakistan.

Pakistanis believed that the real culprit in these decisions was not Radcliffe, but Mountbatten, who was regarded as basically anti-Pakistan and was especially incensed because Jinnah had frustrated his ambition to be the governor-general of both India and Pakistan. It was Mountbatten, they say, who went to the extent of making Radcliffe change in India's favour awards he had already decided to announce.

Pakistanis allege that Calcutta was made over to India as a part of a deal which Mountbatten had made with Congress behind the Muslim League's back. They draw attention to a public speech by Patel at Calcutta on 15 January 1950 in the course of which he recalled, 'We made a condition that we would only agree to partition if we did not lose Calcutta',[95] and conclude that such a condition could have been made only with Mountbatten.

But in fact the British view that Calcutta would have to be allotted to India did not originate with Mountbatten. During his interview with the Cabinet Mission on 16 April 1946, Jinnah demanded to know the reason why Calcutta could not be given to Pakistan and was told by Secretary of State Pethick-Lawrence that 'what the delegation were doing was seeking for a basis of agreement. They did not think that agreement could be reached on the basis that Calcutta was included in Pakistan.'[96]

We have described how Menon and Rau had influenced Wavell and his colleagues in the Cabinet Mission to accept in principle that Gurdaspur district should be allotted to India. But, of course, Radcliffe could have still given it to Pakistan. That he had in fact done so at first and then changed his mind is borne out by no less an authority than the Secretary of State for Commonwealth Relations, Noel-Baker. In a note dated 25 February 1948 to Prime Minister Attlee, Noel-Baker wrote

> There is some reason for thinking that Sir Cyril Radcliffe at the last moment altered his boundary award so as to assign to the E. Punjab a salient in the original demarcation of the W. Punjab boundary which included Gurdaspur. But we have no knowledge that this was done on the advice of Lord Mountbatten.[97]

With regard to Ferozepore district, Pakistanis point out that the Ferozepore Headworks, except for the Bikaner Canal, irrigated mostly Muslim-majority areas in and contiguous to Pakistani Punjab, and they allege that in fact the Muslim-majority *tahsils* of Ferozepore and Zira, contiguous to Pakistan, were at first allotted by Radcliffe to Pakistan and were made over to India as the result of a last minute intervention by Mountbatten.

The truth of this allegation is certified by Radcliffe's own secretary in the Boundary Commission, H. C. Beaumont. The *Daily Telegraph* of 24 February 1992 featured a statement by Beaumont under the caption 'How Mountbatten bent the rules and the Indian border'. One of the present authors (Burke), who had been Beaumont's colleague in the Indian Civil Service in his younger years, got in touch with him. Beaumont was kind enough to respond generously and in the course of the exchanges that followed confirmed that the Muslim-majority *tahsils* of Ferozepore and Zira had at first been allotted by Radcliffe to Pakistan. The change in favour of India was made following a lunch hosted by Ismay from which Beaumont had been excluded. But some years later Beaumont learnt from George Abell, private secretary to Mountbatten at the relevant time, that at the lunch Ismay and Mountbatten had told Radcliffe that if he did not agree to the change it would result in civil war between India and Pakistan.

The Quaid-i-Azam could do no more than to console his countrymen thus

> We have been squeezed in as much as was possible and the last blow that we have received was the Award of the Boundary Commission. It is an unjust, incomprehensible and even perverse Award. It may be wrong, unjust and perverse; and it may not be a judicial

but a political Award, but we have agreed to abide by it and it is binding upon us. As honourable people we must abide by it. It may be our misfortunate but we must bear this one more blow with fortitude, courage and hope.[98]

The Last Year

The Quaid-i-Azam and his sister Fatima flew from New Delhi to Karachi on 7 August 1947. He passed away in the same city on the evening of 11 September 1948. This last year was the most difficult of all his life. He was already mortally ill and his stamina was ebbing away. But he served the country he had fathered with the last ounce of his strength.

At its inaugural session on 11 August 1947, the Pakistani Constituent Assembly elected Jinnah as its president and on the following day it gave formal recognition to his exalted position by resolving that, as from 15 August, he should be addressed as 'Quaid-i-Azam Mohammad Ali Jinnah'.

In his presidential address to the Assembly on 11 August, the Quaid said that the first duty of a government was to maintain law and order so that the life, property and religious beliefs of its subjects are fully protected. Another colossal crime against society that needed to be tackled was black-marketing. People who indulged in this crime undermined the entire system of control and regulation of foodstuffs and essential commodities and thus caused wholesale starvation and want and even death. Thirdly, the evil of nepotism and jobbery which was a legacy from the past needed to be crushed relentlessly. If Pakistanis wanted to make their country happy and prosperous they should 'wholly and solely concentrate on the well-being of the people, and especially of the masses and the poor'.

The Quaid advised Pakistanis to change their past and work together

> ...in a spirit that every one of you, no matter to what community he belongs, no matter what relations he had with you in the past, no matter what is his colour, caste or creed, is first, second and last a citizen of this State with equal rights, privileges and obligations... You may belong to any religion or caste or creed—that has nothing to do with the business of the State... We are starting with this

fundamental principle that we are all citizens and equal citizens of one State... We should keep that in front of us as our ideal and you will find that in due course of time Hindus would cease to be Hindus and Muslims would cease to be Muslims, not in the religious sense, because that is the personal faith of each individual, but in the political sense as citizens of the State.[99]

On the afternoon of 13 August Lord and Lady Mountbatten flew from Delhi to Karachi. Intelligence sources had warned of a plot to throw a bomb at Jinnah during the state procession on the following day, but Jinnah had stated that if Mountbatten was prepared to go through with the drive, then so was he. It was, therefore, decided to leave the arrangements unchanged.

The state procession on 14 August was staged in open cars with Jinnah and Mountbatten in the leading car and Miss Fatima Jinnah and Lady Mountbatten in the next car. Mountbatten addressed the Pakistani Constituent Assembly followed by Jinnah.

In his address Mountbatten reminded the audience

> Your great Emperor Akbar...whose reign was marked by perhaps as great a degree of political and religious tolerance, as has been known before or since...Akbar's tradition has not always been consistently followed by British or Indians, but I pray for the world's sake, that we will hold fast, in the years to come, to the principles that this great ruler taught us.[100]

The Quaid, in his reply pointed out

> The tolerance and goodwill that the Emperor Akbar showed to all the non-Muslims is not of recent origin. It dates back thirteen centuries ago when our Prophet not only by words but by deeds treated the Jews and Christians, after he had conquered them, with the utmost tolerance and regard and respect for their faith and beliefs.[101]

Lord and Lady Mountbatten returned to Delhi on the afternoon of 14 August.

Campbell-Johnson who, as a member of Mountbatten's entourage, had personally witnessed the ceremonies at Karachi, brought back the following impression: 'If Jinnah's personality is cold and remote, it also has a magnetic quality—the sense of leadership is almost overpowering... Here indeed is Pakistan's King Emperor, Archbishop of Canterbury, Speaker and Prime Minister concentrated into one formidable Quaid-i-Azam'.[102]

Pakistan became constitutionally independent at midnight between the 14 and 15 August 1947. The Quaid assumed charge as governor-general on 15 August and the Pakistani Cabinet, with Liaquat Ali Khan as prime minister was sworn in on the same day.

The Quaid's sister watched with sorrow and pain that in this hour of triumph, he was a sick man. He had little or no appetite; he had lost his gift of being able to sleep at will and he passed many sleepless nights; also, his cough increased and with it his temperature. The harrowing tales of the sufferings of the refugees affected him deeply. As brother and sister discussed these mass killings during breakfast, 'his eyes were often moist with tears'.[103] When close to death, he rambled in his unconsciousness: 'Kashmir...Give them...the right...to decide...Constitution...I will complete it...soon...Refugees...give them...all assistance... Pakistan...'[104] Of the numerous disputes with India and domestic worries, it was evidently the unsolved problem of Kashmir, his inability to complete the Constitution of the new State of Pakistan, and the plight of the millions of refugees who had arrived in their new homeland utterly destitute that affected him the most.

The scale of the refugee problem and the depth of its tragedy were indeed heart-rending. The Delhi Correspondent of *The Times* of London reported

> More Indian people have been killed during the short space of the past month than in all the civil broils of the past 50 years. Millions have been rendered homeless. A transfer of populations has been enforced on two administrations reluctant and ill-fitted to cope with it that already dwarfs in scale anything caused by war in Europe.
>
> India lives on a bare margin of subsistence at the best of times, and already the twin evils of pestilence and famine loom large on the horizon. The mood of the people has turned to bitterness and frustration. Men on both sides of the new boundaries talk of the opposite community with a venom and anger that the British rarely expressed towards the Germans or even the Japanese in the worst days of the war.[105]

For Pakistan the problem of coping with the refugees was proportionately far more serious than it was for India. Her territory and resources were much smaller and her administration was still in its infancy. Chaudhri Muhammad Ali who at that time was the Secretary-General of the Government of Pakistan has stated that the number of refugees West Punjab had to accommodate exceeded by some 1.7 million the number of evacuees who had left.[106]

It was not only the plight of the Muslim refugees who had arrived from India that grieved the Quaid-i-Azam deeply. The sad condition of the Hindus in Pakistan hurt him no less. In January 1948 his friend Nusserwanjee accompanied the Quaid to an encampment of Hindus who had stayed on in Pakistan. 'When he saw their misery, he wept. I saw the tears on his cheek,' Nusserwanjee recalled.[107]

A detailed exposition of the Kashmir problem is beyond the scope of this book;[108] we can only outline it. In fact there were three Princely States that formed the subject of disputes between Pakistan and India. These were Junagarh, Hyderabad and Kashmir. To understand the Kashmir problem it is necessary to refer to the other two first.

All the states in the subcontinent except the three named above had acceded either to India or to Pakistan by 14 August 1947. It so happened that all these three were ruled by princes whose own religion was different from that of the majority of their subjects.

Junagarh, a state on the Kathiawar coast had a population of about 700,000 of whom eighty per cent were Hindus. Its ruler was a Muslim. By land it was entirely contiguous to India but it could communicate with Pakistan by sea through its port, Veraval, which is about 300 miles south of Karachi. Its ruler acceded to Pakistan on 15 August. Mountbatten, now Governor-General of India only, protested to Governor-General Jinnah that Junagarh's accession to Pakistan had violated the principle on which the Partition of India had been effected. India solved the problem by invading Junagarh, and occupying it. In February 1948 a referendum conducted by the Indian authorities resulted in India's favour.

Hyderabad was the premier state in India. Its population was about sixteen million, its area was over 82,000 square miles and its revenue was 26 crores of rupees. Its ruler, entitled His Exalted Highness the Nizam, was a Muslim. His subjects were eighty-five per cent Hindus. The state was surrounded on all sides by

India. Because of its size and resources, the Nizam desired to assume sovereign status after the British had relinquished power in India. Nine days after the 3 June 1947 plan had been announced, the Nizam issued a *firman* (proclamation) that upon the departure of the paramount power he would be entitled to 'resume' the status of an independent sovereign. India eventually solved the problem by invading Hyderabad on 13 September, two days after the Quaid's death, and occupying it.

The State of Jammu and Kashmir with an area of 84,417 square miles was the largest Princely State in India. Because of its mountainous terrain it was sparsely populated except in the Valley. According to the 1941 census its population was about 4,000,000 of whom seventy-seven per cent were Muslims. In Kashmir Province the Muslims numbered ninety-three per cent.

The State occupied a strategic position because it had borders with Tibet, China and Afghanistan, and was parted from the Soviet Union only by a strip of under fifty miles. In the subcontinent, Kashmir bordered largely, though not wholly, on Pakistan. Before the Radcliffe Boundary Award which was made on 16 August, it had no road connection with what was to be the territory of independent India. Its only access to the outside world by road was along the Jhelum Valley via Rawalpindi in Pakistan; its only rail link was also with Pakistan at Sialkot. Pakistan's three vital rivers—the Indus, the Jhelum and the Chenab—all originate in Kashmir, and down their waters floated the timber which was Kashmir's most valuable export. Fruit, another important product, was also transported via Rawalpindi. In the reverse direction, Kashmir's necessities of life, including salt, sugar, and petroleum as well as the tourists with their spending money, had all to pass through Pakistan. Thus the two principles of accession—communal majority and geographical contiguity—both demanded that Kashmir should accede to Pakistan. But its ruler was a Dogra Hindu, Sir Hari Singh. Kashmir, moreover, was the ancestral homeland of Prime Minister Jawaharlal Nehru and it was emotionally impossible for him to let it go to Pakistan and he had the full support of Gandhi in this matter. Before Kashmir became the subject of an open dispute between Pakistan and India, Mountbatten wrote in his Personal Report No. 10 dated 27 June 1947 that 'On the subject of States, Nehru and Gandhi are pathological...they were both very anxious that he [the Maharaja of Kashmir] should make no declaration of independence and should, in fact indicate a willingness to join the Constituent Assembly of India'.[109]

The Maharaja signed the Instrument of Accession in favour of India on 27 October 1947, after Indian forces had landed at Srinagar. But he antedated it to read 26 October to make out that the legality of accession had been completed before Indian forces were airlifted to Kashmir.[110]

Even after India had obtained the Instrument of Accession from the Maharaja of Kashmir, she was faced with the problem that Kashmir's accession to India violated both the criteria India had used in all other cases of accession in her favour, religion of the majority of the people in the state and geographical contiguity. According to these principles Kashmir belonged to Pakistan. India got over the problem by resorting to the novel expedient of purporting to accept Kashmir's accession only provisionally. Governor-General Mountbatten wrote to the Maharaja

> Consistently with their policy that in the case of any State where the issue of accession has been the subject of dispute, the question of accession should be decided in accordance with the wishes of the people of the State, it is my Government's wish that as soon as law and order have been restored in Kashmir and her soil cleared of the invader the question of the State's accession should be settled by a reference to the people.[111]

In the course of exchanges between prime ministers Liaquat and Nehru that followed, the latter telegraphed on 4 November 1947

> I wish to draw your attention to the broadcast on Kashmir which I made last evening. I have stated our Government's policy and made it clear that we have no desire to impose our will on Kashmir but to leave final decision to people of Kashmir. I further stated that we have agreed on impartial international agency like United Nations supervising any referendum.[112]

Under Mountbatten's advice, India took the Kashmir dispute to the United Nations. Two resolutions of the United Nations Commission on India and Pakistan (UNCIP) dated 13 August

1948 and 5 January 1949 laid down the framework for a Plebiscite Administrator to carry out a plebiscite. But all efforts to implement the resolutions have been thwarted by India.

In an article 'Nehru in Retrospect' Attlee, on the whole an admirer of Nehru, recalled with regret

> I can recall many long discussions with Mr Nehru on the vexed question of Kashmir, sometimes between the two of us, sometimes with other prime ministers, but they proved fruitless. Although we proposed every possible variant in order to have fair plebiscite, to which he had already agreed in principle, we could not get acceptance from Mr Nehru. I have always considered this the blind spot of a great statesman.[113]

With regard to the Quaid-i-Azam's third main concern—a Constitution for the new state of Pakistan—his sister tells us that he applied his mind to the problem 'as often as he could find time to sit in his study, surrounded by books dealing with constitutions of various countries of the world'.[114] But of course, it was impossible for him to complete this weighty project before he died.

The wisdom of the Quaid's preoccupation with providing a viable Constitution for Pakistan as soon as possible has been vividly demonstrated by subsequent events. His successors did not promulgate Pakistan's first Constitution till 23 March 1956 and there have been alterations from time to time. Constitutional instability has been a marked featured of the country's short history.

To resume the narrative chronologically, the Quaid-i-Azam and Miss Fatima Jinnah flew to Lahore on 26 October 1947 to watch the developments in neighbouring Kashmir. On the night of 27 October, General Douglas Gracey, acting Commander-in-Chief of the Pakistan Army, telephoned to Supreme Commander Field-Marshal Auchinleck in Delhi that he had received orders from Jinnah which, if he obeyed them, would activate the 'Stand Down' order (i.e., the withdrawal of all British officers). Auchinleck flew to Lahore on the following day and met Gracey and Jinnah. Gracey said that the orders which he had not obeyed were to send troops into Kashmir. Auchinleck pointed out to Jinnah the 'incalculable consequences of military violation of what now is territory of the Indian Union in consequences of Kashmir's sudden accession'. Gracey emphasized the military weakness of Pakistan.

Jinnah withdrew the orders but was very angry. He accepted Auchinleck's suggestion that he should meet Mountbatten and Nehru to find a way out of the dangerous situation and Auchinleck conveyed the proposal to Mountbatten.

Mountbatten was in favour of a meeting between the Indian and Pakistani leaders at Lahore on 1 November to resolve the problem amicably but Nehru 'fell suddenly ill' and Mountbatten had to go alone. Jinnah proposed that the two governors-general should jointly conduct a plebiscite in Kashmir, while Mountbatten said a plebiscite should be held by the United Nations; the meeting ended inconclusively. Campbell-Johnson has explained that, 'Jinnah's objection, which he made quite clear at the Lahore meeting, is not to the idea of a plebiscite as such, but to the presence of Indian troops in Kashmir while it is being held, which he claims are likely to prejudice any chance of its being impartial'.

During his stay at Lahore, the Quaid addressed a mammoth rally at the University Stadium and spoke for the first time of death: 'Do not be afraid of death. Our religion teaches us to be always prepared for death... There is no better salvation for a Muslim than the death of a martyr for a righteous cause'.[115]

The Kashmir crisis, the plight of the refugees in Lahore and other anxieties overwhelmed the Quaid-i-Azam. He fell ill and remained confined to bed for several days. It was only on 1 December that he and Fatima could fly back to Karachi. Colonel Birnie, his Military Secretary, who received them at the airport, wrote in his diary, 'I was quite definitely shocked to see him. He left here five weeks ago, looking sixty years of age. Now he looks well over eighty'.[116] But he soon seemed to revive and attended to his duties.

Not long before his last birthday—Christmas Day 1947—he dined with the officers of the Royal Scots before they sailed for home. At the end, first the Princess Royal was toasted in her capacity as the Colonel-in-Chief of the Regiment and then the king. At this special occasion the commanding officer waived the rule that no further toasts are proposed after that of the king. He rose, looked at the Quaid-i-Azam and said, 'Your Excellency, it is such an honour to have you with us that I am going to break tradition. We consider ourselves good fighters: we consider you to be a good fighter also.' The Quaid stood up and responded, 'Gentlemen, may I further break the tradition of your regiment and reply? I shall never forget the British who have stayed in Pakistan to help us begin our work: This I shall never forget.'[117]

In March 1948 he made a strenuous ten-day visit to distant East Pakistan and in April he undertook a heavy programme in the North-West Frontier Province. During an open air meeting at Peshawar, it began to drizzle. His sister advised him to leave but he did not wish to disappoint the thousands who had gathered to honour him. That night he had a running nose, cold and chill, cough and high temperature. When he returned to Karachi he continued to cough and 'when a doctor was forced on him', it was diagnosed that he was suffering from a mild attack of bronchitis. He stayed in bed for a few days but continued to attend to the files which were brought to him.[118]

Under persistent pressure from Dr Rahman, his personal physician, and his sister, he yielded in June so far as to leave the oppressive heat of summer for the cooler hill station of Quetta. There his health improved. Only very important files were permitted to go up for his attention but he accepted some local engagements.

He had already agreed to perform the opening ceremony of the State Bank of Pakistan at Karachi on 1 July. Miss Fatima Jinnah tried to dissuade him from making the trip to Karachi and suggested that his speech be read by someone else but in vain. The air journey from Quetta to Karachi took its toll. On the day of the ceremony, he was confined to bed but got up, got dressed and read his address. The very first sentence showed the importance he attached to the occasion: 'The opening of the State Bank of Pakistan symbolizes the sovereignty of our State in the financial sphere'.[119]

His frailty was apparent as he struggled with the address. His voice was scarcely audible and he paused and coughed as he proceeded. When he returned to the Governor-General's House after the ceremony, he got into bed with his clothes and shoes on. But he fulfilled the promise he had made to attend the reception that evening at the American Ambassador's residence.

After staying at Karachi for five days, brother and sister flew back to Quetta. The next day he showed signs of weariness and fatigue; a slight fever persisted. At Quetta invitations to various functions again began to pour in. He felt dejected that he was unable to accept them and decided that they should move higher up to Ziarat. He hoped that the cooler air and greater seclusion would prove more restful. The Residency where they put up had a pleasant garden. The Quaid enjoyed its quiet charm.

On 21 July, the Quaid's condition suddenly became 'precarious' and Fatima sent for Dr Colonel Ilahi Baksh, an eminent physician of Lahore. She did so without obtaining her brother's permission fearing he might refuse.[120] Ilahi Baksh arrived on the afternoon of 23 July and continued to treat the Quaid-i-Azam till the latter's death. 'Realizing its documentary value' Ilahi Baksh maintained a day to day record of what the Quaid-i-Azam said to him.[121]

Jinnah refused to see the doctor on 23 July and asked him to come at 8 o'clock on the following morning. 'This rather leisurely manner of seeking medical advice caused me some surprise', recorded Illahi Baksh, but it 'wore off later when I discovered the Quaid-i-Azam's lifelong reluctance to undergo a regular treatment'.[122]

When Ilahi Baksh saw the Quaid on the following morning, the latter feebly related his medical history and said that there was nothing wrong with him except that he had got stomach trouble and suffered from exhaustion due to overwork and worry. But on a physical examination the doctor stated that he wished to have him examined further before giving a final diagnosis but hinted that the root cause of the trouble appeared to be lung disease.[123]

Laboratory findings on 25 July confirmed the doctor's suspicions. He gave Miss Jinnah the news but advised her not to let the patient know as it might depress him and have a harmful effect. But she said telling him was the only way of obtaining his cooperation in the treatment.

Thereupon Ilahi Baksh broke the news to the Quaid who received it calmly and asked whether he had told Miss Jinnah. When the doctor replied in the affirmative, the Quaid said, 'No, you shouldn't have done it. After all she is a woman.' The doctor explained that Miss Jinnah had advised him to give the news to her brother to secure his help in the treatment. Jinnah listened patiently and in the end said, 'It doesn't matter, what is done is done'.

Next morning the doctor advised Miss Jinnah to engage a nurse to reduce the strain on herself for looking after the Quaid. The Quaid flatly turned down the suggestion but consented to the engagement of a lady compounder to record his temperature and pulse every four hours. When Illahi Baksh saw Miss Jinnah on the following morning she told him, 'This lady compounder is a very smart and efficient person. Last night when the Quaid-i-Azam asked her what his temperature was, she said she was sorry she could not tell him without the doctor's permission. Instead of being displeased he praised her after she had left'.[124] Being himself a man of principle, Jinnah appreciated the compounder's correct professional attitude.

Ilahi Baksh thought Jinnah's silk pyjamas were not sufficiently warm and ordered thirty yards of Vyella from Karachi. When he told the Quaid what he had done, the latter said, 'Listen doctor, take my advice. When you spend money on anything think twice whether it is necessary, in fact, essential or not.' The doctor replied, 'Sir, in your case whenever I make a decision I think many times before I put it up before you, and I have come to the conclusion that woollen pyjamas are absolutely essential for you'. Thereupon the Quaid said with a smile, 'All right, I give in'. This incident led Ilahi Baksh to hope that he would be able to persuade his patient to do whatever was necessary provided he could offer a sound reason for it. After obtaining this insight into the Quaid's mind all the measures he suggested were duly reasoned out and he never shirked a frank medical discussion. He felt that the Quaid had taken a liking to him.[125]

After X-ray equipment had been brought up from Lahore, the tests revealed that the damage to the lungs was much more than the doctors had guessed before and that the disease must have been going on insidiously for at least two years.[126]

On 9 August the doctors noticed a slight swelling of the feet with a reduction in the urinary output. This led them to propose that Jinnah should be moved to Quetta in the hope that the lower altitude would be beneficial. After some procrastination, the Quaid, finding Ilahi Baksh firm, agreed. The move to the Residency at Quetta by road on 13 August took nearly four hours.

At Quetta he began to show an improvement. On 23 August, the doctors decided that he should make an effort to get up from his bed. It was agreed that he would make the first effort at 8 a.m. on 24 August. That night Ilahi Baksh was kept awake by his son who felt indisposed and reached the Residency at

8.35 a.m. After the routine examination, the doctor asked the Quaid if he was ready to get up and walk. The latter said, 'But I told you to come at 8. I expect my doctors to be punctual.' The doctor apologized and promised to be punctual in the future. The walk was postponed till the evening. A trial for four days showed that taking even a few steps made him breathless. The doctors concluded that he must be taken down to Karachi where his breathing would improve and he could resume the walking exercise. But the Quaid did not approve of the idea and asked the doctors not to hustle him.

One day the Quaid-i-Azam asked Ilahi Baksh if he could smoke. The doctor allowed him to smoke two cigarettes provided he did not inhale the smoke. Next morning the doctor noticed four stumps in the ashtray. He looked at the ashtray and said that the Quaid seemed to enjoy cigarettes. The Quaid ingeniously replied, 'Yes, didn't you tell me that there was no harm in smoking if I didn't inhale?'[127]

On 26 August Ilahi Baksh again pleaded with the Quaid to move down to Karachi. But Jinnah objected to return to the Governor-General's House as an invalid. He said, 'Don't take me to Karachi on crutches. I want to go there when I can walk from the car to my room.'[128]

Two days later the doctors noticed that his appetite was beginning to decrease. They could not account for 'the deterioration in his psychological condition' and the 'baffling depression'.

On 29 August, Ilahi Baksh came to the conclusion that the Quaid-i-Azam had lost his will to live. The doctor expressed the hope that the Quaid would live long enough to see the state he had brought into being firmly established. The Quaid responded, 'You know, when you first came to Ziarat I wanted to live,' adding with an infinitely disillusioned tone, 'now, however, it does not matter whether I live or die.'[129]

On 1 September the doctors noticed minute haemorrhagic spots under the skin of the feet as well as the lower legs; on 5 September the sputum was found to contain germs of pneumonia and the blood showed evidence of an acute infection; on 10 September the doctors informed Miss Jinnah that there was no chance of his survival for more than a day or two.[130]

Ilahi Baksh realized that the fight had been lost and there was no point in keeping the patient in Quetta any longer. It was decided to fly him to Karachi on the afternoon of 11 September. The Quaid too gave his consent to being taken to Karachi. Ilahi Baksh believed that the Quaid had given up his objection to being moved to Karachi because he had himself lost all hope of recovery and had made up his mind to return to the place of his birth.[131]

After a flight of about two hours, the plane carrying the Quaid and his party landed at Mauripur Airport at 4.15 p.m. The ambulance carrying the Quaid had hardly gone four miles when the engine broke down. Another ambulance did not arrive till more than an hour later. The Quaid at last arrived at the governor-general's residence at 6.10 p.m. At about 9.50, Ilahi Baksh said to the Quaid, 'Sir, we have given you an injection to strengthen you, and it will soon have effect. God willing, you are going to live.' The Quaid-i-Azam shook his head and said faintly, 'No, I am not'. These were the last words he spoke to anybody. He breathed his last at 10.20 p.m.[132]

Miss Fatima Jinnah sat near the body of her beloved brother overwhelmed with grief and oblivious to her surroundings. But she recalled that an elderly lady whom she had never met before put her arms around her neck, and quietly whispered into her ear a verse from the Holy Koran, 'From God he came, to God he returned'.

The millions constituting the nation he had fathered mourned the Quaid's death. On 12 September 1948 he was buried in the city in which he had been born nearly seventy-two years before. A magnificent domed mausoleum of marble shelters his mortal remains.

The Quaid-i-Azam's Conception of the State of Pakistan

The Quaid said that there were 'three main pillars which go to make a nation worthy of possessing a territory and running the government'. One is education. The difference between not having education and having it is the same as between darkness and broad daylight. The second is economic and industrial strength because no nation can ever do very much without making herself economically powerful. 'And lastly when you have got that light by means of knowledge by means of education and when you have made yourselves strong economically and industrially, then you have got to prepare yourself for your defence—defence against external aggression and to maintain internal security'.[133] At another time he added a 'fourth pillar' to the list—'social and political uplift'.[134] The people of Pakistan must be prepared for all sacrifices for the collective good and their motto should be 'unity, discipline and faith'.[135]

In October 1947 when destitute Muslim refugees from India were pouring into Pakistan by the hundred-thousand and Muslims who were left behind in India were being slaughtered, the Quaid in his Id-ul-Azha message reminded his people that 'God often tries those who he loves'. He cited the example of Ibrahim (AS) who answered the call and offered to sacrifice his son. 'Today' God was testing the Muslims of Pakistan and India; 'so my message to you all is hope, courage and confidence'.[136]

The main sources of inspiration and guidance for the national effort were Islam and the Prophet (PBUH). 'Islam gives us a complete code', the Quaid said.

> It is not only a religion but it contains laws, philosophy and politics. In fact, it contains everything that matters to a man from morning to night. When we talk of Islam we take it as an all-embracing word. We do not mean any ill-will. The foundation of our Islamic code is that we stand for liberty, equality and fraternity.[137]

In his message on the occasion of Id-ul-Fitr in October 1941, he explained

> The month of Ramazan is the month of fasting, prayer and communication with God. It is in this month that the Holy Quran was revealed. It is primarily a spiritual discipline enjoined upon the Mussulmans but in the performance of this duty, its value in regard to moral discipline and its social and physical value follows in no small degree. It teaches you what hunger means. It teaches you the lesson that you should be prepared for privation and to undergo a hard trial in the performance of duty. That lesson is repeated from day to day for a whole month and its exercise develops in no small degree the moral physical and ethical side of lives... Its physical value also cannot be underrated... It is a scientific fact that all organs of the body are so made that the rest only increases their capacity for

work...Islam lays great emphasis on the social side of things. Every day, the rich and the poor, the great and the small living in a locality are brought five times in a day in the mosque in the terms of perfect equality of mankind and thereby the foundation of a healthy social relationship is laid and established through prayer. At the end of Ramazan comes the new moon, the crescent, as a signal for a mass gathering on the Id day, again in perfect quality of mankind which affects the entire Muslim world.[138]

In an Id message in September 1945, the Quaid-i-Azam pointed out

The Quran is the general code of the Muslims. A religious, social, civil, commercial, military, judicial, criminal, penal code; it regulates everything from the ceremonies of religion to those of daily life; from the salvation of the soul to the health of the body; from the rights of all to those of each individual; from morality to crime, from punishment here to that in the life to come, and our Prophet (PBUH) has enjoined on us that every Mussulman should possess a copy of the Quran and be his own priest. Therefore Islam is not merely confined to the spiritual tenets and doctrines or rituals and ceremonies. It is a complete code regulating the whole Muslim society, every department of life, collective and individual.[139]

The Bar Association of Karachi gave a reception to Quaid-i-Azam Mohammad Ali Jinnah, Governor-General of Pakistan on the Holy Prophet's (PBUH) birthday on 25 January 1948. In his address to the Association the Quaid said he could not understand a section of the people who deliberately wanted to create mischief and made propaganda that the Constitution of Pakistan would not be made on the basis of Shariat. He said

Islamic principles today are as applicable to life as they were 1,300 years ago...Islam and its idealism have taught democracy. Islam has taught equality, justice and fair play for everybody...let us make it [the future Constitution of Pakistan]...The Prophet (PBUH) was a great teacher. He was a great lawgiver. He was a great statesman and he was a great sovereign who ruled.

The Prophet (PBUH) was successful in everything that he put his hand to from businessman to ruler. He was the greatest man that the world had ever seen. Thirteen hundred years ago he laid the foundations of democracy.[140]

The Quaid-i-Azam said that the Muslims of India should not be disheartened because they were a minority in India. He reminded them that 'Thirteen hundred years ago, our Prophet (PBUH) had spread not only his faith in Arabia, Egypt and Europe but also brought them under his suzerainty. If a single Muslim can do all this, what is it which 9 crores of Muslims cannot do.'[141]

With regard to the form of government in Pakistan, the Quaid said

> It is my belief that our salvation lies in following the golden rules of conduct set for us by our own great lawgiver, the Prophet (PBUH) of Islam. Let us lay the foundation of our democracy on the basis of truly Islamic ideals and principles. Our Almighty has taught us that 'our decisions in the affairs of State shall be guided by discussions and consultations'.[142] The Constitution of Pakistan can only be framed by the *millat* and the people; the Constitution and the government will be what the people will decide.[143]

The Quaid felt sure that the Constitution of Pakistan would be 'of a democratic type' embodying the essential principles of Islam. Islam and its idealism had taught the Muslims democracy. It had taught them the equality of man, justice and fair play to everybody. Pakistan was not going to be a theocratic state to be ruled by priests with a divine mission. There were many non-Muslims—Hindus, Christians and Parsees—in Pakistan, but they were all Pakistanis and would enjoy the same rights and privileges as any other citizens and would play their rightful part in the affairs of Pakistan.[144] No injunction was considered by the Holy Prophet (PBUH) more imperative and more divinely binding than the devout but supreme realization by the Muslims of their duty of love and toleration towards all other human beings.[145]

The Quaid-i-Azam believed that economic development and economic power were 'the most important of all the departments of life' and there was 'dire need' for the Muslims to make every possible effort to make up the leeway.[146] He believed Pakistan was blessed with enormous resources and potentialities and it lay with the people to make the best of them.[147]

If Pakistan wished to play her proper role in the world, she must develop industrial potential side by side with its agriculture and give its economy an industrial bias.[148] He felt confident that with the traditions of craftsmanship for which her people were so well-known and with their ability to adjust themselves to new techniques, Pakistan would soon make her mark in the industrial field.[149]

But the Quaid made it clear that Pakistan must follow the Islamic economic system of social justice, not the exploitative economic system of the Western world

> The economic system of the West has created almost insoluble problems for humanity and to many of us it appears that only a miracle can save it from disaster that is now facing the world. It has failed to do justice between man and man and to eradicate friction from the international field. On the contrary, it was largely responsible for the two World Wars in the last half century. The Western world, in spite of its advantages of mechanization and industrial efficiency is today in a worse mess than ever before in history. The adoption of Western economic theory and practice will not help us in achieving our goal of creating a happy and contented people. We must work our destiny in our own way and present to the world an economic system based on true Islamic concept of equality of manhood and social justice.[150]

The paramount objective must be to improve the lot of the poor. The Quaid said that his heart was really with the poor. He was their servant. The Muslims were asking for Pakistan. If that government did not mean equality of manhood, what would be the use of it? The whole underlying principle of the struggle for Pakistan was that 'we want to do everything that is possible for the poor'.[151]

Jinnah reminded his people that the Holy Prophet (PBUH) had enjoined on his followers to go even to China in the pursuit of knowledge.[152] In his view the importance of education and the right type of education could not be over-emphasized. Pakistan's educational policy and programme must be brought on the lines suited to the genius of her people. It had to be consonant with her history and culture and take note of the modern conditions and vast developments that had taken place all over the world. Education did not merely mean academic education. The need was for mobilizing the people and building up the character of future generations. There was an urgent need for training the people in scientific and technical education in order to build up the economic life of the country. It should not be forgotten that Pakistan had to compete with the world which was moving very fast in that direction.[153]

He pointed out that hitherto when the students got their degrees from the universities in thousands, all that they hankered after was government service. They must divert their ambition to other channels. There was no shame in doing manual work. They could learn banking, commerce, trade, etc. New industries, banks, insurance companies and commercial firms were opening and provided new avenues.

The cause of the emancipation of women was close to the Quaid-i-Azam's heart. During the fight for Pakistan he said, 'No nation can make any progress without the cooperation of its women. If Muslim women support their men, as they did in the days of the Prophet of Islam (PBUH), we should soon realize our goal.[154] On another occasion he emphasized that no nation can rise to the height of glory unless

> ...your women are side by side with you... We are victims of evil customs. It is a crime against humanity that our women are shut up within the four walls of the houses as prisoners. I do not mean that we should imitate the evils of Western life. But let us raise the status of our women according to our own Islamic ideas and standards. There is no sanction anywhere for the deplorable conditions in which our women have to live. You should take your women along with you as comrades in every sphere of life avoiding the corrupt practices of Western society. You cannot expect a woman who is herself ignorant to bring up your children properly. The woman has the power to bring up children on right lines. Let us not throw away this asset.[155]

When a vacancy in the Working Committee of the Muslim League occurred because of Shaukat Ali's death, the Quaid nominated the widow of Muhammad Ali to fill it. 'I think the time was come,' he observed, 'when it is necessary to have one who could represent also the views of the women of India and their wants and requirements in the national life of the Mussulmans.'[156]

In this respect he set a personal example by taking his sister Fatima with him everywhere including the sessions of the All-India Muslim League. He acknowledged,

Miss Fatima Jinnah is a constant source of help and encouragement to me. In the days when I was expecting to be taken a prisoner by the British Government, it was my sister who encouraged me, and said hopeful things when revolution was staring me in the face. Her constant care is about my health.[157]

On defence and external affairs, the Quaid said that while giving the fullest support to the principles of the United Nation's Charter, Pakistan could not afford to neglect her defences. However strong the United Nations Organization might be, the primary responsibility for the defence of Pakistan would rest with Pakistanis themselves. The weak and defenceless in this imperfect world invite aggression from others. The best way in which Pakistanis could serve the cause of peace was to remove the temptation from those who thought that Pakistan was weak and they could bully and attack her. The temptation could only be removed if Pakistanis made themselves so strong that no one would dare entertain any aggressive designs against her.[158] At another time he explained that nature's inexorable law was 'the survival of the fittest'.[159] Pakistan's armed forces, he said, were custodians of the life, property and honour of the people of Pakistan; they were the 'most vital of all Pakistan's services'.[160]

Pakistan's foreign policy was one of friendliness and goodwill towards all the nations of the world. Pakistan did not cherish aggressive designs against any country. She believed in the principle of honesty and fair play in national and international dealings and was prepared to make her utmost contribution to the promotion of peace and prosperity among the nations of the world. Pakistan would never be found lacking in extending her material and moral support to the oppressed and suppressed peoples of the world and in upholding the principles of the United Nations Charter.[161]

The Quaid-i-Azam's Place in History

The most persistent criticism against the Quaid-i-Azam is that his scheme of Pakistan did not solve the communal problem. Let us reply to this question in the Quaid's own words.

First what about the Hindus left behind in Pakistan?

> Do you suggest as an argument that because the Hindu minority or minorities in the Muslim zone will be minorities, therefore the 90 million of Muslims should remain as a minority in an artificial 'one India' with unitary form of central government so that you can dominate over them all including those zones where they are in a solid majority?[162]

Next, what about the Muslims left behind in Hindustan?

> The Muslims wherever they are in a minority, cannot improve their position in a united India...whatever happens they would remain a minority...by coming in the way of division of India they do not and cannot improve their own position.[163]

At another time the Quaid-i-Azam rhetorically asked whether the two and a half crores of Muslims left in Hindustan would benefit if the six and a half crores of Muslims in the two Muslim majority zones of the subcontinent continued to stay as a minority in an all-India unitary government.[164]

On yet another occasion he referred to the criticism that Pakistan would not solve the minority problem, he asked, 'Was it the only way to solve the minority problem that 90 millions of Mussulmans should remain a minority for ever in India and under Hindu raj'.[165]

Of course, in the final analysis, it was for the Muslims who were going to be left behind in India to say whether or not they favoured the creation of Pakistan. All the evidence suggests that they were in fact the earliest exponents of Muslim nationalism. Sir Syed Ahmed Khan, the father of Muslim nationalism, who was the first Muslim of all-India stature to call Hindus and Muslims two nations belonged to the Muslim-minority province of the United Provinces. The Muslim League also initially gathered greater strength in the Muslim minority provinces. The Muslim majority provinces of Sind, Bengal, the Punjab and North-West Frontier Provinces were comparatively more recalcitrant. This was logical because living as a minority among the Hindus, the Muslims in the Hindu dominated provinces felt more oppressed by the majority community than their brothers in the Muslim zones.

Ambedkar, the leader of the Untouchables, made a study of

the Pakistan question and published it under the title *Pakistan or The Partition of India*. He affirms that the Muslims of Hindustan clearly said, 'We are not weakened by the separation of Muslims into Pakistan and Hindustan. We are better protected by the existence of separate Islamic States on the Eastern and Western borders of Hindustan than we are by their submersion in Hindustan.'[166]

That East Pakistan revolted in 1971, and with the military intervention of India gained independence, does not provide an argument against the creation of Pakistan. If East Pakistanis had concluded that Partition had been a mistake, they would have gratefully availed of the opportunity and returned to the bosom of Hindustan. They repudiated the domination of West Pakistanis who were geographically nearly a thousand miles away and linguistically, culturally and racially a people apart. But they steadfastly held on to the two-nation concept and gave not the slightest indication that they wished to join India. It is not without significance that even today their relations are far friendlier with Pakistan than they are with India. As a matter of fact there is a steady one-way trickle of Muslims from all over India into Pakistan. Muslims from India who come to Pakistan on a visit endeavour to stay on if they can.

The Quaid-i-Azam is further criticized by some for never having defined the exact boundaries of the proposed state of Pakistan and in the end to have accepted a 'moth-eaten' Pakistan. This too is not a fair criticism. The argument that contiguous Muslim majority areas should form Pakistan implied that non-Muslim areas contiguous to India would have the right to join Hindustan.

Iqbal, in his presidential address at the Allahabad session of the Muslim League in December 1930, recognized that 'the exclusion of Ambala Division and perhaps of some districts where non-Muslims predominate' would make his proposed state 'more Muslim consolidated'.

The Pakistan Resolution of March 1940 also conceded that 'territorial adjustments' may be necessary for forming independent states by grouping together the Muslim majority areas in the north-western and eastern zones of India.

In April 1941, the Quaid issued a statement in reply to that issued by Rajendra Prasad, the Congress leader. He noted that Rajendra Prasad wanted 'full details of the [Pakistan] scheme and then alone the Working Committee of the Congress will be pleased to discuss it'. And commented that

> Babu Rajendra Prasad with his judicial mind ought to know that first the principle of partitioning India must be agreed upon, then alone comes the quest of what ways and means should be adopted to give effect to that decision... Has Babu Rajendra Prasad known any example where the details have been discussed before without the principle having been accepted? Even in the case of partition of joint families, with which Babu Rajendra Prasad is so familiar, there is either an agreement or a decree and then comes the question how best and equitably to divide the property... The latest example in history is that of Ireland. The Constitution of North and South of Ireland was finally agreed upon after the principles and the basis of division was settled. So was the case with Burma. Similarly the decision to separate Sind was taken first and then the details of the scheme were considered and given effect to.[167]

In life, as in card games, it is never wise to disclose your hand. The adversary will always try to take advantage of the disclosure. The drawing of an exact dividing line between disputed territories is a negotiatory as well as a cartographical problem with cartography coming last.

With regard to the criticism that the Quaid achieved only a 'moth-eaten' Pakistan, the real wonder is that he achieved any Pakistan at all. No freedom fighter in history was ever faced with such awesome odds as he was. Normally a national leader has the backing of his entire country against an occupying power. The Quaid-i-Azam had to fight against two adversaries simultaneously, each one of them far stronger than himself and his community. The Hindu community was four times as numerous as the Muslims, was far better organized, had a team of high calibre leaders, was far richer, was better educated and had a far stronger Press. And the second adversary, the British Government, with the power of ultimate decision, was allied with the Hindus in their opposition to the creation of Pakistan. The ailing Quaid fought this overpowering opposition almost single-handedly with unswerving will-power, deep political acumen, brilliant advocacy, the passionate support of the Muslim masses and complete trust in God. Pethick-Lawrence, who as secretary of state for India had turned down the demand for Pakistan, acknowledged: 'He had, of course, immense powers of intellect and also of persuasive eloquence which he used with such effect that the idea [of Pakistan], which was at first an ideal only, became in the end a reality'.[168] Indeed, when the idea of Pakistan was first mooted in 1933 by Rahmat Ali even the Muslim intelligentsia dismissed it out of hand as 'chimerical and impracticable'. The Quaid was not unaware of the seemingly impossible task facing him. He was, therefore, as much surprised and relieved at his own success as everyone else. While walking up the steps of the Government House on arrival at Karachi on 7 August 1947, he said to his ADC, 'Do you know, I never expected to see Pakistan in my lifetime. We have to be very grateful to God for what we have achieved.'[169]

At the critical juncture when the boundaries of the new state of Pakistan were being delineated, the government of India was presided over by a viceroy who was bitterly opposed to the creation of Pakistan, whose most influential political adviser was a Hindu (V. P. Menon) and who did not scruple to influence the Chairman of the Boundary Commission to the detriment of Pakistan.

The independence of India was inevitable. It would have come even if there had been no Gandhi. Before Gandhi assumed the mantle of Congress leadership, the British Government had already declared on 20 August 1917, 'The policy of His Majesty's Government is that of...the gradual development of self-governing institutions with a view to the progressive realizations of responsible government in India'. But without Jinnah there would never have been a Pakistan.

The birthday tribute which M. C. Rajah, a leader of the Hindu Untouchables, paid to the Quaid in 1940 sums up the greatness of the latter's leadership strikingly

> All religions hold the belief that God sends suitable men into the world to work out His plans from time to time, and at critical junctures. I regard Mr Jinnah as the man who has been called upon to correct the wrong ways into which the people of India have been led by the Congress, under the leadership of Mr Gandhi. The Congress did a great service to the country so long as it followed the lines of critical cooperation and cooperative criticism towards the British Government, as laid down by Dadabhai Naoroji and Gokhale. But it took a wrong turn when it adopted wholesale the non-cooperation programme of Mr Gandhi and assumed an attitude of open hostility

towards Britain, and tried to infuse in the minds of the people a spirit of defiance of law and civil disobedience, more or less thinly veiled under a formula of truth and non-violence. Moreover, by 'Mahatmafying' Mr Gandhi, it appealed to the idolatrous superstitions of the Hindus, thus converting the religious adherence of the Hindu section of the population of the Mahatma into political support of his non-cooperation programme. While this strategy was of some avail in hustling the British Government to yield more and more to the demands of Congress, it divided the people into Hindu and non-Hindu sections.

In these circumstances a man was needed to stand up to Congress and tell its leaders that their organization, however powerful numerically and financially, does not represent the whole of India.

I admire Mr Jinnah and feel grateful to him because, in advocating the cause of the Muslims, he is championing the claims of all classes who stand the danger of being crushed under the steam roller of a [caste] Hindu majority, acting under the inspiration and order of Mr Gandhi...[170]

Aga Khan III, who was a contemporary of the Quaid-i-Azam and moved in the highest social and political circles in the world, believed

Of all the the statesmen that I have known in my life—Clemenceau, Lloyd George, Churchill, Curzon, Mussolini, Mahatma Gandhi—Jinnah is the most remarkable. None of these in my view outshone him in strength of character, and in that almost uncanny combination of prescience and resolution which is statecraft.[171]

As these pages are being printed Pakistanis are celebrating the fiftieth anniversary of the birth of the independent country which the Quaid-i-Azam won for them. Their emotional outpouring of gratitude to, and adoration for, the father of their nation are deeply sincere no doubt. But the greatest tribute they can pay to him and the greatest service they can render to themselves and to their country would be to pause and reflect and resolve to follow the Quaid's ideals, advice and example and purge their country of the evils of disunity and malpractices that afflict her. They should always bear in mind the motto he prescribed for them: 'Unity, discipline and faith'.

Taking advantage of Pakistan's recent difficulties, its critics have intensified the criticism that its creation was a mistake.* In reality if only Pakistanis would learn to govern themselves efficiently, theirs would be an impressively thriving land. The country forms an easily traversable rectangular geographical unit with the river Indus and a single railway system as its main arteries. The soil is fertile and the people are intelligent and enterprising. The country is not free from provincial rivalries but the linguistic and racial barriers are tolerable and the almost wholly Muslim population is enjoined by religion to form a cooperative brotherhood.

That Pakistan in fact potentially is one of the leading countries in the world was palpably demonstrated in the Ayub Khan era. At that time it was progressing far faster than India and was cited as a model for economic development. On 18 January 1965 *The New York Times* commented, 'Pakistan may be on its way toward an economic milestone that so far has been reached by only one other populous country, the United States'. There was internal peace and stability and externally Pakistan enjoyed the respect of other nations.

---

*These lines were written before Mian Muhammad Nawaz Sharif steadied the ship of state by winning an overwhelming victory at the polls in February 1997 and set her on a promising course.

Notes

1. *TOP*, IX, op. cit., pp. 773-5.
2. Ibid., pp. 972-4.
3. Alan Campbell-Johnson, *Mission With Mountbatten*, pp. 17-18.
4. Philip Ziegler, *Mountbatten, The Official Biography*, pp. 700-1.
5. Michael Brecher, *Nehru*, p. 412.
6. Pyarelal, *Mahatma Gandhi, The Last Phase*, II, op. cit., p. 75.
7. That Nehru had visited Singapore at the suggestion of Wavell is stated by Campbell-Johnson in *Mission With Mountbatten*, op. cit., on p. 30. This account of the visit given here is taken principally from Ziegler's *Mountbatten*, op. cit., pp. 326-8 and *TOP*, VII, op.cit., pp. 134-6.
8. A general in the Burmese National Army which had been set up by the Japanese to assist in the war against the Allies.
9. Campbell-Johnson, *Mission With Mountbatten*, op. cit., p. 23.
10. Expressed at the Staff Meeting on 4 April 1947. *TOP*, X, p. 115
11. For the text of the Muslim League Working Committee Resolution of 31 January 1947 *see*, *TOP*, IX, op. cit., pp. 586-93.
12. Ibid., pp. 688-9.

PAKISTAN ZINDABAD 379

13. Ibid., p. 785.
14. V. P. Menon, *The Transfer of Power in India*, p. 340.
15. *TOP*, IX, op. cit., p. 829 f.n. 2.
16. *TOP*, X, op. cit., pp. 451-3.
17. 'Death to Pakistan'.
18. 'The Sikhs will rule; no resister will remain'. Penderel Moon, *Divide and Quit*, p. 77. Moon, a member of the Indian Civil Service, was in India at the time of Partition.
19. *TOP*, IX, op. cit., pp. 787-9.
20. Ibid., p. 870.
21. Ibid., p. 901.
22. Ibid., pp. 897-9.
23. Ibid., p. 985.
24. Ibid., p. 916.
25. Pyarelal, *Mahatma Gandhi, The Last Phase*, II, op. cit., pp. 34-35.
26. *TOP*, XII, op. cit., p. 594.
27. After summarizing a rambling interview with Liaquat on 19 April 1947, Mountbatten surmized, 'I have an impression that Mr Liaquat Ali Khan intends to help me find a more reasonable solution than this mad Pakistan'. *TOP*, X, op. cit., p. 333.
28. *TOP*, X, op. cit., p. 11.
29. Campbell-Johnson, *Mission With Mountbatten*, op. cit., p. 45.
30. *TOP*, X, op. cit., p. 12.
31. Ibid., p. 13.
32. Pyarelal, *Mahatma Gandhi, The Last Phase*, II, op. cit., p. 77.
33. *TOP*, X, op. cit., p. 69.
34. Ibid., p. 70.
35. Ibid., pp. 83-84.
36. Ibid., p. 123.
37. Ibid., p. 126.
38. Ibid., p. 197.
39. Ibid., p. 104.
40. Ibid., pp. 137-9.
41. Campbell-Johnson, *Mission With Mountbatten*. op. cit., p. 56.
42. *TOP*, X, op. cit., p. 138.
43. Ibid., p. 143.
44. Ibid., p. 149.
45. Ibid., p. 159.
46. Ibid., pp. 163-4.
47. These six meetings had averaged between two to three hours each. Ibid., p. 298.
48. Ibid., pp. 190-2.
49. Ibid., p. 176.
50. Ibid., p. 242.
51. Ibid., p. 251.
52. Ibid., p. 543-5.
53. Ibid., pp. 533-4.
54. Ibid., p. 756.

55. Ibid., p. 767.
56. Campbell-Johnson, *Mission With Mountbatten,* op. cit., p. 89.
57. *TOP,* X, op. cit., pp. 776-7.
58. Ibid., p. 822.
59. On 23 April 1947, the Earl of Listowel succeeded Lord Pethick-Lawrence as Secretary of State for India.
60. Pyarelal, *Mahatma Gandhi, The Last Phase,* II, op. cit., pp. 184, 187.
61. V. P. Menon, *The Transfer of Power in India,* op. cit., pp. 358-60.
62. *TOP,* X, op. cit., p. 781.
63. V. P. Menon, *The Transfer of Power in India,* op. cit., p. 365.
64. *TOP,* X, op. cit., pp. 841-2.
65. Ibid., p. 826.
66. Ibid., p. 873.
67. Ibid., p. 946.
68. This in effect meant that they were to choose whether they wished to join India or Pakistan.
69. Since the North-West Frontier Province in due course decided to join Pakistan, the 'appropriate successor authority' turned out to be Pakistan.
70. For the text of the Plan of 3 June 1947 *see, TOP,* XI, op. cit., pp. 89-94.
71. For the text of Mountbatten's broadcast *see, TOP,* XI, op.cit., pp. 86-88.
72. *TOP,* XI, op. cit., p. 241.
73. Campbell Johnson, *Mission With Mountbatten,* op. cit., pp. 115-6.
74. *TOP,* XI, op. cit., p. 398.
75. V. P. Menon, *The Transfer of Power in India,* op. cit., p. 386.
76. *TOP,* XI, op. cit., p. 201.
77. Ibid., p. 580.
78. Ibid., pp. 898-900.
79. Ibid., p. 863.
80. Ibid., p. 916.
81. Ibid., p. 921-2.
82. Philip Ziegler, *Mountbatten,* p. 398. Mountbatten's lack of devotion to truth is illustrated by a reference to how he referred to the same incident in an article he contributed to *Pakistan, Past and Present.* At page 41 of that publication he admitted that he was surprised when Jinnah announced that he intended to be the governor-general of Pakistan but claimed that, 'I did not personally resent his decision, as has been the common opinion, for it saved me from the daunting task of having to try and ride separate horses simultaneously'.
83. *TOP,* XI, op. cit., p. 916.
84. *TOP,* X, op. cit., p. 946.
85. *TOP,* XII, op. cit., p. 24.
86. *TOP,* XI, op. cit., p. 164.
87. Chaudhri Muhammad Ali, *The Emergence of Pakistan,* op. cit., p. 178.
88. Mountbatten's 'Report on the Last Viceroyalty' (submitted to His Majesty's Government in September 1948), IOR:L/P and J/5/396, p. 123.
89. H. V. Hodson, *The Great Divide,* p. 535. Hodson had been entrusted with 'all the papers' Mountbatten had brought back from India, and Mountbatten

90. Ibid., p. 512. At a meeting of the Joint Defence Council on 19 March 1948, Nehru and Liaquat decided that the Council should be closed down after that session.
    also assisted him in writing the book by talking with him and finally reading the manuscript.
91. *Jinnah-Attlee Correspondence, September-October 1947*, L/P and J/7/12 508.
92. John Connell, Auchinleck, p. 920. The task of the Supreme Commander was to administer the partition of the Indian Army.
93. For a fuller account of the Radcliffe Boundary Awards *see*, S.M. Burke and Salim AL-Din Quraishi, *The British Raj in India*, op. cit., pp. 536-61.
94. TOP, XII, op. cit., p. 761.
95. *The Hindu*, 16 January 1950.
96. TOP, VII, op. cit., p. 283.
97. PREM 8/821. For a facsimile of this note *see*, S. M. Burke and Salim AL-Din Quraishi, *The British Raj in India*, op. cit., Appendix E.
98. *Quaid-i-Azam Mahomed Ali Jinnah, Speeches as Governor-General of Pakistan*, op. cit., pp. 32-33.
99. For the text of the address *see*, ibid., pp. 6-10.
100. For the text of Mountbatten's address *see*, TOP, XII, op. cit., pp 780-3.
101. For the text of the Quaid's reply *see*, *Speeches as Governor-General of Pakistan*, op. cit., pp. 14-15.
102. Campbell-Johnson, *Mission With Mountbatten*, op. cit., p. 156.
103. Fatima Jinnah, *My Brother*, op. cit., p. 11.
104. Ibid., p. 35.
105. *The Times*, 18 September, 1947.
106. Chaudhri Muhammad Ali, *The Emergence of Pakistan*, op. cit., p. 264.
107. Hector Bolitho, *Jinnah*, op. cit., p. 95.
108. For a fuller account of the Kashmir problem *see*, S. M. Burke and Salim AL-Din Quraishi, *The British Raj in India*, op. cit., pp. 584-608.
109. TOP, XI, op. cit., p. 687. In June 1947 there existed only the Constituent Assembly of India.
110. For an exposition of this fraud *see*, S. M. Burke and Salim AL-Din Quraishi, *The British Raj in India*, op. cit., pp. 594-6.
111. P. L. Lakhanpal, *Essential Documents and Notes on Kashmir Dispute*, p. 57.
112. Ibid., p. 75.
113. *Illustraled Weekly of India*, Sunday 22 November, 1964, p. 31.
114. Fatima Jinnah, *My Brother*, p. 11.
115. *Speeches as Governor-General*, op. cit., p. 30.
116. Quoted by H. Bolitho in *Jinnah*, op. cit., p. 209.
117. Ibid., p. 209.
118. Fatima Jinnah, *My Brother*, p. 18.
119. Ibid., p. 21.
120. Ilahi Baksh, *With the Quaid-i-Azam During His Last Days*, pp. 6, 19. Here Ilahi Baksh states what Miss Jinnah and the Civil Surgeon of Quetta told him.

121. Ibid., p. 4.
122. Ibid., p. 2
123. Ibid., pp. 4-5.
124. Ibid., p. 9.
125. Ibid., pp. 10-11.
126. Ibid., p. 12.
127. Ibid., p. 26.
128. Ibid., p. 28.
129. Ibid., p. 32.
130. Ibid., p. 41.
131. Ibid., p. 44.
132. Ibid., p. 51.
133. Waheed Ahmad, *The Nation's Voice*, II, op. cit., p. 166.
134. Jamil-UD-Din Ahmad, *Speeches and Writings of Mr Jinnah*, I, op. cit., p. 598.
135. Ibid., p. 550.
136. *Quaid-i-Azam Mahomed Ali Jinnah, Speeches as Governor-General of Pakistan*, op. cit., pp. 27-28.
137. Waheed Ahmad, *The Nation's Voice (March 1935-March 1940)*, op. cit., p. 221.
138. Waheed Ahmad, *The Nation's Voice*, II, op. cit., pp. 303-4.
139. Jamil-UD-Din Ahmad, *Speeches and Writings of Mr Jinnah*, II, op. cit., pp. 208-9.
140. M. Rafique Afzal, *Speeches and Statements of the Quaid-i-Azam Mohammad Ali Jinnah*, op. cit., pp. 455-6.
141. Waheed Ahmad, *The Nation's Voice (March 1935-March 1940)*, op. cit., p. 228.
142. *Speeches as Governor-General of Pakistan*, op. cit., p. 58.
143. Pirzada, *Foundations of Pakistan*, II, op. cit., p. 425.
144. *Speeches as Governor-General of Pakistan*, op. cit., p. 67.
145. Waheed Ahmad, *The Voice of the People (March 1935-March 1940)*, p. 413.
146. Jamil-UD-Din Ahmad, *Speeches and Writings of Mr Jinnah*, II, op. cit., p. 29.
147. *Speeches as Governor-General*, op. cit., p. 33.
148. Ibid., p. 20.
149. Ibid., pp. 143-4.
150. Ibid., pp. 160-1.
151. Waheed Ahmad, *The Nation's Voice*, II, pp. 441-2.
152. Jamil-UD-Din Ahmad, *Speeches and Writings of Mr Jinnah*, II, op. cit., p. 161.
153. *Speeches as Governor-General of Pakistan*, op. cit., pp. 36-37.
154. Jamil-UD-Din Ahmad, *Speeches and Writings of Mr Jinnah*, I, op. cit., p. 476.
155. Jamil-UD-Din Ahmad, *Speeches and Writings of Mr. Jinnah*, II, pp. 17-18.
156. Waheed Ahmad, *The Nation's Voice (March 1935-March 1940)*, op. cit., p. 354.
157. *Speeches as Governor-General of Pakistan*, op. cit., p. 5.
158. Ibid., pp. 46-47.

159. Ibid., p. 63.
160. Ibid., p. 154.
161. Ibid., p. 67.
162. Waheed Ahmad, *The Nation's Voice*, II, op. cit., p. 171.
163. Ibid., p. 1.
164. Ibid., p. 125.
165. Ibid., p. 258.
166. Ambedkar, *Pakistan*, op. cit., p. 103.
167. Waheed Ahmad, *The Nation's Voice*, II, op. cit., pp. 228-9.
168. Jamil-UD-Din Ahmad, *Quaid-i-Azam as Seen by His Contemporaries*, op.cit., p. 227.
169. Hector Bolitho, *Jinnah*, op. cit., p. 195.
170. Ibid., pp. 133-4.
171. *The Memoirs of Aga Khan*, p. 292.

Bibliography

Abdul Latif, Saiyid, *The Great Leader*, Lahore, Lion Press, 1946.

Afzal, M. Rafique, *Selected Speeches and Statements of Quaid-i-Azam Mohammad Ali Jinnah*, Lahore, Research Society of Pakistan, 1966.

Aga Khan, H.H., *The Memoirs of Aga Khan*, London, Cassell, 1954.

Albiruni, A.H., *Makers of Pakistan and Modern Muslim India*, Lahore, M. Ashraf, 1950.

Alexander, H.G., *India Since Cripps*, London, Penguin, 1944.

The All-India Moslem League Deputation to the Secretary of State [Meeting Held] in the Council Room of the India Office on 27 January 1909, [London, 1909]

Allana, G., *Pakistan Movement: Historic Documents*, 3rd ed., Lahore, Islamic Book Service, 1977.

———, *Quaid-e-Azam Jinnah*, Lahore, Ferozsons, 1967.

Ambedkar, B.R., *Pakistan or the Partition of India*, 3rd ed., Bombay, Thacker & Co., 1946.

Andrews, C.F. and Mookerjee, Girja, *The Rise and Growth of the Congress in India*, London, Allen and Unwin, 1938.

Attlee, Clement R., *As it Happened*, London, Odhams, 1954.

———, *A Prime Minister Remembers: Memoirs of Prime Minister Clement Attlee*, Compiled by Francis Williams, London, Heinemann, 1962.

Azad, Abul Kalam, *India Wins Freedom*, Bombay, Orient Longman, 1960.

Aziz, K.K., *Rahmat Ali: A Biography*, Lahore, Vanguard, 1987.

———, *History of the Idea of Pakistan*, 4 Vols., Lahore, Vanguard, 1987.

———, *Muslims Under Congress Rule*, 2 Vols. National Commission on Historical and Cultural Research, 1978-1979.

Basham, A.L., *A Cultural History for India*, Oxford, Clarendon Press, 1975.

Batalavi, Ashiq Hussain (ed.), *Liquidation of the British Empire, British Parliamentary Debates on the Indian Independence*, Lahore, Institute of Islamic Culture, 1990.

Besant, Annie, *How India Fought for Freedom*, Madras, Theosophical Publishing House, 1915.

Birkenhead, The Second Earl of, *The Life of F.E. Smith, First Earl of Birkenhead*, Rev. ed., London, Eyre & Spottiswood, 1960.

Bolitho, Henry Hector, *Jinnah, Creator of Pakistan*, London, OUP, 1954.

Bose, Nirmal Kumar, *My Days with Gandhi*, Bombay, Orient Longman, 1974.

Bose, Subhas Chandra, *The Indian Struggle*, New York, Asia Publishing House, 1964.

Brown, J., *Gandhi: Prisoner of Hope*, London, Yale University Press, 1989.

Burke, S.M. and Quraishi, S., *The British Raj: An Historical Review*, Karachi, OUP, 1994.

Campbell-Johnson, A., *Mission with Mountbatten*, London, Hamish Hamilton, 1951.

Chagla, M.C., *Muslims and the Nehru Report*, Bombay, 1972.

———, *Roses in December: An Autobiography*, 8th ed., Bombay, Bharatiya Vidya, 1978.

Callard, Keith B., *Pakistan*, London, Allen and Unwin, 1957.

Chatterjee, Dilip Kumar, *C.R. Das and Indian National Movement*, Calcutta, The Post-Graduate Book Mart, 1965.

Chopra, P.N. (ed.), *Quit India Movement, British Secret Report*, Faridabad, Thomson Press, 1976.

———, *Towards Freedom, Experiment with Provincial Autonomy*, Vol. 1, New Delhi, Indian Council of Historical Research, 1985.

Collins, Larry and Lapierre, Dominique, *Freedom at Midnight*, London, Pan Books, 1975.

Comrade, Selections from Mohammad Ali's Comrade, Compiled and edited by Rais Ahmad Jafri Nadvi, Lahore, Mohammad Ali Academy, 1965.

Conell, John, *Auchinleck*, London, Cassell, 1959.

Coupland, Reginald, *India: A Re-Statement*, London, OUP, 1945.

———, *Indian Politics, 1936-1952*, London, OUP, 1943.

———, *The Indian Problem, 1833-1935*, Oxford, Clarendon Press, 1968.

———, The Future of India, London, OUP, 1943.

Dalal, A.R., *An Alternative to Pakistan*, New Delhi, 1945.

Dani, A.H. (ed.), *Quaid-i-Azam Mohammad Ali Jinnah and Pakistan*, Islamabad, 1981.

———, *World Scholars on Quaid-i-Azam Mohammad Ali Jinnah*. Islamabad, Quaid-i-Azam University, 1979.

Durrani, F.K. Khan, *The Meaning of Pakistan*, Lahore, 1944.

Dwarkadas, Kanji, *Gandhiji Through My Diary Leaves, 1915-1948*, Bombay, Dwarkadas, 1950.

———, *India's Fight for Freedom*, Bombay, Popular Prakashan, 1967.

———, *Ruttie Jinnah, the Story of Great Friendship*, Bombay, Dwarkadas, 1963.

Erikson, Erik H., *Gandhi's Truth*, London, W.W. Norton, 1993.

Estorick, E., *Stafford Cripps: A Biography*, London, Heinemann, 1949.

Fazlul-Huq, Abul Kasem, *Muslim Sufferings under Congress Rule*, Calcutta, 1939.

Fischer, Louis, *The Life of Mahatma Gandhi*, London, Jonathan Cape, 1954.

———, *Gandhi—His Life and Message for the World*, New York, Signet Books, 1954.

Gandhi, M.K., *An Autobiography, or the Story of My Experiments with Truth*, Translated from the original Gujarati by Mahadev Desai, London, Penguin, 1982.

———, *To the Protagonists of Pakistan*, Karachi, Anand T. Hingorani, 1947.

Garratt, G.T., *The Legacy of India*, Oxford, Clarendon Press, 1937.

Gopal, Ram, *Indian Muslims: A Political History*, London, Asia Publishing House, 1959.

Gwyer, Maurice L. and Appadorai, A., *Speeches and Documents on the Indian Constitution, 1921-1947*, 2 Vols. Bombay, OUP, 1957.

Graham. G.F.I., *The Life and Work of Sir Syed Ahmad Khan*, Edinburgh, William Blackwood, 1885.

Halifax, Lord, *Fullness of Days*, London, Collins, 1957.

Hodson, H.V., *The Great Divide*, London, Hutchinson, 1969.

———, *Pakistan, Past and Present*, London, 1977.

Husain, A., *Sir Fazl-i-Husain*, Bombay, Longmans, 1946.

Ikram, S.M., *Modern Muslim India and the Birth of Pakistan*, Lahore, M. Ashraf, 1977.

Ilahi Bakhsh, *With the Quaid-i-Azam During the Last Days*, Karachi, Quaid-i-Azam Academy, 1978.

The Indian National Congress, 1920-1923, Allahabad, Allahabad Law Press, 1924.

Iqbal, Sir Muhammad, *Letters of Iqbal to Jinnah*, Lahore, M. Ashraf, 1943.

———, *Speeches and Statements of Iqbal*, Edited by Shamloo, Lahore, Ghulam Ali, 1948.

Jalal, Ayesha, *The Sole Spokesman: The Muslim League and the Demand for Pakistan*, Cambridge, CUP, 1985.

Jamil-ud-Din Ahmad, *Speeches and Writings of Mr Jinnah*, 7th ed., 2 Vols., Lahore, M. Ashraf, 1968.

———, *Quaid-i-Azam as Seen by His Contemporaries*, Lahore, Publishers United, 1966.

Jinnah, Fatima, *My Brother*, Karachi, Quaid-i-Azam Academy, 1987.

Jinnah, M.A., *Speeches as Governor-General of Pakistan, 1947-1948*, 7th ed., Lahore, Ferozsons, 1976.

Kabir, Humayun, *Muslim Politics, 1906-1942*, Calcutta, Mukhopadhyay, 1969.

Khalid bin Sayeed, *Pakistan—The Formative Phase*, Karachi, Pak Publishing, 1960.

Khaliquzzaman, Choudhry, *Pathway to Pakistan*, Lahore, Longmans, 1961.

Lakhanpal, P.L., *Essential Documents and Notes on Kashmir Dispute*, 2nd ed., Delhi, International Books, 1965.

Lamb, Alastair, *Crisis in Kashmir*, London, Routledge Kegan Paul, 1966.

———, *Kashmir—A Disputed Legacy*, Hertingfordbury, Roxford, 1991.

Linlithgow, Marquis of, *Speeches and Statements, 1936-1943*, New Delhi, Govt. of India, 1945.

Lumby, E.W.R., *The Transfer of Power in India, 1945-47*, London, Allen and Unwin, 1954.

Majumdar, S.K., *Jinnah and Gandhi*, Calcutta, K.L. Mukhopadhyay, 1966.

Majumdar, R.C., *History of the Freedom Movement in India*, 2nd rev. ed., 3 Vols., Calcutta, K.L. Mukhopadhyay, 1977.

Malik, Hafeez, *Political Profile of Sir Sayyid Ahmad Khan*, Islamabad, Institute of Islamic History, Culture and Civilization, Islamic University, 1982.

Masani, R.P., *Dadabhai Naroji*, Delhi, Govt. of India, 1960.

Mende, Tibor, *Conversation with Mr Nehru*, London, Seeker and Warburg, 1956.

Menon, V.P., *Integration of the Indian States*, Bombay, Orient Longman, 1985.

———, *The Transfer of Power in India*, London, Longmans, 1957.

Mohammed Ali, Maulana, *My Life: A Fragment*, Lahore, M. Ashraf, 1942.

———, *Select Writings and Speeches of Maulana Mohamed Ali*, Edited by Afzal Iqbal, Lahore, M. Ashraf, 1944.

Montagu, Edwin S., *An Indian Diary*, London, Heinmann, 1930.

Moon, E. Penderel, *Divide and Quit*, London, Charles and Windus, 1961.

Mosley, L., *The Last Days of the British Raj*, London, Wedenfeld and Nicolson, 1961.

Mountbatten, Earl of, *Time Only to Look Forward: Speeches as Viceroy of India and Governor-General of the Dominion of India*, London, Nicholas Kaye, 1949.

Muhammed Ali, Chaudhri, *The Emergence of Pakistan*, New York, Columbia University Press, 1967.

Mujeeb, M., *Indian Muslims*, New Delhi, Munshiram Manoharlal, 1985.

Mushirul Hasan (ed.), *India's Partition*, Delhi, OUP, 1993.

———, *Mohammed Ali in Indian Politics: Select Writings*, 2 Vols., New Delhi, Atlantic Publishers, 1983.

Naidu, Sarojini, *Mohammed Ali Jinnah—An Ambassador of Unity: His Speeches and Writings, 1912-1917, with a Biographical Appreciation by Sarojini Naidu and a Foreword by the Honr'ble Rajah of Mahmudabad*, Madras, Ganesh, 1918.

Nehru, Jawaharlal, *A Bunch of Old Letters*, Bombay, Asia Publishing House, 1958.

Nehru, Jawaharlal, *An Autobiography*, Delhi, OUP, 1985.

———, *Jinnah-Nehru Correspondence, Including Gandhi-Jinnah and Nehru-Nawab Ismail Correspondence*, Lahore, Book House, 1960.

———, *Discovery of India*, London, Meridian Books, 1946.

———, *Mahatma Gandhi*, Calcutta, Asia Publishing House, 1966.

Nichols, Beverley, *Verdict on India*, London, Jonathan Cape, 1944.

Noman, Mohammad, *Muslim India: Rise and Growth of All India Muslim League*, Allahabad, Kitabistan, 1942.

Noorani, A.G., *Badruddin Tyabji*, New Delhi, Govt. Press, 1969.

O'Malley, L.S.S. (ed.), *Modern India and the West*, London, Royal Institute of International Affairs, 1945.

Pakistan: Past and Present, London, Stacey International, 1971.

Pandit, Vijaya Lakshmi, *The Evolution of India*, London, OUP, 1958.

Panikkar, K.M., *A Survey of Indian History*, London, Asia Publishing House, 1960.

Philips, C.H. (ed.), *The Evolution of India and Pakistan, 1858-1947*, London, OUP, 1962.

Pirzada, Syed Sharifuddin, *The Collected Works of Quaid-i-Azam Mohammad Ali Jinnah*, 3 Vols. Karachi, East and West, 1984-1986.

———, *The Evolution of Pakistan*, Lahore, Royal Book Co., 1995.

———, *The Foundation of Pakistan, All India Muslim League Documents, Vol. 1, 1906-1921; Vol. 2, 1924-1947*, Karachi, National Publishing House, 1970.

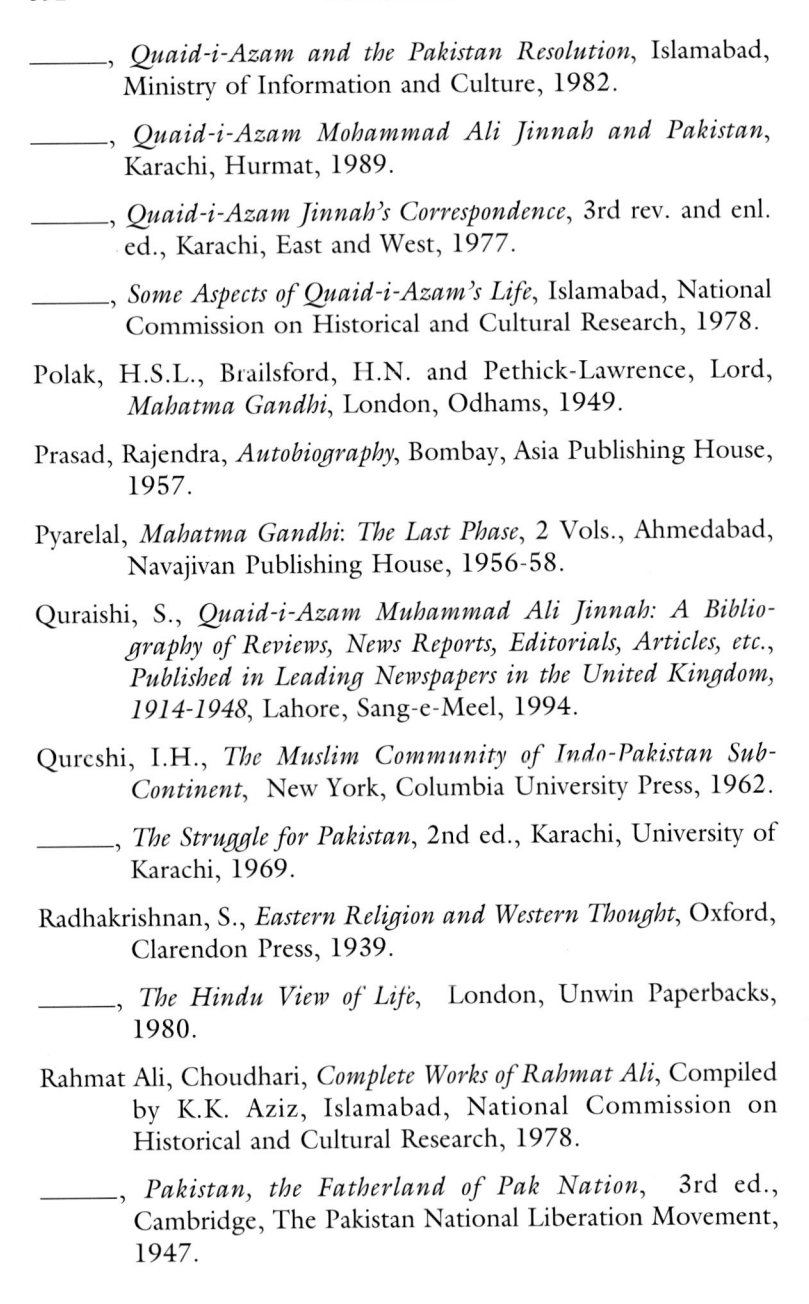

_____, *Quaid-i-Azam and the Pakistan Resolution*, Islamabad, Ministry of Information and Culture, 1982.

_____, *Quaid-i-Azam Mohammad Ali Jinnah and Pakistan*, Karachi, Hurmat, 1989.

_____, *Quaid-i-Azam Jinnah's Correspondence*, 3rd rev. and enl. ed., Karachi, East and West, 1977.

_____, *Some Aspects of Quaid-i-Azam's Life*, Islamabad, National Commission on Historical and Cultural Research, 1978.

Polak, H.S.L., Brailsford, H.N. and Pethick-Lawrence, Lord, *Mahatma Gandhi*, London, Odhams, 1949.

Prasad, Rajendra, *Autobiography*, Bombay, Asia Publishing House, 1957.

Pyarelal, *Mahatma Gandhi: The Last Phase*, 2 Vols., Ahmedabad, Navajivan Publishing House, 1956-58.

Quraishi, S., *Quaid-i-Azam Muhammad Ali Jinnah: A Bibliography of Reviews, News Reports, Editorials, Articles, etc., Published in Leading Newspapers in the United Kingdom, 1914-1948*, Lahore, Sang-e-Meel, 1994.

Qureshi, I.H., *The Muslim Community of Indo-Pakistan Sub-Continent*, New York, Columbia University Press, 1962.

_____, *The Struggle for Pakistan*, 2nd ed., Karachi, University of Karachi, 1969.

Radhakrishnan, S., *Eastern Religion and Western Thought*, Oxford, Clarendon Press, 1939.

_____, *The Hindu View of Life*, London, Unwin Paperbacks, 1980.

Rahmat Ali, Choudhari, *Complete Works of Rahmat Ali*, Compiled by K.K. Aziz, Islamabad, National Commission on Historical and Cultural Research, 1978.

_____, *Pakistan, the Fatherland of Pak Nation*, 3rd ed., Cambridge, The Pakistan National Liberation Movement, 1947.

Rajput, A.B., *Muslim League: Yesterday and Today*, Lahore, M. Ashraf, 1948.

Ray, P.C., *Life and Times of C.R. Das*, London, OUP, 1927.

Riaz Ahmad, *Jinnah and Jauhar*, Islamabad, Quaid-i-Azam University, 1979.

———, *Quaid-i-Azam Mohammad Ali Jinnah: The Formative Years, 1892-1920*, Islamabad, National Institute of Historical and Cultural Research, 1979.

———, *Quaid-i-Azam's Perception of Islam and Pakistan*, Rawalpindi, Alvi Brothers, 1990.

———, *The Works of Quaid-i-Azam Mohammad Ali Jinnah, Vol. 1, 1893-1912*, Islamabad, Quaid-i-Azam University, 1996.

Rizwan Ahmed, *The Quaid-e-Azam Papers*, 2 Vols., Karachi, East and West, 1976.

Rolland, Romain, *Mahatma Gandhi*, London, Garland Publishing, 1973.

Saiyid, M.H., *Mohammad Ali Jinnah*, 2nd ed., Lahore, M. Ashraf, 1953, also rev. ed., Lahore, M. Ashraf, 1962.

Sen, Ranjan and Sen, B.K., *Deshabandhu Chitta Ranjan*, Calcutta, R. Sen, 1926.

Sen, S.P. (ed.), *Dictionary of National Biography*, 4 Vols., Calcutta, Institue of Historical Studies, 1970-1990.

Seth, Hira Lal, *The Khaksar Movement in India*, Delhi, 1973.

Setalvad, Chimanlal H., *Recollections and Reflections*, Bombay, Padma Publications, 1946.

Shan Muhammad, *Khaksar Movement in India*, Meerut, Meenakshi, 1973.

———, *Unpublished Letters of the Ali Brothers*, Delhi, Idarah-yi-Adabiyat-i-Dehli, 1979.

Sharif al-Mujahid, *Quaid-i-Azam Jinnah: Studies in Interpretation*, Karachi, Quaid-i-Azam Academy, 1981.

———, *Quaid-i-Azam: His Times*, Vol. 1, 1876-1937, Karachi, Quaid-i-Azam Academy, 1990.

Sheean, James Vincent, *Nehru*, London, Gollancz, 1960.

Sherwani, Latif Ahmad (ed.), *Pakistan Resolution to Pakistan*, Karachi, National Publishing House, 1969.

Sitaramayya, B. Pattabhi, *History of the Indian National Congress*, 2 Vols., Delhi, S. Chand and Co., 1969.

Stephens, Ian, *Pakistan*, London, Ernest Benn, 1963.

Symonds, Richard, *The Making of Pakistan*, London, Faber and Faber, 1951.

Templewood, Viscount, *Nine Troubled Years*, London, Collins, 1954.

Tendulkar, D.G., *Mahatma: Life of Mohandas Karamchand Gandhi*, 8 Vols., Bombay, V.K. Jhaver and Tendulkar, 1951-54.

Transfer of Power, Edited by Nicholas Mansergh, P. Moon etc., 12 Vols., London, HMSO, 1970-1982.

Tuker, Sir Frances, *While Memory Serves*, London, Cassell, 1950.

Waheed Ahmad (ed.), *Quaid-i-Azam Mohammad Ali Jinnah: The Nation's Voice—Speeches and Statements, March 1935-March 1940*, Karachi, Quaid-i-Azam Academy, 1996.

Waheed-uz-Zaman, *Towards Pakistan*, Lahore, Publishers United, 1964.

Wavell, Lord, *The Viceroy's Journal*, Edited by P. Moon, London, OUP, 1973.

Wolpert, Stanley, *Jinnah of Pakistan*, New York, OUP, 1984.

———, *Tilak and Gokhale: Revolution and Reform in the Making of Modern India*, London, CUP, 1961.

Yajnik, Indulal, *Gandhi as I Knew Him*, Delhi, Danish Mahal, 1943.

Zafrulla Khan, *Tahdis-i-Nimat*, Dacca, Dacca Benevolent Association, 1974, and Lahore, 1994.

Zaidi, A.M. and Zaidi, S.G., *The Encyclopaedia of the Indian National Congress*, 25 Vols., New Delhi, S. Chand and Co., 1980-1981.

Zaidi, A.M., *The Evolution of Muslim Political Thought in India*, 6 Vols., New Delhi, S. Chand and Co., 1979.

Zaidi, Z.H. (ed.), *Jinnah Papers*, 2 Vols., Islamabad, National Archives of Pakistan, 1993.

Zakariya, F., *The Rise of Muslims in Indian Politics*, Bombay, Somaiya Publications, 1970.

Zetland, Second Marquis of, *Essayez: The Memoirs of Lawrence, Second Marquis of Zetland*, London, John Murray, 1956.

Ziegler, Philip, *Mountbatten—An Official Biography*, London, Collins, 1985.

ARTICLES

Campbell-Johnson, A., 'Reflections on the Transfer of Power' in *Asiatic Review*, July 1952.

Jinnah, Fatimah, 'A Sister's Recollections' in *Pakistan Past and Present*, London, Stacey International, 1977.

Jinnah, M.A., 'Two Nations in India' in *Time and Tide*, 9 March 1940.

Moraes, F., 'Gandhi, Ten Years After' in *Foreign Affairs*, January 1958.

'Mr M.A. Jinnah: Creator of Pakistan' in *The Times*, 13 September 1948.

'Nehru in Retrospect' in *Illustrated Weekly of India*, Sunday 22 November 1964.

'The Partition of India', special issue of *Indo-British Review*, Vol. 14, No. 2, 1988.

Quaid-i-Azam Number, *Pakistan Journal of History and Culture*, Islamabad, National Institute of Historical and Cultural Research, Vol. XIV, No. 2, July-Dec. 1993.

Quraishi, S., 'Correspondence between the Quaid-i-Azam and the British Prime Minister Clement Attlee', National Documentation Centre, Islamabad, *Newsletter*, No. 21, Winter 1994.

Radhakrishnan, S., 'Hinduism', in *The Legacy of India*, edited by G.T. Garratt, Oxford, 1937. p. 268.

———, 'Hinduism and the West', in *Modern India and the West*, edited by L.S.S. O'Maley, London, 1945.

Sheean, Vincent, 'The Case for India', in *Foreign Affairs*, October 1951.

NEWSPAPERS

Amrita Bazar Patrika, Calcutta

Comrade, Calcutta

Dawn, Karachi

Hamdard, Delhi.

The Independent, Allahabad, 2 October 1921.

The Times, London 18 September 1947.

Times of India, 24 April 1930

Young India, Ahmedabad.

PROCEEDINGS AND REPORTS

All Parties Conference 1928. Report of the Committee appointed by the Conference to determine the principles of the Constitution for India, together with a summary of the Proceedings of the Conference held at Lucknow. 3rd ed., Allahabad, All India Congress, 1928.

A National Government: Answers to Criticism. Statement issued by the President and Standing Committee of the Non-Party Political Conference, and other papers. Allahabad, 1928.

Non-Party Political Conference. Proceedings of the Non-Party Political Conference held at Bombay on 13 and 14 March 1941. Delhi, 1941.

Report of the Twenty-Second Session of The Indian National Congress held at Calcutta on 26, 27 and 29 December, 1906. Calcutta, 1907.

Report of the Thirty-Second Session of The Indian National Congress held at Calcutta on 26, 27 and 29 December, 1917. Calcutta, 1918.

Report of the Thirty-Third Session of The Indian National Congress held at Delhi on 26, 28 and 29, 30 and 31 December, 1918. Delhi, 1919.

Report of the Thirty-Fourth Session of The Indian National Congress held at Amritsar on 27, 29, 31 December, 1919 and 1 January 1920. Amritsar, 1920.

Report of Thirty-Fifth Session of The Indian National Congress held at Nagpur on 26, 28, 30 and 31 December, 1920. Nagpur, 1920.

Report of the Thirty-Sixth Session of The Indian National Congress held at Ahmedabad on 27 December, 1921. Ahmedabad, 1921.

The Shareef Report. Patna, December 1939.

Report of the Last Viceroyalty, by Rear Admiral The Earl Mountbatten of Burma. 1947. BL: OIOC: L/P&J/5/396.

The Simla Conference. Memorandum by the Secretary of State for India. 8 August 1945. L/P&J/8/524.ff 227.

ACTS OF PARLIAMENT

The Government of India Act, 23 December 1919. 9 and 10 Geo.v.c. 1010.

The Government of India Act, 2 August 1935.
26 Geo. v.c. 2.

The Indian Independence Act, 18 July 1947.
10 and 11 Geo. vi.c. 30

PARLIAMENTARY DEBATES

Minutes and Debates of the Legislative Council of India and its Successors, 1857.

Debates on Indian Affairs, House of Commons and House of Lords, 1857-1947.

Debates on Indian Affairs, House of Lords, Session 1927. BL:OIOC:V/3/1640

PARLIAMENTARY PAPERS

Report on Indian Constitutional Reforms. Montagu-Chelmsford Report, 1918.
cmd., 9109.

Report of the Indian Sedition Committee. Rowlatt Committee Report, 1918.
cmd., 9190.

Report of the Joint Select Committee on the Government of India Bill, 1919.
HC 203.

Report of the Committee Appointed to Investigate Disturbances in the Punjab. Hunter Committee Report, 1920.
cmd., 681.

Report of the Indian Statutory Commission. Simon Commission Report, 1930. Vol. 2. Recommendations.
cmd., 3568.

Report of the Indian Statutory Commission. Simon Commission Report, 1930. Vols. IV-XIV. Memoranda Submitted by

the Government of India and the India office, and by Provincial Governments. London, HMSO, 1930.
cmd., 3568.

East India (Constitutional Reforms). Communal Decision. London, HMSO, 1932.
cmd., 4147.

Proceedings of the Indian Round Table Conference. First Session, 12 November—19 January 1931, London, HMSO, 1931.
cmd., 3772 XII 605

―――― Second Session, 7 September 1931—1 December 1931. Proceedings of the Federal Structure Committee and Minorities Committee. London, HMSO, 1932.
cmd., 3778 XII 91

―――― Third Session, 17 November—24 December 1932. London, HMSO, 1933.
cmd., 4238 XI 169

Joint Committee on Indian Constitutional Reform (Session 1932-33). Report with Minutes of Evidence and Record. 6 Vols. London, HMSO, 1933-34.

India (Lord Privy Seal's Mission) 1942. Statement and Draft Declaration by His Majesty's Government with Correspondence connected therewith. London HMSO, 1942.
cmd., 6350

Correspondence and Documents connected with the Conference between the Cabinet Mission and His Excellency the Viceroy and Representatives of the Congress and the Muslim League, May 1946. London, HMSO, 1946.
cmd., 6829

India; Statement of the Cabinet Mission, 25 May 1946. London, HMSO, 1946.
cmd., 6835

India (Cabinet Mission) Papers relating to (a) the Sikhs, (b) the
    Indian States, (c) the European Community, May-June
    1946. London, HMSO, 1946.
cmd., 6862

India Policy Statement, 20 February 1947.
cmd., 7047

India Policy Statement, 3 June 1947.
cmd., 7136

Index

Act, 1919, Government of India, 115

Act, 1935, Government of India, 208

Act, 1947, Indian Independence, 344

Aga Khan, His Highness the, leads Muslim League Delegation to Viceroy Minto, 74; Delegation was not a put-up show, 75; expresses hope that grant of communal electorates would lead to improvement in Hindu-Muslim relations, 89; presides over Mulsim All-Parties Conference, 160; his estimate of Jinnah's stature as a political leader, 377

Ahmad, Sir Sultan, expelled from Muslim League, 259

Ali Brothers (Muhammad Ali and Shaukat Ali), take up cause of Khilafat, 123; imprisoned, 134; appeal to Muslims not to join Congress in Civil Disobedience Movement, 178

Ali, Chaudhri Muhammad, advises League to take Finance Portfolio in Interim Government, 308

Ali, Chaudhary Rahmat, writes pamphlet *Now or Never* demanding Pakistan, 194; how he coined name Pakistan, 195; Muslim leaders call his demand for Pakistan chimerical, 195; his extravagant schemes, 196; his contribution to achievement of Pakistan, 197.

Ali, Muhammad, his view of Aga Khan delegation 75, 95; explains rationale of Khilafat Movement, 116; leads Khilafat Delegation to London, 124; criticizes Nehru Report, 161; criticizes Gandhi's Civil Disobedience Movement, 178; his speech at First Session of Round Table Conference, 183

All-India Muslim Legislator's Convention, 292

All-India Nationalism, a creation of British rule, 1

Ambedkar, Dr B. R., refutes Gandhi's claim that he represented Untouchables, 188; Muslims in Hindu-majority provinces supported demand for Pakistan, 373

Amery, L. S., criticizes Indian leaders for not making an agreed response to Cripps' Declaration, 263

Attlee, Clement, his goodwill for Congress Party, 211; says minority cannot be allowed to place a veto on advance of majority, 288; Statement of 20 February 1947 on Indian Policy, 317; offers viceroyalty to Mountbatten, 318; hopes partition of India would be reversed, 344; calls Kashmir Nehru's blind spot, 360

Auckinleck, Field Marshal Sir Claude, secret report to London that Indian Cabinet were determined to prevent establishment of Pakistan on a firm basis, 350

Azad, Maulana Abul Kalam, criticizes communal attitude of Congress, 223; criticizes Nehru for sabotaging chance of a League-Congress coalition ministry in the U.P., 224; deplores Nehru's statement sabotaging Cabinet Mission Plan, 303; explains why Congress agreed to let the Muslim League have the Finance portfolio in the Interim Government, 308.

Baksh, Lt. Col. Ilahi, 363

Bande Mataram, 225

Bengal, Partition of 1906, 65; annulment of partition in 1911 stuns Muslims, 90; famine, 268; proposal for a united independent Bengal, 334

Besant, Annie, opens Jinnah Memorial Hall, 111; how Montagu managed to see her, 114; resigns presidentship of Home Rule League, 129.

Birkenhead, Lord, his poor opinion of Indian politicians, 155; challenges Indians to produce an agreed constitution, 155

Bose, Subhas Chandra, secret of Gandhi's charisma, 7-8; calls Gandhi's promise of Swaraj within one year childish, 12; disappointed at meeting with Gandhi, 12; calls for Gandhi's resignation from leadership of Congress, 193; correspondence with Jinnah, 232; takes over command of Indian National Army, 284

Cabinet Mission, appointment of, 288; their statement of 16 May 1946, 295; their plan sabotaged by Nehru, 302

Chagla, M. C., criticizes Gandhi for supporting Khilafat, 25; says in 1919 Jinnah was uncrowned king of Bombay, 111; blames Hindu communal parties for rejecting Delhi Muslim Proposals, 150; praises Jinnah for generous treatment of Ruttie, 169

Chauri Chaura, murder of policemen at, 135

Chelmsford, Lord, sharp exchange with Jinnah, 108; holds war conference attended by Jinnah and Gandhi, 108; unsympathetic reply to Khilafat delegation, 124

Chiang Kai-shek, Marshal, visits India, 260

Churchill, Winston, his picturesque disapproval of Gandhi-Irwin talks, 186; his directive to Wavell and his personal view of policy to be followed in India, 270; favoured partition into Pakistan, Hindustan, Princestan, etc., 277; why he agreed to Simla Conference, 282; message to Jinnah to accept Plan Dominion Status, 337

Non-Cooperation, what it entailed, 129

Communal Award, 190

Congress, Indian National, foundation of, 63; makes Lucknow Pact with Muslim League, 105; demands complete independence, 177; rejects Act of 1935 and demands Constituent Assembly, 212; spurns Jinnah's olive branch, 223; appoints two Hindus as premiers in preference to more deserving non-Muslims, 223; rejects coalition with Muslim League in the U.P., 224; excesses of Congress ministries, 225; reaction to World War II, 236; forms Interim Government, 305; passes resolution on 8 March 1947 asking British Government to partition India, 322; resolution accepting 3 June 1947 Plan, 34

Constituent Assembly, demanded by Congress, 238; Jinnah's objection to convening Constituent Assembly on lines suggested by Congress, 342; boycotted by Muslim League, 312.

Cripps Mission, Cripps' Declaration, 261; proposals rejected first by Congress and then by the Muslim League, 263; result of failure of Mission, 263

Cripps, Sir Stafford, friendly correspondence with Nehru, 218; his surreptitious contacts with Congress leaders when member of Cabinet Mission, 290

Das, C. R., a practical politician desiring Hindu-Muslim unity, 26-7; forms Swarajya Party jointly with Motilal Nehru, 147; passes away, 148

Delhi Muslim Proposals, 149

Dwarkadas, Kanji, witnesses Gandhi's inability to control riotors, 119; finds Gandhi weeping for inability to prevent violence, 135; says Jinnah was popular with Hindus of Bombay, 147; Ruttie continued to love Jinnah even after they had separated, 168; Jinnah rebuffed MacDonald's suggestion of a governor-ship, 53; describes Jinnah's grave illness in 1934, 203; why Jinnah insisted that Gandhi should come to his residence for negotiations, 276

Dyer, Brig.-Gen., R. E. H., orders Jallianwalla massacre, 118; let off lightly by British Government and hailed as a 'saviour of India' by a section of the British public, 125-6.

Emi Bai, 35-6, 42

Fourteen points, enunciated by Jinnah, 166

Gandhi, Mahatma Mohandas Karamchand, he, not Jinnah, was the first one to introduce religion into politics, xv, 8; the secret of his greatness, 7; his unusual ideas, 9-14; his contribution to India's independence, 14; contrast with Jinnah, 16; his dictatorship of the Congress, 20; advocates non-violence for solving international conflicts, 22; undertakes recruiting campaign during World War I, 109; reaction to Rowlatt Act, 118; his 'Himalayan Miscalculation', 118-19; his reasons for supporting cause of Khilafat, 121; launches non-cooperation movement, 126; beginning of Gandhi Era in Indian politics, 128; becomes president of Home Rule League, 129; makes 'childish' promise of Swaraj within one year, 130-1; is unable to control rioters, 119; weeps because of inability to control mob violence, 135; suspends non-cooperation, 135; sentenced to six years imprisonment, 136; released early for reasons of health, 136; salt march, 177; Gandhi-Irwin Pact, 185-6; his arrogant and extravagant claims at Second Session of Round Table Conference, 187-9; fails to bring about communal settlement, 187; asserts Hindu-Muslim differences will disappear when British leave India, 189; resigns permanently from Congress Party, 193; breaks down at prospect of destruction of Houses of British Parliament and Westminster Abbey, 237; launches stayagraha on issue of freedom of speech, 258; opposition to Cripps proposals, 262; leads Quit India rebellion, 265; offers to trade non-violence for immediate independence, 271; his negotiations with Jinnah, 272; calls Pakistan a 'sin', 293; comments on Cabinet Mission plan, 298; end of his dictatorship over Congress party, 324; hollowness of his proposal that Jinnah be asked to form Central Government, 328

George, Lloyd, his promise of sympathetic treatment of Turkey, 123; his unsympathetic reply to Muhammad Ali Khilafat Delegation, 124

Gokhale, Gopal Krishna, supports Muslim demand for separate electorates, 26

Great Calcutta Killing, 304

Hindu-Muslim Riots, 137, 228, 309, 322

Hinduism and Islam, their imcompatibility, 2-6.

Hoare, Sir Samuel, his prejudice against Jinnah, 191-2

Hyderabad, taken over by India, 358.

Interim Government, formed by Congress, 305; Muslim League joins, 306-7.

Iqbal, Sir Muhammad, his presidential address to the Allahabad Session of the Muslim League, 183; recognizes that Jinnah was the only leader who could safely guide the Muslim Community, 185; does not see why Muslims of North-West India and Bengal cannot be considered as nations, 185; praised highly by Jinnah, 185; criticizes Nehru's atheistic socialism, 222

Irwin, Lord, his goodwill for India, 173; his good relations with Jinnah, 173; his declaration of 31 October 1929, 174

Ismay, Lord, says Mountbatten's appointment as Viceroy could be viewed as being pro-Hindu and anti-Muslim League, 320; joins Mountbatten in influencing Radcliffe to change boundary award in favour of India, 353

Jallianwalla Bagh Massacre, the slaughter, 118; Hunter Committee and Congress Committee Reports, 125

Jayakar, Mr opposes Jinnah's amendments to Nehru Report, 160; asks for Dominion Status, 181

Jinnah, Dina, birth, 140.

Jinnah, Miss Fatima, 32, 35, 41-3, 197

Jinnah People's Memorial Hall, 100.

Jinnah, Quaid-i-Azam Mohammad Ali, incompatibility with Gandhi, 16; compatibility with Tilak, C.R. Das and Gokhale, 24, 26-7; parentage and birth, 32; education in India, 33-5; first marriage, 35; education in London, 37-8; his tribute to Naoroji, 38; his spell as an actor, 40; hard start as barrister, 42; his genius in advocacy, 44; integrity as a barrister, 47; joins politics, 48; integrity as politician, 52; independence of India was his life-long passion, 54; his sang-froid, 54; his constitutionalism, 55; his secular politics, 58; reserved but correct, 59; his first Congress (1906), 84; gets Mussalman Wakf Validating Act passed, 84-5; pleads that there should be no reserved quota for safeguarding Muslim representation in higher appointments, 85-6; opposes separate electorates for Muslims, 87; hopeful of Hindu-Muslim unity, 88; advises Muslims not to fear Hindu domination, 88; elected to imperial Legislative Council, 104; sharp exchange with Viceroy Minto, 90; advocates universal elementary education, 91; says he supports the Criminal Law (Amendment) Bill because he is a constitutionalist, 92; invited to attend Muslim League Council Meeting at Bankipur though not yet a member of the Msuslim League, 93; insists that system of self-government must be 'suitable to India', 93; joins Muslim League, 94; reluctantly moves Congress resolution deprecating communal electorates in local bodies, 97; his successful endeavours to have Congress and Muslim League sign the Lucknow Pact, 105; falls in love with Ruttie in 1916, 104; and marries her in 1918, 104; elected to Imperial Legislative Council, 104; presides over Bombay provincial Conference at Ahmedabad and accepts Muslim demand for separate electorates as the mandate of the community, 105; in Indian Legislative Council clashes with Viceroy Chelmsford when demanding equality for Indians with European British subjects as *sine qua non* for helping in war effort, 108; in Bombay War Conference clashes with Governor Willingdon for Willingdon's criticism of Home Rule League, 109; successfully opposes proposal to build a memorial for Governor Willingdon, 110; Jinnah Memorial Hall built by Public subscription, 111; 'uncrowned king of Bombay' (1919), 111; welcomes Montagu's Statement of 20 August 1917, 114; praised by Montagu, 115; his concern for Khilafat, 117; criticizes Montagu-Chelmsford proposals, 117; resigns from Imperial Legislative Council as protest against Rowlatt Act, 120; forwards memorandum on

Khilafat to Lloyd George, 123; resigns from Home Rule League because of differences with Gandhi, 129; resigns from Congress because of differences with Gandhi, 131; is praised by Col. Wedgwood, 131; nature of his differences with Gandhi, 18, 128, 138; resumes efforts to forge Hindu-Muslim unity, 144-5; elected to Legislative Assembly, 146; his popularity among Hindus of Bombay, 147; forms Independent Party in Assembly, 147; serves on Sandhurst Committee, 147; sharp exchange with Gracey, 148; Delhi-Muslim Proposals, 149; unsuccessfully proposes amendments to Nehru Report, 159; formulates Fourteen Points, 166; separation from Ruttie, 168; his grief at Ruttie's death, 169; his good relations with Viceroy Irwin, 173; writes to Prime Minister MacDonald and asks for pledge of Dominion Status and a Round Table Conference and receives a favourable reply, 175; at First Session of Round Table Conference complains of slow pace toward Dominion Status, 181; rebuffs MacDonald at mention of possibility of a governorship, 53; decides to take up residence in London, 197; praises Iqbal highly, 185; why he was not invited to the Third Session of the Round Table Conference, 191; his reasons for self-exile in London, 198; Aziz Group and Hidayat Group of Muslim League heal split and elect Jinnah as president, 202; resumes mission of Hindu-Muslim unity, 202; Himalayan odds facing him, 203; grave illness in 1934, 203; had no central organization at centre till 1943 to assist him, 207; elected to Indian Legislative Assembly, 213; defuses Shahidganj crisis, 214; comments on Act of 1935, 215; comments on election results, 217; rejects Congress suggestion that allegations against Congress ministries be referred to Chief Justice of Federal Court but suggests reference to a Royal Commission, becomes undisputed leader of Muslims of India, 277; argues that British Parliamentary System could not be applied to India and replies to criticism that this view was un-Islamic because Islam believes in democracy, 231-2; correspondence with Bose, 232; points out that constitutionally the Viceroy was entitled to declare war on behalf of India, 236-7; on outbreak of war is received by Viceroy on equal footing with Gandhi, 238-9; seeks assurance from Viceroy that no constitutional changes would be made without the consent of both the Msulim and Hindu communities and receives satisfactory assurance, 241; his objection to Constitutent Assembly on lines suggested by Congress, calls Hindus and Muslims two nations in an article published in *Time and Tide*, 246; expounds rationale for the creation of Pakistan, 247; defuses Khaksar crisis, 251; his advocacy in support of creation of Pakistan, 251; in retrospect feels relieved that Providence had frustrated his efforts to bring about a Hindu-Muslim constitutional accord, 251; criticizes Chiang Kahi-shek's statement, 260; criticizes Quit India Rebellion, 266; suffers a murderous attack by a Khaksar, 267; criticizes Wavell for calling India a natural unit, 270; rift with Khizar, 270; Jinnah-Gandhi Negotiations 272-6; his demand at First Simla Conference, 280; criticizes Gandhi's role at Simla Conference, 282; his handicaps when negotiating with the Cabinet Mission, 289; reply to Attlee's statement that minority cannot be allowed to place a veto on the advance of majority, 291; in interviews with Cabinet Mission claims five provinces for Pakistan, 294; reaction to Cabinet Mission Plan, 298; agrees to Muslim League joining the Interim Government, 306; tells Mountbatten that the only constitutional solution for India was a 'surgical operation', 328; after two meetings makes Mountbatten realize that eventually a 'truncated' Pakistan would emerge, 329; appeals to Mountbatten not to give him a 'moth-eaten' Pakistan, 329; calls proposal to partition Bengal and the Punjab 'a sinister move', 331; demands 800 mile corridor to link West and East Pakistan, 338; his broadcast message accepting 3 June 1947 plan, 341; attempt on his life by Khaksars on 9 June 1947, 342; his wisdom in preventing Mountbatten from becoming Governor-General of Pakistan, 345; letter to Attlee that topmost Hindu leaders were trying to make Pakistan submit to India, 350; his disappointment at Radcliffe Boundary Awards, 353; his first address as President of the Constituent Assembly of Pakistan, 354; his address to Assembly during the transfer of power ceremony, 355; Campbell-Johnson calls his sense of leadership 'overpowering', 355; his worsening illness, 356; his three principal concerns — Kashmir, a constitution for Pakistan and the plight of refugees, 356; the plight of Hindu refugees in Pakistan moves him equally, 357; speaks of death for the first time, 361; moves to Quetta, 362; moves up to Ziarat, 362; his condition becomes precarious, 363; confirmation that he is suffering from lung disease, 363; comes down to Quetta, 364; loses his will to live, 365; is flown down to Karachi, 366; death, 366; his conception of the state of Pakistan, 366; prescribes 'unity, faith and discipline' as motto for Pakistanis, 367; says Islam is a complete code for life, 367-8; says Prophet was the greatest man that the world has seen, 368; says Pakistan's constitution must be founded on Islamic ideals and principles, 369;

Pakistan must adopt Islamic system of social justice, not the Western exploitative economic system, 370; his concern for the poor, 370; education did not mean only academic education, 370; women must be emancipated, 371; his view of defence and external affairs policies for Pakistan, 372; his place in history, 372; his replay to the criticism that the creation of Pakistan did not solve the communal problem of the Indian subcontinent, 372-3; unfairness of criticism that he did not define the precise boundaries when demanding Pakistan, 374; unfairness of criticism that he could achieve only a 'moth-eaten' Pakistan, 375; birthday tribute from the Untouchable leader M. C. Rajah, 376; estimate of his stature as leader by the Aga Khan 377; need for Pakistanis to follow his example and his advice, 377-8

Jinnah, Poonja, 32

Jinnah, Ruttie (*nee* Petit), patriotic and self-respecting, 140; separates from Jinnah, 168; loved Jinnah even after they had separated, 169; death, 169.

Junagadh, taken over by India, 357.

Kashmir, a summary of the Kashmir dispute between Pakistan and India, 358-60; Attlee calls Kashmir Nehru's blind spot, 360

Khaksars, crisis defused by Jinnah, 251; murderous attack on Jinnah, 267; attempted attack on Jinnah, 342

Khaliquzzaman, Choudhry, how Nehru frustrated proposed Congress-League coalition ministry in the U.P., 224; how Hindu press bestowed name of Pakistan Resolution on Lahore Resolution, 248

Khan, Abdul Ghaffar, the power behind the throne, 222

Khan, Khizar Hayat, rift with Jinnah and expulsion from Muslim League, 270-1; calls Attlee's statement of 20 February 1947 'the work of lunatics', 321

Khan, Liaquat Ali, appointed Finance Minister in Interim Government, 307-8; sworn in as first Prime Minister of Pakistan, 356

Khan, Muhammad Zafrulla, his recommendation that Jinnah be invited to the Third Session of the Round Table Conference rejected by Secretary of State Hoare, 191

Khan Sahib, Dr, heads Congress ministry in North-West Frontier Province, 222; decline of his popularity, 323, 333

Khan, Sir Syed Ahmed, father of Muslim nationalism in India, 68; founds M.A.O. College, 70; declares English representative system not suitable for India, 71; calls Hindus and Muslims two nations of India, 73; proposes communal electorates for Muslims, 73

Khilafat, rationale explained by Muhammad Ali, 116; delegation

awaits on Viceroy, 124; its effect on Hindu-Muslim relations, 138-9
Lal, Chaman, his article on Jinnah, 154
Linlithgow, Lord, declares war on behalf of India, 236; war aims and war effort, 239; 8 August 1940 offer, 256; his comments on course of Quit India Rebellion, 266
Lucknow Pact, between Congress and Muslim League, 105.
MacDonald, James Ramsay, his reply to Jinnah's letter, 175; rebuffed by Jinnah at hint of offering him a governorship, 53; rebukes Gandhi for ducking communal question, 188; makes Communal Award, 190
MacPherson, Sir John Molesworth, 43
Mehta, Sir Pherozeshah, 84
Minto, Lord, receives Aga Khan Delegation and gives sympathetic reply to their demands, 74-5; sharp exchange with Jinnah, 90
Mithibai, 32, 33, 34, 42
Mohani, Maulana Hasrat, criticizes Jinnah, 57
Montagu, Edwin, his statement of 20 August 1917, 24-5; visits India, 114; how he contrived to meet Mrs. Besant, 114; praises Jinnah, 115
Moplahs, rise in rebellion, 134
Mountbatten, Lady Edwina, her friendship with Nehru, 319
Mountbatten of Burma, Rear-Admiral the Earl, appointed Viceroy, 318; his character, 319; cultivates friendly relations with Nehru during the latter's visit to Singapore in March 1946, 320; regards Nehru indispensable for peaceful transfer of power, 321; Ismay says his appointment could be viewed as being pro-Hindu and anti-Muslim League, 320; his relations with Congress get off to a flying start, 326; refers to demand for Pakistan as 'this mad Pakistan', 326; after first meeting with Nehru calls the latter 'most sincere', 327; Gandhi's proposal to invite Jinnah to form the Central Government and its hollowness, 327; says at their first meeting found Jinnah 'most frigid, haughty and disdainful, 28; after two meetings with Jinnah realizes that 'eventually a truncated Pakistan would emerge', 329; his frustration at failure to budge Jinnah from his demand for Pakistan, 330; his dismay at Nehru's rejection of Plan Balkan, 332; his broadcast message introducing 3 June 1947 Plan, 341; frustration at not being able to become Governor-General of Pakistan, 346-7; his strategy for undoing partition, 349; influences Radcliffe to change boundary awards in favour of India, 352-3; his address to Pakistani Constituent Assembly during transfer of power ceremony, 355
Muslim All-Parties Conference, 160
Muslim League, foundation, 77; adopts self-government as aim, 93; its decline, 139; splits into two on issue of boycotting the Simon Commission, 152; Aziz

Group and Hidayat Group decide to unite under one banner with Jinnah as president, 202; lays down programme of rejuvenation at Bombay session, 216; had no central organization to assist Jinnah till 1943, 207; attitude toward 1935 Act, 215; election manifesto, 216; reaction to rule of Congress ministries, 229; passes direct action resolution, 234; reaction to outbreak of World War II, 239; passes Pakistan Resolution, 247; attitude toward Quit India resolution of Congress, 264; at first accepts Cabinett Mission Plan, 300; withdraws acceptance of Cabinet Mission Plan, 303; joins Interim Government, 306-7; boycotts Constitutent Assembly, 312; resolution accepting 3 June 1947 Plan, 342

Naidu, Sarojini, her pen portrait of Jinnah calling him An Ambassador of Unity, 61; describes Jinnah's brilliance as an advocate, 44

Naoroji, Dadabhai, Jinnah learnt politics 'at his feet', 38; elected to House of Commons, 39

Naval Mutiny, Bombay, 285

Nawaz, Begum Shah, expelled from Muslim League, 259

Nehru, Jawaharlal, calls Gandhi permanent super-president of Congress, 20; friendly correspondence with Cripps, 218; his make-up, 219; underrates Jinnah, 220-1; criticized by Iqbal, 222; sabotages chance of Congress-League coalition in the U.P., 224; sabotages Cabinet Mission Plan, 302; lays foundation of friendship with Mountbatten during visit to Singapore in March 1946, 320; calls Attlee's statement of 20 February 1947 'a courageous document', 321; establishes rapport with Viceroy Mountbatten at very first meeting, 327; disparages Jinnah, 327; rejects Plan Balkan, 332; broadcasts message accepting 3 June 1947 Plan, 341; Attlee calls Kashmir his blind spot, 360

Nehru, Motilal, forms Swarajya Party jointly with C. R. Das, 147; presides over Nehru Committee which produces the Nehru Report, 156

Nehru Report, origin of Nehru Committee, 154; Nehru Report, 157; burial of Nehru Report, 160; its legacy, 164

Nichols, Beverley, 17, 207

North-West Frontier Province, reason for having a Congress ministry, 222; swing against Congress, 323, 333; referendum in favour of joining Pakistan,

Nusserwanjee, Jamshed, finds Jinnah in tears after his amendments to Nehru Report were rejected, 160; saw Jinnah in tears at plight of Hindu refugees left behind in Pakistan, 60-1, 357

Non-Cooperation Movement, launched by Gandhi, 118, 126; its programme, 129; an assessment of its impact, 132-135

Pakistan, demanded by Rahmat Ali, 194; how Rahmat Ali invented the name, 195; called chimerical by Muslim leaders,

195; a step toward Pakistan, 233; Pakistan Resolution by Muslim League, 247; demand for Pakistan criticized by Hindus and British but welcomed by Muslims, 249; how Hindu press bestowed name of Pakistan Resolution on Lahore Resolution, 238

Paneli, 32

Panikkar, K.M., concedes two nations came into being as soon as Islam came to India, 254

Parliamentary Delegation, 286

Pethick-Lawrence, Lord, leads Cabinet Mission, 288; describes his own and Cripps' friendship with Congress leaders, 289; attends Gandhi's prayer meetings, 290; praises Jinnah for winning Pakistan, 375

Petit, Sir Dinshaw, 104

Poonja, See Jinnahbhai Poonja

Provincial nationalism, xiv.

Quaid-i-Azam, see Jinnah, Mohammad Ali,

Quit India Rebellion, 264

Rai, Lala Lajput, declares Hindu-Muslim unity is impossible and proposes division of India, 253

Rajah, M.C., his perceptive tribute to Jinnah's greatness as a political leader, 376

Rajagopalachari, C.R., recommends that Muslim League's claim for partition of India be recognized, 264; his 'formula' for Jinnah-Gandhi negotiations, 272-3

Romain, Rolland, 16, 24.

Round Table Conferences, First Session decides Indian form of government must be federal, 180; First and Second Sessions fail to solve communal problem, 181, 187, 198; Third Session takes no important decision, 190

Rowlatt, Report and Act, 117

Sapru, Sir Tej Bahadur, pleads for acceptance of Jinnah's amendments to the Nehru Report, 159

Satyagraha, defined by Gandhi, 9

Savarkar, V., concedes Hindus and Muslims are two nations, 254

Separate Electorates, as viewed by Coupland and Zetland, 87

Setavald, Sir Chimanlal, quoted 165

Shafi, Sir Muhammad, splits from Jinnah Section of the Muslim League on issue of boycotting Simon Commission, 152; contradicts Gandhi at Round Table Conference, 188

Simla, The Simla Conference, 276

Simon Commision, appointment, 150; its report, 178

Singh, Master Tara, his inflammatory shout, 322

Tilak, Bal Gangadhar, a practical politician who helps Jinnah to make the Lucknow Pact, 24; criticizes Gandhi as a politician, 24

Time and Tide, publishes article by Jinnah, 246

Tyabji, Badruddin, 82

Wakf Validating Act, 85

Wavell, Field-Marshal Earl, appointed Viceroy, 269; calls India a natural unit, 270; stages first Simla Conference, 277; his Breakdown Plan, 286; criticizes Pethick-Lawrence's and Cripps' partiality to Congress, 290

Wedgwood, Col., praises Jinnah, 131

Willingdon, Lord, clash with Jinnah at War Conference, 109; Jinnah successfully opposes proposal to build a memorial to commemorate his governorship, 100

World War I, India's voluminous aid to the allies, 100; expectations of steps toward self-government, 101

World War II, India's reaction to outbreak of, 235; repercussions in India of German Blitzkrieg, 254

Zetland, Lord, his comment on separate electorates, 87